The Daily Telegraph

CRICKET
YEAR BOOK 91

GW00496962

The Daily Telegraph
CRICKET
YEAR BOOK 91

Norman Barrett

Michael Melford

Wendy Wimbush

Foreword by Trevor Bailey

Pan

Editor Norman Barrett
Consultant Editor Michael Melford
Statistics Wendy Wimbush
Other contributors:
Trevor Bailey, Mike Beddow, Edward Bevan, Tony Cozier
(West Indies), Peter Deeley, Clive Ellis, Cathy Harris,
John Fogg, David Green, Neil Hallam, Don Cameron (New
Zealand), R. Mohan (India), Michael Owen-Smith (South
Africa), Qamar Ahmed (Pakistan), Charles Randall,
D.J. Rutnagur, Alan Shiell (Australia), Sa'adi Thawfeeq
(Sri Lanka), Rob Wildman

Acknowledgements Thanks are due to David Armstrong
for supplying the data for the Minor Counties and to Tim
Lamb and the TCCB for making the first-class fixtures
available. The Coopers Deloitte Ratings are published by
kind permission of Coopers & Lybrand Deloitte.
    The photographs appearing in this book are reproduced
by permission of Patrick Eagar, Allsport, Bill Smith,
The Hulton Picture Company, and the N.S. Barrett
Collection.
    The editors particularly wish to thank Radford Barrett,
former Sports Editor of *The Daily Telegraph*, proof-readers
Fred and Kathie Gill, and Kate Jenkins of the TCCB for
their help, and the Editors of *The Telegraph* newspapers for
permission to reproduce articles and reports by
E.W. Swanton, Tony Lewis, Peter Deeley, John Major,
Derek Pringle, Trevor Bailey, Charles Randall, Sunil
Gavaskar, Don Cameron, and Tony Becca, as well as the
obituaries.

Published 1991 by Pan Books Ltd
Cavaye Place, London SW10 9PG
in association with *The Daily Telegraph*

9 8 7 6 5 4 3 2 1
ISBN 0 330 31665 6

Typeset by Michael Weintroub Graphics Ltd,
Kenton, Middx.
Printed and bound in Great Britain by
Richard Clay Ltd, Bungay, Suffolk

Contents

Foreword

The last two decades have witnessed a marked decline in standards of behaviour at international and county matches by both players and spectators. What happened on England's last tour to Pakistan could never have occurred in the 1950s, when the offending players would have been sent home and fined, not given a £1,000 bonus. At one time, three policemen were adequate to control a capacity crowd at Lord's; now a brigade, plus an army of stewards, is necessary.

Cricket at this level has, of course, never been the gentle sporting game that some would have us believe, as it has always contained a ruthless streak. But this was usually kept below the surface and not allowed to explode. There were occasional exceptions, with the 1932-33 Bodyline tour to Australia the classic example. This was a tactically brilliant exercise and did not break the Laws, though these had to be subsequently amended, but it certainly offended against the spirit of the game. Ironically, Bodyline was not nearly as physically dangerous as the constant barrage of short-pitched bowling that has been allowed to dominate so much of modern cricket and has gone unpenalized. Far more batsmen were hit and felled in the 1988 Melbourne Test than in the entire 1932-33 series. This does not mean that the fast bowlers of the forties and fifties were more worried when they injured a batsman, but they were more selective. They reckoned to bowl out the tailender, not knock him out. Yet they were quite happy to send down the occasional beamer, more difficult to deliver than the bouncer, but much more lethal, until it was eventually outlawed.

Sledging

This marked increase in what might be termed a meanness of spirit, or 'sledging', has made rather a mockery of that time-honoured phrase 'not cricket'. These days, it is common practice for the fielding side to pressure the umpires by incessant appealing, by using bat and pad fielders who have acting ability, as well as agility, and indicating dramatically why they felt the batsman was out, with the occasional thirty-yard dash from the slips up to the other end to emphasize the point.

There is too much calculated intimidation by fast bowlers. Batsmen are inclined to make their displeasure obvious when adjudged out. Deliberately slow over-rates do not add to the harmony, so that at times 'sledging' had led to animosity, almost hatred, between individual players and teams in what is intended to be a civilized game embellished with skill and coloured with laughter. As a result, on some tours a sporting arena has been transformed into an ugly battlefield.

What has gone wrong? Today's cricketers are certainly no worse nor better than their predecessors. To some extent it stems from the many changes that have occurred in the outside world. Things that were clearly unacceptable in the fifties are now considered acceptable. This applies to what we see on television, read in the press, some sports sponsorship, the clothes we wear, and a decline in discipline at home and in the schools. Sex and language are now more explicit on the box. Sports writers are often more interested in describing a player's performance off the field than the century he has scored on it. Cricket today could not exist in its present form without a massive injection of cash from sponsorship. Jeans have become the universal uniform of mediocrity. Many football fans no longer go to watch the football and there is a big increase in mindless violence. All these factors have contributed to cricketers' tending to have less self-discipline, and consequently more likely to become involved in unsavoury incidents, which the media are only too delighted to blow up.

The marked growth of player power has also meant that they are less willing to accept the dictates of authority. The financial rewards are far higher, which has automatically given them more independence. But the extra cash has brought with it extra pressure, which they sometimes forget.

Gamesmanship

Gamesmanship has always been part, often a highly amusing part, of the game, with W.G. Grace one of its most expert practitioners. I shall always treasure the look on Jim Laker's face when I told him to appeal against the light on one of the

sunniest days Headingley has ever experienced. We were
fighting a rearguard action and my objective was to avoid
another over before lunch, which the obligatory consultation by
the equally astonished umpires achieved. I also enjoyed the
moments when an Australian on the next tour appealed against
the sun and later against sawdust blowing in his face. However,
nobody would have ever considered bowling an underarm
sneak to prevent the chance of a six being struck off the last ball
of a one-day international: that would have transgressed against
our unwritten code and shown a meanness which was
unacceptable. Likewise, I cannot imagine Ray Lindwall or
Keith Miller deliberately charging into an opposing batsman,
the stumps, or an umpire, or Denis Compton threatening to rap
his bat over a bowler's head.

There is nothing remotely new about players who lose their
temper, batsmen who are never out, bowlers who, having been
struck to the boundary, automatically want to pin the
perpetrator to the sight-screen with their next delivery, and
fielders who invariably have difficulty in determining whether a
catch is clean.

The language on the field has always been colourful. I cursed
myself whenever I bowled a bad ball and might have suggested,
when an edge bisected them at catchable height, that my two
slips had been born out of wedlock. Although on many
occasions it might have been justified, nobody ever swore
directly at me throughout my career, because we abided by a
code of conduct that forbade personalized swearing at a
member of the opposition, let alone at an umpire. As captain of
Essex I only once reported an opposing player, because he had
verbally abused a young tail-ender. Today 'mouthing' at
newcomers has become almost commonplace, but I still believe
primitive oral abuse to be both unnecessary and unacceptable.
It cannot be easy to socialize at close of play with an opponent
who has deliberately insulted your wife.

Over-rates

In 1948 Essex bowled out the Australians in a day that started at

11.30 a.m. and ended with the fall of their 10th wicket at 6.28 p.m. In this period, the tourists scored 721 runs, which meant that boundaries were rather frequent, but we still managed to bowl 128 overs. These days it is not unusual to find teams having problems to maintain 13 overs per hour. Over-rates did not become a serious tactical weapon until the fifties, when we began to speed them up when wickets were falling, and slow them down when the runs were flowing. I found I could easily adjust the length of an over from three-and-a-half to five minutes. All that was required was to follow through a little further, wait until the ball was returned, and walk back a little slower. But we still expected to average around 17 overs per hour in a full day's play. The trend in recent years has become far, far slower, with teams regularly bowling 12 overs per hour and often under 72 overs in a full day, which clearly robs spectators of a large amount of cricket.

A slow over-rate can benefit any team with an attack based on four pacemen, as the West Indies have so often demonstrated. It reduces the chances of bowlers losing their nip or becoming tired, and means they will be fresh on the second day. On good pitches it also means that a batting side, averaging 3 runs per over, will use up two-fifths of a Test to reach a total in excess of 450. England and India have also achieved draws with deliberately slow overs, using slow bowlers, plus frequent field changes, consultations, and interruptions.

Anyone doubting the tactical importance of over-rates should turn to Law 17/6, which states that a minimum of 20 overs shall be bowled in the last hour. This Law was introduced to prevent time wasting at every level of the game and has proved effective. However, it might be argued that stipulating 20 overs in the last hour of a match that has been allowed to meander along at 13 does not make too much sense. In addition, the success and the popularity of the one-day game would not have occurred without the over restriction.

Reluctance to act

It is sad that the ICC have taken so long to realize the harm that ultra-slow over-rates and the excessive use of fast short-pitched bowling have done to Test cricket. The reluctance and the slowness to act that the governing bodies have shown is one of the main reasons that some unsavoury features have been allowed to creep into what is essentially a beautiful game. Their reluctance has stemmed from a combination of financial, political, and social causes, plus self and parochial interests, while it has to be admitted that there are several chairmen at both international and county level whose knowledge of first-class cricket and its requirements is distinctly limited – and that is being very kind.

TREVOR BAILEY

1989-90
LOOKING BACK

Review of the Season
by Peter Deeley

After four depressing years, English cricket at last lifted itself out of the doldrums in 1990, inspired by a highly unexpected Test victory in the West Indies and another golden summer which saw the balance at last swing back in favour of bat over ball.

Graham Gooch and his side had been written off as 'no hopers' before they set off for the Caribbean in January. Though they eventually lost the series 2-1, the side emerged hardened by experience, and the success they achieved was reflected during the summer by one of the most entertaining and trouble-free domestic seasons in recent memory.

'Success' is a small word, but the win at Sabina Park, Kingston, was responsible for the general resurgence of optimism that at last seemed to pervade the game after all the bitterness and rancour of recent years.

Gone was the back-biting and recriminations that the selectors, and successive England captains, had endured over the years of failure. In the new climate Gooch prospered considerably as both captain and batsman, and the knock-on effect was noticeable throughout the game.

England's revival was nowhere better illustrated than in the emergence of Michael Atherton as a Test player of true quality. His patience and level-headedness enabled him to construct many a long innings with an almost old-fashioned attention to detail. Before his death in September at the age of 74, Sir Leonard Hutton had spoken highly of the young Lancastrian. With the loss of one of the game's all-time greats, is it premature to express the belief that we are seeing the beginnings of another outstanding talent?

It is to be hoped that Atherton's correctness of technique – not least his preference for the orthodox stance and admirably straight stroke-play – and the consequent success it brought, will not be lost on some of his colleagues whose deficiencies had been so exposed by the highest class of seam bowling as personified by the likes of Australia's Terry Alderman and New Zealand's Sir Richard Hadlee?

Tours to England

The knighthood for the great all-rounder at the end of his long and distinguished career, which took his final tally of Test wickets to 431 – a total which may not be overtaken for many seasons – gave a lift to the early part of the season, when New Zealand were the first of the two touring sides.

They and India, who followed, had each been granted a series of three Tests, and both countries made clear their view that these short rubbers were not entirely to their liking. Although there was some sympathy within the Test and County Cricket Board for full five-Test recognition for both sides, such decisions are taken these days largely in the light of the likely ensuing financial benefit.

The sight of two touring sides back-to-back, as it were, at least gave the public at home an idea of the great diversity in standards of present-day international cricket.

New Zealand, save for Hadlee and the performance of Mark Greatbatch with centuries in each of the Texaco one-days, were hard-working but of only moderate quality. Six players, including Hadlee, announced their impending retirement or future non-availability during the series for future tours, and New Zealand's short-term prospects were not particularly promising when they left these shores.

Of their captain, John Wright, however, there was unstinting admiration from all who came in contact with him. A gentleman off the field as well as on it, Wright conducted himself in a manner that makes one wonder whether New Zealand have produced a better 'ambassador at large'.

Almost as much could be said for the gentle and charming Indian captain, Mohammed Azharuddin, whose 'princely' qualities with the bat won as much approval as his unfailing courtesy away from the field of play. Azharuddin, new to leadership of his country in 1990, had the advantage – though some might consider it a double-edged sword – of three former captains in Shastri, Kapil Dev, and Vengsarkar.

In the event, India's batting, if sometimes capable of self-destruction, was as exciting as New Zealand's had been dour. Sachin Tendulkar, the 17-year-old student who has modelled himself on Sunil Gavaskar, even down to the 'little master's' oversized, dis-coloured batting pads, scored a maiden Test century and gave notice that we were witnessing the ripening of an astonishing talent.

Batsmen benefit from TCCB edicts

After the glorious summer of 1989, it was hard to believe that 1990 would be as dry and sun-kissed. Yet so it proved, and batsmen around the counties profited to an unprecedented degree.

They were aided by TCCB edicts, one which limited the size and prominence of the seam on the ball and another, a fresh set of instructions to county groundsmen, on the preparation of pitches. This laid down that there should be no inconsistent bounce, and that wickets should be as dry as the conditions allow and without any obvious greenness or mat of grass.

The purpose was to reverse the drift of previous seasons, when bowlers were felt to be taking too many cheap wickets on greenish tops and the ball was considered too helpful for them. In short, what we saw last summer were 'smooth balls and white pitches'. Groundsmen were setting the blades on their mowers so low that by the end of the season, on some grounds, the grass was no longer strong enough to bind together to prevent part of the surface from breaking up.

The overall result of these changes was to restore the dominance of bat over ball to an unreal extent. Where before bowlers of only moderate ability had reaped rewards beyond their due, now batsmen of no outstanding merit collected hundreds almost at will.

Championship format

The biggest debate within county circles had taken place before the season began. Moves by the TCCB to change to an undiluted four-day championship format in 1991 were unceremoniously thrown out by the counties. It was an issue that provoked much public acrimony that at times seemed to descend into an argument about which should come first: county or country.

The outcome was a severe setback for Ted Dexter and his colleagues on the England Committee. They believed that four-day cricket provided the best 'proving ground' for players with Test potential: the counties, on the other hand, were fearful that the loss of some days' championship play would mean a downturn in revenue as well as ruin the traditional cricket 'weeks'.

Early in the season, a further attempt was made by the Board to win support for a modified proposal that would have increased the number of four-day games from six to eight in 1991. This time the vote was tied 9-9, but the Board chairman, Raman Subba Row, declined to exercise his casting vote. So the status quo remains.

At times, the England Committee – entrusted with responsibility for restoring the country's diminished status in the Test arena – and their 'masters', the counties, seemed to be pulling in different directions.

There was a feeling among some clubs that they had been presented with a *fait accompli* by the board's introduction of a plan to reschedule the county programme in 1991. The long-established routine of starting three-day games on Wednesdays and Saturdays is being dropped in favour of matches beginning on Tuesdays and Fridays. This will enable players called up for England duty to have two days together before the start of a Test.

Both Gooch and the England team manager, Micky Stewart, believe very strongly in the value of pre-preparation, and this change in the starting day is but one plank in their long-term scheme to reshape England's whole approach to the international game.

Test umpires

These changes, significant though they may be for the future, are scarcely more wide-reaching than the proposals now being studied by the International Cricket Council for a fundamental reappraisal of the role of the umpire in Test cricket.

We shall probably not know until shortly before the 1991 season has started whether the system for a panel of international umpires is yet in place, along with a third, an 'arbitrator', who would be there to assist the others, mainly in matters of off-field dispute – but *not* to have the power to overrule on-field decisions.

ICC set up a panel of chief executives, drawn from the Test-playing countries, to meet during the winter in England and Australia, with a brief to get the changes into operation by April 1991.

They are also considering the idea of run penalties for sides who do not meet the daily quota of Test overs, and powers to show players the equivalent of the 'red' card – or sending-off – for misdemeanours such as too much intimidatory bowling and 'sledging'.

The idea of 'international' umpires is the most radical proposition in this package. Care, rightly, has been taken not to call them 'neutral', since in the context of the job that would be unecessarily tautologous – even an insult to their tradition of objectivity. Among the many hurdles that remained to be overcome was the cost of the scheme in terms of travel and remuneration. A search was under way for a sponsor to underwrite the operation.

Commercialism in cricket

Money is an influence that overlays all major decisions in today's game. The BBC lost its monopoly of domestic television coverage as BSB were given the Benson & Hedges and Sky the Refuge Sunday League.

The Test and County Cricket Board itself explored previously uncharted areas of commercial opportunity. For the final Test of the summer against India at the Oval, we saw, for the first time at this level of the game in England, an advertising logo painted on the ground at either end behind the stumps. This was the emblem of the series sponsors, Cornhill Insurance, and was in its way a tester for the public's appetite for this innovation.

The Board also decided to hand the 'marketing' of the England team to a professional agency, as is already the case with other countries' Test teams. "If it comes to a choice between a million pounds for opening a supermarket and a nets practice, the tins of beans will win out," was the wry comment of an England selector.

There were also moves afoot to sell advertising space on the shirts of England players. We were assured these would be 'unobtrusively' displayed on shirt collars and sleeves.

Ground redevelopment

Of more immediate concern on the home front for those who would still seek to enjoy, untrammelled, their cricket at first hand were the problems of ground redevelopment associated with Lord's and the Oval.

The rebuilding of the stands, to be called Compton and Edrich when they are complete, at Lord's Nursery End, dragged out the whole of the summer with much associated disruption. The stands were expected to be ready by the end of April, but by mid-September the view of the historic ground from the pavilion was still disfigured by scaffolding and tarpaulin sheets – not to mention the noise of building works. The loss of the extra seating during the summer was estimated to have cost cricket somewhere in the region of a million pounds in lost revenue.

There was also a continuing problem with MCC's public image after the revelation that Sunil Gavaskar, a year before, had turned down an invitation to become an honorary life member in protest at his treatment over the years by Lord's petty officialdom. He said that at times during his playing career he had been made to feel 'like a trespasser'.

This led to a vitriolic open letter from the Indian team manager Bishen Bedi, attacking Gavaskar's attitude. It may not have been entirely unrelated to the fact that Gavaskar, in a syndicated column in an Indian newspaper the previous week, had called for Bedi to be dismissed from his post.

At the Oval, redevelopment work sufficiently progressed for the extension to the pavilion to be open by the time of the India Test in late August. But the discovery of pockets of methane gas in the lower levels caused delays in the construction of the cricket school and the postponement of an official opening by HM the Queen.

South Africa

The season as a whole was remarkable for the absence of the South African dimension, which for years had hung like a millstone around the international game. ICC's decision in effect to wipe clean the slate of past involvement in the game in that country meant that England could undertake their tour of the West Indies free of demonstrations and threats of disruption which had marred previous visits.

Simultaneously, Mike Gatting had led a party of his countrymen to South Africa on a private tour which led to five-year bans from Test cricket. But with the changing political situation there, the South African Cricket Union later announced that it had called off a second tour by the same players for the winter of 1990-91.

At last there seems hope for the future of a return by South African cricket to the brotherhood of Test nations. With social reform on the way, the possibility is that well before the end of this decade of the 1990s, a South African side based on multiracial selection will be taking its place once more in the international arena.

All in all, 1990 was a summer of rich promise for the seasons that will follow.

Forget 1990: It was a cricketing phoney
by Tony Lewis

Should this last season be struck from the record books? Congratulations to the batsmen who filled their boots with runs, but the sight of an outstanding fast bowler unleashing a ball which bounced twice before the wicketkeeper was evidence that the competition has been phoney. The balance between bat and ball disappeared.

You will know that the seam of the ball was made less prominent and bowlers proved that only on exceptional days did it swing or move off the seam. Mostly it bounced conveniently to be struck by the middle of the bat, regardless of a batsman getting his foot to the pitch of the ball or not.

I watched Glamorgan chasing 495 to beat Worcestershire on the last day at Abergavenny and getting as far as 493-6 when time ran out. I also saw Alan Donald last week at Edgbaston; a genuinely fast bowler, rarely seeing his bowling rise above stump height. He bowled double-bouncers to the wicket-keeper on a lifeless pitch.

Pitch or ball? Which is to blame for the summer's distortion? The TCCB made a mistake. A more sensible experiment would have been to change either one or the other. Not both. Then it would have been a simple process of elimination. Many cricketers believe that the best formula is to return to the ball with the higher seam but still play on pitches as they are, carefully prepared to be dry and not to incur a 25-point penalty in the Championship.

At the same time, the lobby for uncovering pitches grows stronger and you must seriously consider the argument that it may be wrong to keep the turf so dry. On these super-safe, chip-dry pitches ordinary batsmen looked very good, and the very good looked brilliant.

On the other hand, the TCCB would argue that 1990 was the season when the bowlers learned the lesson vital to England cricket that they were not half as good as they had appeared to be. No more landing the ball anywhere in the batsman's half to see it deviate off the seam every other ball. Bowlers this summer have suffered if they have not commanded a good and consistent length.

Angus Fraser survived: Philip DeFreitas did not. Those who just waited for things to come right again got their wickets expensively. Those who had the sense to school themselves with coaches, recovered and ended respectably.

The unhelpful surface and alien ball also meant bowlers had to experiment to get some lateral movement. County captains screamed out for variation in attack and most counties played two spinners. The cry for the return of spinners was answered. So there was greater concentration on the art of bowling and this must be the most salutary effect of the changes. Take a look at the national averages and see how those bowlers established as craftsmen still led the field.

The Board knows that good comes out of bad, and bad out of good. And so it has already anticipated the next trends. Firstly, fast bowling could become extinct. Just look at India. The reason why there are no fast bowlers in India is that it is the most unrewarding job when pitches provide no bounce. Could our young cricketers similarly soon prefer being clever, medium-fast bowlers and spinners to toiling with unproductive flat-out speed.

Secondly, the effect on batting may be equally damaging. This past season technique has gone out of the window when approximate footwork suffices to deal with balls which do not move at all over after over. A batting average of 35 once meant a useful county contribution, now only 50-plus registers.

Of course, batting is much more than a bat and pad jammed together, but generations have proved before that it is a sideways game when played most consistently. So the question is: How long will it be before batting becomes the simple exercise bowling became before the changes: just a matter of getting on the field fit and going through the motions? Would it be wrong to make changes quickly, and to what? In which direction should the game go?

The advocates for uncovered wickets believe rain-affected pitches will bring back the spinners. That is not entirely correct. Often the most effective bowlers after rain are faster bowlers.

They do believe that the more natural surface will breed better batsmen and better bowlers. They see the return of variety. I am with them as long as uncovered pitches mean a bounce which mirrors the efforts a bowler has exerted.

Strong voices urge no change at all, arguing that the lessons of 1990 are yet to be learned. So within the game there are three voices: for the old ball but present pitches, for uncovered pitches and for the status quo. Now that should make for a fascinating winter!

Personally, I am not for tinkering with the ball as much as I favour serious change in the surfaces on which the game is played. That sight of Alan Donald's embarrassing double-bouncing has lingered with me the longer.

Equally, the sight of batsmen of limited talent looking like world-beaters – or as Geoff Boycott puts it, "Bad players gettin' 'undreds" – persuades me that uncovered pitches will be best for the game.

Cricket is rich because of its variety. Since pitches have been dry, some of the zest has gone out of the game. The Board have been guilty of too much change in a short space of time. As a result, we have years of discussion ahead about pitch-covering, of seams on balls, and of three-day and four-day cricket.

The balance between bat and ball is delicate, and is achieved by a gentler touch than tinkering with the lot at once.

The Sunday Telegraph, 23 September

Young Australians give education in 'sledging'
by E.W. Swanton

"The young Australians have just been here and have proved too good for our lads...I'm afraid there were reports of typical Aussie 'sledging' which took our boys, none of them yet *educated* (!) in the ways of the modern first-class game, by surprise. Not a promising omen for the Test series to follow." So writes Tony Cozier to me from Barbados, banishing at a stroke my euphoric thoughts about this unforgettable summer.

His comment is depressing though not surprising to me, as I had heard from the Worcestershire secretary, the Rev M.D. Vockins, how the England Under-19 side which he managed in Australia last winter had been persistently abused on the field.

Of all the modern elements in the game, old cricketers probably find sledging the most incomprehensible and contemptible. It is largely, though not be any means wholly, an Australian product, the word seemingly a contraction of sledge-hammering – distracting and offensive expletives and chat into the ears and minds of batsmen.

Last year Russell Davies in *The Sunday Telegraph* was telling us how in Australia the newcomers to Test cricket, the Sri Lankans, were *racially* abused by some of the Australians.

When I taxed Bobby Simpson, the Australian coach, on the subject last summer he, of course, deplored it, but said he hoped he had silenced all but two members of his side. He did not name names, but one offender will come to everyone's mind.

Sledging is, of course, punishable under the Unfair Play Law 42 (paragraphs 1 and 13), and I trust that Peter Lush, the England manager, on his arrival in Australia next month will request the ACB to remind umpires and captains of their duties under the law.

Just one English ray of light on this sombre subject: After this, his first full summer of county cricket, a young player answered my inquiry by saying that though some badinage had passed to and fro he had not at any time encountered an attempt to put him off his game. That perhaps counterbalances some evidence that sledging has infiltrated certain clubs playing league cricket, especially those infiltrated by Australians.

The Daily Telegraph, 24 September

A foretaste of paradise and purgatory
by John Major

When we are very old we may babble about the marvellous cricket in the summer of 1990. It has been a foretaste of paradise for batsmen, but not for bowlers, for whom it has been purgatory. They have persevered, perspired but seldom prevailed. And that imbalance is the impediment to declaring the season a vintage one.

But there is no doubt it has been memorable. Early in the summer I was planning a day at the Oval when, as so often, Treasury business detained me. I missed the day; I also missed Ian Greig amassing 291 and I cursed. For 38 years I have watched Surrey and have never seen a score like that for the county. And, what is more, I thought I had also missed the highest individual score of the year. I was wrong; the next day Neil Fairbrother scored 366 in the same match and later, of course, Graham Gooch scored his 333 against India at Lord's.

I also saw, at the Oval, a small cameo that showed why Gooch has become such a success as captain. On the fourth morning England were following on with Gooch and Atherton batting as lunch approached. Off the first ball of the pre-lunch over, Gooch squirted the ball behind square leg. It looked like a single that would have left Gooch safely at the non-striker's end; instead, he sprinted two and played out the rest of the over hemmed in by close fieldsmen. Captaincy by example.

Throughout the season, the runs have kept coming: double centuries; hundreds; fifties have scarcely counted. Glorious stroke-play, particularly to the off side. And one of the most memorable factors has been the golden year enjoyed by some of the unsung heroes of cricket without whom the county game would never survive. Among them, the greatest pleasure for me has been the mid-career blossoming of David Ward, of Surrey, who has batted out of his socks all summer. His bat has been all middle and no edges.

Nothing is perfect

But nothing is ever perfect, and on the perverse principle of the grass being greener on the other side, I think we have still missed several things in this rich summer harvest for batsmen. Where are the pace bowlers who will pitch the ball up and swing it? Swing used to be a staple part of an opening bowler's armoury and yet this season it has seemed redundant.

It is hard to understand why. Only a few years ago Ian Botham wrecked numerous Test sides with swing. So did Geoff Arnold a few years earlier, while Bob Massie, of Australia, was quite unplayable in the remarkable 1972 Test at Lord's. Where are the off-spinners? Must Eddie Hemmings be preserved in aspic forever as the last of the breed?

Where have all the tail-enders gone? Has cricketing myxomatosis wiped out the tail-end rabbit whose appearance emptied the tea tent and brought fun to the dullest of days? Not quite, while Devon Malcolm plays, but very nearly.

We have enjoyed two Test series this summer, although the New Zealand tour was a quiet affair made memorable only by the knighthood for Richard Hadlee. But the Indians were a delight, with Azharuddin and Tendulkar, in particular, leaving lasting images. And the Indian series also revived another tradition, that the fifth day mattered.

Looking ahead

Ahead of England this winter lie the Australians and the perennial fascination of the struggle for the Ashes. Notwithstanding Alderman, England may score a packet of runs, but it will not be easy to bowl out Taylor, Boon, Border, and Co, twice on good wickets unless our attack perform above expectations.

Fraser, I suspect, will earn his wickets on any pitch through sheer dogged line and length, while Malcolm's pace may get its true reward on Australia's harder pitches. There could be some equally absorbing cricket in the A-team tour of Pakistan. Last winter's 'A' tour helped bring on Michael Atherton as a fully fledged Test player this summer, and we must hope for similar good fortune again.

Pakistan have been lucky of late. Wasim Akram and Waqar Younis have emerged from the nets and local park as international players. So did Tendulkar for India. This rapid emergence of real class has few parallels in England, but it does raise an intriguing question: Are all the best players in county cricket?

We know we have some fine young players in county cricket, and some fine young players coming along – Ilott, Thorpe, Ramprakash, Tufnell, the Bicknells, Crawley – but we do not know if there are others of equal potential playing for club sides.

There's a thought as we settle down for the last few day's cricket this season. Do enjoy it. As for me . . . I'm off to the park to look. After all, who knows?

The Daily Telegraph, 17 September

All-rounders' era is at an end
by Derek Pringle

During the 1980s the emergence of some great all-rounders has given Test cricket a long-awaited popularity boost. Whether it has been Botham for England, Imran for Pakistan, Hadlee for New Zealand, or Kapil Dev for India, the star billing has often been – certainly in the contrived consciousness of the tabloid press – the confrontations between these individuals rather than those of the teams, such has been their dominating presence.

But as the new decade unfurls, most of these greats are close to retirement, with barely any worthy successors in sight. Does modern Test cricket perhaps preclude the need for a top-class all-rounder? Or are the all-rounders of Test class simply made with time and rarely if ever show equal aptitude with bat and ball from the outset?

Bits and pieces cricketers

One-day cricket is fairly littered with all-rounders who could be filed under 'bits and pieces' cricketers. But with no more than 10 or so overs to cope with when bowling and rarely ever more than 30 overs to bat, a sustained performance is hardly necessary.

So a quick 30 here and a tight 10 overs there are all that is ever required from the one-day all-rounder. At Test level, however, there is usually no room for a player who is nearly Test standard at either batting or bowling. The longer game requires consistent performance sustainable sometimes for days at a time.

What is required is a specialist in one sphere who can perhaps do a bit of the other to near Test standard. Often it is the brilliance of one aspect that allows the other, unfettered by pressure of performance, to improve, sometimes quite dramatically.

The 'easier' route, and one that is borne out by the great all-rounders of the 80s, has been to begin as a bowler of indisputable class, then improve the batting so that as powers with the ball wane, prowess with the bat comes to the fore. Both Imran and Botham have followed this route at the latter stages of their careers.

It is a lot more difficult to improve one's bowling at Test level, if one is a front-line batsman. There is no scope for letting the opposition off the hook to give a potential all-rounder a bowl, though Michael Atherton may in time disprove this contention.

A class bowler, batting down the order, is often afforded the opportunity to relax and play his shots, hoping in the end to gain confidence and generally get a feel for batting at this level. Here, there is the opportunity for nurturing technique and confidence.

Once accomplished at both batting and bowling, the all-rounder works virtually twice as hard as the specialist. Given today's demanding schedules, burn-out must be another factor in the scarcity of class all-rounders.

For similar reasons, most bowling all-rounders tend to be stroke-players and not batsmen who expend a lot of time and energy building their scores. They do not want to be batting for five hours, then spending the next day and a half in the field trying to bowl a side out.

Spinners as all-rounders are even rarer, while batsmen who can bowl have not been in vogue since Garfield Sobers. The West Indians haven't had a class all-rounder for a time, though Marshall, and to a lesser extent Harper, come closest.

The top all-rounders

Here, then, is an assessment of the top all-rounders of the decade with one or two likely heirs thrown in.

For most of the past decade **Ian Botham**, having always relinquished doubt, ambiguity, and self-inquiry in favour of aggressive self-championing belief, has dominated English Test cricket. His deeds have always inspired others.

Starting off as an aggressive fast-medium bowler who could swing the ball mainly away from the right-handers, Test scalps were never slow in coming. With some successful, aggressive knocks down the order and his *annus mirabilis* 1981 Ashes series, came the recognition of a special all-round talent.

As the bowling began to wane, the batting became more technically sound though less scintillating. With injury and perhaps a smidgin of existential dread creeping in, Botham has not been quite the force with either bat or ball in the last couple of years, but he is just as aggressive as ever in wanting to prove the doubters wrong.

Sir Richard Hadlee started his all-roundership along similar lines. As plain old 'Paddles' he opened the bowling, strove for pace, and batted low down the order.

While Hadlee was initially fairly successful with the ball, his batting, particularly against the faster short-pitched delivery, held no clues to the incarnation that was to occur. Being analytical and less reliant upon the Botham adrenalin/oppression approach, he realized that at Test level and on Test pitches in particular, pressure had to be maintained upon batsmen through persistence of line and length.

What ensued was a very methodical, mechanical grooving of his run-up and action, in tandem with a highly disciplined and blinkered mental approach. With constant fine tuning over the years, and a lean, wiry physique to boot, longevity at Test level and a metronomic consistency have given Hadlee the greatest number of Test wickets.

His batting has come on nicely too. It is said that the advent of the helmet was a major catalyst in the transformation of Hadlee the tail-ender to Hadlee the awesomely clean stroke-player that emerged during the 80s. In fact Hadlee's batting is a complete foil to his bowling, dashing, full of risk and bravura, as if the method, concentration, and discipline that go with his bowling are gleefully jettisoned in favour of some light mental relief.

Imran Khan began his first-class career as a medium-paced swing bowler who probably batted more effectively than he bowled. Unlike Hadlee, he decided an injection of dynamism and pace was what was needed for him to compete more favourably in the Test arena.

Initially, and at the expense of his batting, Imran worked hard on his fitness and all the components that he felt were necessary to bowl fast successfully – muscle strength, suppleness, smooth run-up, and powerful action of which the famous leap became a hallmark.

He always possessed the ability to swing the ball, and the new-found pace rapidly thrust him to the fore in Test cricket. Not content with the successes his bowling was bringing him, he began to work on the batting that had got left behind.

Improving his technique allowed him to build an innings patiently, a route that the other all-rounders have not favoured. No doubt the expectations of his countrymen and the burdens of captaincy contribute to this 'sensible' batting approach.

Heir apparent

An heir apparent has arrived in the shape of **Wasim Akram**. A bowler of genuine pace and talent, he also possesses an uncommon ability to adapt his bowling to conditions, such is his range of swing and deceptive change of pace. His batting, always notable for its awesome striking, seemed to come of age with a century against Australia last winter, where, by all accounts, the range of strokes and exquisite timing had Test-hardened journalists searching for superlatives.

At present, he is comfortably the best one-day performer in world cricket and if able to stay fit with an action that stresses both groin and shoulder – and also able to improve on his batting – records could tumble.

Hailing from the other side of the Punjab, **Kapil Dev** has always possessed an enviable ability to improvise with bat and ball often turning Test matches India's way.

Swinging the ball mainly away from the right-hander with neither Imran's pace nor Hadlee's persistent accuracy, Kapil Dev has been a consistent wicket-taker who thrives on inspired spells. His batting needs similar stimulus, for when in full flow there is no batsman with a greater range and audacity of shot. He is a master of the brief cameo of 70 or 80 runs.

Though not knowing him well, I get the impression that his confidence and approach is akin to that of Botham, for they are aggressively similar – a player who can disappoint or enthral in equal measure, and one who possibly has not done his batting talents full justice.

These are the great Test all-rounders of the last decade. There have been others less successful, such as Ravi Shastri, Greg Matthews, Steve Waugh, and David Capel. It is no coincidence, though, that they are either spinning all-rounders or batsmen who bowl less well than they bat.

Today's cricket offers little scope for becoming an all-rounder in the mould of Sobers, a phenomenal batsman who bowled pretty well.

The route of the bowler who learns to improve his batting in unstressful situations is the most likely to succeed. That is why Chris Lewis could be the long-term answer for England.

Their Test Records

	Kapil	Imran	Botham	Hadlee
Tests	106	82	97	86
Innings	153	118	154	134
Not outs	12	22	5	19
Runs	4301	3541	5119	3124
Average	30.50	36.88	34.35	27.16
Highest score	163	136	208	151*
100s	6	6	14	2
50s	22	15	22	15
Runs per Test	41	43	53	36
Catches	54	28	112	39
Balls bowled	22270	19290	21281	21918
Runs	10754	8188	10633	9612
Wickets	364	358	376	431
Average	29.54	22.87	28.27	22.30
Best bowling	9-83	8-58	8-34	9-52
5 wkts in innings	21	23	27	36
10 wkts in match	2	6	4	9
Strike rate	61.18	53.88	56.59	50.85
Runs per 100 balls	48.28	42.44	49.96	43.85
Wickets per Test	3.4	4.4	3.9	5.01

The Daily Telegraph, 11 July

Umpires and Umpiring
by Trevor Bailey

Watching football's World Cup on television, I kept thinking that if these were the best referees in the world then there must be some very bad ones about. This did not surprise me because, having covered football for more than 30 years, I have seen some very indifferent officials.

Probably the main reason why the standard of refereeing is so poor is that the vast majority of the officials have never played the game at a serious level. The outcome is that, although they know the rules backwards, forwards, and sideways, they have problems differentiating between a deliberate foul and a perfectly executed fall, or in anticipating trouble before it occurs.

Finest in the world

I believe that the practical knowledge gained as a player is unbeatable and unteachable, which is why the best boxing referees are usually ex-boxers, the best rugby referees former players, and why our county umpires are probably regarded as the finest in the world.

The average county umpire enjoys two great advantages over his counterpart in other countries.

Firstly, he has usually been a first-class cricketer. Though his knowledge of the laws may initially sometimes be shaky and his marks from a written exam less than those obtained by a club umpire, it is a very different story when it comes to the practical decision out in the middle. For example, did the short ball down the leg side flick the glove or the shirt? Or, when making an lbw decision, what was the position of the bowler's front foot? His experience as a player also enables him to scent trouble and take the appropriate action.

Secondly, he is a professional who stands regularly and whose every performance is judged. Though it could be argued that this should not be done by two captains, this has proved an effective system. It is noticeable how our Test umpires demonstrate their skill regularly by finishing with the highest marks.

Smelling them out

My favourite umpire was Alex Skelding, a lovable figure wearing a long white coat, cricket boots, the thickest pebble glasses imaginable, and a smile. There may have been some doubts about his eyesight and his hearing, but none about the correctness of his decisions. He smelled them out.

His presence automatically brought a happy atmosphere to every game. Removing the bails at close of play, he would loudly pronounce: "And that, gentlemen, concludes the entertainment for today," before making his way back to the pavilion and a well-deserved pint. Just as Father Christmas is a friend to every child, Alex was a friend to every cricketer.

Rapport with players

The present umpire comes under far more pressure, but it helps enormously if he can establish a rapport with the players – one reason why Dickie Bird has been so successful – and thus avoid those incidents, still mercifully few in this country but too common overseas. In addition to his normal duties, which anyone who has tried umpiring will agree are extremely demanding, he has to cope with a marked decline in standards of behaviour by both players and the media, deliberate intimidation by fast bowlers, and bad language directed at opponents plus large sums of money at stake and that all-seeing eye of television.

It is impossible to over-estimate the value of good umpiring, because bad umpiring can ruin a tour. I have often felt that the umpires do not receive sufficient support from governing bodies. This was certainly the case during the throwing purge of the 1950s, when they were blamed for not calling offenders, when the real culprits were the clubs who had picked the offenders in the first place.

Every umpire will make some mistakes

Every umpire will make some mistakes. Indeed, rather too many occurred last summer against Australia. Though I believe we have the best in the world, the finest sustained umpiring I encountered as a player was by Messrs Elphinston and Barlow in Australia.

They never made an incorrect decision in the 1950-51 Test series – and that, coming from a losing tourist, is praise indeed, as tourists never forget an error, indeed tend to dwell on them forever.

The Daily Telegraph, 16 July

Great names, great games,

The Daily Telegraph
Century of County Cricket
The 100 Best Matches

The first ever collection of reports, scorecards and analysis of the 100 best county cricket matches played since 1890, as told by correspondents of *The Daily Telegraph* and *The Sunday Telegraph*.

Edited by **Simon Heffer**
Introduction by **E.W. SWANTON**

INCLUDES

*The most famous feats in county cricket – from Archie Maclaren's 424 for Lancashire in 1895 to Graeme Hick's 405 for Worcestershire in 1988
*The great controversies – did Holmes and Sutcliffe *really* score 555 for the first wicket against Essex in 1932?
*The great names – Grace, Fry, Hobbs, Hammond, Edrich, Botham and many, many more – as seen by *Telegraph* correspondents at the time
*The great writers – E.W. Swanton, Thomas Moult and Colonel Philip Trevor and many more – and their descriptions of the time
*Full scorecards for each game
*Many historic action photographs

SIDGWICK & JACKSON

Price: £15.95 (hardback)

Dexter joins campaign to expose the cover-up
by E.W. Swanton

As readers must know by now, it is my firm view that one of the most crucial ways of putting English county cricket back on the right track would be to take the covers off the pitches in first-class matches.

In my last Commentary, quoting two wise heads who thought likewise, R.E.S. Wyatt and M.J.K. Smith, I said I hoped to name someone of even greater authority who felt the same way. I can, and it is Ted Dexter, chairman of the TCCB's England Committee.

Thus we have Mr Dexter and the TCCB's Inspector of Pitches, Harry Brind, of the same opinion, and if there were to be a poll of past county cricketers on the subject I have no doubt a big majority would be in agreement, headed by Sir Leonard Hutton and Denis Compton. So indeed are at least a handful of the county committees.

The majority of present players might need some persuading, partly, I suppose, from an instinctive reluctance to face new problems, and also because they dislike the prospect of confronting fast bowlers who, in certain conditions, could make the ball fly. In answer to that, one might say they get confronted with too much bowling flying around their helmets at times as things are, and when pitches are made soft by rain, it should normally be the spinners and the cutters who come into their own.

Mr Dexter added: "Mind you, they must go out and play as soon as possible after rain, and not wait until all the surrounds are bone dry." Every spectator will say "Here, here" to that, and would add that the umpires are also far too pernickety about offering the batsmen the light, which they, as though working to rule, almost always accept.

As to the uncovering issue, let me repeat – without going over all the arguments again – that bowlers' run-ups would not be protected, only (as always in modern times) the crease areas and any worn places around old pitches.

The conditions would be just those which have produced since time began the best English batsmen and bowlers until the universal covering, started in 1980, was followed by the leanest decade for talent in our history.

If the chairman – who is far from aloof to suggestions – would instigate a seminar on public relations involving the three essential elements – the umpires, the county chairmen, and the captains – before the start of next season, as well as serious courses on the techniques, involving players and coaches, he would be doing the most valuable job possible.

The Daily Telegraph, 30 July

The Daily Telegraph Cricketers Of the Year

Michael Melford, thankfully recovering from a mild stroke, was well enough to select **Graham Gooch** as the England Cricketer of the Year. Not a difficult choice in view of his prolific season at the crease, but Melford emphasized Gooch's leadership of England, in the dressing-room as well as on the field.

Alan Shiell made **Mark Taylor** the Australian choice for his remarkable consistency in Tests, his fine slip fielding, and his record in domestic cricket – he headed the list of run-scorers and, in the absence of the injured Geoff Lawson, led New South Wales to victory over Queensland in the Sheffield Shield final, scoring a hundred in each innings.

It is difficult to follow the exploits of Gooch and Taylor, but Michael Owen-Smith makes out a good case for **Adrian Kuiper**, who was the outstanding player in South African cricket, both at domestic level and against Mike Gatting's tourists: "He captured the imagination of the public whenever he went to the crease, most notably when he made a century off 49 balls at Bloemfontein against the tourists, and he is the biggest drawcard in the South African game since the retirement of Graeme Pollock." (He didn't do so well in England for Derbyshire, though!)

The West Indies choice was **Curtly Ambrose**, for, as Tony Cozier points out, his splendid spell of bowling (8-45) in the Barbados Test, which broke England's spirit, and for his 22 wickets in the Red Stripe Cup, a major factor in Leeward Islands' winning it for the first time.

For India, R. Mohan (writing before India's tour of England) chose **Sachin Tendulkar**, "a callow youth", for "standing up bravely to an unremitting bouncer attack by Imran Khan and Wasim Akram in the Sialkot Test which Sachin, bloodied by blows, helped save". After his performances in England, one cannot argue with this.

Qamar Ahmad had no doubts about the Pakistan choice – **Wasim Akram**, now surely established as a leading international all-rounder, for his maiden Test hundred at Adelaide as well as for his performances with the ball (including two hat-tricks in one-day internationals).

It was an easy choice, too, for Sa'adi Thawfeeq, who felt that **Aravinda de Silva's** "phenomenal batting achievements" in Sri Lanka's two-Test series against Australia's best bowlers – 167, 75, and 72 – speak for themselves.

The Daily Telegraph Schools Cricket Awards
by Charles Randall

Christopher Gates had his skull fractured in a road accident last summer and lingered in intensive care close to death – which made his achievement of winning the Under-19 batting prize in this season's *Daily Telegraph* Schools Cricket Awards all the more remarkable. Mike Gatting, Middlesex's captain, presented Gates with his inscribed trophy during a special luncheon for the schoolboy award-winners and their cricket masters at Lord's on 7 September.

Last summer Gates, an exceptional all-round sportsman from Brighton College, was knocked over by a car and had to miss his 'A' levels, but his extra year at school won him a place at Exeter University and representative honours for Sussex at rugby union and hockey – rounded off by his exceptional cricket season. Last term he hit four hundreds, including 178 not out against Ipswich School, and finished with 1,378 runs, second only to Neil Lenham in the college's all-time list.

Jonathan Whittington, the Eton left-arm spinner, took the Under-19 bowling award for his total of 71 wickets, which included 22 for Berkshire Schools. He will be captaining the school side in his final year, starting with the three-week tour of Australia and New Zealand at Christmas.

Gary Keedy, the Under-15 bowling award-winner from Garforth Comprehensive in Leeds, is another left-arm spinner, and his success seems to prove that a good leg-break is better than a good off-break. Gary's identical twin brother Ian is – according to Gary – just as good a cricketer, but he bowls off-spin. This 'laboratory test' reveals that Gary, with 34 wickets, has been much more successful at school and club level.

At Under-15 level the winners are decided on representative matches only, and Michael Vaughan's remarkable aggregate of 990 runs reflects his steady progress up through the representative batting ladder in Yorkshire and the North. Vaughan, from Silverdale Comprehensive in Sheffield, is a Lancastrian by birth and could well join a long list of boys whose ambition to play for Yorkshire, his home county, is denied by the 'Yorkshire-born only' policy.

The four national winners each collected a trophy, a Duncan Fearnley bat, and £1,000 worth of Fearnley equipment for his school. The 16 regional winners earned a trophy each, plus £250 worth of equipment for their schools.

1989-90

ENGLAND'S WINTER TOURS

England in West Indies

Soon after the England players had arrived in the West Indies, they ordered a colourful T-shirt made to their own design. On the back it read: "They tell me it's HELL out there." On the front was a palm tree and beneath it three stumps being smashed by a ball.

If asked for their views three months later, after losing a Test series by 2-1, the players will tell you: "Well, it wasn't hell. But it certainly wasn't heaven either."

The bottom line of this England performance must be that they did a whole lot better than anyone expected. They might have been singed, but they were not burned.

When the side left home in January, the prophets of doom were to be heard on all sides. Gooch and his team manager, Micky Stewart, had picked, largely, young terriers who would work and worry the hearts out of the opposition. Old hands such as Botham and Gower had been discarded. The South African rebel tour had eliminated Gatting and Emburey and the first-choice opening attack, Foster and Dilley.

It was a golden opportunity for Mr Stewart to rebuild a side much more in his own image – fit, aggressive, and ready to "fight fire with fire", though half-way through the tour the manager went back on those words of Ted Dexter, chairman of the England Committee.

No touring party could have pulled together better than this one. None could have been better led by example than Graham Gooch, a workaholic of the cricket world. That is, until the tragic moment in Trinidad when, with England coasting in high gear towards a 2-0 lead, a ball reared up from Ezra Moseley and broke a finger of Gooch's left hand.

In that moment, the spell which the side had cast over their opponents for more than half this Cable and Wireless Test series was broken. England had lost a leader and a batting anchor and Gooch was robbed by the fickleness of fortune.

Port-of-Spain was a watershed in the team's fortunes in more senses than one. At the end, it was called off in awful light with England 31 runs away from their second win and five wickets in hand. So near and yet so far. And never anywhere near again.

In a side of gambles, the biggest was the choice of Devon Malcolm who, in his only previous Test, last summer, had shown the control of a man shying at a fairground coconut.

How he and his mentors must have worked on his line and length for this tour – 19 wickets in seven innings in the series and the scalp of Viv Richards three times. But there was bound to be a game when he failed. After five wickets in Jamaica and 10 in Trinidad (the man-of-the match award here), his Waterloo came in Barbados.

Gladstone Small also measured up to everything England asked of him. He was incisive, accurate (except on the second day in Antigua, where something seemed to affect all the attack), and had a good haul of wickets: 17. But the loss of Angus Fraser was a mortal blow in the final two games. He went for not much more than an average of two runs an over and collected 11 wickets.

Mr Stewart stuck to his game plan of an attack solely composed of quickish bowlers, but there was too little variety. It is one thing to stay with a winning formula, but when you have lost ingredient "X" it is time to re-make the potion. At Barbados, Hemmings had bowled brilliantly in the one-day international and really should have played, if only to take some of the burden off the fast men.

The call-up and stand-down of David Gower was not well handled. Again, there seemed a stubborn determination to stay with the original party. Maybe in that there was a studied refusal to admit the selectors had been wrong in the first place to omit Gower.

The media circus – more than 50 English journalists at some time or other were on the tour – was bound to inject controversy, and did. So, too, did some of the television commentary with the need to "hype" the action. Desmond Haynes remained unprovoked by his "Dirty Des" tag; Richards was predictably more volatile and threatened to "whack a reporter" at a time when he should have been on the field.

The umpiring was often very good, erring occasionally but not worthy of condemnation. The most worrying feature was the slow over-rate. Expecting 90 overs a day in the Caribbean, given the propensity towards pace attacks, is ludicrous. If all 18 days of the Tests had gone their normal six hours, something like 300 overs would have been lost.

Equally, it was ridiculous to set a limit and not impose any kind of sanction. The paying customer demands his money's worth today.

PETER DEELEY
The Daily Telegraph, 18 April

West Indies viewpoint

The West Indies' reign as world champions could come to an end when they next face England in the summer of 1991 – unless they find at least one good opening batsman, a middle-order batsman, two fast bowlers, and a wicket-keeper who can bat. Apart from Ian Bishop, it was the ageing and experienced players who made the difference in the series against England. But Gordon Greenidge, Desmond Haynes, Viv Richards, and even Curtly Ambrose cannot go on forever.

The West Indies have always over the years found a young star or two just when they were needed. But if it proved nothing else, this series showed up a lack of support in their cricket. Apart from one face-saving innings by Gus Logie and one brilliant display by Carlisle Best, the world champions were forced to depend on the old brigade to pull them out of the fire and rescue their reputation.

In celebrating their sixth successive victory over England, therefore, the West Indies should count their blessings, and in doing so prepare for the testing days ahead. For now that they have proven to be back in the company of mere mortals, every team in the world will be hunting their scalp.

The series could easily have gone the other way but for the weather and injuries. Fortune, it is said, favours the brave. But this time around it abandoned England, and after looking ready and prepared for whatever the West Indies could come up with, the tourists were hit two crunching blows with the injuries to Graham Gooch and Angus Fraser – injuries which put them out of the crucial fourth and fifth Test matches.

It is true that the West Indies had their share of injuries, with fast bowler Ambrose missing the first Test, and Malcolm Marshall and Viv Richards the third. But based on the strengths of the two teams, the absence of their top batsman and their main bowler affected England tremendously.

The absence of Gooch destroyed any chance England had of even drawing the series, as, apart from being the team's top batsman, he was also the motivating force behind his relatively young and inexperienced players.

With Richards playing only one innings of merit, he must be numbered among those who failed. The performances that opened the door for the victory were those of Bishop and Ambrose at Queen's Park Oval. They were on top at Kensington Oval and the Antigua recreation ground, but the job was really done at Queen's Park Oval.

TONY BECCA

Diary of the Tour

Sep 7: Graham Gooch, who declined to play for England in the fifth Test against Australia, is appointed captain for the West Indies tour. He replaces David Gower, who led England against Australia in the summer.

8: England tour party announced. Gower, to his anguish, is omitted, as is Ian Botham. Ricardo Ellcock, who bowled only 182 overs for Middlesex all summer, is a surprise fast-bowling choice. Devon Malcolm, one for 166 in his one Ashes Test, is also included. Nassar Hussain wins place to gain experience.

Jan 24: The England tour party fly into Barbados.

25: Nets in Bridgetown are washed out by torrential rain.

Feb 4: Hussain reprimanded after twice showing dissent at umpiring decisions in his second innings against Leeward Islands at St Kitts. In first incident, he is recalled after disputing fairness of bat-pad catch.

7: Ellcock breaks down with back trouble in his first serious net practice, which precedes Windward Islands game at St Lucia.

8: Chris Lewis, of Leicestershire, is summoned from the England 'A' tour party in Kenya to replace Ellcock.

11: England lose to Windwards by one wicket after collapsing to Mervin Durand, a left-arm spinner making his first-class debut, who takes seven for 15 off 19.4 overs in the first innings.

19: Gooch scores 239 and Larkins hits a century in 115 minutes against Jamaica.

24: England stun the cricketing world by dismissing West Indies for 164 in their first innings of the first Test at Kingston, Jamaica. Angus Fraser takes five for 28.

25: Allan Lamb extends England's unexpected dominance with 132.

28: England endure frustration when, with victory within their grasp, fourth day is washed out by rain. West Indies are only 29 ahead with two wickets remaining.

Mar 1: The sun shines and the series catches fire as England wrap up victory by nine wickets. Devon Malcolm, in the island of his birth, leaves nobody in doubt about his extra pace in taking 4 for 77, with the wicket of Richards in both innings.

12: Hussain, who made his England debut at Kingston, sprains wrist playing tennis and misses next two Tests.

15: The second Test in Guyana – where West Indies have not won a Test in 25 years – is rained off without a ball being bowled. Rob Bailey bats for the first time in six weeks and makes 42 in hastily arranged one-day game.

21: England beat the President's XI by 113 runs in Trinidad after Robin Smith, with 99, turns round a probable defeat.

23: Richards and Malcolm Marshall miss third Test in Trinidad with fitness problems and England take a grip from the first day after dismissing West Indies for 199.

27: Malcolm takes three wickets in four deliveries as West Indies reach the fourth-day close just 145 ahead with one wicket standing. He finishes the innings with 6 for 77 and 10 wickets in the match.

28: The turning point of the tour. It is the dry season, but rain cruelly lops three hours' play off the final day and the match is drawn. Gooch has his hand broken by an Ezra Moseley delivery, and England, on 73 for one, see their 'easy' target of 151 to win suddenly look difficult. It becomes impossible as Bailey completes a 'pair' and the West Indies send down only 17 overs in 100 minutes. On-field behaviour deteriorates as Desmond Haynes, standing in as West Indies captain, harangues Alec Stewart and Lamb at the end of a session. Larkins and Stewart finish with badly bruised fingers.

30: Gower, on tour as a journalist, is called in to play against Barbados.

31: When Bailey is unable to continue as substitute wicket-keeper against Barbados because of bruising on his hands, David Bairstow, on tour with Yorkshire, goes behind the stumps. Gower is caught for four.

Apr 1: David Smith, of Sussex, arrives from England as a replacement opener for Gooch, who will miss the last two Tests.

2: Angus Fraser breaks down with a side strain, which will keep him out of the last two Tests.

3: England lose the fifth one-day international in Barbados and the series 3-0. David Smith, in his first innings for England, has his thumb damaged by Moseley and will miss the remainder of the tour.

5: The selectors decide against selecting Gower for the fourth Test in Barbados. Lamb, in his first match as captain of England, puts West Indies in, but Carlisle Best hits a maiden century (164) on his home ground. Malcolm is left with none for 142 off 33 overs as West Indies rush towards 446 with ominous speed.

7: Lamb makes 119, but only Robin Smith (62) can support him. The cracks are showing, even though England make 358 in reply.

8: Controversy as Bailey is given out caught behind – television replays suggest the ball hit thigh pad, not bat – and umpire Barker delays his decision until Richards, back as captain, has danced jubilantly

towards him from slip. BBC Radio commentator Christopher Martin-Jenkins becomes the centre of a furore after he alludes to Richards' actions being akin to cheating and suggests Barker changed his mind. The umpire threatens to sue for defamation. Earlier Haynes had made 109, a warning of even better things to come for the West Indies.

10: England lose by 164 runs, and the series is levelled 1-1. Curtly Ambrose, with eight for 45, skittles England for 191, exposing their batting as desperately thin without Gooch.

12: Final Test, in Antigua, and there is no time to stop the downhill plunge of England's bandwagon. The bouncers fly as England slip to 203 for six on a good batting pitch.

14: England's worst day of the tour. Richards is again in the news, climbing to the press box to remonstrate with a journalist about a newspaper article in England while his side take the field without him. England are dismissed for 260 then Gordon Greenidge (118 not out) and Haynes (101 not out) put on 228 in only 51.4 overs before the close. The mocking calypso rings out: "London Bridge is falling down."

15: Greenidge (149) and Haynes (167) take their partnership to 298 before the West Indies reach 446 (Richards is out for one). England lose Larkins before the close.

16: All over with a day to spare. England, with Robin Smith retiring with an injured finger – broken while batting four days earlier – are dismissed for 154, losing the Test by an innings and 32 runs and the series 2-1. As the home crowd celebrates and Richards receives the Antiguan Order of Distinction, the rain begins to pour down on the St John's ground.

West Indies v England 1989-90 1st Test

England won by 9 wickets
Played at Sabina Park, Kingston, 24, 25, 26, 28(np) February, 1 March
Toss: West Indies. Umpires: L.H. Barker and S. Bucknor
Debuts: England – N. Hussain, A.J. Stewart

West Indies

C.G. Greenidge	run out (Malcolm/ Russell)	32	c Hussain b Malcolm	36
D.L. Haynes	c & b Small	36	b Malcolm	14
R.B. Richardson	c Small b Capel	10	lbw b Fraser	25
C.A. Best	c Russell b Capel	4	c Gooch b Small	64
C.L. Hooper	c Capel b Fraser	20	c Larkins b Small	8
I.V.A. Richards*	lbw b Malcolm	21	b Malcolm	37
P.J.L. Dujon†	not out	19	b Malcolm	15
M.D. Marshall	b Fraser	0	not out	8
I.R. Bishop	c Larkins b Fraser	0	c Larkins b Small	3
C.A. Walsh	b Fraser	6	b Small	2
B.P. Patterson	b Fraser	0	run out (Capel/Malcolm)	2
Extras	(B9, LB3, NB4)	16	(B14, LB10, NB1)	26
		164		**240**

England

G.A. Gooch*	c Dujon b Patterson	18	c Greenidge b Bishop	8
W. Larkins	lbw b Walsh	46	not out	29
A.J. Stewart	c Best b Bishop	13	not out	0
A.J. Lamb	c Hooper b Walsh	132		
R.A. Smith	c Best b Bishop	57		
N. Hussain	c Dujon b Bishop	13		
D.J. Capel	c Richardson b Walsh	5		
R.C. Russell†	c Patterson b Walsh	26		
G.C. Small	lbw b Marshall	4		
A.R.C. Fraser	not out	2		
D.E. Malcolm	lbw b Walsh	0		
Extras	(B23, LB12, W1, NB12)	48	(LB1, NB3)	4
		364	(1 wkt)	**41**

England	O	M	R	W	O	M	R	W
Small	15	6	44	1	22	6	58	4
Malcolm	16	4	49	1	21.3	2	77	4
Fraser	20	8	28	5	15	5	31	1
Capel	13	4	31	2	15	1	50	0

West Indies	O	M	R	W	O	M	R	W
Patterson	18	2	74	1	3	1	11	0
Bishop	27	5	72	3	7.3	2	17	1
Marshall	18	3	46	1				
Walsh	27.2	4	68	5	6	0	12	0
Hooper	6	0	28	0				
Richards	9	1	22	0				
Best	4	0	19	0				

Fall of Wickets

Wkt	WI 1st	E 1st	WI 2nd	E 2nd
1st	62	40	26	35
2nd	81	60	69	–
3rd	92	116	87	–
4th	92	288	112	–
5th	124	315	192	–
6th	144	315	222	–
7th	144	325	222	–
8th	150	339	227	–
9th	164	364	237	–
10th	164	364	240	–

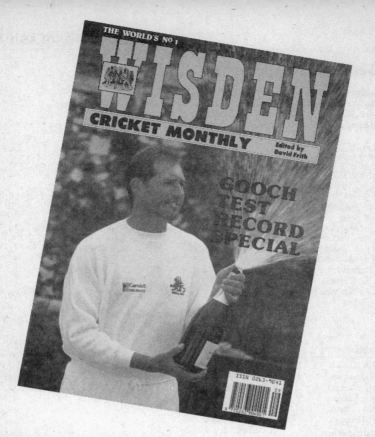

West Indies v England 1989-90 3rd Test

Match Drawn
Played at Queen's Park Oval, Port-of-Spain, 23, 24, 25, 27, 28 March
Toss: England. Umpires: L.H. Barker and C.E. Cumberbatch
Debuts: West Indies – E.A. Moseley

West Indies

C.G. Greenidge	c Stewart b Malcolm	5	lbw b Fraser	42
D.L. Haynes*	c Lamb b Small	0	c Lamb b Malcolm	45
R.B. Richardson	c Russell b Fraser	8	c Gooch b Small	34
C.A. Best	c Lamb b Fraser	10	lbw b Malcolm	0
P.J.L. Dujon†	lbw b Small	4	b Malcolm	0
A.L. Logie	c Lamb b Fraser	98	c Larkins b Malcolm	20
C.L. Hooper	c Russell b Capel	32	run out (Smith/Russell)	10
E.A. Moseley	c Russell b Malcolm	0	c Lamb b Malcolm	26
C.E.L. Ambrose	c Russell b Malcolm	7	c Russell b Fraser	18
I.R. Bishop	b Malcolm	16	not out	15
C.A. Walsh	not out	8	lbw b Malcolm	1
Extras	(LB4, NB7)	11	(B2, LB13, W1, NB12)	28
		199		**239**

England

G.A. Gooch*	c Dujon b Bishop	84	retired hurt	18
W. Larkins	c Dujon b Ambrose	54	c Dujon b Moseley	7
A.J. Stewart	c Dujon b Ambrose	9	c Bishop b Walsh	31
A.J. Lamb	b Bishop	32	lbw b Bishop	25
R.A. Smith	c Dujon b Moseley	5	lbw b Walsh	2
R.J. Bailey	c Logie b Moseley	0	b Walsh	0
D.J. Capel	c Moseley b Ambrose	40	not out	17
R.C. Russell†	c Best b Walsh	15	not out	5
G.C. Small	lbw b Bishop	0		
A.R.C. Fraser	c Hooper b Ambrose	11		
D.E. Malcolm	not out	0		
Extras	(B10, LB9, W3, NB16)	38	(B2, LB7, NB6)	15
		288	(5 wkts)	**120**

Note: G.A. Gooch retired hurt at 37-1.

England	O	M	R	W	O	M	R	W
Small	17	4	41	2	21	8	56	1
Malcolm	20	2	60	4	26.2	4	77	6
Fraser	13.1	2	41	3	24	4	61	2
Capel	15	2	53	1	13	3	30	0

West Indies	O	M	R	W	O	M	R	W
Ambrose	36.2	8	59	4	6	0	20	0
Bishop	31	6	69	3	10	1	31	1
Walsh	22	5	45	1	7	0	27	3
Hooper	18	5	26	0				
Moseley	30	5	70	2	10	2	33	1

Fall of Wickets

Wkt	WI 1st	E 1st	WI 2nd	E 2nd
1st	5	112	96	27
2nd	5	125	100	74
3rd	22	195	100	79
4th	27	214	100	85
5th	29	214	142	106
6th	92	214	167	–
7th	93	243	200	–
8th	103	244	200	–
9th	177	284	234	–
10th	199	288	239	–

West Indies v England 1989-90 4th Test

West Indies won by 164 runs
Played at Kensington Oval, Bridgetown, 5, 6, 7, 8, 10 April
Toss: England. Umpires: D.M. Archer and L.H. Barker
Debuts: nil

West Indies

C.G. Greenidge	c Russell b DeFreitas	41		lbw b Small	3
D.L. Haynes	c Stewart b Small	0		c Malcolm b Small	109
R.B. Richardson	c Russell b Small	45		lbw b DeFreitas	39
C.A. Best	c Russell b Small	164			
I.V.A. Richards*	c Russell b Capel	70	(4)	c Small b Capel	12
A.L. Logie	c Russell b Capel	31	(5)	lbw b DeFreitas	48
P.J.L. Dujon†	b Capel	31	(8)	not out	15
M.D. Marshall	c Lamb b Small	4	(7)	c Smith b Small	7
C.E.L. Ambrose	not out	20		c Capel b DeFreitas	1
I.R. Bishop	run out (Hussain)	10		not out	11
E.A. Moseley	b DeFreitas	4	(6)	b Small	5
Extras	(LB8, NB18)	26		(LB12, W1, NB4)	17
		446		(8 wkts dec)	**267**

England

A.J. Stewart	c Richards b Moseley	45		c Richards b Ambrose	37
W. Larkins	c Richardson b Bishop	0		c Dujon b Bishop	0
R.J. Bailey	b Bishop	17		c Dujon b Ambrose	6
A.J. Lamb*	lbw b Ambrose	119	(6)	c Dujon b Moseley	10
R.A. Smith	b Moseley	62	(7)	not out	40
N. Hussain	lbw b Marshall	18	(8)	lbw b Ambrose	0
D.J. Capel	c Greenidge b Marshall	2	(9)	lbw b Ambrose	6
R.C. Russell†	lbw b Bishop	7	(5)	b Ambrose	55
P.A.J. DeFreitas	c & b Ambrose	24	(10)	lbw b Ambrose	0
G.C. Small	not out	1	(4)	lbw b Ambrose	0
D.E. Malcolm	b Bishop	12		lbw b Ambrose	4
Extras	(B14, LB9, W3, NB25)	51		(B8, LB9, W1, NB15)	33
		358			**191**

England	O	M	R	W	O	M	R	W
Malcolm	33	6	142	0	10	0	46	0
Small	35	5	109	4	20	1	74	4
DeFreitas	29.5	5	99	2	22	2	69	3
Capel	24	5	88	3	16	1	66	1

West Indies	O	M	R	W	O	M	R	W
Bishop	24.3	8	70	4	20	7	40	1
Ambrose	25	2	82	2	22.4	10	45	8
Moseley	28	4	114	2	19	3	44	1
Marshall	23	5	55	2	18	8	31	0
Richards	9	4	14	0	10	5	11	0
Richardson					2	1	3	0

Fall of Wickets

Wkt	WI 1st	E 1st	WI 2nd	E 2nd
1st	6	1	13	1
2nd	69	46	80	10
3rd	108	75	109	10
4th	227	268	223	71
5th	291	297	228	97
6th	395	301	238	166
7th	406	308	238	173
8th	411	340	239	181
9th	431	340	–	181
10th	446	358	–	191

West Indies v England 1989-90 5th Test

West Indies won by an innings and 32 runs
Played at Recreation Ground, St. John's, 12, 14, 15, 16 April
Toss: England. Umpires: D.M. Archer and A.E. Weekes
Debuts: nil

England

A.J. Stewart	c Richards b Walsh	27		c Richardson b Bishop	8
W. Larkins	c Hooper b Ambrose	30		b Ambrose	10
R.J. Bailey	c Dujon b Bishop	42	(4)	c Dujon b Bishop	8
A.J. Lamb*	c Richards b Ambrose	37	(5)	b Baptiste	35
R.A. Smith	lbw b Walsh	12	(6)	retired hurt	8
N. Hussain	c Dujon b Bishop	35	(7)	c Dujon b Bishop	34
D.J. Capel	c Haynes b Bishop	10	(8)	run out (Ambrose/Dujon/ Greenidge)	1
R.C. Russell†	c Dujon b Bishop	7	(9)	c Richardson b Ambrose	24
P.A.J. DeFreitas	lbw b Bishop	21	(10)	c Greenidge b Ambrose	0
G.C. Small	lbw b Walsh	8	(3)	b Ambrose	4
D.E. Malcolm	not out	0		not out	1
Extras	(B5, LB11, NB15)	31		(B1, LB8, W1, NB11)	21
		260			**154**

R.A. Smith retired hurt at 61-4.

West Indies

C.G. Greenidge	run out (Small)	149
D.L. Haynes	c Russell b Small	167
R.B. Richardson	c Russell b Malcolm	34
C.L. Hooper	b Capel	1
I.V.A. Richards*	c Smith b Malcolm	1
A.L. Logie	c Lamb b DeFreitas	15
P.J.L. Dujon†	run out (Bailey/Malcolm)	25
E.A.E. Baptiste	c Russell b Malcolm	9
C.E.L. Ambrose	c DeFreitas b Capel	5
I.R. Bishop	not out	14
C.A. Walsh	b Malcolm	8
Extras	(LB5, NB13)	18
		446

West Indies	O	M	R	W	O	M	R	W
Bishop	28.1	6	84	5	14	2	36	3
Ambrose	29	5	79	2	13	7	22	4
Walsh	21	4	51	3	10	1	40	0
Baptiste	13	4	30	0	10	1	47	1

England	O	M	R	W
Small	31	3	123	1
Malcolm	34.5	3	126	4
Capel	28	1	118	2
DeFreitas	27	4	74	1

Fall of Wickets

Wkt	E 1st	WI 1st	E 2nd
1st	42	298	16
2nd	101	357	20
3rd	143	358	33
4th	167	359	37
5th	167	382	86
6th	195	384	94
7th	212	415	148
8th	242	417	148
9th	259	433	154
10th	260	446	154

Test Match Averages: West Indies v England 1989-90

West Indies

Batting and Fielding	M	I	NO	HS	R	Avge	100	50	Ct/St
D.L. Haynes	4	7	0	167	371	53.00	2	–	1
C.A. Best	3	5	0	164	242	48.40	1	1	3
C.G. Greenidge	4	7	0	149	308	44.00	1	–	3
A.L. Logie	3	5	0	98	212	42.40	–	1	1
I.V.A. Richards	3	5	0	70	141	28.20	–	1	4
R.B. Richardson	4	7	0	45	195	27.85	–	–	4
P.J.L. Dujon	4	7	2	31	109	21.80	–	–	15/-
I.R. Bishop	4	7	3	16	69	17.25	–	–	1
C.L. Hooper	3	5	0	32	71	14.20	–	–	3
C.E.L. Ambrose	3	5	1	20*	51	12.75	–	–	1
E.A. Moseley	2	4	0	26	35	8.75	–	–	1
M.D. Marshall	2	4	1	8*	19	6.33	–	–	–
C.A. Walsh	3	5	1	8*	25	6.25	–	–	–

Also batted: E.A.E. Baptiste (1 match) 9; B.P. Patterson (1 match) 0, 2 (1ct).

Bowling	O	M	R	W	Avge	Best	5wI	10wM
C.E.L. Ambrose	132	32	307	20	15.35	8-45	1	1
I.R. Bishop	162.1	37	419	21	19.95	5-84	1	–
C.A. Walsh	93.2	14	243	12	20.25	5-68	1	–
E.A. Moseley	87	14	261	6	43.50	2-70	–	–

Also bowled: E.A.E. Baptiste 23-5-77-1; C.A. Best 4-0-19-0; C.L. Hooper 24-5-54-0; M.D. Marshall 59-16-132-3; B.P. Patterson 21-3-85-1; I.V.A. Richards 28-10-47-0; R.B. Richardson 2-1-3-0.

England

Batting and Fielding	M	I	NO	HS	R	Avge	100	50	Ct/St
A.J. Lamb	4	7	0	132	390	55.71	2	–	7
G.A. Gooch	2	4	1	84	128	42.66	–	1	2
R.A. Smith	4	7	2	62	186	37.20	–	2	2
W. Larkins	4	8	1	54	176	25.14	–	1	4
A.J. Stewart	4	8	1	45	170	24.28	–	–	2
R.C. Russell	4	7	1	55	139	23.16	–	1	14/-
N. Hussain	3	5	0	35	100	20.00	–	–	1
D.J. Capel	4	7	1	40	81	13.50	–	–	2
R.J. Bailey	3	6	0	42	73	12.16	–	–	–
P.A.J. DeFreitas	2	4	0	24	45	11.25	–	–	1
D.E. Malcolm	4	6	3	12	17	5.66	–	–	1
G.C. Small	4	6	1	8	17	3.40	–	–	3

Also batted: A.R.C. Fraser (2 matches) 2*, 11.

Bowling	O	M	R	W	Avge	Best	5wI	10wM
A.R.C. Fraser	71.1	18	161	11	14.63	5-28	1	–
G.C. Small	161	33	505	17	29.70	4-58	–	–
D.E. Malcolm	161.4	21	577	19	30.36	6-77	1	1
P.A.J. DeFreitas	78.5	11	242	6	40.33	3-69	–	–
D.J. Capel	124	17	436	9	48.44	3-88	–	–

Statistical Highlights of the Tests

1st Test, Kingston. England beat West Indies for the 1st time since the last match of the 1973-74 series. It was West Indies' 1st defeat at Sabina Park since Australia won there in 1954-55. Fraser took 5 wickets for 1st time. Lamb scored his 10th Test hundred, his 5th against West Indies, and his 1st overseas. Walsh took 5 wickets for 5th time, his 1st against England. In the 2nd innings, Richards at 22* reached 7,892 Test runs and passed Javed Miandad. Larkins played his 7th Test, his 1st since Oval 1981 against Australia, during which time England played 85 Tests.

2nd Test, Georgetown. This was the 5th Test to be abandoned without a ball bowled, and the 1st instance in West Indies.

3rd Test, Port-of-Spain. Logie scored his 4th Test score in the nineties. Malcolm took 5 wickets for 1st time and reached 10 wickets/match for the 1st time in his first-class career.

4th Test, Bridgetown. Best scored his 1st Test hundred. Russell was the 1st England wicket-keeper to take 5 catches against West Indies. Lamb scored his 11th Test hundred, his 6th against West Indies, equalling Cowdrey. He was the 2nd England player to make 100 in his 1st Test as captain (A.C. MacLaren 109 v Australia, SCG 1897-98). Haynes scored his 13th Test hundred, his 4th against England. Greenidge at 31* reached 6,972 Test runs and passed Hutton. Ambrose took 5 wickets for 2nd time as he recorded his best career bowling. It gave him 10 wickets/match for the 1st time. It is the best bowling for West Indies against England in the West Indies. Richards played his 110th Test, equalling Lloyd in most appearances for West Indies.

5th Test, St. John's. Bishop took 5 wickets for 2nd time, his 1st against England. Greenidge became the 11th player (3rd West Indian) to play 100 Tests. He was the 3rd after Cowdrey and Javed Miandad to score 100 in his 100th Test and, like Javed Miandad, he also achieved this in his 1st and 100th Tests. At 12* he reached 6,997 Test runs and passed Bradman. At 15* he reached 7,000 Test runs, the 12th player to do so. At 126* he reached 7,111 and passed G.S. Chappell to stand 11th in world list. Haynes, meanwhile, was scoring his 14th Test hundred, his 5th against England. Greenidge's hundred was his 18th and 7th against England. The partnership reached 298, a record 1st-wicket total for West Indies against England. Dujon ended the series with 223 dismissals and passed Evans (219). Richards played a record 111th Test for West Indies.

One-Day Internationals

14 February at Queen's Park Oval, Port-of-Spain, Trinidad. MATCH ABANDONED. Toss: England. West Indies 208-8 (50 overs) (R.B. Richardson 51). England 26-1 (13 overs).

17 February at Queen's Park Oval, Port-of-Spain, Trinidad. MATCH ABANDONED. Toss: England. West Indies 13-0 (5.5 overs).

3 March at Sabina Park, Kingston, Jamaica. WEST INDIES beat ENGLAND by 3 wickets. Toss: England. England 214-8 (50 overs) (R.A. Smith 43, A.J. Lamb 66; I.R. Bishop 10-1-28-4). West Indies 216-7 (50 overs) (R.B. Richardson 100*). Award: R.B. Richardson (100*).

7 March at Bourda, Georgetown, Guyana. WEST INDIES beat ENGLAND by 6 wickets. Toss: West Indies. England 188-8 (48 overs). West Indies 191-4 (45.2 overs) (C.A. Best 100, D.L. Haynes 50). Award: C.A. Best (100).

3 April at Kensington Oval, Bridgetown, Barbados. WEST INDIES beat ENGLAND by 4 wickets. Toss: West Indies. England 214-3 (38 overs) (R.A. Smith 69, A.J. Lamb 55*). West Indies 217-6 (37.3 overs) (D.L. Haynes 45, R.B. Richardson 80, C.A. Best 51). Award: R.B. Richardson (80).

The following match was played when the second Test was abandoned without a ball bowled. It was not part of the official series.
15 March at Bourda, Georgetown, Guyana. WEST INDIES beat ENGLAND by 7 wickets. Toss: West Indies. ENGLAND 166-9 (49 overs) (G.A. Gooch 42, R.J. Bailey 42; C.E.L. Ambrose 9-1-18-4). West Indies 167-3 (40.2 overs) (C.G. Greenidge 77, C.B. Lambert 48).

England Tour of West Indies 1989-90

First-Class Matches: Played 10; Won 2, Lost 3, Drawn 4, Abandoned 1
All Matches: Played 16; Won 2, Lost 7, Drawn 4, Abandoned 3

First-Class Averages

Batting and Fielding	M	I	NO	HS	R	Avge	100	50	Ct/St
G.A. Gooch	6	11	1	239	616	61.60	1	4	6
A.J. Lamb	7	12	0	132	549	45.75	2	1	9
W. Larkins	8	16	2	124*	524	37.42	2	1	4
R.A. Smith	9	16	3	99*	477	36.69	–	4	5
A.J. Stewart	9	18	1	125	516	30.35	1	1	4
N. Hussain	6	10	1	70*	260	28.88	–	1	2
R.C. Russell	8	15	5	55	269	26.90	–	1	24/2
D.J. Capel	8	15	3	65	245	20.41	–	2	5
R.J. Bailey	6	12	1	52	177	16.09	–	1	3
P.A.J. DeFreitas	6	11	4	24	108	15.42	–	–	2
C.C. Lewis	2	3	0	21	33	11.00	–	–	1
K.T. Medlycott	3	3	0	21	24	8.00	–	–	1
D.E. Malcolm	7	9	3	12	29	4.83	–	–	3
A.R.C. Fraser	4	5	1	11	17	4.25	–	–	2
G.C. Small	5	6	1	8	17	3.40	–	–	4
E.E. Hemmings	4	6	1	6	13	2.60	–	–	2

Also batted: D.I. Gower (1 match) 4.

Bowling	O	M	R	W	Avge	Best	5wI	10wM
E.E. Hemmings	108.1	30	301	15	20.06	5-77	1	–
A.R.C. Fraser	122.2	27	353	17	20.76	5-28	1	–
G.C. Small	201	41	644	23	28.00	4-58	–	–
D.E. Malcolm	258.4	37	948	32	29.62	6-77	1	–
K.T. Medlycott	110.2	12	425	13	32.69	4-36	–	–
P.A.J. DeFreitas	196.4	26	697	21	33.19	4-54	–	–
D.J. Capel	201	26	733	14	52.35	3-88	–	–

Also bowled: G.A. Gooch 3-0-6-1; C.C. Lewis 35-6-128-2.

England 'A' in Zimbabwe

Quality was the missing ingredient during the unofficial five-day Test series between Zimbabwe and Mark Nicholas's England side, which was regarded by both cricket authorities as a 'learning process'. There is a big difference between Test cricket and two teams spinning a match out for five days, and it was underlined during Zimbabwe's three-match unofficial series against England.

Nicholas, as captain, and Keith Fletcher, as coach, pursued a policy of attrition, a dress-rehearsal for Test cricket, and the prize was a 1-0 series success. The price was grindingly slow batting on sound batting strips, the rate of just over two runs an over, occasionally descending to a level which could only be described as crass; in the 'dead' final day of the Bulawayo Test, England scored 123 runs off 82 overs.

The five-day game was unknown territory for Zimbabwe, who have started a five-year probationary period towards full test status. Their players, mostly amateurs who travel vast distances for a match, had to switch from a near continuous diet of one-day weekend cricket to the longest game.

Zimbabwe have three professional cricketers – David Houghton, their captain, and the two Flower brothers, Andy and Grant. The rest are an assortment of farmers, lawyers and salesmen. Players of adequate quality in Zimbabwe number fewer than 50, very few of them black, and the tradition of cricket has been hard to sustain since 'the troubles' ended 10 years ago and Rhodesia became Zimbabwe.

Houghton, director of ZCU coaching, estimates it will take 15 years or more to create a nucleus of black players of sufficient quality. In the meantime, the country needs Test status to prevent the sport folding into oblivion. This argument is difficult to resist.

Zimbabwe want that recognition, not to challenge the West Indies in the Caribbean, but to attract brief stop-overs from major countries on tour – for example, England on their way to Australia. They are unlikely to win a Test match for perhaps 20 years, but this is regarded as a subsidiary consideration.

Bob Bennett, Lancashire's chairman, was an inspired choice as manager of the Touring side and Fletcher, as coach, revelled in the talent available to him.

The three-match whitewash in the one-day series knocked the stuffing out of Zimbabwe, and England were never in danger in the five-day series.

The star of the tour was undoubtedly vice-captain Mike Atherton. In the first 'Test' at Harare, his hundred in the first innings followed by a spell of 3 for 4 in six overs with his loopy leg-breaks ensured a 10-

wicket win for England. Another hundred at Bulawayo helped to build up an impregnable score, and he missed the last match through injury. He was the only batsman in the party obviously ready for Test cricket, posing the big question: Why on earth was he not in the West Indies?

Yorkshire's Richard Blakey also caught the eye at the crease, sharing two big stands with Atherton. He scored 92 at Harare and then 221 in 10 hours at Bulawayo, showing the mental toughness and determination required of a Test cricketer, but perhaps at this stage of his career lacking the full range of strokes. His wicket-keeping skills, however, are a bonus. The number one wicket-keeper Steve Rhodes confirmed his standing as a capable deputy to Jack Russell and seemed to find runs easy to score.

The captain, Nicholas, made some solid contributions at the crease, but the only other batsman to enhance his reputation was Graham Thorpe of Surrey. As his confidence increased, he unzipped mellow strokes all round the wicket and hit the ball harder than anyone else during his two Test innings of 44 and 98.

Of the bowlers, Alan Igglesden of Kent was the most effective, taking 13 wickets in the three 'Tests' and twice destroying Zimbabwe in one-day internationals. Martin Bicknell of Surrey also impressed as an England candidate of the future, looking capable of getting a wicket with every delivery, except when he failed to control his outswingers.

When MCC decided to give only the 'Tests' first-class status, it robbed Atherton of the distinction of leading both batting and bowling tour averages. Outside limited-overs games, he scored 438 runs at an average of 109.50 and took 11 wickets at 17.36 apiece.

CHARLES RANDALL

One-day Internationals

24 February at Harare Sports Club. ENGLAND 'A' beat ZIMBABWE on faster scoring rate. Toss: England 'A'. Zimbabwe 134-6 (50 overs). England 'A' 118-4 (41.5 overs).

25 February at Harare Sports Club. ENGLAND 'A' beat ZIMBABWE by 61 runs. Toss: Zimbabwe. England 'A' 245-5 (50 overs) (D.J. Bicknell 70, R.J. Blakey 73, G.P. Thorpe 50*). Zimbabwe 184-8 (50 overs) (D.L. Houghton 88).

18 March at Bulawayo Athletic Club. ENGLAND 'A' beat ZIMBABWE by 28 runs. Toss: Zimbabwe. England 'A' 247-5 (50 overs) (M.A. Atherton 101, G.P. Thorpe 66*). Zimbabwe 219 (49.1 overs) (D.G. Goodwin 60; A.P. Igglesden 10-1-34-4).

Before the Zimbabwe tour, England 'A' played two one-day matches in Kenya:

10 February at Nairobi Club. ENGLAND 'A' beat KENYA by 5 wickets. Kenya 180-8 (55 overs). England 'A' 186-5 (52.2 overs) (Stephenson 65).

11 February at Nairobi Gymkhana. KENYA beat ENGLAND 'A' by 5 wickets. England 'A' 271-3 (55 overs) (Atherton 96, D.J. Bicknell 73). Kenya 'A' 275-5 (53.5 overs) (Odumbe 58, Tikolo 45*, Tariq 41).

First 'Test': Harare, 3, 4, 5, 7, 8 March
England 'A' won by 10 wickets

Nicholas could not have been feeling too happy about his decision to field when, at the end of the first day, Zimbabwe were 253 for 3. Ali Shah (98) had put on 130 for the third wicket with Houghton, still there on 103. But they had lost opener Arnott, his finger broken by a delivery from Igglesden, and on the second day it was the Kent quickie who brought about an immediate collapse with 3 for 4, and Zimbabwe were all out for 290. After openers Bicknell and Stephenson had gone for only 13, Atherton (103) and Blakey (92) slowly pulled England 'A' round with a stand of 185. Solid contributions from Nicholas and Thorpe helped England to a lead of 76. By the end of the fourth day Zimbabwe were 12 runs behind with 3 wickets down, but they collapsed again on the last day, Atherton finishing them off with 3 for 4 from his leg-breaks, so that England had the easy task of knocking off 43 for victory.

Second 'Test': Bulawayo, 10, 11, 12, 14, 15 March
Match drawn

Nicholas decided to bat and, although the openers went cheaply again, Atherton (122) and Blakey (221) once more shored up the England innings with a stand of 154, ground out with painstaking concentration. Blakey batted for nigh on 10 hours before he was out first ball on the third day. Nicholas, who made another fifty, declared on 529 for 9. Martin Bicknell took three quick wickets and Zimbabwe were soon 52 for 4, but any thoughts of another easy victory were dispelled by Zimbabwe captain Houghton (202) and Paterson (93), who put on 177 in 77 overs for the 5th wicket. Both were eventually caught off the unlikely bowling of Stephenson (3-22), but they had saved the follow-on and a draw was the only result. Nevertheless, England's batsmen received heavy criticism from many quarters for their performance on the last day, scoring at 1½ runs an over, with Blakey the main culprit, taking 47 overs to compile his 18.

Third 'Test': Harare, 24, 25, 26, 28, 29 March
Match drawn

Houghton chose to bat first, but any hopes of drawing the series were dashed by Igglesden, who took 5 for 33 in 20 overs and helped to skittle Zimbabwe out for 149. England, without the injured Atherton, lost 4 wickets for 85. But they found a new hero in bowler Richard Illingworth, who came in as nightwatchman at the fall of the first wicket and stayed for 6 hours for 106. Thorpe (98) and wicket-keeper Rhodes (86) made sure England had a first-innings lead of 228, but fifties from Andy Flowers, Pycroft, and the inevitable Houghton earned Zimbabwe a draw.

Zimbabwe v England 'A' 1989-90 1st Match

England won by 10 wickets
Played at Harare Sports Club, Harare, 3, 4, 5, 7, 8 March
Toss: Zimbabwe. Umpires: J.H. Hampshire and I. Robinson

Zimbabwe

K.J. Arnott	not out	0	(9) c Thorpe b Atherton		6
A.H. Shah	c Rhodes b Pringle	98	b Afford		15
C.M. Robertson	c Blakey b Afford	2	(1) c Afford b Pringle		23
A.J. Pycroft	lbw b Afford	8	c Atherton b Igglesden		14
D.L. Houghton*	c Watkin b Igglesden	108	(6) c Pringle b Watkin		0
A. Flower†	lbw b Igglesden	28	(3) b Watkin		15
G.A. Paterson	c Atherton b Igglesden	0	lbw b Atherton		23
E.A. Brandes	c Rhodes b Watkin	14	lbw b Afford		0
A.J. Traicos	lbw b Pringle	11	(5) C. Atherton b Igglesden		6
M.P. Jarvis	run out	3	not out		12
K.G. Duers	c Rhodes b Pringle	0	c Rhodes b Atherton		0
Extras	(LB7, W1, NB10)	18	(LB3, NB1)		4
		290			**118**

In 1st innings, Arnott retired hurt at 9-0 and returned at 286-9.

England 'A'

D.J. Bicknell	lbw b Brandes	0	not out	22
J.P. Stephenson	c A. Flower b Brandes	2	not out	21
M.A. Atherton	b Shah	103		
R.J. Blakey	c Robertson b Jarvis	92		
M.C.J. Nicholas*	c sub b Shah	53		
G.P. Thorpe	c A. Flower b Brandes	44		
S.J. Rhodes†	c Traicos b Duers	20		
D.R. Pringle	b Duers	27		
A.P. Igglesden	c Houghton b Duers	7		
S.L. Watkin	c A. Flower b Duers	0		
J.A. Afford	not out	0		
Extras	(B10, LB6, W2,)	18		
		366	(0 wkt)	**43**

England	O	M	R	W	O	M	R	W
Igglesden	24	8	50	3	23	7	47	2
Watkin	16.3	3	64	1	19	8	35	2
Pringle	33	11	70	3	10	5	11	1
Afford	37	12	58	2	15	8	18	2
Atherton	15	1	41	0	5.2	4	4	3

Zimbabwe	O	M	R	W	O	M	R	W
Brandes	36	7	92	3				
Jarvis	41	13	99	1	6	0	20	0
Duers	38.2	8	66	4	3	1	7	0
Shah	21	10	22	2				
Traicos	68	34	71	0	3	0	11	0
Pycroft					1	0	5	0

Fall of Wickets

Wkt	Zim 1st	Eng 1st	Zim 2nd	Eng 2nd
1st	35	0	36	–
2nd	57	13	40	–
3rd	187	198	58	–
4th	260	218	66	–
5th	260	287	67	–
6th	261	321	82	–
7th	279	344	89	–
8th	284	355	95	–
9th	286	365	110	–
10th	290	366	118	–

Zimbabwe v England 'A' 1989-90 2nd Match

Match Drawn
Played at Bulawayo Athletic Club, Bulawayo, 10, 11, 12, 14, 15 March
Toss: England 'A'. Umpires: E. Gilmour and J.H. Hampshire

England 'A'

D.J. Bicknell	c Houghton b Traicos	26	c Paterson b Shah		3
J.P. Stephenson	c & b Jarvis	21	c Paterson b Jarvis		22
M.A. Atherton	c Pycroft b Duers	122	(4) c A. Flower b Duers		25
R.J. Blakey	c Pycroft b Jarvis	221	(5) c Pycroft b G.W. Flower		18
M.C.J. Nicholas*	c Jarvis b Traicos	50	(6) not out		37
J.J. Whitaker	c Traicos b Shah	19	(3) lbw b Jarvis		19
S.J. Rhodes†	lbw b Jarvis	41	not out		6
D.R. Pringle	c A. Flower b Jarvis	7			
M.P. Bicknell	c Houghton b Jarvis	0			
A.P. Igglesden	not out	10			
J.A. Afford	did not bat				
Extras	(LB10, NB2)	12	(NB3)		3
	(9 wkts dec)	529	(5 wkts)		133

Zimbabwe

A.H. Shah	lbw b M.P. Bicknell	1
D.G. Goodwin	lbw b M.P. Bicknell	15
C.M. Robertson	b M.P. Bicknell	0
A.J. Pycroft	b Pringle	21
D.L. Houghton*	c sub (R.K. Illingworth) b Stephenson	202
G.A. Paterson	c Blakey b Stephenson	93
A. Flower†	lbw b M.P. Bicknell	37
G.W. Flower	c Rhodes b Stephenson	14
A.J. Traicos	b Igglesden	1
M.P. Jarvis	not out	5
K.G. Duers	b Igglesden	0
Extras	(B2, LB9, W1, NB2)	14
		403

Zimbabwe	O	M	R	W	O	M	R	W
Jarvis	56.5	20	157	5	26	15	29	2
Duers	52	8	149	1	25	10	36	1
Shah	36	14	88	1	15.3	3	28	1
Traicos	59	24	93	2	17	11	10	1
G.W. Flower	9	2	32	0	8	1	30	1

England	O	M	R	W
Igglesden	34.4	7	99	2
M.P. Bicknell	32	10	74	4
Atherton	24	10	62	0
Pringle	29	10	77	1
Afford	27	6	58	0
Stephenson	12	4	22	3

Fall of Wickets

	Eng	Zim	Eng
Wkt	1st	1st	2nd
1st	29	2	15
2nd	80	2	38
3rd	234	26	49
4th	358	52	76
5th	435	229	108
6th	480	328	–
7th	498	384	–
8th	498	397	–
9th	529	403	–
10th	–	403	–

Zimbabwe v England 'A' 1989-90 3rd Match

Match Drawn
Played at Harare Sports Club, Harare, 24, 25, 26, 28, 29 March
Toss: Zimbabwe. Umpires: J.H. Hampshire and K. Kanjee

Zimbabwe

G.W. Flower	c Blakey b Igglesden	21	c Thorpe b Igglesden		52
D.G. Goodwin	c Whitaker b Igglesden	4	c Watkin b M.P. Bicknell		0
A. Flower†	c Whitaker b M.P. Bicknell	36	lbw b Stephenson		78
A.J. Pycroft	c Nicholas b Igglesden	15	(5) lbw b M.P. Bicknell		70
D.L. Houghton*	b Watkin	29	(4) b Watkin		57
C.M. Robertson	c M.P. Bicknell b Illingworth	7	run out		0
G.A. Paterson	c Whitaker b Illingworth	4	run out		0
E.A. Brandes	lbw b Igglesden	12	not out		23
A.J. Traicos	c Rhodes b Watkin	8	not out		0
M.P. Jarvis	not out	1			
K.G. Duers	c & b Igglesden	0			
Extras	(B1, LB3, W5, NB3)	12	(B4, LB8, W1, NB3)		16
		149	(7 wkts)		**296**

England 'A'

D.J. Bicknell	c Goodwin b Brandes	0
J.P. Stephenson	c Brandes b Traicos	24
R.K. Illingworth	lbw b Jarvis	106
R.J. Blakey	c Pycroft b Brandes	6
J.J. Whitaker	c A. Flower b Brandes	2
M.C.J. Nicholas*	c Goodwin b Brandes	38
G.P. Thorpe	st A. Flower b Traicos	98
S.J. Rhodes	b Traicos	86
M.P. Bicknell	c Houghton b Jarvis	10
A.P. Igglesden	not out	0
S.L. Watkin	not out	0
Extras	(LB6, W1,)	7
	(9 wkts dec)	**377**

England	O	M	R	W	O	M	R	W
Igglesden	20	7	33	5	36	6	86	1
M.P. Bicknell	16	4	35	1	29	12	49	2
Watkin	26	8	43	2	38	8	91	1
Stephenson	4	1	6	0	12	3	28	1
Illingworth	23	12	28	2	43	24	30	0

Zimbabwe	O	M	R	W
Brandes	42	9	119	4
Traicos	49	18	81	3
Jarvis	42	7	109	2
G.W. Flower	3	0	12	0
Duers	31	12	50	0

Fall of Wickets

	Zim	Eng	Zim
Wkt	1st	1st	2nd
1st	5	0	0
2nd	60	70	138
3rd	78	81	138
4th	89	85	233
5th	109	171	233
6th	123	197	239
7th	123	333	294
8th	146	367	–
9th	148	377	–
10th	149	–	–

Unofficial Test Averages: Zimbabwe v England 'A' 1989-90

Zimbabwe

Batting and Fielding	M	I	NO	HS	R	Avge	100	50	Ct/St
D.L. Houghton	3	5	0	202	396	79.20	2	1	4
A. Flower	3	5	0	78	194	38.80	–	1	6/1
A.H. Shah	2	3	0	98	114	38.00	–	1	–
G.W. Flower	2	3	0	52	87	29.00	–	1	–
A.J. Pycroft	3	5	0	70	128	25.60	–	1	4
G.A. Paterson	3	5	0	93	120	24.00	–	1	2
M.P. Jarvis	3	4	3	12*	21	21.00	–	–	2
E.A. Brandes	2	4	1	23*	49	16.33	–	–	1
A.J. Traicos	3	5	1	11	26	6.50	–	–	2
C.M. Robertson	3	5	0	23	32	6.40	–	–	1
D.G. Goodwin	2	3	0	15	19	6.33	–	–	2

Also batted: K.J. Arnott (1 match) 0rh, 6; K.G. Duers (3 matches) 0, 0, 0, 0.

Bowling	O	M	R	W	Avge	Best	5wI	10wM
E.A. Brandes	78	16	211	7	30.14	4-119	–	–
A.H. Shah	72.3	27	138	4	34.50	2-22	–	–
M.P. Jarvis	171.5	55	414	10	41.40	5-157	1	–
K.G. Duers	149.2	39	308	6	51.33	4-66	–	–
A.J. Traicos	196	87	266	5	53.20	3-81	–	–

Also bowled: G.W. Flower 20-3-74-1; A.J. Pycroft 1-0-5-0.

England 'A'

Batting and Fielding	M	I	NO	HS	R	Avge	100	50	Ct/St
R.J. Blakey	3	4	0	221	337	84.25	1	1	3
M.A. Atherton	2	3	0	122	250	83.33	2	–	3
M.C.J. Nicholas	3	4	1	53	178	59.33	–	2	1
S.J. Rhodes	3	4	1	86	153	51.00	–	1	6/-
J.P. Stephenson	3	5	1	24	90	22.50	–	–	–
J.J. Whitaker	2	3	0	19	40	13.33	–	–	3
D.J. Bicknell	3	5	1	25	51	12.75	–	–	–

Also batted: J.A. Afford (2 matches) 0* (1ct); M.P. Bicknell (2 matches) 0, 10 (1ct); A.P. Igglesden (3 matches) 7, 10*, 0* (1ct); R.K. Illingworth (1 match) 106; D.R. Pringle (2 matches) 27, 7 (1ct); G.P. Thorpe (2 matches) 44, 98 (2ct); S.L. Watkin (2 matches) 0 (2ct).

Bowling	O	M	R	W	Avge	Best	5wI	10wM
J.P. Stephenson	28	8	56	4	14.00	3-22	–	–
M.P. Bicknell	77	26	158	7	22.57	4-74	–	–
A.P. Igglesden	137.4	35	315	13	24.23	5-33	1	–
D.R. Pringle	72	26	158	5	31.60	3-70	–	–
J.A. Afford	79	26	134	4	33.50	2-18	–	–
S.L. Watkin	99.3	27	233	6	38.83	2-35	–	–

Also bowled: M.A. Atherton 44.2-15-107-3; R.K. Illingworth 66-36-58-2.

England Young Cricketers in Australia

In a packed six-week tour of Australia, England Young Cricketers played three Youth Tests and three one-day internationals. Australia maintained their record of never having lost a youth series. They won the Barclays Bank Youth International series for the Tim Caldwell Trophy 1-0, taking the last Youth Test by an innings, and won the one-day series 3-0. England played six other matches, winning four, with one drawn and one abandoned.

England's successes included John Crawley (Lancs), with a Test average of 42 (no other batsman reached 30), Jeremy Hallett (Somerset), who took 16 Test wickets at 16.50 apiece, and captain and wicket-keeper Wayne Noon (Northants). Hallett shared the Barclays Bank Cricketer of the Series award with Australian opening bat Jason Young, who scored 295 runs (avge 59.00). Five Australian batsmen averaged over 50, and Steve Cottrell took 14 wickets (avge 20.21), including 10-100 in the deciding Test when he ripped the England first innings apart with 6-40 in 11 overs.

Youth Tests

14-17 January at North Sydney Oval. MATCH DRAWN. Toss: England YC. Australia YC 410-6 dec (Gallian 158*, Ruddell 64, Harper 61, Vowles 40, Mann 40*) and 220-6 dec (Martyn 71*, Young 65), England YC 319 (Grayson 110, Crawley 52, Noon 40) and 145-3 (Butler 54*, Crawley 44*).

25-28 January at Kardinia Park, Geelong. MATCH DAWN. Toss: England YC. England YC 279 (Keech 49, Holloway 40; Gallian 4-46) and 236 (Crawley 48, Keech 40; Castle 4-44, Martyn 4-27). Australia YC 288 (Young 134, Mann 57; Batty 5-60) and 64-3.

6-8 February at the WACA, Perth. AUSTRALIA YC beat ENGLAND YC by an innings and 2 runs. Toss: Australia YC. England YC 71 (Cottrell 6-40) and 272 (Holloway 44, Crawley 43; Cottrell 4-60, Oliver 4-95). Australia YC 345 (Young 69, Ruddell 68, Harper 53, Adlam 46*, Mann 40; Hallett 5-73).

One-day Internationals

19 January at Manuka Oval, Canberra. AUSTRALIA YC beat ENGLAND YC by 8 wickets. England YC 184 (49 overs) (Holloway 89). Australia YC 186-2 (42.1 overs) (Martyn 69*, Young 45, Gallian 42*).

23 January at MCG. AUSTRALIA YC beat ENGLAND YC by 7 wickets. England YC 238-7 (55 overs) (Crawley 87, Holloway 56). Australia YC 239-3 (45.2 overs) (Vowles 102, Young 93).

4 February at Fremantle. AUSTRALIA YC beat ENGLAND YC by 77 runs. Australia YC 211 (53.1 overs) (Mann 54). England YC 134 (45.5 overs) (Vowles 4-18).

English XI in South Africa

The controversial and ill-fated 'rebel' tour to South Africa by Mike Gatting and his 'mercenaries', which cost the participants a five-year Test ban, was called off before it was finished, and the second leg, due to take place in 1991, was later cancelled. As the result of harassment and demonstrations at all the tourists' matches (three 3-day warm-up games and one 5-day 'Test'), the South African Cricket Union reached a compromise with the organizers of the opposition, the National Sports Congress. They cancelled the second 'Test' and agreed to play just four of the six scheduled one-day games.

The English XI lost the low-scoring 'Test' in three days and were beaten 3-1 in the one-day series. There were few notable performances in the first-class matches. No English batsman made a hundred, and Gatting topped the averages with 47.00. The only English win was against a Combined Bowl XI, David Graveney taking 10-65 in the match.

South African XI v English XI

8, 9, 10 February at Wanderers, Johannesburg. SOUTH AFRICAN XI beat ENGLISH XI by 7 wickets. Toss: South African XI. English XI 156 (B.C. Broad 48, A.A.Donald 4-30, R.P. Snell 4-38) and 122 (A.A. Donald 4-29). South African XI 203 (A.P. Kuiper 84; R.M. Ellison 4-41) and 76-3.

One-day Internationals

16 February at Centurion Park, Verwoerdburg (floodlit). SOUTH AFRICA beat ENGLISH XI by 5 wickets. English XI 217 (54.5 overs) (M.W.Gatting 55, B.N. French 43). South Africa 218-5 (52 overs) (S.J. Cook 73).

18 February at Kingsmead, Durban. SOUTH AFRICA beat ENGLISH XI by 14 runs. South Africa 219-5 (55 overs) (H.R. Fotheringham 51, C.E.B. Rice 43*, T.R. Madsen 42*). English XI 205-7 (55 overs) (K.J. Barnett 76, C.W.J. Athey 44).

20 February at Springbok Park, Bloemfontein (floodlit). SOUTH AFRICA beat ENGLISH XI by 207 runs. South Africa 301-7 (55 overs) (S.J. Cook 73, P.N. Kirsten 40, A.P. Kuiper 117). English XI 94 (C.W.J. Athey 50).

22 February at Wanderers, Johannesburg. ENGLISH XI beat SOUTH AFRICA by 134 runs. English XI 296-8 (55 overs) (K.J. Barnett 136, C.W.J. Athey 49). South Africa 162 (37.2 overs) (H.R. Fotheringham 58, R.F. Pienaar 52; M.W. Gatting 6.2-0-26-6).

1990

BRITANNIC ASSURANCE CHAMPIONSHIP

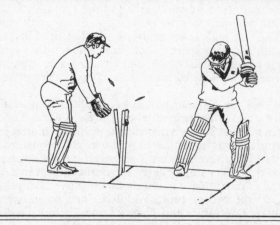

Britannic Assurance County Championship

Middlesex showed they were the side most competent, by some distance, at dealing with the prevailing conditions of the summer, and they won the Championship by 31 points. Under the astute positive captaincy of Mike Gatting, they conjured up 10 wins during a season in which imagination was an essential attribute for tacticians and bowlers alike to deal with an explosion of runs.

Essex came second again with eight wins, compared with 13 in 1989, when they finished runners-up to Worcestershire because of a 25-point penalty imposed by the Test and County Cricket Board pitches committee. They suffered again in 1990 over pitches, this time because their Chelmsford strip was too bland and exposed their lack of depth in bowling behind Neil Foster, the season's most prolific wicket-taker in first-class cricket with 94. The low-seamed ball – with nine strands in the seam's flax instead of the 13 of the previous year – meant that only the best, most varied attacks were likely to succeed on the white, dry strips the TCCB required.

Middlesex possessed accurate seamers, led by Angus Fraser and Neil Williams, and the best spin attack in John Emburey and Philip Tufnell. With two matches to play, only Essex could overtake Middlesex, and Gatting's team made sure by beating Sussex in the final game with a day to spare. Their knack of bowling teams out burnt off their pursuers one by one, and in their last four games they managed three victories by dismissing their opponents twice in the match.

Suspicions that the summer would be weighted in favour of the batsmen were quickly confirmed when, in early May, Lancashire piled up 863 in reply to Surrey's declaration of 707 for nine at Foster's Oval, scattering records like confetti. And over at Chelmsford, Essex were amassing 761 for seven against Leicestershire at the same time.

Notts made the early running at the top of the table, but could not establish a lead of more than a handful of points over Hampshire and Derbyshire. By the end of June, Middlesex had taken over, challenged briefly by Lancashire and Warwickshire, before a late charge by Essex brought them unexpectedly into the picture.

Hampshire, strengthened by the arrival of David Gower from Leicestershire, fought hard for third place and achieved it in the last game by making 446 in their second innings against Gloucestershire at Southampton, winning by two wickets after the highest successful run-chase in their history. Notts fell away badly, along with the form of their talented West Indian all-rounder Franklyn Stephenson, while Lancashire became distracted by their remarkable success in the limited-overs competitions. However, the presence of a spin attack of

Middlesex's quality would undoubtedly have kept Lancashire interested longer than they were. Sussex began their campaign with a victory over Surrey, but the fact that their bowlers conceded, in successive first innings, 425 runs, 465, 600, 402, and 500 from the start of the season warned of a wearisome summer. Sussex won only two more matches and finished bottom.

The Championship season produced 28 double centuries and two 300s. Neil Fairbrother, of Lancashire, led the list with 366 in the infamous four-day game against Surrey, who at one stage looked set to become the first county to concede 1,000 runs in an innings, on a pitch, one might add, that remained unmarked. Fairbrother also made 203 not out against Warwickshire.

Despite the batsmen's summer, the TCCB did find a sub-standard pitch that merited official sanction. The authorities deducted 25 points from Derbyshire for the pitch at the Racecourse Ground after Middlesex had been demolished by 171 runs in August. It was the champions' only defeat. Middlesex's second-innings total of 99 at Derby was the fourth lowest overall in a year not noted for low scores. Northampton was the venue for the smallest total, when early in the season the home side, with three men short due to injury, were dismissed for 50 by Derbyshire.

Though the conditions helped moderate batsmen to shine, just as run-of-the-mill bowlers advanced to prominence in 1989, the cricket in the Championship was usually interesting. Pitches rarely suited spinners, but captains tended to use them heavily, probably because there was no viable alternative, and spectators benefited accordingly.

Richard Illingworth, of Worcestershire, finished top of the spin pile with 75 wickets, followed by Tufnell and Richard Davis, of Kent, each of these left-armers bowling a colossal number of overs by recent standards. Tufnell sent down more than 1,000 overs in all first-class cricket, and Lancashire's Mike Atherton was permitted 434 overs of leg-spin, which reaped 45 wickets. Perhaps, in some people's eyes, a golden era has arrived.

Fast-bowlers of quality remained the match-winners, and this was underlined by the startling emergence of Waqar Younis from 'nowhere' to rejuvenate Surrey. The 18-year-old had in fact already played Test cricket for Pakistan, but his arrival at Surrey on Imran Khan's recommendation was a pleasant surprise, and he became one of the few bowlers who looked effective on any sort of pitch. A yorker is a yorker. Courtney Walsh, with eight for 58 against Northamptonshire at Cheltenham, recorded the best bowling return of the season, and Malcolm Marshall's fast-bowling artistry could still turn a match.

The championship summer was full of interest and variety and, apart from a surfeit of declarations in the three-day games, the TCCB experiment with ball and pitch was broadly successful.

CHARLES RANDALL

Britannic Assurance County Championship 1990

Final Table	P	W	L	D	1st Innings Points Batting	Bowling	Total Points
1 MIDDLESEX (3)	22	10	1	11	73	55	288
2 Essex (2)	22	8	2	12	73	56	257
3 Hampshire (6)	22	8	4	10	67	48	243
4 Worcestershire (1)	22	7	1	14	70	58	240
5 Warwickshire (8)	22	7	7	8	55	64	231
6 Lancashire (4)	22	6	3	13	65	56	217
7 Leicestershire (13)	22	6	7	9	61	53	210
8 Glamorgan (17)	22	5	6	11	64	48	192
9 Surrey (12)	22	4	3	15	54	64	190†
10 Yorkshire (16)	22	5	9	8	52	55	187
11 Northamptonshire (5)	22	4	9	9	61	60	185
12 Derbyshire (7)	22	6	7	9	58	52	181★
=13 Nottinghamshire (11)	22	4	8	10	51	58	173
=13 Gloucestershire (9)	22	4	7	11	51	58	173
15 Somerset (14)	22	3	4	15	73	45	168
16 Kent (15)	22	3	6	13	69	35	152
17 Sussex (10)	22	3	9	10	51	44	143

1989 positions in brackets.
† includes 8 points for drawn match in which scores finished level.
★ Derbyshire had 25 points deducted for a sub-standard pitch.

Points

For a win: 16 points, plus any first innings points. For winning a match reduced to a single innings because it started with less than eight hours' playing time remaining: 12 points. First innings points are awarded during the first 100 overs of each first innings:

Batting		Bowling	
150 to 199 runs	1	3 or 4 wickets	1
200 to 249 runs	2	5 or 6 wickets	2
250 to 299 runs	3	7 or 8 wickets	3
300 runs and over	4	9 or 10 wickets	4

Final Positions 1890-1990

	D	E	Gm	Gs	H	K	La	Le	M	Nh	Nt	Sm	Sy	Sx	Wa	Wo	Y
1890	—	—	—	6	—	3	2	—	7	—	5	—	1	8	—	—	3
1891	—	—	—	9	—	5	2	—	3	—	4	5	1	7	—	—	8
1892	—	—	—	7	—	7	4	—	5	—	2	3	1	9	—	—	6
1893	—	—	—	9	—	4	2	—	3	—	6	8	5	7	—	—	1
1894	—	—	—	9	—	4	4	—	3	—	7	6	1	8	—	—	2
1895	5	9	—	4	10	14	2	12	6	—	12	8	1	11	6	—	3
1896	7	5	—	10	8	9	2	13	3	—	6	11	4	14	12	—	1
1897	14	3	—	5	9	12	1	13	8	—	10	11	2	6	7	—	4
1898	9	5	—	3	12	7	6	13	2	—	8	13	4	9	9	—	1
1899	15	6	—	9	10	8	4	13	2	—	10	13	1	5	7	12	3
1900	13	10	—	7	15	3	2	14	7	—	5	11	7	3	6	12	1
1901	15	10	—	14	7	7	3	12	2	—	9	12	6	4	5	11	1
1902	10	13	—	14	15	7	5	11	12	—	3	7	4	2	6	9	1
1903	12	8	—	13	14	8	4	14	1	—	5	10	11	2	7	6	3
1904	10	14	—	9	15	3	1	7	4	—	5	12	11	6	7	13	2
1905	14	12	—	8	16	6	2	5	11	13	10	15	4	3	7	8	1
1906	16	7	—	9	8	1	4	15	11	11	5	11	3	10	6	14	2
1907	16	7	—	10	12	8	6	11	5	15	1	14	4	13	9	2	2
1908	14	11	—	10	9	2	7	13	4	15	8	16	3	5	12	6	1
1909	15	14	—	16	8	1	2	13	6	7	10	11	5	4	12	8	3
1910	15	11	—	12	6	1	4	10	3	9	5	16	2	7	14	13	8
1911	14	6	—	12	11	2	4	15	3	10	8	16	5	13	1	9	7
1912	12	15	—	11	6	3	4	13	5	2	8	14	7	10	9	16	1
1913	13	15	—	9	10	1	8	14	6	4	5	16	3	7	11	12	2
1914	12	8	—	16	5	3	11	13	2	9	10	15	1	6	7	14	4
1919	9	14	—	8	7	2	5	9	13	12	3	5	4	11	15	—	1
1920	16	9	—	8	11	5	2	13	1	14	7	10	3	6	12	15	4
1921	12	15	17	7	6	4	5	11	1	13	8	10	2	9	16	14	3
1922	11	8	16	13	6	4	5	14	7	15	2	10	3	9	12	17	1
1923	10	13	16	11	7	5	3	14	8	17	2	9	4	6	12	15	1
1924	17	15	13	6	12	5	4	11	2	16	6	8	3	10	9	14	1
1925	14	7	17	10	9	5	3	12	6	11	4	15	2	13	8	16	1
1926	11	9	8	15	7	3	1	13	6	16	4	14	5	10	12	17	2
1927	5	8	15	12	13	4	1	7	9	16	2	14	6	10	11	17	3
1928	10	16	15	5	12	2	1	9	8	13	3	14	6	7	11	17	4
1929	7	12	17	4	11	8	2	9	6	13	1	15	10	4	14	16	2
1930	9	6	11	2	13	5	1	12	16	17	4	13	8	7	15	10	3
1931	7	10	15	2	12	3	6	16	11	17	5	13	8	4	9	14	1
1932	10	14	15	13	8	3	6	12	10	16	4	7	5	2	9	17	1
1933	6	4	16	10	14	3	5	17	12	13	8	11	9	2	7	15	1
1934	3	8	13	7	14	5	1	12	10	17	9	15	11	2	4	16	5
1935	2	9	13	15	16	10	4	6	3	17	5	14	11	7	8	12	1
1936	1	9	16	4	10	8	11	15	2	17	5	7	6	14	13	12	3
1937	3	6	7	4	14	12	9	16	2	17	10	13	8	5	11	15	1
1938	5	6	16	10	14	9	4	15	2	17	12	7	3	8	13	11	1
1939	9	4	13	3	15	5	6	17	2	16	12	14	8	10	11	7	1
1946	15	8	6	5	10	6	3	11	2	16	13	4	11	17	14	8	7
1947	5	11	9	2	16	4	3	14	1	17	11	11	6	9	15	7	7
1948	6	13	1	8	9	15	5	11	3	17	14	12	2	16	7	10	4
1949	15	9	8	7	16	13	11	17	1	6	11	9	5	13	4	3	1
1950	5	17	11	7	12	9	1	16	14	10	15	7	1	13	4	6	3
1951	11	8	5	12	9	16	3	15	7	13	17	14	6	10	1	4	2
1952	4	10	7	9	12	15	3	6	5	8	16	17	1	13	10	14	2
1953	6	12	10	6	14	16	3	3	5	11	8	17	1	2	9	15	12
1954	3	15	4	13	14	11	10	16	7	7	5	17	1	9	6	11	2
1955	8	14	16	12	3	13	9	6	5	7	11	17	1	4	9	15	2
1956	12	11	13	3	6	16	2	17	5	4	8	15	1	9	14	9	7
1957	4	5	9	12	13	14	6	17	7	2	15	8	1	9	11	16	3
1958	5	6	15	14	2	8	7	12	10	4	17	3	1	13	16	9	11
1959	7	9	6	2	8	13	5	16	10	11	17	12	3	15	4	14	1
1960	5	6	11	8	12	10	2	17	3	9	16	14	7	4	15	13	1
1961	7	6	14	5	1	11	13	9	3	16	17	10	15	8	12	4	2
1962	7	9	14	4	10	11	16	17	13	8	15	6	5	12	3	2	1
1963	17	12	2	8	10	13	15	16	6	7	9	3	11	4	4	14	1
1964	12	10	11	17	12	7	14	16	6	3	15	8	4	9	2	1	5

Final Positions 1890-1990

	D	E	Gm	Gs	H	K	La	Le	M	Nh	Nt	Sm	Sy	Sx	Wa	Wo	Y
1965	9	15	3	10	12	5	13	14	6	2	17	7	8	16	11	1	4
1966	9	16	14	15	11	4	12	8	12	5	17	3	7	10	6	2	1
1967	6	15	14	17	12	2	11	3	7	9	16	8	4	13	10	5	1
1968	8	14	3	16	5	2	6	9	10	13	4	12	15	17	11	7	1
1969	16	6	1	2	5	10	15	14	11	9	8	17	3	7	4	12	13
1970	7	12	2	17	10	1	3	15	16	14	11	13	5	9	7	6	4
1971	17	10	16	8	9	4	3	5	6	14	12	7	1	11	2	15	13
1972	17	5	13	3	9	2	15	6	8	4	14	11	12	16	1	7	10
1973	16	8	11	5	1	4	12	9	13	3	17	10	2	15	7	6	14
1974	17	12	16	14	2	10	8	4	6	3	15	5	7	13	9	1	11
1975	15	7	9	16	3	5	4	1	11	8	13	12	6	17	14	10	2
1976	15	6	17	3	12	14	16	4	1	2	13	7	9	10	5	11	8
1977	7	6	14	3	11	1	16	5	1	9	17	4	14	8	10	13	12
1978	14	2	13	10	8	1	12	6	3	17	7	5	16	9	11	15	4
1979	16	1	17	10	12	5	13	6	14	11	9	8	3	4	15	2	7
1980	9	8	13	7	17	16	15	9	1	12	3	5	2	4	14	11	6
1981	12	5	14	13	7	9	16	8	4	15	1	3	6	2	17	11	10
1982	11	7	16	15	3	13	12	2	1	9	4	6	5	8	17	14	10
1983	9	1	15	12	3	7	12	4	2	6	14	10	8	11	5	16	17
1984	12	1	13	17	15	5	16	4	3	11	2	7	8	6	9	10	14
1985	13	4	12	3	2	9	14	16	1	10	7	17	6	7	15	5	11
1986	11	1	17	2	6	8	15	7	12	9	4	16	3	14	13	5	10
1987	6	12	13	10	5	14	2	3	16	7	1	11	4	17	15	9	8
1988	14	3	17	10	15	2	9	7	8	12	5	11	4	16	6	1	13
1989	6	2	17	9	6	15	4	13	3	5	11	14	12	10	8	1	16
1990	12	2	8	13	3	16	6	7	1	11	13	15	9	17	5	4	10

Derbyshire

Derbyshire finished well adrift of the top-five Championship position predicted by their captain Kim Barnett, but 1990 was still a season of encouraging achievement and potent memories. The deduction of 25 points for an unsatisfactory pitch against Middlesex at Derby in August – and the consequent effect on morale – condemned Derbyshire to mid-table.

But Barnett was more accurate with his pre-season forecast that they would lift a one-day trophy. They found their metier in a tense Refuge Assurance Sunday League which saw them claim the title on the final day – only the third trophy in their 120-year history.

The forceful batting of Barnett and Morris was crucial. The captain topped 1,600 runs despite a lean late-season spell, overtaking Denis Smith's county record of 30 first-class centuries. Morris's eight hundreds in all competitions underwrote his graduation to the England side. Resources were strained when Morris joined Malcolm on Test duty, but Bowler confirmed his reliability and, by keeping wicket in one-day cricket, offered valuable flexibility in selection.

Kuiper, the South African all-rounder, arrived with a reputation for fierce hitting. He found county cricket a taxing business, but redeemed sketchy Championship form with several match-winning assaults in limited-overs matches. The enigmatic Roberts overcame an unproductive mid-season spell to become the fourth player past 1,000 runs, and with Adams maturing in technique and temperament and the impressive O'Gorman available again after law studies, Derbyshire's batting was often destructive if occasionally prone, as against Essex, to abject collapse.

Neutered pitches conspired against Bishop and Malcolm, the latter's form jaded by sore shins. But they remained as fearsome as any new-ball partnership and, along with the admirably accurate Mortensen, finished well up the national averages. Mortensen was especially vital in confining batsmen in one-day cricket, and Warner's ability to suppress late flurries in the Sunday League compensated for the waywardness of Base and the limited effectiveness of Kuiper's medium pace. Miller's off-spin has rarely looked better than in a match-winning display against Yorkshire before injuries eroded his value. His rejection of a match contract for 1991 left an obvious gap in attacking options. India's captain Azarhuddin replaces Bishop as the overseas player in 1991. Wicket-keeper Krikken, while still a novice, confirmed high potential. And the development of Cork, the Young England seamer, also underwrote Derbyshire's confidence in emerging young talent.

NEIL HALLAM

Britannic Assurance County Championship: 12th; Won 6, Lost 7, Drawn 9
All First-Class Matches: Played 24: Won 7, Lost 8, Drawn 9
NatWest Bank Trophy: Lost to Lancashire in 2nd round
Benson & Hedges Cup: Failed to qualify for quarter-final (4th in Group B)
Refuge Assurance League: 1st; Won 12, Lost 3, No Result 1
Refuge Assurance Cup: Lost to Middlesex in final

County Averages

Batting and Fielding	M	I	NO	HS	R	Avge	100	50	Ct/St
J.E. Morris	17	27	4	157*	1373	59.69	6	6	9
K.J. Barnett	24	39	6	141	1648	49.93	5	9	14
P.D. Bowler	22	39	5	210	1428	42.00	3	7	17
A.M. Brown	8	12	2	139*	413	41.30	1	1	7
T.J.E. O'Gorman	7	12	1	100	448	40.72	1	4	4
G. Miller	14	14	8	47*	233	38.83	–	–	7
B. Roberts	24	38	7	124*	1108	35.74	2	4	23
C.J. Adams	23	34	4	111*	932	31.06	2	5	25
I.R. Bishop	13	16	4	103*	333	27.75	1	–	2
A.P. Kuiper	12	17	0	68	407	23.94	–	2	10
S.J. Base	13	13	2	58	215	19.54	–	2	4
K.M. Krikken	22	29	2	77*	488	18.07	–	2	60/3
S.C. Goldsmith	12	17	1	51	267	16.68	–	1	9
M. Jean-Jacques	12	13	5	25	107	13.37	–	–	2
O.H. Mortensen	12	11	9	5*	20	10.00	–	–	5
A.E. Warner	14	19	2	59	160	9.41	–	1	2
D.E. Malcolm	10	7	2	20*	44	8.80	–	–	–

Also batted: D.G. Cork (2 matches) 2*, 7; F.A. Griffith (1 match) 1; Z.A. Sadiq (1 match) 0.
B.J.M. Maher played in one match but did not bat.

Hundreds (21)

6 J.E. Morris: 121 & 109 v Somerset (Taunton); 103 v Notts (Derby); 103* v Warwick (Derby); 157* v Hants (Portsmouth); 109 v Yorks (Scarborough)

5 K.J. Barnett: 141 v Yorks (Chesterfield); 131 v Warwicks (Derby); 107 v Glos (Derby); 123 v Sussex (Hove); 109 v Lancs (Liverpool)

3 P.D. Bowler: 120 v Warwicks (Derby); 115* v Lancs (Liverpool); 210 v Kent (Chesterfield)

2 C.J. Adams: 111* v Camb. Univ. (Cambridge); 101 v Yorks (Scarborough)
  B. Roberts: 124* v Yorks (Chesterfield); 100* v Kent (Chesterfield)

1 I.R. Bishop: 103* v Yorks (Scarborough)
  A.M. Brown: 130 ret hurt v Northants (Chesterfield)
  T.J.E. O'Gorman: 100 v Leics (Derby)

Bowling	O	M	R	W	Avge	Best	5wI	10wM
I.R. Bishop	407.3	92	1124	59	19.05	6-71	3	–
O.H. Mortensen	316.2	91	785	35	22.42	4-22	–	–
K.J. Barnett	293.3	55	757	26	29.11	4-28	–	–
A.P. Kuiper	125.3	29	393	12	32.75	4-69	–	–
D.E. Malcolm	289.4	45	983	30	32.76	4-63	–	–
G. Miller	461	114	1308	35	37.37	6-45	1	–
S.J. Base	414.3	68	1402	35	40.05	6-105	2	–
A.E. Warner	393.3	67	1330	33	40.30	3-56	–	–
M. Jean-Jacques	300	42	1106	25	44.24	6-60	1	–
S.C. Goldsmith	128	22	383	7	54.71	2-105	–	–

Also bowled: P.D. Bowler 11-0-81-1; C.J. Adams 14-1-56-2; D.G. Cork 39-8-123-2; F.A. Griffith 11-2-20-1; J.E. Morris 27-0-170-1; B. Roberts 19-5-52-3.

Essex

Robbed of the County Championship they deserved by the TCCB for a sub-standard pitch in 1989, Essex again had to settle for second place, which this time was due to their own insipid start and poor finish. In these two bleak periods they ignored that old cricket saying that, 'catches win matches'. They put down far too many, especially in the slips, dropping a possible 22 in those three vital games against Northants and Kent, in the closing stages, but usually their fielding was excellent, with Prichard, Shahid, Waugh, and Hussain outstanding.

At full strength, Essex probably possessed the most powerful batting line-up in the county circuit. Gooch averaged over 100 and Waugh plundered over 2,000 runs, and in their very different styles they were a delight. Prichard enjoyed his best ever season, while Stephenson made more runs than in the previous summer when capped by England, making his exclusion from the 'A' side to Pakistan rather strange. Shahid forced himself into the team by scoring runs whenever included. As a result, Hardie in his last season was unable to command a regular place, despite averaging over 70.

In support they had an aggressive and resilient middle order, in which Pringle, Garnham and Foster played valuable innings when runs were really needed. This meant that the absence of Hussein with a broken wrist for the first part of the season, and his subsequent failure to score heavily until the last match, did not matter too much. Emphasizing still further the batting potential for the future was a 2nd XI brimming with talent, as illustrated by the century Lewis made on his first-team debut.

The Essex attack was less impressive, which was hardly surprising in a year dominated by batsmen. Nevertheless, despite a smaller seam, fast outfields, and rather too many pitches on which a result could not be obtained without declarations, Foster, with 94 wickets, was the leading wicket-taker in the country. Pringle remained among the best seamers and Andrew, after an unhappy start, proved a useful acquisition. But Topley lost his place. The most significant feature long term was the arrival of Ilott, who looked as good a prospect as John Lever at the same age. Although both spinners, Childs and Such, proved useful and economical, they lacked the penetration required.

Everything suggests that in the 90s, as in the 80s, Essex will be among the best sides and will secure some of the honours that eluded them in 1990, especially if they can discover, or sign, a high-class, match-winning bowler. It is also to be hoped that they will retain that sense of humour that made them a popular as well as a successful county.

TREVOR BAILEY

Britannic Assurance County Championship: 2nd; Won 8, Lost 2, Drawn 12
All First-Class Matches: Played 24: Won 9, Lost 2, Drawn 13
NatWest Bank Trophy: Lost to Hampshire in 2nd round
Benson & Hedges Cup: Lost to Nottinghamshire in quarter-final
Refuge Assurance League: 12th; Won 6, Lost 9, No Result 1

County Averages

Batting and Fielding	M	I	NO	HS	R	Avge	100	50	Ct/St
G.A. Gooch	12	19	3	215	1688	105.50	8	5	9
M.E. Waugh	22	33	6	207*	2072	76.74	8	8	18
B.R. Hardie	12	17	7	125	728	72.80	2	4	11
J.P. Stephenson	24	39	7	202*	1730	54.06	3	13	15
P.J. Prichard	22	32	3	245	1407	48.51	5	4	9
N. Shahid	18	27	7	125	964	48.20	1	6	22
A.C. Seymour	3	5	2	89	131	43.66	–	1	1
N. Hussain	15	22	2	197	715	35.75	1	2	15
D.R. Pringle	17	15	2	84	443	34.07	–	3	9
M.A. Garnham	24	28	7	84*	615	29.28	–	2	48/2
N.A. Foster	22	22	2	101	530	26.50	1	2	13
P.M. Such	11	5	3	27	44	22.00	–	–	2
T.D. Topley	9	6	2	23*	78	19.50	–	–	6
M.C. Ilott	9	10	2	42*	123	15.37	–	–	1
S.J.W. Andrew	18	16	7	35	119	13.22	–	–	1
J.H. Childs	23	16	5	26	123	11.18	–	–	7

Also batted: J.J.B. Lewis (1 match) 116* (1ct); A.W. Lilley (1 match) 1;
K.O. Thomas (1 match) 2.

Hundreds (30)

8 **G.A. Gooch:** 137 v Middlesex (Lord's); 215 v Leics (Chelmsford); 121 v Worcs (Worcester); 120 v Middlesex (Ilford); 102 ret hurt v New Zealanders (Chelmsford); 177 v Lancs (Colchester); 174 & 126 v Northants (Northampton).

M.E. Waugh: 166* v Worcs (Worcester); 125 v Hants (Southampton); 204 v Glos (Ilford); 103 v Warwicks (Edgbaston); 126 v Derbys (Colchester); 103* v Sussex (Chelmsford); 207* v Yorks (Middlesbrough); 169 v Kent (Chelmsford).

5 **P.J. Prichard:** 245 v Leics (Chelmsford) 116 v Camb. Univ. (Cambridge); 115 v Somerset (Bath); 103 v Derbys (Derby); 102 v Kent (Chelmsford).

3 **J.P. Stephenson:** 202* v Somerset (Bath); 147 v New Zealanders (Chelmsford); 131* v Leics (Leicester).

2 **B.R. Hardie:** 125 v Hants (Southampton); 110* v Glos (Ilford).

1 **N.A. Foster:** 101 v Leics (Chelmsford).

N. Hussain: 197 v Surrey (Foster's Oval).

J.J.B. Lewis: 116* v Surrey (Foster's Oval).

N. Shahid: 125 v Lancs (Colchester).

Bowling	O	M	R	W	Avge	Best	5wI	10wM
N.A. Foster	819.2	175	2502	94	26.61	6-32	6	1
D.R. Pringle	358.3	90	994	34	29.23	5-66	1	–
T.D. Topley	223	33	713	22	32.40	4-67	–	–
M.C. Ilott	322.1	65	1036	31	33.41	5-34	2	–
P.M. Such	272.4	67	715	20	35.75	3-34	–	–
S.J.W. Andrew	503	75	1897	46	41.23	5-55	1	–
J.H. Childs	655.5	212	1590	27	58.88	4-56	–	–
N. Shahid	106.2	18	413	7	59.00	3-91	–	–
M.E. Waugh	191	33	771	12	64.25	5-37	1	–

Also bowled: G.A. Gooch 35-8-1125-0; B.R. Hardie 1-0-16-0; N. Hussain 12-2-62-0; A.W. Lilley 1-0-7-0; P.J. Prichard 1.4-0-11-0; J.P. Stephenson 111-24-451-4; K.O. Thomas 18.2-3-81-0.

Glamorgan

After occupying bottom place for two successive seasons, Glamorgan rose nine places to eighth in 1990. They had another disappointing Sunday League season, but reached the quarter-finals of the other two one-day competitions. Their improvement coincided with Viv Richards's arrival. He scored seven championship centuries, while his presence was an inspiration to others, especially the younger players in the team.

Alan Butcher and Hugh Morris had excellent seasons, and although Morris was appointed captain of the England 'A' team to tour Pakistan, both players were unlucky not to be chosen for the tour to Australia. Morris broke almost every Glamorgan batting record, including the most centuries (10) in the season, while his season's aggregate surpassed Javed Miandad's record set in 1981. Butcher also scored over 2,000 runs for the first time, and the opening pair's prolific form was a contributing factor to the team's improvement.

Richards played some memorable innings, including a match-winning effort of 164 not out against Hampshire at Southampton. Glamorgan, who had been set 364 to win, were struggling at 139 for 5, but Richards took on the opposition's attack almost single-handed, ensuring his team a victory by 4 wickets. Maynard, who benefited from Richards's guidance, experienced a much improved season, while Cottey reached 1,000 runs for the first time in his career.

Steve Watkin was again Glamorgan's leading wicket-taker, while Mark Frost, with 59 wickets in his first season, was a valuable acquisition from Surrey. The county, however, missed the services of Barwick, who played in only three championship games because of a knee injury, while Cowley, the former Hampshire off-spinner, was also troubled by injury. Robert Croft, however, the 20-year-old all-rounder, made a considerable impression in his first year in county cricket. He bowled his off-spin effectively as well as contributing in the middle order. An innings of 91 not out almost won the game against Worcestershire at Abergavenny, where Glamorgan chased an improbable 495 for victory and ended two runs short.

Steve James, who was Cambridge University's most successful batsman, had a disappointing county season, although Adrian Dale, another University graduate, who will also be available full-time next season, is a promising young all-rounder who played some useful innings. Glamorgan, however, do not possess an established left-arm spinner, and in four-day games on true pitches this type of bowler is essential. There is also a need of an opening bowler with real pace to strengthen an attack that is rarely able to bowl a side out twice in a three-day game.

EDWARD BEVAN

Britannic Assurance County Championship: 8th; Won 5, Lost 6, Drawn 11
All First-Class Matches: Played 26: Won 5, Lost 6, Drawn 15
NatWest Bank Trophy: Lost to Middlesex in quarter-final
Benson & Hedges Cup: Lost to Worcestershire in quarter-final
Refuge Assurance League: 15th; Won 4, Lost 11, No Result 1

County Averages

Batting and Fielding	M	I	NO	HS	R	Avge	100	50	Ct/St
I.V.A. Richards	18	28	5	164*	1425	61.95	7	3	8
A.R. Butcher	23	41	5	151*	2116	58.77	6	15	8
H. Morris	25	46	5	160*	2276	55.51	10	10	13
R.D.B. Croft	16	26	11	91*	672	44.80	–	4	2
M.P. Maynard	23	41	7	125*	1501	44.14	2	11	15
G.C. Holmes	10	15	4	125*	465	42.27	1	2	2
N.G. Cowley	14	17	4	76	536	41.23	–	6	9
I. Smith	7	10	2	112*	328	41.00	1	2	1
P.A. Cottey	20	35	5	156	1001	33.36	3	4	13
M.J. Cann	6	10	0	64	206	20.60	–	2	2
M.L. Roberts	4	5	1	25	79	19.75	–	–	10/-
A. Dale	9	14	0	92	229	16.35	–	1	7
C.P. Metson	23	27	5	50*	352	16.00	–	1	58/-
H.A.G. Anthony	6	8	0	39	127	15.87	–	–	–
S.L. Watkin	23	24	8	25*	173	10.81	–	–	6
S.P. James	5	10	0	47	79	7.90	–	–	4
S. Bastien	12	9	3	12	47	7.83	–	–	–
M. Frost	20	18	8	12	42	4.20	–	–	2
S.J. Dennis	14	8	1	6	23	3.28	–	–	3

Also batted: S.R. Barwick (5 matches) 0*, 2*; M. Davies (1 match) 5* (1ct);
J. Derrick (1 match) 28*; R.N. Pook (1 match) 0, 0*.

Hundreds (30)

10 **H. Morris:** 103 v Oxf. Univ. (Oxford); 100* v Kent (Swansea); 102 v Yorks (Cardiff); 119 v Worcs (Abergavenny); 106 v Warwicks (Swansea); 100 v Middlesex (Lord's); 110 & 102* v Notts (Worksop); 126 v Sri Lankans (Ebbw Vale); 160* v Derbys (Cardiff).

7 **I.V.A. Richards:** 119 v Leics (Cardiff); 118* v Sussex (Hove); 109 v Northants (Northampton); 164* v Hants (Southampton); 111 & 118* v Essex (Southend); 127 v Notts (Worksop).

6 **A.R. Butcher:** 139 v Sussex (Hove); 151* v Kent (Swansea); 115 v Leics (Hinckley); 130 v Worcs (Abergavenny); 116 v Warwicks (Swansea); 121* v Notts (Worksop).

3 **P.A. Cottey:** 156 v Oxf. Univ. (Oxford); 125 v Leics (Hinckley); 100* v Worcs (Abergavenny).

2 **M.P. Maynard:** 125* v Northants (Northampton); 115 v Notts (Worksop).

1 **G.C. Holmes:** 125* v Somerset (Cardiff).
  I. Smith: 112* v Lancs (Colwyn Bay).

Bowling	O	M	R	W	Avge	Best	5wI	10wM
S. Bastien	317.1	57	1187	39	30.43	6-75	2	–
M. Frost	557.1	74	2047	59	34.69	5-40	2	1
H.A.G. Anthony	132.4	32	466	12	38.83	3-95	–	–
S.L. Watkin	767.1	130	2629	65	40.44	5-100	1	–
R.D.B. Croft	397.1	83	1335	28	47.67	3-10	–	–
A. Dale	90	13	338	7	48.28	3-21	–	–
S.J. Dennis	322	61	1071	22	48.68	5-76	1	–
S.R. Barwick	158.4	43	441	9	49.00	3-29	–	–
N.G. Cowley	316.3	64	900	12	75.00	3-84	–	–
I.V.A. Richards	137	26	426	5	85.20	2-27	–	–

Also bowled: A.R. Butcher 25.3-2-153-1; M.J. Cann 35-3-162-1; P.A. Cottey 18-0-116-1; M. Davies 8-1-16-0; J. Derrick 9-2-58-0; G.C. Holmes 42-10-132-4; M.P. Maynard 29-2-184-0; H. Morris 6-0-62-0; R.N. Pook 8-3-19-0; I. Smith 39-3-181-1.

Gloucestershire

Gloucestershire, who propped up the Championship table for the first half of the season, failed to record a victory until the end of July. They rallied towards the latter part of the season, winning three games in the last five weeks, but overall it was a disappointing summer on the field amid rumours of further discontent in the dressing room.

Despite the appointment of Eddie barlow as Chief Coach, Gloucestershire dropped four places to 13th in the Championship. They also failed to win any of their Benson & Hedges games, while they suffered a record defeat against Lancashire in the quarter-final of the NatWest Trophy. Their Sunday League form improved, enabling them to win seven games and occupy a respectable eighth position.

Dean Hodgson took the opportunity to establish himself in his first full season as Gloucestershire's regular opener by scoring 1,300 runs. Wright, however, had a dismal season, failing to score a thousand runs, and the pressures of captaincy obviously affected his form. Athey experienced a much better summer, and was the county's leading runs scorer. Curran and Bainbridge also passed a thousand runs, following Athey in the averages. But neither will be returning in 1991. Curran, by mutual consent, is to join another county. The Zimbabwean all-rounder has an outstanding talent, but too often his temperament has caused dissent among his fellow players. Bainbridge, who was frequently troubled by injury, declined the offer of a one-year contract.

Stovold played only two games and from next season will captain the 2nd XI. Despite an innings of 256, against Northants, and a century against Surrey, Mark Alleyne totalled only 854 runs in 21 innings, and he needs consistency to match his ability.

Courtney Walsh was again Gloucestershire's leading bowler with 72 wickets at 28.08. He will be missed by Gloucestershire in 1991, when he will be in the West Indies touring party. Lawrence and Curran represented a steady seam attack, but the spin department was far less prosperous. There was a reluctance to play Graveney after his injury, but he proved a point by taking 15 wickets in the final three Championship games. His retirement, however, was not unexpected following the club's attitude towards him over the past three years. Lloyds' off-spin was expensive, while Ball, the young off-spinner who played for young England two years ago, took only three wickets in four first-glass games.

With Terry Alderman unlikely to play in 1991, much will depend on Lawrence's fitness, while there will be further opportunities for the youthful trio of Barnes, Bell, and Pooley.

EDWARD BEVAN

Britannic Assurance County Championship: =13th; Won 4, Lost 7, Drawn 11
All First-Class Matches: Played 25: Won 5, Lost 7, Drawn 13
NatWest Bank Trophy: Lost to Lancashire in quarter-final
Benson & Hedges Cup: Failed to qualify for quarter-final (4th in Group A)
Refuge Assurance League: 9th; Won 7, Lost 7, No Result 2

County Averages

Batting and Fielding	M	I	NO	HS	R	Avge	100	50	Ct/St
C.W.J. Athey	23	35	7	131	1474	52.64	3	9	18
K.M. Curran	23	33	8	144*	1267	50.68	3	5	15
P. Bainbridge	20	28	3	152	1107	44.28	2	5	4
R.C. Russell	11	16	1	120	651	43.40	2	3	28/-
M.W. Alleyne	13	21	0	256	854	40.66	2	3	11
J.W. Lloyds	24	34	12	93	839	38.13	–	4	15
G.D. Hodgson	24	40	4	126	1320	36.66	2	10	12
I.P. Butcher	12	19	4	102	513	34.20	1	2	4
R.C.J. Williams	8	8	4	50*	132	33.00	–	1	27/4
P.W. Romaines	7	11	2	95	295	32.77	–	2	2
C.A. Walsh	20	20	3	63*	464	27.29	–	3	6
A.J. Wright	23	38	3	112	911	26.02	1	5	23
G.A. Tedstone	6	5	0	23	88	17.60	–	–	9/1
D.A. Graveney	13	13	4	46*	107	11.88	–	–	7
D.V. Lawrence	22	23	3	35	159	7.95	–	–	7
M.C.J. Ball	4	5	0	15	39	7.80	–	–	4
S.N. Barnes	10	9	3	12*	23	3.83	–	–	3

Also batted: R.M. Bell (2 matches) 0, 0; K.B.S. Jarvis (2 matches) 0*, 1*; E.T. Milburn (2 matches) 35, 11*, 0, 3*; P.A. Owen (3 matches) 1, 1; A.W. Stovold (2 matches) 4, 74, 7, 19. M.W. Pooley played in one match but did not bat.

Hundreds (16)

3 C.W.J. Athey: 131 v Sussex (Hove); 108* & 122 v Warwicks (Bristol).

  K.M. Curran: 103* v Somerset (Bristol); 144* v Sussex (Bristol); 101* v Hants (Southampton).

2 M.W. Alleyne: 118 v Surrey (Cheltenham); 256 v Northants (Northampton).

  P. Bainbridge: 152 v Yorks (Cheltenham); 129 v Worcs (Bristol).

  G.D. Hodgson: 126 v Zimbabweans (Bristol); 109 v Worcs (Bristol).

  R.C. Russell: 120 v Somerset (Bristol); 103* v Notts (Trent Bridge).

1 I.P. Butcher: 102 v Middlesex (Lord's).

  A.J. Wright: 112 v Northants (Cheltenham).

Bowling	O	M	R	W	Avge	Best	5wI	10wM
M.W. Alleyne	112	29	391	16	24.43	3-23	–	–
C.A. Walsh	611.1	107	2022	72	28.08	8-58	3	1
K.M. Curran	598.3	111	1961	64	30.64	5-63	1	–
D.V. Lawrence	471.2	52	1874	56	33.46	5-51	2	–
S.N. Barnes	207	45	602	16	37.62	4-51	–	–
D.A. Graveney	485.4	137	1189	31	38.35	5-45	3	1
P. Bainbridge	162.4	30	515	11	46.81	3-23	–	–
J.W. Lloyds	382.5	59	1429	25	57.16	4-11	–	–

Also bowled: C.W.J. Athey 50.5-10-145-2; M.C.J. Ball 62-15-201-3; R.M. Bell 44-7-114-3; K.B.S. Jarvis 34-3-142-3; E.T. Milburn 32.3-4-150-3; P.A. Owen 57-7-239-4; M.W. Pooley 16-1-67-2; P.W. Romaines 6-0-30-1; G.A. Tedstone 2-1-1-0; A.J. Wright 0.5-0-7-0.

Hampshire

Hampshire's glorious end to the Championship season, when they reached an improbable victory target of 445 to beat Gloucestershire, was a final reminder of the bat's utter dominance over ball in 1990. The win enabled Hampshire to finish in a highly creditable third place, though there were times during the year when a first Championship title since 1973 seemed feasible. At the start of August they were tucked in behind Middlesex and Essex, but five matches without a Hampshire victory enabled the top two to build an unbridgeable gap.

It was always likely that batting would be Hampshire's strong suit, even allowing for the plethora of artificially inflated averages around the country, and for half a season they gave an efficient impersonation of impregnability. They were into their 12th Championship match, with July almost over, before Derbyshire became the first side to bowl them out.

If the overall success of Hampshire's batting was predictable, the make-up of the high scores did not always follow the expected script. Middleton, who had not come close to establishing himself in the side since his debut in 1984, scored a maiden century against Kent in the first match and, with four more hundreds, commanded a first-team place for much of the season. The Smith brothers again excelled – though Robin's appearances were severely restricted by England duties – but Gower had a rather patchy first season and will have been disappointed to have scored only one Championship hundred.

One of the most satisfying aspects of Hampshire's season was the emergence of Marshall as a front-line batsman, which in turn seemed to breathe new fire and enthusiasm into his bowling. The distinct bonus for the county was that Marshall reconsidered his decision to retire at the end of the season and committed himself to another two years at least.

The lack of bowling support for Marshall explained Hampshire's failure to win a title – Bakker, Connor, and Maru were the only other bowlers to exceed 20 championship wickets and all three proved expensive.

Ayling was restored to fitness after missing the whole of the 1989 season, but his return was followed almost immediately by the long-term absence of James. It was all the more galling for the all-rounder as he scored fifty and an unbeaten hundred in his one and only game of the summer.

For the third successive year Hampshire faltered at the semi-final stage in the NatWest Trophy, but a late surge on Sundays brought them close to a top-four place in the Refuge Assurance League.

CLIVE ELLIS

Britannic Assurance County Championship: 3rd; Won 8, Lost 4, Drawn 10
All First-Class Matches: Played 25: Won 9, Lost 4, Drawn 12
NatWest Bank Trophy: Lost to Northamptonshire in semi-final
Benson & Hedges Cup: Failed to qualify for quarter final (4th in Group C)
Refuge Assurance League: 5th; Won 9, Lost 5, No Result 2

County Averages

Batting and Fielding	M	I	NO	HS	R	Avge	100	50	Ct/St
L.A. Joseph	6	5	4	69*	152	152.00	–	1	1
A.N. Aymes	5	8	4	75*	317	79.25	–	3	9/3
T.M. Tremlett	8	5	3	78	143	71.50	–	1	1
R.A. Smith	12	19	4	181	941	62.73	4	3	8
C.L. Smith	22	38	7	148	1886	60.83	4	12	14
T.C. Middleton	18	29	3	127	1238	47.61	5	5	9
J.R. Ayling	9	11	3	62*	368	46.00	–	3	2
M.D. Marshall	18	24	3	117	962	45.80	2	6	7
R.M.F. Cox	4	7	2	104*	220	44.00	1	–	3
D.I. Gower	17	26	3	145	972	42.26	2	3	17
V.P. Terry	22	35	3	165	1332	41.62	5	4	24
M.C.J. Nicholas	23	35	10	104	895	35.80	1	5	9
R.J. Maru	25	20	2	59	520	28.88	–	3	30
C.A. Connor	22	10	4	46	148	24.66	–	–	10
S.D. Udal	7	6	2	28*	79	19.75	–	–	2
R.J. Parks	20	21	10	36*	216	19.63	–	–	49/4
P-J. Bakker	16	9	4	20	95	19.00	–	–	3
R.J. Scott	6	10	2	71	144	18.00	–	1	4

Also batted: K.D. James (1 match) 50, 104*; K.J. Shine (7 matches) 24* (1ct);
I.J. Turner (5 matches) 14, 1, 0* (2ct); J.R. Wood (2 matches) 17, 11 (1ct).

Hundreds (25)

5 T.C. Middleton: 127 v Kent (Canterbury); 104* v Essex (Southampton); 123 v Northants (Bournemouth); 117* v Worcs (Worcester); 104 v Kent (Bournemouth).
  V.P. Terry: 107 v Kent (Canterbury); 112 v Oxf. Univ. (Oxford); 119* v Warwicks (Edgbaston); 165 v Northants (Bournemouth); 120 v Sri Lankans (Southampton).
4 C.L. Smith: 148 v Oxf. Univ. (Oxford); 128 v Essex (Southampton); 132* v Sussex (Arundel); 111 v Surrey (Southampton).
  R.A. Smith: 181 v Sussex (Southampton); 114* v Surrey (Foster's Oval); 153 v Glamorgan (Southampton); 124 v Glos (Southampton).
2 D.I. Gower: 145 v Sussex (Southampton); 126* v Indians (Southampton).
  M.D. Marshall: 117 v Yorks (Headingley); 112 v Leics (Leicester).
1 R.M.F. Cox: 104* v Worcs (Worcester).
  K.D. James: 104* v Kent (Canterbury).
  M.C.J. Nicholas: 104 v Indians (Southampton).

Bowling	O	M	R	W	Avge	Best	5wI	10wM
M.D. Marshall	554.2	141	1381	72	19.18	7-47	4	2
C.L. Smith	28	9	97	5	19.40	3-35	–	–
R.J. Scott	36.4	5	165	5	33.00	2-5	–	–
R.J. Maru	852.1	219	2420	66	36.66	6-97	2	–
C.A. Connor	510.1	88	1791	47	38.10	5-96	1	–
P-J. Bakker	436.2	90	1439	37	38.89	5-101	1	–
K.J. Shine	156.4	30	550	14	39.28	4-52	–	–
T.M. Tremlett	120.5	30	393	10	39.30	3-33	–	–
S.D. Udal	233.3	46	900	22	40.90	4-139	–	–
I.J. Turner	148.2	39	424	9	47.11	2-60	–	–
J.R. Ayling	171.2	46	572	11	52.00	2-48	–	–
L.A. Joseph	102	16	462	7	66.00	2-28	–	–

Also bowled: R.M.F. Cox 1-0-1-0; K.D. James 28-8-74-1; T.C. Middleton 5-0-29-0; M.C.J. Nicholas 69.2-9-276-2; R.A. Smith 0.3-0-5-0; V.P. Terry 1-0-19-0.

Kent

Chris Cowdrey's six-year reign as captain of Kent ended with his side finishing 16th in the Championship table, the lowest place since 1980, when the county were also second bottom. While the batsmen accumulated a respectable 69 batting points – the fifth best – the bowlers mustered just 35 bonus points, the worst of all the counties.

Cowdrey had a miserable season, with injury restricting his Championship appearances to 12 games. It was unfortunate timing that his decision to quit was announced during one of the few high spots of the summer, when Kent defeated Leicestershire at Dartford on a spinners' wicket (which, incidentally, attracted the attention of the TCCB pitch inspectors).

That success over Leicestershire was one of Kent's three victories in the Championship. Each of these featured the left-arm spin bowling of Richard Davis, who enjoyed his best summer since joining the county in 1986. He bowled more than 900 overs and took 73 wickets, propelling himself to the edge of England recognition for one of the winter tours.

Davis returned his best match figures of 10 for 142 against Leicestershire, and was joined in tandem by Minal Patel, the county's other left-arm slow bowler, who also took best figures of 10 for 148. Such achievements were not matched on the seam side, where Kent struggled to field a regular, fit and willing trio from De Villiers, Merrick, Ellison, Penn, and Igglesden.

Such problems did not exist on the batting front, where Kent enjoyed their fair share of runs in a rich summer for batsmen. Neil Taylor topped the county averages, falling just short of 2,000 for the season in all first-class games. His seven centuries included a career best 204 in the first innings against Surrey at Canterbury in September that was followed by a further 142 in the second.

Taylor was backed up by the usual consistency of openers Mark Benson and Simon Hinks, and there were also increased contributions from Graham Cowdrey and Matthew Fleming. The former made more than 1,500 runs and the latter was 20 short of joining the 1,000 brigade.

Kent's batsmen are capable run getters, but they lack the firepower to chase big totals – a fact that was emphasized by the county's 13 drawn games. Unfortunately, such obduracy does not win titles, and the new captain, Benson, has much to work on. He will have the support of Chris Cowdrey, who remains as a player, and he will also be hoping for a greater contribution from overseas players.

ROB WILDMAN

Britannic Assurance County Championship: 16th; Won 3, Lost 6, Drawn 13
All First-Class Matches: Played 24: Won 4, Lost 7, Drawn 13
NatWest Bank Trophy: Lost to Gloucestershire in 2nd round
Benson & Hedges Cup: Failed to qualify for quarter-final (3rd in Group A)
Refuge Assurance League: 11th; Won 7, Lost 8, No Result 1

County Averages

Batting and Fielding	M	I	NO	HS	R	Avge	100	50	Ct/St
N.R. Taylor	22	37	5	204	1979	61.84	7	10	9
M.R. Benson	15	24	1	159	1119	48.65	5	4	5
G.R. Cowdrey	22	39	6	135	1576	47.75	3	8	9
C.S. Cowdrey	13	24	6	107*	733	40.72	3	2	9
R.M. Ellison	15	19	7	81	473	39.41	–	3	6
M.V. Fleming	19	32	6	102	980	37.69	1	5	6
S.G. Hinks	24	43	0	234	1588	36.93	4	6	8
S.A. Marsh	24	35	8	114*	911	33.74	1	5	49/5
T.R. Ward	15	28	1	175	863	31.96	2	5	14
V.J. Wells	8	15	0	58	352	23.46	–	2	8
P.S. De Villiers	12	15	3	37	264	22.00	–	–	6
R.P. Davis	24	32	3	59	504	17.37	–	2	27
C. Penn	7	6	2	23*	66	16.50	–	–	2
M.M. Patel	9	12	5	41*	104	14.85	–	–	2
A.P. Igglesden	14	17	9	24	105	13.12	–	–	5
D.J.M. Kelleher	5	8	0	44	101	12.62	–	–	2
T.A. Merrick	7	8	2	35	66	11.00	–	–	1
T.M. Wren	5	5	2	16	23	7.66	–	–	2

Also batted: M.C. Dobson (1 match) 0, 6; M.A. Ealham (2 matches) 0, 13*.
N.J. Llong played one match but did not bat (1ct).

Hundreds (26)

7 **N.R. Taylor:** 106 v Glamorgan (Swansea); 124* v Yorks (Tunbridge Wells); 120 v Camb. Univ. (Cambridge); 107 v Indians (Canterbury): 152* v Middlesex (Canterbury); 204 & 142 v Surrey (Canterbury).
5 **M.R. Benson** 109 v Sussex (Folkestone): 116 v Somerset (Canterbury): 159 v Essex (Maidstone); 107 v Leics (Dartford); 115 ret hurt v Sussex (Hove).
4 **S.G. Hinks:** 107 v Glamorgan (Swansea); 120 v Surrey (Guildford); 234 v Middlesex (Canterbury); 163 v Leics (Leicester).
3 **C.S. Cowdrey:** 107 v Hants (Canterbury): 102* v Camb. Univ. (Cambridge); 107* v Northants (Northampton).
  G.R. Cowdrey: 116 v Essex (Maidstone): 119* v Surrey (Guildford); 135 v Leics (Leicester).
2 **T.R. Ward:** 124 v Derbys (Chesterfield); 175 v Hants (Bournemouth).
1 **M.V. Fleming:** 102 v Notts (Tunbridge Wells).
  S.A. Marsh: 114* v Notts (Tunbridge Wells).

Bowling	O	M	R	W	Avge	Best	5wI	10wM
V.J. Wells	85	19	257	12	21.41	5-43	1	–
T.A. Merrick	184.3	45	488	17	28.70	4-66	–	–
A.P. Igglesden	326	47	1150	32	35.93	4-79	–	–
R.P. Davis	905.1	221	2844	73	38.95	6-40	5	1
P.S. De Villiers	304.5	58	992	25	39.68	6-70	1	–
M.M. Patel	297.5	72	836	20	41.80	6-57	2	1
M.V. Fleming	394.5	94	1072	22	48.72	3-65	–	–
R.M. Ellison	291.5	51	963	19	50.68	4-76	–	–
D.J.M. Kelleher	112.5	20	398	7	56.85	3-148	–	–
C. Penn	186	35	636	11	57.81	3-45	–	–
T.M. Wren	122	14	489	6	81.50	2-78	–	–

Also bowled: M.R. Benson 8-2-46-1; C.S. Cowdrey 61-12-192-4; G.R. Cowdrey 6.3-1-44-0; M.C. Dobson 3.1-1-7-0; M.A. Ealham 34.2-5-120-3; S.G. Hinks 15-2-60-2; N.J. Llong 7-1-24-0; S.A. Marsh 8.4-0-36-2; N.R. Taylor 21-5-57-1; T.R. Ward 53-6-225-4.

Lancashire

Lancashire's triumphant season, in which they became the first side to win the NatWest Trophy and the Benson & Hedges Cup in the same summer, and also finished 2nd in the Refuge Assurance League, confirmed their position among the foremost counties. Only in the Britannic Assurance Championship, were they dropped back to finish sixth after making a strong early challenge, did they appear at a disadvantage. That said, sixth place represented an advance from ninth the previous season.

Lancashire's inability to win more than six championship matches stemmed from the one weakness in the composition of their team. They lacked a class spin bowler, and hence had difficulty in winkling sides out twice on placid pitches. That apart, they were pretty well armed at all points. Their batting alternated solid players with stroke-makers; their seam bowling, at least when all were fit, was accurate and varied; and their fielding, underpinned by Warren Hegg's efficient wicket-keeping, was notably sharp.

Two batsmen in Michael Atherton and Neil Fairbrother had outstanding seasons. Throughout, Fairbrother scored with an ease and fluency that make his failures at Test level difficult to understand. His 366 against Surrey was the second highest ever by an Englishman, behind Archie MacLaren's 424 for Lancashire at Taunton in 1895. Atherton effortlessly bridged the gap between county and Test cricket. His Championship batting average of 75 reflects his high skill and, in addition, his leg-spinners brought him 42 Championship victims.

Mendis had another very consistent year, and though Fowler was below par in the Championship he made plenty of one-day runs. Graham Lloyd impressed at times, and the lower middle order of Mike Watkinson, Philip DeFreitas and Hegg contributed valuably.

In the Championship, the bowling was not quite so satisfactory. Wasim Akram, a dominant cricketer in one-day matches, was prevented by niggling strains from giving of his best in three- and four-day games, and his penetrative fast left-arm swing bowling was particularly missed. But Watkinson, who switched occasionally from seam to off-spin, did well enough with 47 wickets, Patterson had his days, and Paul Allott, though not so sharp as in his prime, was very steady.

While the advance of Peter Martin, a tall 21-year-old fast bowler, was encouraging, the finger-spin department was disappointing, with off-spinner Dexter Fitton's lack of success forcing skipper David Hughes to employ his own rather rusty slow left-arm.

The batting, though, is abundantly healthy, and with Lloyd, Nick Speak, and the Crawley brothers challenging the established players, the county's selectors were troubled as much by whom to leave out as whom to select.

DAVID GREEN

Britannic Assurance County Championship: 6th; Won 6, Lost 3, Drawn 13
All First-Class Matches: Played 25: Won 6, Lost 3, Drawn 16
NatWest Bank Trophy: Winners
Benson & Hedges Cup: Winners
Refuge Assurance League: 2nd; Won 11, Lost 3, No Result 2
Refuge Assurance Cup: Lost to Middlesex in semi-final

County Averages

Batting and Fielding	M	I	NO	HS	R	Avge	100	50	Ct/St
N.H. Fairbrother	19	27	6	366	1681	80.04	4	9	19
M.A. Atherton	13	19	4	191	1170	78.00	5	6	17
G.D. Mendis	21	35	6	180	1551	53.48	4	8	16
N.J. Speak	6	9	0	138	409	45.44	1	3	3
G.D. Lloyd	14	20	2	96	796	44.22	–	8	9
T.E. Jesty	17	24	6	98	785	43.61	–	7	6
W.K. Hegg	20	21	6	100*	617	41.13	1	2	47/2
P.A.J. DeFreitas	16	18	3	102	608	40.53	2	2	7
M. Watkinson	19	23	2	138	754	35.90	1	4	8
G. Fowler	21	35	6	126	938	32.34	2	2	14
I.D. Austin	13	15	6	58	276	30.66	–	1	–
P.J.W. Allott	13	6	2	55*	114	28.50	–	1	9
S.P. Titchard	3	5	0	80	129	25.80	–	1	–
D.P. Hughes	18	17	7	57	237	23.70	–	1	13
J.D. Fitton	15	13	5	25*	133	16.62	–	–	3
Wasim Akram	8	11	0	32	135	12.27	–	–	–
P.J. Martin	10	7	3	21	44	11.00	–	–	5
B.P. Patterson	10	4	1	4*	5	1.66	–	–	2

Also batted: S. Bramhall (2 matches) 0*, 0, 1* (2 ct); J.P. Crawley (3 matches) 1, 76*, 26 (1ct); M.A. Crawley (1 match) 42, 48; I. Folley (3 matches) 47*, 5; J. Gallian (1 match) 17*; S.N.V. Waterton (1 match) 3 (4ct); G. Yates (5 matches) 2*, 42, 15, 106* (1ct).
R. Irani (1 match) and J. Stanworth (2 matches, 3ct) did not bat.

Hundreds (21)

5 **M.A. Atherton:** 191 v Surrey (Foster's Oval); 117 v Oxf. Univ. (Oxford); 101 v Kent (Maidstone); 108* v Essex (Colchester); 108 v Yorks (Old Trafford).
4 **N.H. Fairbrother** 366 v Surrey (Foster's Oval); 105 v Oxf. Univ. (Oxford); 203* v Warwicks (Coventry); 109* v Leics (Leicester).
　G.D. Mendis: 102 v Surrey (Foster's Oval); 113 v Leics (Old Trafford); 114 v Middlesex (Old Trafford); 180 v Notts (Southport).
2 **P.A.J. DeFreitas:** 102 v Oxf. Univ. (Oxford); 100* v Northants (Northampton).
　G. Fowler: 115* v Leics (Old Trafford); 126 v Glos (Old Trafford).
1 **W.K. Hegg:** 100* v Essex (Colchester).　　　　　**M. Watkinson:** 138 v Yorks (Old Trafford).
　N.J. Speak: 138 v Zimbabweans (Old Trafford).　　**G. Yates:** 106 v Notts (Trent Bridge).

Bowling	O	M	R	W	Avge	Best	5wI	10wM
M.A. Atherton	395.3	94	1220	44	27.27	6-78	3	–
M. Watkinson	508.2	122	1578	47	33.57	5-65	3	–
B.P. Patterson	282.4	45	1015	29	35.00	4-52	–	–
P.A.J. DeFreitas	429.5	100	1265	34	37.20	6-39	1	–
D.P. Hughes	280.4	61	918	24	38.25	4-25	–	–
P.J. Martin	275.3	52	868	22	39.45	4-68	–	–
Wasim Akram	204	44	640	16	40.00	3-76	–	–
P.J.W. Allott	266	77	730	18	40.55	4-23	–	–
G. Yates	167	38	420	8	52.50	4-94	–	–
I.D. Austin	245	76	662	12	55.16	3-42	–	–
I. Folley	114.1	18	397	6	66.16	2-18	–	–
J.D. Fitton	454.4	91	1447	14	103.35	3-69	–	–

Also bowled: M.A. Crawley 14-3-25-0; N.H. Fairbrother 7-0-29-0; G. Fowler 4.1-2-33-1; J. Gallian 21-8-65-1; R. Irani 22-7-73-2; T.E. Jesty 8-3-27-1; G.D. Lloyd 3.1-0-29-0; N.J. Speak 5-0-26-1.

Leicestershire

Leicestershire, who finished out of the Championship's top ten in 1989 for only the second time in 19 seasons, regained lost ground in 1990 without suggesting they could challenge for honours. First-round dismissal from the NatWest Trophy followed a fall at the first hurdle in the Benson & Hedges Cup, and 16th place in the Sunday League added to the impression of under-achievement in one-day cricket.

In the Championship, however, they improved from 13th position to 7th, with much credit to Briers, who failed by only four runs to become the first batsman to reach 2,000 in a season for the county since 1961 – all the more commendable since it came in a season in which he took over the captaincy and had the further distraction of a busy testimonial. Whitaker, with more than 1,700 runs, and Boon, with over 1,500, benefited from improved pitches at Grace Road, and Willey and Potter, with fewer chances to build long innings, topped 1,000.

Eight players yielded 17 first-class centuries, compared with six from three batsman in 1989, but Benson's progress seemed hindered by flimsy concentration and Hepworth's career stagnated with negligible opportunity. Whitticase's summer was blighted by injuries, but Nixon deputized capably behind the wicket as well as making useful runs. The benefits of fitness training under new team manager Bobby Simpson could be seen in sharper fielding.

Blander pitches and thinner seams compromised an attack more reliant on movement than sheer pace, and Benjamin, who is quitting county cricket, was only fitfully effective. Agnew overcame a limp start to play a major part in a strong mid-season revival, and his retirement and that of Taylor made the impressive emergence of Millns, who produced genuine pace in the last two months of the season, something of a relief.

Parsons, less frantic and more controlled, also prospered in the final weeks, and Lewis, whose batting bore the gloss of true class, reminded them of the other qualities they missed while he was on international duty by claiming 6-58 in the final game against Derbyshire.

Mullally, a left-arm-seamer born in Southend and raised in Australia, earned rich praise, but still had to be viewed in terms of potential rather than achievement and spin was a little used weapon. Willey's off-spin was mainly seen in grudging, one-day mode, and he rejected the offer of a new one-year contract at the end of the season. But there are high hopes of Hawkes, a left-arm-spinner and former *Daily Telegraph* Young Bowler of the Year. NEIL HALLAM

Britannic Assurance County Championship: 7th; Won 6, Lost 7, Drawn 9
All First-Class Matches: Played 24: Won 6, Lost 7, Drawn 11
NatWest Bank Trophy: Lost to Hampshire in 1st round
Benson & Hedges Cup: Failed to qualify for quarter final (3rd in Group D)
Refuge Assurance League: 16th; Won 4, Lost 11, No Result 1

County Averages

Batting and Fielding	M	I	NO	HS	R	Avge	100	50	Ct/St
N.E. Briers	24	44	4	176	1996	49.90	5	11	7
J.J. Whitaker	24	45	6	124*	1767	45.30	4	8	14
T.J. Boon	24	45	4	138	1539	37.53	2	11	13
C.C. Lewis	14	23	5	189*	661	36.72	1	2	11
J.D.R. Benson	18	27	6	106	725	34.52	1	3	12
P. Willey	22	40	6	177	1150	33.82	2	5	10
W.K.M. Benjamin	12	15	2	101*	437	33.61	1	4	3
L. Potter	23	38	5	109*	1080	32.72	1	7	23
P.N. Hepworth	4	8	2	55*	185	30.83	–	1	1
M.I. Gidley	5	5	1	73	113	28.25	–	1	2
P.A. Nixon	19	23	8	46	411	27.40	–	–	49/1
G.J.F. Ferris	6	6	0	35	104	17.33	–	–	1
J.P. Agnew	22	26	5	46*	257	12.23	–	–	5
G.J. Parsons	10	13	3	20	112	11.20	–	–	4
A.D. Mullally	19	18	6	29	113	9.41	–	–	4
P.J. Whitticase	5	7	2	11*	39	7.80	–	–	13/-
D.J. Millns	9	10	5	10*	23	4.60	–	–	3

Also batted: C. Hawkes (1 match) 3, 2* (1ct); B.F. Smith (2 matches) 4, 15* (1ct).
L.B. Taylor played in one match but did not bat.

Hundreds (17)

5 **N.E. Briers:** 104 v Essex (Chelmsford); 157* v Notts (Leicester); 150* v Indians (Leicester); 111 v Worcs (Leicester); 176 v Northants (Leicester).

4 **J.J. Whitaker:** 107* v Lancs (Old Trafford); 124* v Oxf. Univ. (Oxford); 116 v Derbys (Leicester); 100 v Kent (Leicester).

2 **T.J. Boon:** 128 v Somerset (Leicester); 138 v Glos (Gloucester).
  P. Willey: 177 v Oxf. Univ. (Oxford); 112 v Sussex (Leicester).

1 **W.K.M. Benjamin:** 101* v Derbys (Leicester).
  J.D.R. Benson: 106 v Indians (Leicester).
  C.C. Lewis: 189* v Essex (Chelmsford).
  L. Potter: 109* v Yorks (Sheffield).

Bowling	O	M	R	W	Avge	Best	5wI	10wM
D.J. Millns	206.4	36	662	31	21.35	6-63	2	–
C.C. Lewis	430.2	86	1289	47	27.42	6-55	2	1
G.J. Parsons	304.5	77	963	35	27.51	6-75	2	–
W.K.M. Benjamin	284.3	63	858	28	30.64	5-73	2	–
J.P. Agnew	612	108	2196	59	37.22	5-54	5	–
A.D. Mullally	487.2	117	1446	38	38.05	4-59	–	–
G.J.F. Ferris	138.2	29	482	12	40.16	4-44	–	–
P. Willey	421.4	119	1091	23	47.43	2-7	–	–
L. Potter	181	40	623	7	89.00	2-2	–	–

Also bowled: J.D.R. Benson 39.5-3-157-1; T.J. Boon 6.5-0-39-0; M.I. Gidley 94-27-309-1; C. Hawkes 14-3-40-0; L.B. Taylor 9-1-34-0.

Middlesex

Middlesex came close to their best season in modern times when they won the Britannic Assurance County Championship, almost won the Sunday League for the first time, and reached the semi-finals of the NatWest Trophy. They won the Refuge Assurance Cup, as their 40-over consolation, and only in the Benson & Hedges Cup did they perform below expectation.

The ineligibility of Mike Gatting and John Emburey for Test cricket, because of their ill-fated excursion to South Africa in the winter, meant that Middlesex had their captain and vice-captain available for nearly every game, with a strong nucleus of consistent batting at their disposal. Compared with their five other Championship-winning sides in 14 previous seasons, they remained relatively free of international call-ups. Only Angus Fraser, so effective as an accurate opening bowler, was frequently unavailable because of his England duties, though Neil Williams, free of injury at last, was called up for his Test debut.

Quick runs, and plenty of them, became a hallmark of Middlesex, and Gatting was never afraid to turn off the tap if there was a chance of victory. Desmond Haynes, the West Indies opener, enjoyed a sparkling season, inspiring those around him with the joy of hitting the ball hard.

Haynes piled up 2,346 runs in first-class cricket at an average of exactly 69. He collected eight centuries, including two double-hundreds, and smashed another three centuries in limited-overs games. Perhaps the most disappointing match of the season was at Old Trafford, when Middlesex failed to reach the NatWest Trophy final after scoring 296 for four, Haynes amassing 149 not out in a rain-affected tie.

Haynes's presence helped Roseberry, his opening partner, advance his career. But it was Mark Ramprakash of the younger batsmen who caught the eye. Ramprakash, who turned 21 in September, produced four championship hundreds, including three in successive innings – two in the Kent match at Canterbury. He also emerged as a highly effective one-day player. Keith Brown, who made his debut in 1984, was capped at the start of the season. He hit five championship centuries, including 200 not out against Nottinghamshire, and gave Middlesex's middle order a reassuringly reliable look.

The emergence of Philip Tufnell as a left-arm spin-bowler proved important to the Middlesex momentum during the height of the summer on bland pitches when seam-bowlers could not impose themselves. Gatting used him extensively in every match he played, often in tandem with Emburey's accurate off-spin. Tufnell's variations and patience earned him 65 Championship wickets and a ticket aboard England's plane for the Ashes trip, while Emburey's haul of 57 wickets was the best for an off-spinner in the country by a considerable margin.

CHARLES RANDALL

Britannic Assurance County Championship: 1st; Won 10, Lost 1, Drawn 11
All First-Class Matches: Played 24: Won 10, Lost 1, Drawn 13
NatWest Bank Trophy: Lost to Lancashire in semi-final
Benson & Hedges Cup: Lost to Somerset in quarter-final
Refuge Assurance League: 3rd; Won 10, Lost 5, No Result 1
Refuge Assurance Cup: Winners

County Averages

Batting and Fielding	M	I	NO	HS	R	Avge	100	50	Ct/St
D.L. Haynes	23	39	5	255*	2346	69.00	8	7	14
M.W. Gatting	23	37	7	170*	1704	56.80	4	9	20
K.R. Brown	24	36	8	200*	1505	53.75	5	8	30
M.R. Ramprakash	24	42	10	146*	1541	48.15	5	6	6
M.A. Roseberry	24	44	4	135	1593	39.82	3	11	23
J.E. Emburey	23	32	7	111*	702	28.08	1	2	33
P.R. Downton	16	24	2	63	587	26.68	–	4	42/3
A.R.C. Fraser	12	11	2	97	213	23.66	–	1	3
P.C.R. Tufnell	22	21	9	37	271	22.58	–	–	8
P. Farbrace	8	8	2	79	124	20.66	–	1	17/2
N.F. Williams	20	23	3	55*	410	20.50	–	2	4
S.P. Hughes	17	18	5	23*	111	8.53	–	–	3
N.G. Cowans	17	16	6	31	81	8.10	–	–	3

Also batted: R.O. Butcher (2 matches) 29*, 32, 0, 22* (3ct); J.C. Pooley (1 match) 8, 13 (1ct); C.W. Taylor (2 matches) 13, 0*; N.R. Taylor (1 match) 0 (1ct); P.N. Weekes (3 matches) 22, 51, 2 (3ct). M.J. Thursfield played 2 matches but did not bat.

Hundreds (26)

8 D.L. Haynes: 116 v Essex (Lord's); 181 & 129 v New Zealanders (Lord's); 220* v Essex (Ilford); 108 v Somerset (Uxbridge); 173 v Glamorgan (Lord's); 255* v Sussex (Lord's); 131 v Yorks (Headingley).

5 K.R. Brown: 141 v Essex (Lord's); 109* v Yorks (Uxbridge); 120 v Glamorgan (Lord's); 200* v Notts (Lord's); 116* v Sussex (Hove).

　M.R. Ramprakash: 118* v Camb. Univ. (Cambridge); 146* v Somerset (Uxbridge); 100* & 125 v Kent (Canterbury); 132 v Notts (Lord's).

4 M.W. Gatting: 170* v Somerset (Uxbridge); 101 v Kent (Canterbury); 169* v Notts (Trent Bridge); 119* v Derbys (Derby).

3 M.A. Roseberry: 122 v Surrey (Lord's); 135 v Essex (Ilford); 115 v Northants (Luton).

1 J.E. Emburey: 111* v Hants (Bournemouth).

Bowling	O	M	R	W	Avge	Best	5wI	10wM
M.W. Gatting	56	21	138	7	19.71	4-2	–	–
C.W. Taylor	47.5	7	139	6	23.16	5-33	1	–
A.R.C. Fraser	436.5	103	1073	41	26.17	6-30	2	–
N.F. Williams	489.1	93	1470	52	28.26	7-61	2	–
N.G. Cowans	442	119	1208	38	31.78	5-67	1	–
J.E. Emburey	942.3	272	1957	61	32.08	5-32	2	–
P.C.R. Tufnell	1039.5	279	2622	74	35.43	6-79	2	–
S.P. Hughes	386.2	73	1287	33	39.00	5-101	1	–

Also bowled: K.R. Brown 16-4-65-1; R.O. Butcher 2-0-2-0; P.R. Downton 1.1-0-4-1; D.L. Haynes 35-7-113-2; J.C. Pooley 2-0-11-0; M.R. Ramprakash 41-7-164-2; M.A. Roseberry 22-5-115-2; N.R. Taylor 14-5-44-3; M.J. Thursfield 42-11-130-2; P.N. Weekes 80-17-264-4.

Northamptonshire

Apart from carrying off the Benson & Hedges Cup in the first year, the 80s, in terms of honours won, were a barren and disappointing period for Northants, despite having some fine players. However, it looked as if 1990 would mark the commencement of a bright new era, as on paper they had one of the most accomplished sides on the county circuit, a side capable of lifting them clear of the ruck in the middle of the table and joining the five strongest clubs at the top.

Four of the Northants team – Lamb, Bailey, Larkins, and Capel – had been on the tour of the West Indies last winter, while Ambrose, an important member of the opposition, is a world-class pace bowler when in the mood. This surely represented a more than useful nucleus for any county, while they also possessed good and experienced support. Davis would be an automatic choice for most Test teams, and Cook and Thomas were both capped for England not so long ago. Williams is an accomplished all-rounder, Ripley a very competent keeper, as well as a useful lower-order batsman, and Robinson a highly promising pace bowler who can move the ball away from the bat. An additional bonus was the discovery of a new opening pair, Fordham and Felton.

Their team had depth in batting, including several exciting stroke-makers, while their captain, Lamb, is a quite exceptional improviser in limited-overs cricket. Their attack appeared to have pace and penetration, plus the balance of two contrasting spinners. Yet it proved to be another trophy-less summer for Northants.

They were beaten by Scotland in the Benson & Hedges Cup and, almost unbelievably, finished bottom of the Refuge Assurance League. They were unable to make any impression in the County Championship, in which they lost the same number of matches as the bottom club, a depressing nine, and only won four. What went wrong?

They certainly suffered from injuries, but this does not really explain either their failure to play to their potential or their inconsistency. Both these weaknesses were all too apparent in the NatWest Final at Lords, where they allowed their one chance of glory to be taken from them far too easily. Lamb was unlucky to lose the toss and have to bat on a pitch which gave too much assistance to the bowlers in the first hour. Then, attempts to achieve a rescue by Capel and Ambrose were both ended with unlucky run-outs. So Lancashire were able to cruise home. However, missed catches, which so nearly cost them the semi-final, made the task much easier. It demonstrated how Northants were liable to crack under pressure and still lacked the steel required to win an honour.

TREVOR BAILEY

Britannic Assurance County Championship: 11th; Won 4, Lost 9, Drawn 9
All First-Class Matches: Played 24: Won 4, Lost 9, Drawn 11
NatWest Bank Trophy: Lost to Lancashire in final
Benson & Hedges Cup: Failed to qualify for quarter-final (5th in Group D)
Refuge Assurance League: 17th; Won 3, Lost 12

County Averages

Batting and Fielding	M	I	NO	HS	R	Avge	100	50	Ct/St
A.J. Lamb	11	18	3	235	1103	73.53	4	3	5
R.J. Bailey	23	39	8	204*	1987	64.09	7	9	16
D.J. Capel	18	29	6	123	1092	47.47	3	7	16
A. Fordham	24	42	2	206*	1767	44.17	4	9	22
N.A. Felton	22	39	2	122	1538	41.56	4	9	19
A.L. Penberthy	12	17	3	101*	435	31.07	1	3	8
D. Ripley	21	28	6	109*	656	29.81	1	2	28/6
W. Larkins	15	25	0	207	701	28.04	2	2	8
R.G. Williams	17	26	5	96	566	26.95	–	4	6
G. Cook	9	12	1	87	287	26.09	–	1	2
W.W. Davis	9	7	1	47	101	16.83	–	–	2
C.E.L. Ambrose	15	18	5	55*	203	15.61	–	1	1
J.G. Thomas	12	13	3	48	152	15.20	–	–	9
N.G.B. Cook	19	19	8	30	143	13.00	–	–	10
J.G. Hughes	4	7	0	2	4	0.57	–	–	–
M.A. Robinson	19	16	10	1*	3	0.50	–	–	5

Also batted: S.J. Brown (4 matches) 2, 4* (2ct); J.W. Govan (3 matches) 3, 17, 4, 17;
W.M. Noon (3 matches) 2, 2, 2 (5ct/1st); A.R. Roberts (2 matches) 5, 0, 0 (1ct);
D.J. Wild (2 matches) 20, 43, 17, 0.

Hundreds (26)

7 **R.J. Bailey:** 101 v Somerset (Taunton); 138* v Kent (Northampton); 204* v Sussex (Northampton); 134* v Derbys (Chesterfield); 105 v Glos (Northampton); 108 v Essex (Northampton); 107 v Essex (Chelmsford).

4 **N.A. Felton:** 119* v Notts (Trent Bridge); 122 v Glamorgan (Northampton); 101 v Somerset (Taunton); 106 v Yorks (Northampton).

A. Fordham: 206* v Yorks (Headingley); 128 v Somerset (Taunton); 172 v Lancs (Northampton); 159 v Essex (Chelmsford).

A.J. Lamb: 235 v Yorks (Headingley); 135* v Sussex (Northampton); 134 v Essex (Northampton); 165 v Essex (Chelmsford).

3 **D.J. Capel:** 113 v Glamorgan (Northampton); 123 v New Zealanders (Northampton); 103* v Derbys (Chesterfield).

2 **W. Larkins:** 107 v Surrey (Foster's Oval); 207 v Essex (Northampton).

1 **A.L. Penberthy:** 101* v Camb. Univ. (Cambridge).

D. Ripley: 109* v Leics (Leicester).

Bowling	O	M	R	W	Avge	Best	5wI	10wM
C.E.L. Ambrose	503.4	127	1413	61	23.16	7-89	5	1
J.W. Govan	47	14	142	5	28.40	2-12	–	–
D.J. Capel	234	51	711	25	28.44	5-74	1	–
N.G.B. Cook	527.1	167	1364	40	34.10	5-44	2	–
A.L. Penberthy	207.4	29	791	22	35.95	4-91	–	–
R.G. Williams	432.3	119	1204	31	38.83	4-94	–	–
J.G. Thomas	305.2	51	1171	29	40.37	7-75	1	–
S.J. Brown	73	17	250	6	41.66	1-11	–	–
M.A. Robinson	559.1	104	1889	40	47.22	3-47	–	–
R.J. Bailey	168.2	29	604	11	54.90	3-82	–	–
W.W. Davis	237.5	28	812	13	62.46	3-28	–	–

Also bowled: N.A. Felton 19-1-113-1; A. Fordham 10-0-43-1; J.G. Hughes 66-12-293-3;
W. Larkins 10-1-45-00; A.R. Roberts 63-14-207-3; D.J. Wild 21.5-6-74-1.

Nottinghamshire

Nottinghamshire's fall from a mid-summer high to mediocrity was one of the features of the season. By mid-June they led the Championship and had reached the semi-finals of the Benson & Hedges Cup. Yet by the end, Notts had slipped to 13th in the table and had failed to win a one-day trophy.

With Tim Robinson, Chris Broad, and Bruce French banned from Test cricket after taking part in the unofficial tour of South Africa, Notts had, in theory, one of the strongest squads. Their failure, primarily, was the lack of consistency among the batsmen, leading to their following on six times during the Championship.

Though Broad enjoyed a record season, Notts' top batsmen failed to hit form together, with too often only one making a big score. Broad made 2,226 runs in all first-class games. He hit nine centuries, equalling a feat by Dodge Whysall (1938) and Mike Harris (1971).

Robinson contributed 1,747 runs, and ended the summer by making four centuries in consecutive matches. Paul Johnson hit 1,518 runs and earned a place in the England under-25 side against the Indians. But the other batsmen struggled, with Derek Randall hit by injury and Mike Newell and Paul Pollard out of sorts.

The decline in performance of Franklyn Stephenson was another factor. He scored 800 runs and captured 54 wickets, but the sharpness and match-winning flair of the two previous seasons had gone. There were some plus factors; Andy Pick gained a place on the England 'A' tour to Pakistan with his haul of 51 wickets, and all-rounder Kevin Evans showed marked improvement.

Notts will hope that Pick does not suffer a fall in performance after an England tour, as did Andy Afford last season. The left-armer toured Zimbabwe in the winter of 1990 but was expected to do better on his return than 42 wickets at a cost of 46.28.

If Notts are to recapture their reputation as one of the best county sides, it is down to the likes of Afford, Pick, and Evans to improve further. They are among a group of young players who must be nurtured by John Birch, the former player, who has been appointed manager.

Birch will have the support of Ken Taylor, the former manager, as consultant next season. Like Robinson, Taylor harboured great hopes at the start of the season, but four victories was a dismal return. Performances fluctuated wildly — from chasing 354 to win at Scarborough against Yorkshire, to losing by 10 wickets against Essex at Southend.

ROB WILDMAN

Britannic Assurance County Championship: = 13th; Won 4, Lost 8, Drawn 10
All First-Class Matches: Played 25: Won 4, Lost 8, Drawn 13
NatWest Bank Trophy: Lost to Northamptonshire in 2nd round
Benson & Hedges Cup: Lost to Worcestershire in semi-final
Refuge Assurance League: 4th; Won 10, Lost 5, No Result 1
Refuge Assurance Cup: Lost to Derbyshire in semi-final

County Averages

Batting and Fielding	M	I	NO	HS	R	Avge	100	50	Ct/St
B.C. Broad	22	43	2	227*	2226	54.29	9	3	7
K.P. Evans	15	25	9	100*	738	46.12	1	4	13
R.T. Robinson	23	45	5	220*	1747	43.67	4	8	12
P. Johnson	22	41	3	165*	1514	39.84	3	9	14
D.W. Randall	15	28	1	178	987	36.55	2	5	14
M. Newell	15	27	2	112	851	34.04	1	6	4
M. Saxelby	8	15	4	73	335	30.45	–	2	3
D.J.R. Martindale	17	28	3	138	751	30.04	2	2	5
F.D. Stephenson	20	35	7	121	807	28.82	1	4	5
E.E. Hemmings	11	14	4	83	230	23.00	–	1	2
P. Pollard	7	13	0	72	277	21.30	–	1	5
R.A. Pick	17	16	6	35	204	20.40	–	–	6
B.N. French	22	34	9	105*	506	20.24	1	–	47/10
R.J. Evans	3	5	2	21*	37	12.33	–	–	1
K.E. Cooper	21	26	6	35*	227	11.35	–	–	9
G.W. Mike	4	5	1	18*	45	11.25	–	–	4
K. Saxelby	5	6	0	20	42	7.00	–	–	3
J.A. Afford	22	22	7	5	16	1.06	–	–	7

Also batted: M.G. Field-Buss (3 matches) 0, 0; D.R. Laing (1 match) 2; C.W. Scott (3 matches) 67*, 13*, 31 (1ct).

Hundreds (24)

9 **B.C. Broad:** 180 v Derbys (Trent Bridge); 119 v Warwicks (Edgbaston); 227* v Kent (Tunbridge Wells); 112* v Leics (Trent Bridge); 126 v Yorks (Scarborough); 122 v Lancs (Southport); 140 v Middlesex (Trent Bridge); 156 v Worcs (Trent Bridge); 122 v Lancs (Trent Bridge).

4 **R.T. Robinson:** 125* v Somerset (Weston-super-Mare); 123 v Glos (Trent Bridge); 105 v Middlesex (Lord's); 220* v Yorks (Trent Bridge).

3 **P. Johnson:** 165* v Northants (Trent Bridge); 112* v Oxf. Univ. (Oxford); 149 v Yorks (Scarborough).

2 **D.J.R. Martindale:** 108 v Northants (Trent Bridge); 138 v Camb. Univ. (Cambridge).

  D.W. Randall: 120 v Leics (Leicester); 178 v Kent (Tunbridge Wells).

1 **K.P. Evans:** 100* v Somerset (Weston-super-Mare).

  B.N. French: 105* v Derbys (Derby).

  M. Newell: 112 v Sri Lankans (Cleethorpes).

  F.D. Stephenson: 121 v Leics (Trent Bridge).

Bowling	O	M	R	W	Avge	Best	5wI	10wM
R.A. Pick	494.5	83	1657	51	32.49	7-128	1	1
K.P. Evans	356	78	1232	34	36.23	4-50	–	–
F.D. Stephenson	610.4	94	2098	54	38.85	6-84	2	–
E.E. Hemmings	443.3	127	1175	30	39.16	5-99	1	–
K.E. Cooper	703.4	153	2203	54	40.79	5-56	3	–
K. Saxelby	91.4	15	319	7	45.57	4-92	–	–
J.A. Afford	688	209	1944	42	46.28	4-137	–	–

Also bowled: R.J. Evans 6-1-24-0; M.G. Field-Buss 48.5-16-99-3; P. Johnson 1-0-1-0; D.R. Laing 5-1-21-0; G.W. Mike 60.2-10-263-2; M. Newell 8.2-3-35-1; M. Saxelby 61.4-9-270-3.

Somerset

Somerset's season very closely resembled that of 1989 in terms of results. They dropped one place in the Championship from 14th to 15th, climbed two to 8th in the Refuge Assurance League, and again reached the Benson & Hedges semi-finals. This was not unexpected, for their basic strengths and weaknesses were not altered by some changes in personnel. They remained one of the strongest batting sides, but were also less likely than most to bowl sides out on last season's pitches.

Once more the leading batsman was the South African Jimmy Cook, whose appetite for runs was undiminished at 37. He increased his Championship aggregate from 2,173 to 2,432, and, in scoring 902 Sunday League runs, broke Clive Rice's 1977 record of 814. Only Gooch exceeded Cook's first-class aggregate of 2,608. His consistent scoring in one-day competitions brought his total run tally to within 50 or so of 4,000, a remarkable feat even in so fine a summer.

In addition to Cook, Somerset had four other batsmen with Championship averages above 50, a feat matched by no other county. And their total of 73 batting points was excelled by none and equalled only by the champions Middlesex and second-placed Essex.

Major pluses were the form of Andy Hayhurst, signed from Lancashire in the close season, the continued improvement of Richard Harden, who scored quickly and consistently at No. 5, and the tremendous hitting of the improving Graham Rose. Hayhurst had to wait a while for his chance, but having gained it at the expense of Jon Hardy, he showed excellent technique, concentrated fiercely, and revealed an effective range of strokes in making the No. 3 position his own.

Chris Tavaré and Peter Roebuck both had profitable seasons, and if runs were needed lower down Rose and Burns could usually be relied on. Burns again kept wicket pretty well, but the bowling was a different story.

Though Neil Mallender's haul of 51 wickets at 30 apiece was a noble effort on the pitches prevailing, and Rose bowled well enough, Jones too frequently wasted the new ball. None of the trio regularly took early wickets, a vital ingredient of success. Roland Lefebvre, a Dutch international, lent support with steady medium pace, but lacked hostility, and though the off-spinner Ian Swallow, signed from Yorkshire, was adequate in a containing role he rarely troubled batsmen when they were set.

There were promising appearances from the young seamer Jeremy Hallett, and Richard Bartlett showed signs of returning confidence after a prolific 2nd XI season. But little obvious progress was made by other young players.

DAVID GREEN

Britannic Assurance County Championship: 15th; Won 3, Lost 4, Drawn 15
All First-Class Matches: Played 24: Won 3, Lost 5, Drawn 16
NatWest Bank Trophy: Lost to Worcestershire in 2nd round
Benson & Hedges Cup: Lost to Lancashire in semi-final
Refuge Assurance League: 8th; Won 8, Lost 8

County Averages

Batting and Fielding	M	I	NO	HS	R	Avge	100	50	Ct/St
S.J. Cook	24	41	7	313*	2608	76.70	9	11	10
R.J. Harden	24	31	7	104*	1460	60.83	3	12	18
C.J. Tavaré	24	32	4	219	1638	58.50	3	12	16
A.N. Hayhurst	22	35	8	170	1559	57.74	4	8	9
G.D. Rose	24	29	11	97*	1000	55.55	–	8	13
P.M. Roebuck	18	28	5	201*	1134	49.30	2	6	7
N.D. Burns	24	34	10	166	951	39.62	1	5	43/1
J.J. Hardy	9	16	5	91	361	32.81	–	1	6
N.A. Mallender	20	10	3	87*	177	25.28	–	1	3
A.N. Jones	22	9	5	41	100	25.00	–	–	6
I.G. Swallow	23	17	7	32	187	18.70	–	–	12
R.P. Lefebvre	17	16	3	53	214	16.46	–	1	8
H.R.J. Trump	7	5	1	4*	11	2.75	–	–	3

Also batted: R.J. Bartlett (1 match) 73, 12; J.C. Hallett (3 matches) 0; G.T.J. Townsend (2 matches) 0, 0*, 15, 6 (3ct).

Hundreds (22)

9 S.J. Cook: 313* v Glamorgan (Cardiff); 117* v New Zealanders (Taunton); 197 v Sussex (Taunton); 112 ret hurt v Northants (Taunton); 137 v Warwicks (Taunton); 152 v Middlesex (Uxbridge); 116* v Surrey (Weston-super-Mare); 114 v Hants (Taunton); 143 v Worcs (Taunton).

4 A.N. Hayhurst: 110* v Glamorgan (Cardiff); 170 v Sussex (Taunton); 119 v Worcs (Worcester); 170 v Yorks (Scarborough).

3 R.J. Harden: 104 v New Zealanders (Taunton); 101 v Yorks (Scarborough); 104* v Surrey (Weston-super-Mare).

C.J. Tavaré: 120* v Glamorgan (Cardiff); 156 v New Zealanders (Taunton); 219 v Sussex (Hove).

2 P.M. Roebuck: 114* v Warwicks (Taunton); 201* v Worcs (Worcester).

1 N.D. Burns: 166 v Glos (Taunton).

Bowling	O	M	R	W	Avge	Best	5wI	10wM
N.A. Mallender	554.2	116	1585	51	31.07	5-46	2	–
A.N. Jones	572.4	92	2055	56	36.69	6-75	2	–
G.D. Rose	571.4	99	1951	53	36.81	5-52	1	–
J.C. Hallett	65.5	9	238	6	39.66	2-40	–	–
R.P. Lefebvre	506.1	137	1281	31	41.32	5-30	1	–
R.J. Harden	67	6	276	6	46.00	2-39	–	–
H.R.J. Trump	164	41	520	9	57.77	3-58	–	–
I.G. Swallow	689.1	161	2174	34	63.94	3-88	–	–
A.N. Hayhurst	321.2	50	1087	17	63.94	3-58	–	–
P.M. Roebuck	182.3	42	529	8	66.12	2-34	–	–

Also bowled: N.D. Burns 0.3-0-8-0; S.J. Cook 8-0-42-2; C.J. Tavaré 17.2-0-162-0.

Surrey

Harry Brind and the pitches he prepared at Foster's Oval tended to dominate Surrey's season, which, in achievement terms, proved to be unremarkable. Brind, as the Test and County Cricket Board's pitches inspector, needed to be above criticism in following the official policy of dry, pale strips. Surrey, in the words of their captain Ian Greig, had to 'learn to bowl', and Martin Bicknell used his experience of 1990 to secure a seam-bowler's place on England's tour to Australia.

The start of Surrey's home season produced a match against Lancashire that stunned everyone who watched it, as runs flowed with machine-gun rapidity. Greig, batting at seven, smote 291 off 251 deliveries before he declared at 707 for nine, and history records that Lancashire replied with 863. Things could only get better for Surrey's bowlers.

The improvement did happen, to an extent almost beyond belief, when Imran Khan suggested Surrey give an 18-year-old Pakistan fast-bowler a try-out as a second overseas registration to cover for the injury-prone Tony Gray. Waqar Younis, with his powerful arm action, made his Championship debut in early June and finished the season with a five-year contract. The presence of Waqar Younis and his deadly swinging yorkers took the pressure of expectation off Bicknell and they formed a classy opening attack on the fast, true 'Harry's'.

The supporting seam-bowling proved fairly modest, and Keith Medlycott's left-arm spin was not as effective as in the previous season. Accordingly, Surrey won only four Championship matches, while improving their 1989 position of 12th to ninth.

They lost their first three Refuge Assurance League games, but, with Waqar Younis aboard, improved steadily to reach seventh position, one lower than 1989.

Individual feats continued to capture the imagination – none more so than the 2,072 runs David Ward scored, the first Surrey batsman to pass the two-thousand mark since John Edrich in 1962. He hit seven first-class hundreds, including innings of 263 and 208, and all this from a player who had managed only three previous centuries since his debut in 1985. Some observers wondered if Ward should have gone on the Ashes tour instead of his team-mate Alec Stewart, whom he replaced as wicket-keeper and eclipsed as a batsman.

Darren Bicknell, between breaks for injury and illness, improved markedly as an opening batsman, but Stewart, Monte Lynch, and Graham Thorpe all missed the runs feast. But Bicknell, with 186, and Ward, 263, put on 413 together against Kent at Canterbury, breaking Surrey's third-wicket record that had stood since 1919.

The regeneration of the Oval ground is complete, with its impressive new £2 million stand and indoor cricket centre.

CHARLES RANDALL

Britannic Assurance County Championship: 9th; Won 4, Lost 3, Drawn 15
All First-Class Matches: Played 24: Won 4, Lost 3, Drawn 17
NatWest Bank Trophy: Lost to Middlesex in 2nd round
Benson & Hedges Cup: Lost to Lancashire in quarter-final
Refuge Assurance League: 7th; Won 9, Lost 6, No Result 1

County Averages

Batting and Fielding	M	I	NO	HS	R	Avge	100	50	Ct/St
D.M. Ward	24	34	7	263	2072	76.74	7	3	32/3
D.J. Bicknell	15	23	4	186	1317	69.31	5	6	2
I.A. Greig	24	29	6	291	1259	54.73	2	5	16
R.I. Alikhan	11	16	2	138	726	51.85	2	4	3
A.J. Stewart	14	24	6	100*	837	46.50	1	8	19
G.S. Clinton	20	32	4	146	1292	46.14	1	8	6
M.A. Lynch	24	32	5	104	1227	45.44	1	9	30
M.P. Bicknell	20	16	8	50*	310	38.75	–	1	8
K.T. Medlycott	22	25	9	44	410	25.62	–	–	14
G.P. Thorpe	17	26	6	86	585	29.25	–	3	9
M.A. Feltham	15	16	3	101	379	29.15	1	2	11
Waqar Younis	14	9	7	14	56	28.00	–	–	4
J.D. Robinson	8	10	0	72	175	17.50	–	1	1
N.M. Kendrick	13	12	4	52*	124	15.50	–	1	14
A.J. Murphy	12	6	3	4*	6	2.00	–	–	1

Also batted: P.D. Atkins (1 match) 23, 0*; A.H. Gray (7 matches) 11, 11 (7ct); N.F. Sargeant (3 matches) 1, 18 (6ct/1st).

Hundreds (20)

7 **D.M. Ward:** 181 v Oxf. Univ. (Oxford); 129* v Hants (Foster's Oval); 154* v Notts (Trent Bridge); 126 v Warwicks (Foster's Oval); 191 v Hants (Southampton); 263 v Kent (Canterbury); 208 v Essex (Foster's Oval).

5 **D.J. Bicknell:** 169 v Northants (Foster's Oval); 143 v Sussex (Guildford); 111 v Leics (Foster's Oval); 186 v Kent (Canterbury); 114 v Middlesex (Foster's Oval).

2 **R.I. Alikhan:** 119 v Middlesex (Foster's Oval); 138 v Essex (Foster's Oval).

I.A. Greig: 291 v Lancs (Foster's Oval); 123* v Somerset (Weston-super-Mare).

1 **G.S. Clinton:** 146 v Northants (Foster's Oval).

M.A. Feltham: 101 v Middlesex (Foster's Oval).

M.A. Lynch: 104 v Somerset (Weston-super-Mare).

A.J. Stewart: 100* v Hants (Foster's Oval).

Bowling	O	M	R	W	Avge	Best	5wI	10wM
Waqar Younis	423	70	1357	57	23.80	7-73	3	1
M.P. Bicknell	640.1	149	1751	64	27.35	5-34	1	–
M.A. Feltham	349.4	61	1150	40	28.75	6-53	2	–
A.H. Gray	239.5	43	666	19	35.05	4-83	–	–
K.T. Medlycott	734.5	169	2307	59	39.10	7-92	3	–
A.J. Murphy	404.2	76	1367	30	45.56	5-67	2	–
N.M. Kendrick	348	66	1194	25	47.76	4-110	–	–
I.A. Greig	216.1	21	858	13	66.00	3-60	–	–
J.D. Robinson	146.3	28	476	7	68.00	2-84	–	–

Also bowled: R.I. Alikhan 20-1-83-1; D.J. Bicknell 9-1-20-0; M.A. Lynch 27-5-130-1; A.J. Stewart 5-0-32-0; G.P. Thorpe 23-7-99-1.

Sussex

There is rarely an advance sense of inevitability about the result of a Championship match, but there was little surprise shown at Sussex's capitulation against Middlesex. The innings victory gave Middlesex the title and condemned Sussex to last place at the end of a season that highlighted their glaring inadequacies as a bowling side.

It was certainly no coincidence that the two sides finishing at the bottom of the table – Sussex and Kent – were the ones whose attacks proved consistently impotent. Sussex's lack of firepower was illustrated perfectly against Gloucestershire in their penultimate match, when a score of 82 for 5 was converted into an all-out total of 467 and an innings victory for Gloucestershire.

Pigott may have topped the county averages, but each Championship wicket cost more than 37, and Dodemaide and Salisbury were the only other bowlers to take a substantial number of wickets. Salisbury's figures did not exactly make a cut-and-dried case for the inclusion of a leg-break bowler at all times, but in a seam-dominated world it was encouraging to see his promise rewarded with a place on the England 'A' tour.

The batting was not as consistent as it had been in 1989, but Sussex supporters could draw some comfort from the progress made by three of the younger players. Lenham, held back over the past few years by a succession of broken fingers, stayed fit for most of the season and scored four centuries to average more than 40. Hall took advantage of Smith's extended absence through injury to force his way into the side as an opener, and though he was prone to long spells of strokelessness he revealed a sound technique and great application. Speight's contributions were much more fluent, and he enjoyed a particularly fruitful first six weeks of the season.

Parker, the captain, began the season with centuries in Sussex's first two matches, but he was frustrated subsequently by a persistent hamstring injury. Alan Wells had another successful year with the bat, but his brother Colin fell below the standards he has set himself as an all-rounder.

Dodemaide, the Australian, was caught up in the welter of speculation about which overseas players the county would engage for 1991. But it was just reward for his whole-hearted commitment to the struggle – the one-day competitions brought no consolation – that he was retained. His bowling is not penetrative enough for him to be regarded as spearhead of the attack, but in bowling more overs than any other Sussex player and scoring over 1,000 first-class runs he showed his value.

CLIVE ELLIS

Britannic Assurance County Championship: 17th; Won 3, Lost 9, Drawn 10
All First-Class Matches: Played 25: Won 3, Lost 11, Drawn 11
NatWest Bank Trophy: Lost to Glamorgan in 2nd round
Benson & Hedges Cup: Failed to qualify for quarter-final (3rd in Group B)
Refuge Assurance League: 13th; Won 5, Lost 9, No Result 2

County Averages

Batting and Fielding	M	I	NO	HS	R	Avge	100	50	Ct/St
K. Greenfield	3	6	2	102*	230	57.50	1	1	1
P.W.G. Parker	14	24	4	107	892	44.60	2	5	7
A.P. Wells	24	44	7	144*	1611	43.54	4	7	12
N.J. Lenham	22	41	1	123	1663	41.57	4	9	6
M.P. Speight	23	41	7	131	1375	40.44	2	11	14
A.I.C. Dodemaide	24	38	8	112	1001	33.36	2	4	9
C.M. Wells	20	33	5	113*	933	33.32	2	4	5
J.W. Hall	20	37	2	125	1140	32.57	2	5	6
B.T.P. Donelan	11	13	6	53	211	30.14	–	1	4
D.M. Smith	9	16	2	71	353	25.21	–	2	2
I.D.K. Salisbury	20	23	10	68	313	24.07	–	1	13
I.J. Gould	8	12	2	73	235	23.50	–	2	8
P. Moores	25	36	4	106*	694	21.68	1	2	53/10
A.C.S. Pigott	21	29	5	64*	451	18.79	–	4	11
A.R. Hansford	4	6	1	29	55	11.00	–	–	1
R.A. Bunting	15	13	5	24*	85	10.62	–	–	2
J.A. North	4	5	1	19*	41	10.25	–	–	1

Also batted: A.M. Babington (3 matches) 20, 8 (2ct); R. Hanley (2 matches) 2, 29, 2, 0;
C.C. Remy (2 matches) 4*. P.W. Threlfall played one match but did not bat.

Hundreds (20)

4 N.J. **Lenham:** 121 v Hants (Southampton); 108 v Somerset (Taunton); 109* v Surrey (Guildford);
123 v Somerset (Hove).
  A.P. **Wells:** 137 v Camb. Univ. (Hove); 102* v Northants (Northampton); 144* v Warwicks (Eastbourne);
109* v Leics (Leicester).
2 A.I.C. **Dodemaide:** 110* v New Zealanders (Hove); 112 v Somerset (Hove).
  J.W. **Hall** 120* v New Zealanders (Hove); 125 v Notts (Trent Bridge).
  P.W.G. **Parker:** 100 v Surrey (Hove); 107 v Kent (Folkestone).
  M.P. **Speight:** 131 v Glamorgan (Hove); 108 v Surrey (Guildford).
  C.M. **Wells:** 113* v New Zealanders (Hove); 107 v Hants (Arundel).
1 K. **Greenfield:** 102* v Camb. Univ. (Hove).
  P. **Moores:** 106* v Glamorgan (Hove).

Bowling	O	M	R	W	Avge	Best	5wI	10wM
P.W. Threlfall	30	8	89	5	17.80	3-45	–	–
A.C.S. Pigott	541	94	1997	54	36.98	5-52	3	–
J.A. North	83.1	17	236	6	39.33	2-43	–	–
A.I.C. Dodemaide	763.1	130	2457	61	40.27	6-106	1	–
C.C. Remy	54	6	224	5	44.80	4-63	–	–
I.D.K. Salisbury	601.1	113	2075	42	49.40	5-32	2	–
B.T.P. Donelan	304.4	56	1000	20	50.00	3-79	–	–
R.A. Bunting	360	61	1314	26	50.53	2-36	–	–
A.R. Hansford	123.5	21	425	7	60.71	3-91	–	–
N.J. Lenham	95	19	317	5	63.40	2-26	–	–
C.M. Wells	374	68	1237	17	72.76	3-48	–	–

Also bowled: A.M. Babington 63-7-256-3; I.J. Gould 5.4-0-19-0; K. Greenfield 0.3-0-8-0;
P.W.G. Parker 8-0-59-0; A.P. Wells 39-8-169-3.

Warwickshire

Warwickshire spent all of August in the top three in the Championship, but their challenge faded with three defeats in a row, and a damp and frustrating last match at Old Trafford dropped them to fifth. This was three places higher than in 1989, but Bob Cottam, the manager-coach who drastically reshaped the playing staff in three seasons, accepted that they were still a little short of being a championship-winning squad. "It's the batting, always the batting, which lets us down," he said after a heavy defeat at Worcester. Yet Warwickshire had one of the most consistent openers in Andy Moles and a reliable middle-order prop in Dermot Reeve, who averaged 55, mainly with only the tail-end for company.

There was also a glimpse of a rising world-class talent in Tom Moody, who made five centuries in his seven Championship appearances. The giant Australian completed the fastest 1,000 runs in the club's history, in 12 innings, and scored a world-record century in 26 minutes against Glamorgan. However, under the new TCCB cutback on overseas players, he had to be released at the end of the season.

Warwickshire were unable to spread any consistency around their three leading scorers. Andy Lloyd, the captain, had a lean time in his benefit year, Paul Smith missed half the season through injury, and Asif Din was rarely able to build on his good starts.

With Alvin Kallicharran and Geoff Humpage announcing their retirement, Warwickshire will need to find runs from a group of promising young players. There is above-average potential in opening batsman Jason Ratcliffe, 21, and Dominic Ostler, 19, who was never overawed in his first season as a professional. Keith Piper, 20, succeeded Humpage and proved himself to be a naturally gifted wicket-keeper as well as scoring a maiden century.

Warwickshire alternated between three spin bowlers with only minimal success, but there was considerable strength in their pace bowling. Tim Munton maintained his progress as one of the most accurate and hard-working seamers and was rewarded with selection for the England 'A' tour to Pakistan. Joey Benjamin, a late developer at 29, was a lively new-ball bowler until his contribution was curtailed by a neck injury. He had filled the gap when Allan Donald, who will continue as the overseas player, was absent with a recurring back strain. Gladstone Small suffered a temporary loss of form, which cost him his Test place in the series against India. But he came back strongly and merited inclusion in the tour party to Australia.

In summary, it was a mildly encouraging season, though there was a fall-off in one-day performances after winning the NatWest Trophy in 1989.

MIKE BEDDOW

Britannic Assurance County Championship: 5th; Won 7, Lost 7, Drawn 8
All First-Class Matches: Played 25: Won 7, Lost 8, Drawn 10
NatWest Bank Trophy: Lost to Yorkshire in 2nd round
Benson & Hedges Cup: Failed to qualify for quarter-final (5th in Group A)
Refuge Assurance League: 14th; Won 5, Lost 10, No Result 1

County Averages

Batting and Fielding	M	I	NO	HS	R	Avge	100	50	Ct/St
T.M. Moody	9	15	2	168	1163	89.46	7	1	4
D.A. Reeve	24	37	12	202*	1373	54.92	3	5	26
A.J. Moles	24	46	8	224*	1854	48.78	4	10	12
G.W. Humpage	13	22	4	74	628	34.88	–	5	30/-
P.A. Smith	12	20	4	117	520	32.50	1	3	1
N.M.K. Smith	10	14	2	83*	370	30.83	–	1	4
J.D. Ratcliffe	16	31	3	81*	780	27.85	–	3	7
J.E. Benjamin	15	14	7	41	188	26.85	–	–	4
D.P. Ostler	11	19	2	71	510	30.00	–	5	9
Asif Din	22	39	4	100*	974	27.82	1	5	10
R.C. Twose	6	10	1	64*	241	26.77	–	3	3
T.A. Lloyd	15	27	1	101	646	24.84	1	4	7
A.I. Kallicharran	7	10	1	72	221	24.55	–	2	5
K.J. Piper	16	21	1	111	461	23.05	1	1	39/4
P.A. Booth	10	16	2	60	240	17.14	–	2	3
A.R.K. Pierson	11	9	5	16*	57	14.25	–	–	1
G.C. Small	12	18	2	55	212	13.25	–	1	3
A.A. Donald	16	22	6	25*	148	9.25	–	–	–
T.A. Munton	24	24	9	29*	125	8.33	–	–	9

Also batted: S.J. Green (1 match) 44, 0; G. Smith (1 match) 30 (1ct).

Hundreds (18)

7 T.M. Moody: 147 v Camb. Univ. (Cambridge); 106 v New Zealanders (Edgbaston); 168 v Derbys (Derby); 103* v Glamorgan (Swansea); 101* v Hants (Edgbaston); 110 v Sussex (Eastbourne); 117 v Leics (Edgbaston).

4 A.J. Moles: 128* v Middlesex (Lord's); 100* v Lancs (Coventry); 224* v Glamorgan (Swansea): 117 v Sri Lankans (Edgbaston).

3 D.A. Reeve: 102* v Camb. Univ. (Cambridge); 202* v Northants (Northampton); 121* v Lancs (Old Trafford).

1 Asif Din: 100* v Camb. Univ. (Cambridge).
   T.A. Lloyd: 101 v Glamorgan (Swansea).
   K.J. Piper: 111 v Somerset (Edgbaston).
   P.A. Smith: 117 v Glamorgan (Edgbaston).

Bowling	O	M	R	W	Avge	Best	5wI	10wM
P.A. Smith	148.5	34	497	20	24.85	5-48	1	–
D.A. Reeve	364.4	107	900	33	27.27	4-42	–	–
J.E. Benjamin	388.3	68	1205	43	28.02	5-29	4	–
T.A. Munton	792.1	184	2179	77	28.29	5-33	2	–
G.C. Small	321.4	78	900	27	33.33	6-94	2	–
A.A. Donald	391	89	1089	29	37.55	3-28	–	–
A.R.K. Pierson	302.4	55	965	25	38.60	5-101	1	–
P.A. Booth	250.5	75	636	13	48.92	4-55	–	–
Asif Din	159.1	30	635	10	63.50	3-17	–	–
N.M.K. Smith	177.5	37	535	7	76.42	2-76	–	–

Also bowled: G.W. Humpage 9-3-35-0; T.A. Lloyd 9-1-58-1; A.J. Moles 25-2-133-2; T.M. Moody 59-15-212-3; G. Smith 26.5-3-81-4; R.G. Twose 53-12-185-4.

Worcestershire

There was a poignant moment at New Road when the Britannic Assurance Championship trophy was taken out of its display case an hour after Worcestershire had demolished Glamorgan in their last match. If the handful of members who witnessed this ceremony grieved over the departure of the cup after two years in residence, at least there was consolation in that their team had finished the season in the style of champions.

Fourth place in the Championship and an appearance in the Benson & Hedges Cup final added up to a satisfactory season by most standards, although for Worcestershire it represented a decline after the silver and glitter of previous years.

Though they lost only one Championship match, it was some while before they found true consistency. On July 20, when Middlesex had completed half their programme, Worcestershire were second from bottom. But they won five of their last 12 matches and went very close to victory on three other occasions.

Probably no side suffered more with injuries. They began with their four leading seamers playing together for the first time in a year, but only Phil Newport stayed fit for any length of time.

Graham Dilley's right knee required two more operations, Neal Radford had stomach muscle surgery, and Ian Botham's availability was limited by a knee operation and latterly by a hamstring problem.

This did create a plus point in providing further opportunities for Steve McEwan, who performed the hat-trick against Leicestershire, and Stuart Lampitt, a wicket-taking medium-pacer and a promising batsman.

No one appeared in every championship fixture, but Graeme Hick, Richard Illingworth, and Steve Rhodes recovered quickly from broken bones and contributed heavily to the strong run at the end of the season. Hick became the youngest player to score 50 first-class centuries, and in 1991 will be available for England. Worcestershire have signed Tom Moody, the Australian batsman, as their overseas player.

Illingworth, the leading English-qualified slow bowler in the national averages, was considered unfortunate not to make the England tour to Australia. Rhodes, too, may have felt hard done by when, again, the selectors decided not to take a specialist wicket-keeper as understudy to Jack Russell.

Tim Curtis, Damian D'Oliveira, and Gordon Lord enjoyed their most successful seasons at the top of the batting order. Phil Neale, in his ninth season as captain, also delivered his customary quota of valuable innings.

MIKE BEDDOW

Britannic Assurance County Championship: 4th; Won 7, Lost 1, Drawn 14
All First-Class Matches: Played 24: Won 7, Lost 2, Drawn 15
NatWest Bank Trophy: Lost to Northamptonshire in semi-final
Benson & Hedges Cup: Lost to Lancashire in final
Refuge Assurance League: 10th; Won 7, Lost 8, No Result 1

County Averages

Batting and Fielding	M	I	NO	HS	R	Avge	100	50	Ct/St
G.A. Hick	21	35	9	252*	2347	90.26	8	14	26
T.S. Curtis	22	39	8	197*	1731	55.83	4	7	12
G.R. Dilley	10	8	4	45*	185	46.25	–	–	2
G.J. Lord	13	24	2	190	1003	45.59	3	5	4
S.J. Rhodes	22	25	10	96	672	44.80	–	5	60/8
P.A. Neale	21	32	10	122	976	44.36	2	3	12
D.B. D'Oliveira	23	35	2	155	1263	38.27	2	7	33
P.J. Newport	21	18	6	98	424	35.33	–	3	6
I.T. Botham	13	18	1	113	595	35.00	1	4	7
R.K. Illingworth	22	22	6	117	532	33.25	1	3	7
P. Bent	7	12	0	79	346	28.83	–	2	–
D.A. Leatherdale	4	6	0	70	154	25.66	–	2	2
S.M. McEwan	15	12	5	54	164	23.42	–	1	5
S.R. Lampitt	22	24	5	45*	356	18.73	–	–	10
N.V. Radford	12	8	1	43*	118	16.85	–	–	6
C.M. Tolley	6	6	1	29	79	15.80	–	–	2
M.J. Weston	6	10	1	38*	90	10.00	–	–	1

Also batted: S.R. Bevins (2 matches) 6*, 10, 1 (6ct); R.D. Stemp (2 matches) 3*, 0* (1ct).

Hundreds (21)

8 G.A. Hick: 106* v Lancs (Old Trafford); 117* v Somerset (Worcester); 252* & 100* v Glamorgan (Abergavenny); 102 v Leics (Leicester); 110 v Glos (Bristol); 154 v Somerset (Taunton); 138* v Glamorgan (Worcester).

4 T.S. Curtis: 111* v Glamorgan (Abergavenny); 151* v Leics (Leicester); 197* v Warwicks (Worcester); 156 v Somerset (Taunton).

3 G.J. Lord: 101 v Lancs (Kidderminster); 190 v Hants (Worcester); 127 v Glamorgan (Worcester).

2 D.B. D'Oliveira: 155 v Lancs (Old Trafford); 121 v Glamorgan (Abergavenny).

  P.A. Neale: 122 v Notts (Worcester); 119* v Kent (Canterbury).

1 I.T. Botham: 113 v Surrey (Foster's Oval).

  R.K. Illingworth: 117 v Notts (Worcester).

Bowling	O	M	R	W	Avge	Best	5wI	10wM
R.K. Illingworth	834.5	272	1998	74	27.00	5-59	1	–
I.T. Botham	194.4	38	614	21	29.23	4-65	–	–
S.M. McEwan	375.2	75	1189	38	31.28	3-31	–	–
S.R. Lampitt	539.3	96	1794	57	31.47	5-34	2	–
P.J. Newport	626.2	117	2001	63	31.76	6-54	4	–
G.A. Hick	208.5	41	654	20	32.25	5-37	1	–
G.R. Dilley	224.2	30	818	24	34.08	5-62	2	–
C.M. Tolley	88	14	326	5	65.20	2-66	–	–
N.V. Radford	302	49	1195	18	66.38	4-55	–	–

Also bowled: T.S. Curtis 5.3-1-43-0; D.B. D'Oliveira 11.3-1-80-2; R.D. Stemp 45-14-123-1; M.J. Weston 21-3-74-1.

Yorkshire

Yorkshire, having in the winter appointed Steve Oldham as cricket manager and Martyn Moxon to succeed Phil Carrick as captain, will look back on the past season with satisfaction over some areas and with concern over others. On the positive side, they won five championship matches and moved up the table from 16th to 10th, while in the Refuge Assurance League they climbed five places to 6th, advances which partially compensated for early exits from the Benson & Hedges and the NatWest.

Four of their five championship wins came from successful fourth-innings chases, which would indicate that their batting was satisfactory. In fact, in a season which admittedly greatly favoured batsmen, three players had best-ever figures. These were Ashley Metcalfe – who became the first Yorkshire player to score 2,000 runs since Geoff Boycott in 1971, and incidentally did not score the first of his five centuries till 21 July – Moxon, and Phil Robinson.

Moxon himself has stressed the increasing importance of last-innings chases: 'If the wickets and the balls are unchanged next season, we should do well in this area, particularly as this year we got very close to three other targets.' However, with Richard Blakey having a moderate year and David Byas and Simon Kellett struggling to establish themselves, the three major batsmen were grateful for the runs scored by Phil Carrick and Chris Pickles lower down. Blakey's comparative failure may have had something to do with his taking over the wicket-keeping virtually full-time – the long-serving David Bairstow made only a handful of appearances – but Blakey's class was recognized by selection for the 'A' tour of Pakistan.

Yorkshire's bowlers found it harder than most to cope with the demands of unresponsive pitches and the reduced seam. None took 50 championship wickets, and the lowest average was Carrick's at 34.13. The greatest disappointment was the form of Paul Jarvis. Though still only 25, he looked distinctly weary at times. The cost of his 37 wickets approached 40 runs apiece, and not once in the season did he take five wickets in an innings.

With Arnie Sidebottom's doubtful fitness confining his activities almost entirely to the one-day competitions, more rested with Stuart Fletcher and Peter Hartley, the latter responding well enough by capturing 48 county wickets. Carrick bowled his slow left-arm as well as he has done for some years, and it was good to see opportunities given to young spinners in Jeremy Batty, Phil Berry, and Paul Grayson, all of whom might have benefited from longer runs in the side.

DAVID GREEN

Britannic Assurance County Championship: 10th; Won 5, Lost 9, Drawn 8
All First-Class Matches: Played 24: Won 5, Lost 9, Drawn 10
NatWest Bank Trophy: Lost to Hampshire in quarter-final
Benson & Hedges Cup: Failed to qualify for quarter-final (3rd in Group C)
Refuge Assurance League: 6th; Won 9, Lost 6, No Result 1

County Averages

Batting and Fielding	M	I	NO	HS	R	Avge	100	50	Ct/St
A.A. Metcalfe	23	44	4	194*	2047	51.17	6	7	10
M.D. Moxon	21	39	6	218*	1621	49.12	3	7	14
P.E. Robinson	23	39	7	150*	1402	43.81	1	12	20
K. Sharp	9	13	5	53*	318	39.75	–	1	1
P.A. Grayson	5	8	4	44*	145	36.25	–	–	2
C.S. Pickles	16	22	8	57*	478	34.14	–	3	6
S.A. Kellett	16	28	3	75*	774	30.96	–	6	8
D.L. Bairstow	5	6	0	61	179	29.83	–	1	9
R.J. Blakey	24	42	8	111	993	29.20	1	6	44/8
D. Byas	19	29	4	83	704	28.16	–	5	21
A. Sidebottom	3	4	0	38	104	26.00	–	–	1
P. Carrick	18	22	2	64	515	25.75	–	3	7
P.W. Jarvis	15	16	4	43*	212	17.66	–	–	2
P.J. Hartley	17	15	1	75	218	15.57	–	1	8
C. White	10	11	2	38	127	14.11	–	–	4
D. Gough	14	17	6	24	123	11.18	–	–	1
J.D. Batty	7	5	2	21	30	10.00	–	–	4
S.D. Fletcher	11	13	3	19	39	3.90	–	–	3

Also batted: P.J. Berry (2 matches) 4*, 31*, 6*, 4* (1ct); C. Chapman (2 matches) 5, 17, 20, 5 (2ct); I.J. Houseman (3 matches) 0*. M.J. Doidge played in one match but did not bat.

Hundreds (11)

6 **A.A. Metcalfe:** 162 v Glos (Cheltenham); 102 v Somerset (Scarborough); 146 v Lancs (Headingley); 150* v Derbys (Scarborough); 194* & 107 v Notts (Trent Bridge).
3 **M.D. Moxon:** 130 v Zimbabweans (Headingley); 123 v Notts (Scarborough); 218* v Sussex (Eastbourne).
1 **R.J. Blakey:** 111 v Somerset (Scarborough).
  P.E. Robinson: 150* v Derbys (Scarborough)

Bowling	O	M	R	W	Avge	Best	5wI	10wM
P. Carrick	601	173	1570	46	34.13	5-49	3	–
P.J. Hartley	491	80	1781	52	34.25	6-57	2	–
S.D. Fletcher	292.5	59	1035	29	35.68	5-94	1	–
D. Gough	279.4	49	1037	28	37.03	4-68	–	–
P.W. Jarvis	405.2	68	1393	37	37.64	4-53	–	–
C.S. Pickles	325.1	72	1163	28	41.53	3-56	–	–
C. White	159	23	608	13	46.76	5-74	1	–
J.D. Batty	195	29	722	12	60.16	4-76	–	–

Also bowled: P.J. Berry 44.3-4-172-2; D. Byas 96-19-358-4; M.J. Doidge 24-5-106-0; P.A. Grayson 80-19-270-1; I.J. Houseman 50-9-198-2; A.A. Metcalfe 9.1-0-88-0; M.D. Moxon 57-9-175-3; P.E. Robinson 3.3-0-28-1; A. Sidebottom 60.5-11-190-4.

SUBSCRIBE TO CRICKET WORLD

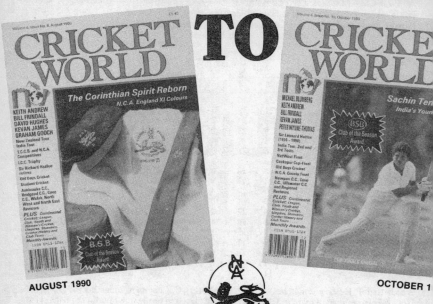

AUGUST 1990

OCTOBER 1

MONTHLY NEWS FROM
THE NATIONAL CRICKET ASSOCIATION

THE BEST READ IN CRICKET

THE ONLY CRICKET MAGAZINE REPORTING THE GAME FROM
VILLAGE GREEN TO TEST CRICKET, UNDER-11s TO OVER-50s

BILL FRINDALL, DAVID HUGHES, RAVI SHASTRI, PETER WYNNE-THOMAS AND KEVAN JAME
WRITE MONTHLY IN *CRICKET WORLD*

Send cheques payable to THE CLUB CRICKETER LTD,
Heathfield House, London Road, Windlesham, Surrey GU20 6PJ
£18.00 UK and BFPO, £28.00 Overseas Airmail (Europe and surface elsewhere), £36.00 Airmail (Rest of the Wor

Visa/Access Card No. ☐☐☐☐☐☐☐☐☐☐☐☐☐☐☐☐

Expiry Date: _____

Name _____ Signature _____

Address _____

_____ Postcode _____

Club, School, College _____

Date for subscription to commence _____

Binder Offer £6 p.&p. _____

only £12 fo,
Schools Polytec
Universities
Colleges an
Under-18†
cricketers

*Discount for Clubs £70.00 for five copies, £100.00 for ten copies (U.K. only).
†Under-18, 1st May 1990.

1990
TOURS TO ENGLAND

Tours to England

Engand played hosts to two major touring teams in the summer of 1990, New Zealand and India each playing a three-Test series. England, fresh from their losing but exhilarating series in the West Indies, won both series 1-0. In the two Tests they won, the opposing captain put England in to bat, first John Wright of New Zealand and then Mohammad Azharuddin of India.

In the Texaco Trophy one-day internationals, England and New Zealand won one match each, with England taking the series on a superior run rate, but England lost both their matches against India. In all four of these 55-over games, the side winning the toss fielded first and then completed a successful run chase.

In a record English summer, the New Zealanders were unlucky with the weather, the first two Tests, played in June, being inconclusive. The Indians, on the other hand, enjoyed perfect weather, but it was the perfect batting pitches that prevented results in their last two Tests.

The two tours produced some memorable moments . . . two young players in Atherton and Tendulkar scoring their maiden Test hundreds and showing great maturity in the Test arena . . . the great Hadlee, bowing out as Sir Richard, thrilling the Lord's crowd with 86 in 84 balls and in his last Test, at Edgbaston, taking another eight wickets to bring his record Test haul to 431 . . . Azharuddin also thrilling the Lord's crowd with his superb, flowing 121 in 111 balls . . . Kapil Dev, in the same innings, striking Hemmings with breathtaking audacity for four consecutive sixes to save the follow-on . . . David Gower's sparkling 157 not out at the Oval to revive his Test career. . . . But, above all, it will be remembered as Gooch's summer. He not only led England to two series victories after their long spell of failure, but he achieved unprecedented personal success at the crease. In the six Tests he amassed 1,058 runs, passing Sir Donald Bradman's 60-year-old record for an English summer of 974 made, albeit, in five Tests and only seven innings (to Gooch's 11). Gooch averaged 96.18 in the six Tests.

Atherton and Robin Smith also compiled impressive averages over the two series. Atherton scored 735 runs at 66.81, and Smith 513 at 73.28. England's leading wicket-takers were Malcolm (22) and Hemmings (21), both of whom played in all six Tests. But whereas their wickets cost them each about 32 runs apiece, Fraser was the most successful bowler. Missing the New Zealand series because of injury, he played only against the run-happy Indians and picked up 16 wickets at 28.75.

Three other countries sent touring sides to England in 1990, Sri Lanka, who did not play a Test, Zimbabwe, and Pakistan Under-19s.

New Zealand in England

O ver the last decade or so, New Zealand have fashioned a proud Test record. But the evidence of Edgbaston, where England won the only conclusive Test of the tour, is that New Zealand will be very vulnerable over the next few years.

They will be without the very senior players, Sir Richard Hadlee, John Wright, and Martin Snedden, while John Bracewell could be counting his remaining Test days, too. Jeff Crowe must be near the end of his very curious international carreer, and Ian Smith will soon be heading for the television commentator's seat.

To make matters worse, four of the new breed, Martin Crowe, Andrew Jones, Mark Greatbatch, and Danny Morrison, performed indifferently against England.They accepted failure too easily and did not seem hungry or determined to occupy the crease. Trevor Franklin made progress as a steadfast opening batsman, but the only other batsman with a respectable Test average was John Wright. Stand-in wicket-keeper Adam Parore looks an interestingly eager young man, and Mark Priest may soon be at the head of a rather modest list of all-rounders.

Over the next few months the New Zealanders must learn to live without Hadlee, and fashion a new coach, a new captain, and new supply of young players. Wright was the best ambassador for the sport that any touring side have sent for many a year, and in some ways his going will be as big a blow as Hadlee's.

England, on the other hand, are moving onward and upward on their improvement curve. They are perhaps only two or three players away from being a very strong side – and they may reach that level by the time they get to Australia later this year.

They found a new opening partnership in Gooch and Atherton, one or both of whom made at least fifty in all five innings, and the younger man outscored his captain over the series. But after England's victory at Edgbaston, Gooch observed that "there is still a lot of room for improvement in this side".

The obvious area was in the middle order (after the openers, the next name in the test averages was Gladstone Small). However, only Neil Fairbrother could be said to have failed, and he has probably had his last chance, although Alec Stewart's performances were uninspiring. David Gower failed in the Texaco Trophy matches but began to show the county form that the selectors required for a recall.

In the fast-bowling department, Malcolm impressed with 15 wickets in the series at under 18 apiece, and Fraser's return to fitness signalled that he was ready to be recalled. Small did not look his normal, economical self, but both DeFreitas and Lewis showed good form.

First Test: Trent Bridge, 7, 8, 9, 11, 12 June
Match Drawn

New Zealand stuttered to 208 all out over two days and part of the third morning as the rain took its toll. On a slow, soft pitch, DeFreitas took 5 for 53 as only Martin Crowe looked comfortable. Before rain finally stopped play on the Saturday, Hadlee had Gooch lbw for 0, but his opening partner Mike Atherton, in only his third Test, dominated the last two days, compiling 151 in 8 hours 21 minutes at the crease. New Zealand batted out the last 1¼ hours for the loss of two wickets.

Second Test: Lord's, 21, 22, 23, 25, 26 June
Match Drawn

While the headquarters of cricket honoured Sir Richard Hadlee's knighthood, the weather was not so kind. Wright put England in and Atherton soon edged Morrison onto his stumps for a duck, but rain stopped play after 50 minutes with England 27-1. On the second day England stroked their way to another 302 runs, with fifties from Gooch, Stewart, and Smith, but sadly Fairbrother failed again. New Zealand mopped up the last three England wickets for 5 runs on the Saturday and then Franklin and Wright proceeded to make the England attack look very ordinary with an unbeaten opening stand of 156. They were finally parted on the Monday after putting on 185, but Hadlee stole the show with 86 in 84 balls. New Zealand declared on the last morning with a lead of 128, but with Hadlee resting a 'lazy hamstring' after bowling Gooch for 37, the game ended in anticlimax.

Third Test: Edgbaston, 5, 6, 7, 9, 10 July
England won by 114 runs

Wright again put England in after winning the toss for the third time, but must have regretted it at the end of the day when England stood at 191-1. After a much delayed start, Gooch and Atherton (82) put on 170 in 205 minutes, England's highest opening partnership for nearly four years. On the second day, England lost 4 wickets for 63 runs, but Gooch (154), with no little help from the tailenders, steered his side to their highest total, 435, in three years. The next day Malcolm and Lewis broke the back of the New Zealand innings before Eddie Hemmings spun out the last six batsmen, but not before they had saved the follow-on. The Monday saw Sir Richard Hadlee bowl his way out of Test cricket in heroic style with 5-53. After a spirited start by Gooch and Atherton, England's wickets tumbled first to spinner Bracewell and then to Hadlee. But 158 was enough to give them a lead of 344. New Zealand knocked off 101 by the close for the loss of their openers, but on the final day England's bowlers, especially Malcolm (5-46), kept on top to give England their first home series win for five years.

England v New Zealand 1990 1st Test

Match Drawn
Played at Trent Bridge, 7, 8, 9, 11, 12 June
Toss: New Zealand   Umpires: H.D. Bird and J.H. Hampshire
Debuts: New Zealand – M.W. Priest
Man of Match: M.A. Atherton (G. Boycott)

New Zealand

T.J. Franklin	b Malcolm	33	not out		22
J.G. Wright*	c Stewart b Small	8	c Russell b Small		1
A.H. Jones	c Stewart b Malcolm	39	c Russell b DeFreitas		13
M.D. Crowe	b DeFreitas	59			
M.J. Greatbatch	b Hemmings	1			
M.W. Priest	c Russell b DeFreitas	26			
M.C. Snedden	c Gooch b DeFreitas	0			
J.G. Bracewell	c Gooch b Small	28			
R.J. Hadlee	b DeFreitas	0			
I.D.S. Smith†	not out	2			
D.K. Morrison	lbw b DeFreitas	0	(4) not out		0
Extras	(B1, LB10, W1)	12			
		208	(2 wkts)		**36**

England

G.A. Gooch*	lbw b Hadlee	0
M.A. Atherton	c Snedden b Priest	151
A.J. Stewart	c Smith b Hadlee	27
A.J. Lamb	lbw b Hadlee	0
R.A. Smith	c Smith b Bracewell	55
N.H. Fairbrother	c Franklin b Snedden	19
R.C. Russell†	c Snedden b Morrison	28
P.A.J. DeFreitas	lbw b Bracewell	14
G.C. Small	c Crowe b Hadlee	26
E.E. Hemmings	not out	13
D.E. Malcolm	not out	4
Extras	(B2, LB3, NB3)	8
	(9 wkts dec)	**345**

England	O	M	R	W	O	M	R	W
Small	29	9	49	2	6	2	14	1
Malcolm	19	7	48	2	7	2	22	0
Hemmings	19	6	47	1	2	2	0	0
DeFreitas	22	6	53	5	2	2	0	1

New Zealand	O	M	R	W
Hadlee	33	6	89	4
Morrison	22	3	96	1
Snedden	36	17	54	1
Bracewell	35	8	75	2
Priest	12	4	26	1

Fall of Wickets

Wkt	NZ 1st	E 1st	NZ 2nd
1st	16	0	8
2nd	75	43	36
3rd	110	45	–
4th	121	141	–
5th	170	168	–
6th	174	260	–
7th	191	302	–
8th	191	306	–
9th	203	340	–
10th	208	–	–

England v New Zealand 1990 2nd Test

Match Drawn
Played at Lord's, 21, 22, 23, 25, 26 June
Toss: New Zealand   Umpires: M.J. Kitchen and D.R. Shepherd
Debuts: nil
Man of Match: Sir Richard Hadlee (V.J. Marks)

England

G.A. Gooch*	c & b Bracewell	85	b Hadlee		37
M.A. Atherton	b Morrison	0	c Bracewell b Jones		54
A.J. Stewart	lbw b Hadlee	54	c sub (M.W. Priest)		
			b Bracewell		42
A.J. Lamb	lbw b Snedden	39	not out		84
R.A. Smith	c Bracewell b Morrison	64	hit wicket b Bracewell		0
N.H. Fairbrother	c Morrison b Bracewell	2	not out		33
R.C. Russell†	b Hadlee	13			
P.A.J. DeFreitas	c Franklin b Morrison	38			
G.C. Small	b Morrison	3			
E.E. Hemmings	b Hadlee	0			
D.E. Malcolm	not out	0			
Extras	(LB13, W1, NB22)	36	(B8, LB8, NB6)		22
		334	(4 wkts dec)		**272**

New Zealand

T.J. Franklin	c Russell b Malcolm	101
J.G. Wright*	c Stewart b Small	98
A.H. Jones	c Stewart b Malcolm	49
M.D. Crowe	c Russell b Hemmings	1
M.J. Greatbatch	b Malcolm	47
K.R. Rutherford	c Fairbrother b Malcolm	0
Sir Richard Hadlee	b Hemmings	86
J.G. Bracewell	run out	
	(DeFreitas/Russell)	4
I.D.S. Smith†	c Small b Malcolm	27
M.C. Snedden	not out	13
D.K. Morrison	not out	2
Extras	(B12, LB15, W2, NB5)	34
	(9 wkts dec)	**462**

New Zealand	O	M	R	W	O	M	R	W
Hadlee	29	5	113	3	13	2	32	1
Morrison	18.4	4	64	4	16	0	81	0
Snedden	21	4	72	1				
Bracewell	21	3	72	2	34	13	85	2
Jones					12	3	40	1
Rutherford					3	0	18	0

England	O	M	R	W
Malcolm	43	14	94	5
Small	35	4	127	1
DeFreitas	35.4	1	122	0
Hemmings	30	13	67	2
Gooch	13	7	25	0
Atherton	1	1	0	0

Fall of Wickets

	E	NZ	E
Wkt	1st	1st	2nd
1st	3	185	68
2nd	151	278	135
3rd	178	281	171
4th	216	284	175
5th	226	285	–
6th	255	408	–
7th	319	415	–
8th	322	425	–
9th	332	448	–
10th	334	–	–

England v New Zealand 1990 3rd Test

England won by 114 runs
Played at Edgbaston, 5, 6, 7, 9, 10 July
Toss: New Zealand. Umpires: J.W. Holder and B.J. Meyer
Debuts: England – C.C. Lewis. New Zealand – A.C. Parore
Man of Match: D.E. Malcolm (T.W. Graveney)

England

G.A. Gooch*	c Hadlee b Morrison	154	b Snedden		30
M.A. Atherton	lbw b Snedden	82	c Rutherford b Bracewell		70
A.J. Stewart	c Parore b Morrison	9	lbw b Bracewell		15
A.J. Lamb	c Parore b Hadlee	2	st Parore b Bracewell		4
R.A. Smith	c Jones b Bracewell	19	c & b Hadlee		14
N.H. Fairbrother	lbw b Snedden	2	lbw b Bracewell		3
R.C. Russell†	b Snedden	43	c sub (J.J. Crowe) b Hadlee		0
C.C. Lewis	c Rutherford b Bracewell	32	c Parore b Hadlee		1
G.C. Small	not out	44	not out		11
E.E. Hemmings	c Parore b Hadlee	20	b Hadlee		0
D.E. Malcolm	b Hadlee	0	lbw b Hadlee		0
Extras	(B4, LB15, NB9)	28	(LB6, NB4)		10
		435			**158**

New Zealand

T.J. Franklin	c Smith b Hemmings	66	lbw b Malcolm		5
J.G. Wright*	c Russell b Malcolm	24	c Smith b Lewis		46
A.H. Jones	c Russell b Malcolm	2	c Gooch b Small		40
M.D. Crowe	lbw b Lewis	11	lbw b Malcolm		25
M.J. Greatbatch	b Malcolm	45	c Atherton b Hemmings		22
K.R. Rutherford	c Stewart b Hemmings	29	c Lamb b Lewis		18
Sir Richard Hadlee	c Atherton b Hemmings	8	b Malcolm		13
J.G. Bracewell	b Hemmings	25	(9) c Atherton b Malcolm		0
A.C. Parore†	not out	12	(8) c Lamb b Lewis		20
M.C. Snedden	lbw b Hemmings	2	not out		21
D.K. Morrison	b Hemmings	1	b Malcolm		6
Extras	(B9, LB11, W2, NB2)	24	(LB9, W1, NB4)		14
		249			**230**

New Zealand	O	M	R	W	O	M	R	W
Hadlee	37.5	8	97	3	21	3	53	5
Morrison	26	7	81	2	3	1	29	0
Snedden	35	9	106	3	9	0	32	1
Bracewell	42	12	130	2	16	5	38	4
Jones	1	0	2	0				

England	O	M	R	W	O	M	R	W
Small	18	7	44	0	16	5	56	1
Malcolm	25	7	59	3	24.4	8	46	5
Lewis	19	5	51	1	22	3	76	3
Hemmings	27.3	10	58	6	29	13	43	1
Atherton	9	5	17	0				

Fall of Wickets

Wkt	E 1st	NZ 1st	E 2nd	NZ 2nd
1st	170	45	50	25
2nd	193	67	87	85
3rd	198	90	99	111
4th	245	161	129	125
5th	254	163	136	155
6th	316	185	141	163
7th	351	223	146	180
8th	381	230	157	180
9th	435	243	158	203
10th	435	249	159	230

Test Match Averages: England v New Zealand 1990

England

Batting and Fielding

	M	I	NO	HS	R	Avge	100	50	Ct/St
M.A. Atherton	3	5	0	151	357	71.40	1	3	3
G.A. Gooch	3	5	0	154	306	61.20	1	1	3
G.C. Small	3	4	2	44*	84	42.00	–	–	1
A.J. Lamb	3	5	1	84*	129	32.25	–	1	2
R.A. Smith	3	5	0	64	152	30.40	–	2	2
A.J. Stewart	3	5	0	54	147	29.40	–	1	5
R.C. Russell	3	4	0	43	84	21.00	–	–	7/-
N.H. Fairbrother	3	5	1	33*	59	14.75	–	–	1
E.E. Hemmings	3	4	1	20	33	11.00	–	–	–
D.E. Malcolm	3	4	2	4*	4	2.00	–	–	–

Also batted: P.A.J. DeFreitas (2 matches) 14, 38; C.C. Lewis (1 match) 32, 1.

Bowling

	O	M	R	W	Avge	Best	5wI	10wM
D.E. Malcolm	118.4	38	269	15	17.93	5-46	2	–
E.E. Hemmings	107.3	44	215	10	21.50	6-58	1	–
P.A.J. DeFreitas	59.4	9	175	6	29.16	5-53	1	–
G.C. Small	104	27	290	5	58.00	2-49	–	–

Also bowled: M.A. Atherton 10-6-17-0; G.A. Gooch 13-7-25-0; C.C. Lewis 41-8-127-4.

New Zealand

Batting and Fielding

	M	I	NO	HS	R	Avge	100	50	Ct/St
T.J. Franklin	3	5	1	101	227	56.75	1	1	2
J.G. Wright	3	5	0	98	177	35.40	–	1	–
M.J. Greatbatch	3	4	0	47	115	28.75	–	–	–
A.H. Jones	3	5	0	49	143	28.60	–	–	1
R.J. Hadlee	3	4	0	86	107	26.75	–	1	2
M.D. Crowe	3	4	0	59	96	24.00	–	1	1
M.C. Snedden	3	4	2	21*	36	18.00	–	–	2
K.R. Rutherford	2	3	0	29	47	15.66	–	–	2
J.G. Bracewell	3	4	0	28	57	14.25	–	–	3
D.K. Morrison	3	5	2	6	9	3.00	–	–	1

Also batted: A.C. Parore (1 match) 12*, 20 (4ct/1st); M.W. Priest (1 match) 26; I.D.S. Smith (2 matches) 2*, 27 (2ct).

Bowling

	O	M	R	W	Avge	Best	5wI	10wM
R.J. Hadlee	133.5	24	384	16	24.00	5-53	1	–
J.G. Bracewell	148	41	400	12	33.33	4-38	–	–
M.C. Snedden	101	30	264	6	44.00	3-106	–	–
D.K. Morrison	85.4	15	351	7	50.14	4-64	–	–

Also bowled: A.H. Jones 13-3-42-1; M.W. Priest 12-4-26-1: K.R. Rutherford 3-0-18-0.

Statistical Highlights of the Tests

1st Test, Trent Bridge. DeFreitas took 5 wickets for 2nd time to record his best Test bowling. Atherton scored his 1st Test hundred. Stewart became Smith's 150th test dismissal (142ct, 8st).

2nd Test, Lord's. Smith at 61* reached 1,000 Test runs in his 25th innings. Franklin scored his 1st Test hundred in his 14th Test. Franklin and Wright added 185 for 1st wicket, a record for New Zealand against England in England. Greatbatch and Hadlee added a record 123 for 6th wicket New Zealand against England. Malcolm took 5 wickets for 2nd time.

3rd Test, Edgbaston. England registered their 20th win over New Zealand in the 37 Tests played in England. It was the 1st home series win since 1985 against Australia. Gooch scored his 9th Test hundred, his 2nd against New Zealand and his 1st as England captain. At 26* he became the 11th England batsman to score 5,000 Test runs. At 146* he reached 5,120 and passed Botham. He and Atherton put on 170 for the 1st wicket, the highest for England in any Test at Edgbaston. Playing his 41st Test, Bracewell at 24* reached 1,000 Test runs and in the 2nd innings dismissed Lamb to get his 100th Test wicket. He became the 2nd New Zealand player to have 1,000 runs and 100 wickets. Only Kapil Dev (25th Test) did this in the same Test. Hemmings took 5 wickets for 1st time to give his best Test return and the best bowling for England against New Zealand at Edgbaston. Gooch in 2nd innings at 11* reached 5,139 Test runs and passed J.H. Edrich. England's total is their lowest against New Zealand in England. Hadlee, in his last Test, took 5 wickets for 36th time, his 8th against England, to end his career with 431 wickets. Malcolm took 5 wickets for 3rd time, his 2nd against New Zealand.

England v New Zealand
1st Texaco Trophy International

New Zealand won by 4 wickets
Played at Headingley, Leeds, 23 May
Toss: New Zealand. Umpires: B.J. Meyer and N.T. Plews
Man of the Match: M.J. Greatbatch (Adjudicator: F.S. Trueman)

England		Runs	Mins	Balls	6	4
G.A. Gooch*	c Millmow b Pringle	55	121	88	1	4
D.I. Gower	c Priest b Hadlee	1	15	8	–	–
R.A. Smith	c Crowe b Hadlee	128	196	168	–	16
A.J. Lamb	run out (Greatbatch/Smith)	18	36	25	–	2
A.J. Stewart	lbw b Morrison	33	33	25	1	3
D.R. Pringle	not out	30	31	17	–	5
R.C. Russell†	c Crowe b Pringle	13	4	5	–	3
P.A.J. DeFreitas	not out	1	6	1	–	–
C.C. Lewis	did not bat					
G.C. Small	"					
E.E. Hemmings	"					
Extras	(LB10, W1, NB5)	16				
	(55 overs; 224 minutes)	**295-6**				

New Zealand		Runs	Mins	Balls	6	4
J.G. Wright*	c Stewart b Gooch	52	95	77	–	8
A.H. Jones	st Russell b Gooch	51	87	66	–	4
M.D. Crowe	c Russell b Lewis	46	78	48	–	3
M.J. Greatbatch	not out	102	131	104	2	9
K.R. Rutherford	lbw b Lewis	0	1	2	–	–
R.J. Hadlee	c Lamb b Lewis	12	24	18	–	1
M.W. Priest	c Gower b Small	2	6	4	–	–
I.D.S. Smith†	not out	17	25	11	–	2
J.P. Millmow	did not bat					
D.K. Morrison	"					
C. Pringle	"					
Extras	(B5, LB7, W3, NB1)	16				
	(54.5 overs; 226 minutes)	**298-6**				

New Zealand	O	M	R	W
Hadlee	11	4	46	2
Pringle	11	2	45	2
Morrison	11	0	70	1
Millmow	11	0	65	0
Priest	11	0	59	0

England	O	M	R	W
Small	11	1	43	1
DeFreitas	10.5	0	70	0
Pringle	7	0	45	0
Lewis	11	0	54	3
Hemmings	11	0	51	0
Gooch	4	0	23	2

Fall of Wickets

Wkt	E	NZ
1st	5	97
2nd	118	106
3rd	168	224
4th	225	224
5th	261	254
6th	274	259
7th	–	–
8th	–	–
9th	–	–
10th	–	–

England v New Zealand, 2nd Texaco Trophy International

England won by 6 wickets
Played at The Foster's Oval, London, 25 May
Toss: England. Umpires: D.J. Constant and J.H. Hampshire
Man of the Match: D.E. Malcolm (Adjudicator: R.G.D. Willis)
Men of the Series: G.A. Gooch (England) & M.J. Greatbatch (New Zealand)

New Zealand		Runs	Mins	Balls	6	4
J.G. Wright*	c Small b Malcolm	15	37	41	–	2
A.H. Jones	run out (Stewart/Hemmings)	15	55	31	–	1
M.D. Crowe	c Russell b Lewis	7	46	31	–	–
M.J. Greatbatch	c Smith b Malcolm	111	158	130	1	10
K.R. Rutherford	retired hurt	0	3	3	–	–
R.J. Hadlee	retired hurt	9	43	24	–	–
M.W. Priest	c Smith b DeFreitas	24	62	51	–	–
I.D.S. Smith†	not out	25	28	17	1	2
C. Pringle	b Small	1	10	2	–	–
J.P. Millmow	did not bat					
D.K. Morrison	,,					
Extras	(LB2, W3)	5				
	(55 overs; 227 minutes)	**212-6**				

England		Runs	Mins	Balls	6	4
G.A. Gooch*	not out	112	207	152	–	15
D.I. Gower	b Hadlee	4	3	3	–	1
R.A. Smith	c Smith b Hadlee	5	14	12	–	1
A.J. Lamb	lbw b Pringle	4	5	4	–	1
A.J. Stewart	c Morrison b Priest	28	80	57	–	3
R.C. Russell†	not out	47	98	71	–	5
C.C. Lewis	did not bat					
P.A.J. DeFreitas	,,					
G.C. Small	,,					
E.E. Hemmings	,,					
D.E. Malcolm	,,					
Extras	(LB7, W5, NB1)	13				
	(49.3 overs; 207 minutes)	**213-4**				

England	O	M	R	W
DeFreitas	11	1	47	1
Malcolm	11	5	19	2
Lewis	11	1	51	1
Small	11	0	59	1
Hemmings	11	2	34	0

New Zealand	O	M	R	W
Hadlee	11	2	34	2
Pringle	9.3	0	53	1
Millmow	9	1	47	0
Morrison	9	0	38	0
Priest	11	2	34	1

Fall of Wickets

Wkt	NZ	E
1st	25	5
2nd	34	15
3rd	53	29
4th	174	104
5th	202	–
6th	212	–
7th	–	–
8th	–	–
9th	–	–
10th	–	–

Note: Rutherford retired hurt at 53-3
Hadlee retired hurt at 93-3

New Zealand Tour of England 1990

Tests: Played 3; Lost 1, Drawn 2
First-Class Matches: Played 12; Won 4, Lost 2, Drawn 6
All Matches: Played 19; Won 8, Lost 5, Drawn 6

First-Class Averages

Batting and Fielding	M	I	NO	HS	R	Avge	100	50	Ct/St
M.D. Crowe	9	13	3	123*	537	53.70	1	5	5
A.H. Jones	10	16	3	121*	692	53.23	1	5	3
J.G. Wright	9	15	2	121	653	50.23	1	5	2
K.R. Rutherford	8	13	5	68*	376	47.00	–	1	7
T.J. Franklin	11	17	1	103	731	45.68	2	5	3
J.J. Crowe	8	15	4	132	493	44.81	1	2	6
M.W. Priest	9	11	3	72	345	43.12	–	3	6
M.J. Greatbatch	10	14	1	85	448	34.46	–	4	5
R.J. Hadlee	5	6	0	90	204	34.00	–	2	4
J.G. Bracewell	8	8	3	40*	169	33.80	–	–	5
S.A. Thomson	5	5	4	20	32	32.00	–	–	5
A.C. Parore	7	6	1	43	131	26.20	–	–	14/1
I.D.S. Smith	6	4	1	34	65	21.66	–	–	5/-
M.C. Snedden	7	6	3	21*	38	12.66	–	–	3
D.K. Morrison	9	6	2	6	14	3.50	–	–	3

Also batted: J.P. Millmow (5 matches) 2* (2ct); C. Pringle (4 matches) 6 (2ct); W. Watson (2 matches) 17*.

Bowling	O	M	R	W	Avge	Best	5wI	10wM
R.J. Hadlee	201.5	39	586	24	24.41	5-27	2	–
M.C. Snedden	231.5	56	633	23	27.52	5-63	1	–
J.G. Bracewell	383.3	102	1120	34	32.94	7-120	2	1
J.P. Millmow	105	14	391	11	35.54	3-66	–	–
D.K. Morrison	234.4	36	889	21	42.33	4-64	–	–
C. Pringle	130	31	398	8	49.75	2-67	–	–
M.W. Priest	312.4	90	907	14	64.78	3-35	–	–
S.A. Thomson	106.2	18	435	5	87.00	2-84	–	–

Also bowled: M.D. Crowe 8-3-20-0; A.H. Jones 26-4-87-3; K.R. Rutherford 42-3-196-0; W. Watson 54-10-177-3.

Results († One-Day Match)

† Duchess of Norfolk XI (Arundel)	Won by 7 wickets
† MCC (Lord's)	Lost by 6 wickets
† Ireland (Downpatrick)	Won by 7 wickets
† Ireland (Belfast)	Won by 40 runs
Worcestershire (Worcester)	Won by 6 wickets
Somerset (Taunton)	Won by 5 wickets
Middlesex (Lord's)	Drawn
† ENGLAND (Headingley)	Won by 4 wickets
† ENGLAND (The Foster's Oval)	Lost by 6 wickets
Sussex (Hove)	Won by 7 wickets
Warwickshire (Edgbaston)	Drawn
Derbyshire (Derby)	Won by 82 runs
ENGLAND (Trent Bridge)	Drawn
† Leicestershire (Leicester)	Lost by 4 wickets
Northamptonshire (Northampton)	Drawn
ENGLAND (Lord's)	Drawn
Oxford & Cambridge (Cambridge)	Lost by 2 wickets
Essex (Chelmsford)	Drawn
ENGLAND (Edgbaston)	Lost by 114 runs

Hundreds (6)

2 – T.J. Franklin: 103 v Somerset, Taunton;
101 v England, Lord's
1 – J.J. Crowe: 132 v Oxford & Cambridge, Cambridge

M.D. Crowe: 123* v Essex, Chelmsford
A.H. Jones: 121* v Derbyshire, Derby
J.G. Wright: 121 v Essex, Chelmsford

India in England

Most people who followed the Tests between England and India would believe that the Indian captain Mohammad Azharuddin's decision to ask England to bat at Lord's cost India the series. That certainly was one reason, but not the major reason, because the Indians, chasing England's 653, had avoided the follow-on in the most marvellous manner possible. However, they seemed to get carried away by this approach and destroyed themselves in the second innings by playing reckless shots to lose the game long before tea on the last day. That cavalier, thoughtless approach to the second innings was the major reason the Indian team lost that game and, therefore, the series.

They had a very good chance to draw level at the Oval, but found themselves one bowler short. Hirwani tried manfully but looked bereft of ideas once the batsmen got through his first five or six overs. Though he has variation in the form of a top-spinner, a flipper, and a 'wrong 'un', he pitches them on the same spot. Accuracy in a leg-spinner is not always the virtue it should be, for it makes him predictable, and a good batsman can thus anticipate what might be coming, even though he may not have read it from the bowler's hand. That was Hirwani's fate in the final Test as, after the initial doubt and uncertainty, every batsman played him well.

The series was dominated by the batsmen of both sides. The brilliant summer dried out the wickets and made them into batting paradises, and every batsman worth his salt added plenty of runs and centuries to his Test aggregate.

The tone was set by Graham Gooch, the England captain. He showed his appreciation of his counterpart's invitation to bat first at Lord's by scoring 333, sending statisticians scurrying for their record books.

England's biggest plus of the summer had to be Mike Atherton. Every time I saw him on the field, the impression was more and more favourable. The young man has, apart from a fine technique, an equally calm temperament and looks destined for greatness if he carries on in the same manner. His leg-spinners, however, have a long way to go before they are successful at Test level.

The one bowler to shine in a series dominated by batsmen was Angus Fraser. He was the perfect new-ball bowler, with just enough pace to make the batsmen think twice before coming onto the front foot. With a nagging line on or outside the off-stump, his ability to bowl long spells was a bonus for the team, for one end was thus just about blocked up.

From the Indian viewpoint, the tour was a bit of a let-down, although their performances with the bat sent everyone back from the grounds longing for more. Here, too, Azharuddin led by example. He finally showed the consistency with which he had signalled his arrival in Test cricket five years ago.

As a captain, he brought great dignity to the job with his demeanour on and off the field.

As a tactician, he was hampered by having to keep one eye on the dressing-room balcony for approval of his tactics, which was seldom forthcoming, and thus he was not as positive as his batting was. He is still fairly new to the job and with greater experience and confidence will be the kind of captain India need.

Ravi Shastri, his deputy, had already won a Test match as captain and looked more certain about his tactics on the field when he was in charge. It was as an opening batsman that he was a revelation. He still shuffles too much, often leaving his leg-stump exposed, but his two centuries on the tour, and especially the last effort at the Oval, will have done him no harm at all in his attempts to re-establish himself in the side.

Sachin Tendulkar and Kapil Dev scored their centuries in different styles. While Tendulkar's century augurs well for the future of the Indian middle-order, Kapil's superb hundred may be a pointer to where his future priorities may lie.

Manjrekar played well at Manchester, but seemed generally consumed by the attacking Indian approach to batting, getting out in an untypical manner. As for the Indian bowlers, they tried very hard. But on this summer's pitches, they never looked like dismissing England twice. All the games of the series were England's, while India are back to square one.

SUNIL GAVASKAR
The Daily Telegraph, 30 August

First Test: Lord's, 26, 27, 28, 30, 31 July
England won by 247 runs

Azharuddin's decision to put England in is history, as is Gooch's 333. England scored 359 on the first day in 360 minutes, for the loss of two wickets. The next day Gooch and Lamb took their stand to 308 before Lamb went, and another big stand with Smith allowed Gooch to declare. India's openers Shastri and Sidhu survived the final 63 minutes. Shastri went on to make his 100, but the Saturday will always be remembered for Azharuddin's glorious unbeaten 117 made off 106 balls. On Monday, it was Kapil Dev's turn to take centre stage. He saved the follow-on in dramatic style by hitting Hemmings for four consecutive sixes. But Gooch had the last word, breaking several more records with his 123 off 113 balls and putting on 204 for the first wicket with Atherton. England declared with a lead of 471 and took two Indian wickets for 57 in the final hour. The next day it was all over in 3¼ hours.

Second Test: Old Trafford, 9, 10, 11, 13, 14 August
Match Drawn

England fielded an unchanged side, but India brought in leg-spinner Kumble for Sharma. Gooch won the toss, batted, and continued as he had left off at Lord's, hitting his third Test century in as many innings. Atherton also scored a hundred, and the pair passed their Lord's record with 225 for the opening partnership. Gower again disappointed, but at the close England were a healthy 322-3. They increased this to 519 the next day thanks to an unbeaten hundred by Smith, and then Fraser left India in tatters at 77-3. On Saturday, Azharuddin, 179, led a heroic fightback, leaving England with a lead of only 87. Gooch went quickly on Monday, but Atherton and Lamb, 109, pulled England round and they were able to declare after half an hour on the last day with a lead of 407. At 127-5, things looked bleak for India, but they were saved by a marvellously mature maiden Test century from the teenage wonderboy Tendulkar.

Third Test: The Foster's Oval, 23, 24, 25, 27, 28 August
Match Drawn

With Neil Williams making his debut as a last-minute replacement for Lewis (migraine), England found themselves toiling in the field and suffering the indignity of following on. India, 324-4 on the first day, went on to make 606-9, thanks largely to Shastri's 187 and a hundred by Kapil Dev. England lost Atherton before the close, and although Gooch made 85, it was thanks to fifties by Smith and Hemmings that they followed on only 266 behind. But Gooch and Atherton, with a stand of 176, took the sting out of the Indian attack, and Gower came good at last to make the situation safe with an unbeaten 157.

England v India 1990 1st Test

England won by 247 runs
Played at Lord's, 26, 27, 28, 30, 31 July
Toss: India. Umpires: H.D. Bird and N.T. Plews
Debuts: England – R.E. Morris

England

G.A. Gooch*	b Prabhakar	333	c Azharuddin b Sharma	123
M.A. Atherton	b Kapil Dev	8	c Vengsarkar b Sharma	72
D.I. Gower	c Manjrekar b Hirwani	40	not out	32
A.J. Lamb	c Manjrekar b Sharma	139	c Tendulkar b Hirwani	19
R.A. Smith	not out	100	b Prabhakar	15
J.E. Morris	not out	4		
R.C. Russell†	did not bat			
C.C. Lewis	"			
E.E. Hemmings	"			
A.R.C. Fraser	"			
D.E. Malcolm	"			
Extras	(B2, LB21, W2, NB4)	29	(LB11)	11
	(4 wkts dec)	653	(4 wkts dec)	272

India

R.J. Shastri	c Gooch b Hemmings	100	c Russell b Malcolm	12
N.S. Sidhu	c Morris b Fraser	30	c Morris b Fraser	1
S.V. Manjrekar	c Russell b Gooch	18	c Russell b Malcolm	33
D.B. Vengsarkar	c Russell b Fraser	52	c Russell b Hemmings	35
M. Azharuddin*	b Hemmings	121	c Atherton b Lewis	37
S.R. Tendulkar	b Lewis	10	c Gooch b Fraser	27
M. Prabhakar	c Lewis b Malcolm	25	lbw b Lewis	8
Kapil Dev	not out	77	c Lewis b Hemmings	7
K.S. Moré†	c Morris b Fraser	8	lbw b Fraser	16
S.K. Sharma	c Russell b Fraser	0	run out (Gooch)	38
N.D. Hirwani	lbw b Fraser	0	not out	0
Extras	(LB1, W4, NB8)	13	(B3, LB1, NB6)	10
		454		224

India	O	M	R	W	O	M	R	W
Kapil Dev	34	5	120	1	10	0	53	0
Prabhakar	43	6	187	1	11.2	2	45	1
Sharma	33	5	122	1	15	0	75	2
Shastri	22	0	99	0	7	0	38	0
Hirwani	30	1	102	1	11	0	51	0

England	O	M	R	W	O	M	R	W
Malcolm	25	1	106	1	10	0	65	2
Fraser	39.1	9	104	5	22	7	39	3
Lewis	24	3	108	1	8	1	26	2
Gooch	6	3	26	1				
Hemmings	20	3	109	2	21	2	79	2
Atherton					1	0	11	0

Fall of Wickets

	E	I	E	I
Wkt	1st	1st	2nd	2nd
1st	14	63	204	9
2nd	141	102	207	23
3rd	449	191	250	63
4th	641	241	272	114
5th	–	288	–	127
6th	–	348	–	140
7th	–	393	–	158
8th	–	430	–	181
9th	–	430	–	206
10th	–	454	–	224

England v India 1990 2nd Test

Match Drawn
Played at Old Trafford, 9, 10, 11, 13, 14 August
Toss: England. Umpires: J.H. Hampshire and J.W. Holder
Debuts: India – A. Kumble

England

G.A. Gooch*	c Moré b Prabhakar	116	c Moré b Prabhakar	7
M.A. Atherton	c Moré b Hirwani	131	lbw b Kapil Dev	74
D.I. Gower	c Tendulkar b Kapil Dev	38	b Hirwani	16
A.J. Lamb	c Manjrekar b Kumble	38	b Kapil Dev	109
R.C. Russell†	c Moré b Hirwani	8	(7) not out	16
R.A. Smith	not out	121	(5) not out	61
J.E. Morris	b Kumble	13	(6) retired hurt	15
C.C. Lewis	b Hirwani	3		
E.E. Hemmings	lbw b Hirwani	19		
A.R.C. Fraser	c Tendulkar b Kumble	1		
D.E. Malcolm	b Shastri	13		
Extras	(B2, LB9, W1, NB6)	18	(LB15, NB7)	22
		519	(4 wkts dec)	**320**

India

R.J. Shastri	c Gooch b Fraser	25	b Malcolm	12
N.S. Sidhu	c Gooch b Fraser	13	c sub (C.J. Adams) b Fraser	0
S.V. Manjrekar	c Smith b Hemmings	93	c sub (C.J. Adams) b Hemmings	50
D. B. Vengsarkar	c Russell b Fraser	6	b Lewis	32
M. Azharuddin*	c Atherton b Fraser	179	c Lewis b Hemmings	11
S.R. Tendulkar	c Lewis b Hemmings	68	not out	119
M. Prabhakar	c Russell b Malcolm	4	(8) not out	67
Kapil Dev	lbw b Lewis	0	(7) b Hemmings	26
K.S. Moré†	b Fraser	6		
A. Kumble	run out (Morris)	2		
N.D. Hirwani	not out	15		
Extras	(B5, LB4, NB12)	21	(B17, LB3, NB6)	26
		432	(6 wkts)	**343**

India	O	M	R	W	O	M	R	W
Kapil Dev	13	2	67	1	22	4	69	2
Prabhakar	25	2	112	1	18	1	80	1
Kumble	43	7	105	3	17	3	65	0
Hirwani	62	10	174	4	15	0	52	1
Shastri	17.5	2	50	1	9	0	39	0

England	O	M	R	W	O	M	R	W
Malcolm	26	3	96	1	14	5	59	1
Fraser	35	5	124	5	21	3	81	1
Hemmings	29.2	8	74	2	31	10	75	3
Lewis	13	1	61	1	20	3	86	1
Atherton	16	3	68	0	4	0	22	0

Fall of Wickets

	E	I	E	I
Wkt	1st	1st	2nd	2nd
1st	225	26	15	4
2nd	292	48	46	35
3rd	312	57	180	109
4th	324	246	248	109
5th	366	358	–	127
6th	392	364	–	183
7th	404	365	–	–
8th	434	396	–	–
9th	459	401	–	–
10th	519	432	–	–

Note: Morris retired hurt at 290-4 in the 2nd innings

England v India 1990 3rd Test

Match Drawn
Played at Foster's Oval, 23, 24, 25, 27, 28 August
Toss: India. Umpires: N.T. Plews and D.R. Shepherd
Debuts: England – N.F. Williams

India

R.J. Shastri	c Lamb b Malcolm	187
N.S. Sidhu	c Russell b Fraser	12
S.V. Manjrekar	c Russell b Malcolm	22
D.B. Vengsarkar	c & b Atherton	33
M. Azharuddin*	c Russell b Williams	78
M. Prabhakar	lbw b Fraser	28
S.R. Tendulkar	c Lamb b Williams	21
Kapil Dev	st Russell b Hemmings	110
K.S. Moré†	not out	61
A.S. Wassan	b Hemmings	15
N.D. Hirwani	not out	2
Extras	(B7, LB8, W6, NB16)	37
	(9 wkts dec)	**606**

England

G.A. Gooch*	c Shastri b Hirwani	85	c Vengsarkar b Hirwani	88
M.A. Atherton	c Moré b Prabhakar	7	lbw b Kapil Dev	86
N.F. Williams	lbw b Prabhakar	38		
D.I. Gower	lbw b Wassan	8	(3) not out	157
J.E. Morris	c Moré b Wassan	7	(4) c Moré b Wassan	32
A.J. Lamb	b Kapil Dev	7	(5) c Shastri b Kapil Dev	52
R.A. Smith	c Manjrekar b Shastri	57	(6) not out	7
R.C. Russell†	run out (Wassan)	35		
E.E. Hemmings	c Vengsarkar b Prabhakar	51		
A.R.C. Fraser	c Moré b Prabhakar	0		
D.E. Malcolm	not out	15		
Extras	(B8, LB9, W4, NB9)	30	(B16, LB22, W5, NB12)	55
		340	(4 wkts dec)	**477**

England	O	M	R	W				
Malcolm	35	7	110	2				
Fraser	42	17	112	2				
Williams	41	5	148	2				
Gooch	12	1	44	0				
Hemmings	36	3	117	2				
Atherton	7	0	60	2				

India	O	M	R	W	O	M	R	W
Kapil Dev	25	7	70	1	24	5	66	2
Prabhakar	32.4	9	74	4	25	8	56	0
Wassan	19	3	79	2	18	2	94	1
Hirwani	35	12	71	1	59	18	137	1
Shastri	12	2	29	1	28	2	86	0

Fall of Wickets

Wkt	I 1st	E 1st	E 2nd
1st	16	18	176
2nd	61	92	251
3rd	150	111	334
4th	289	120	463
5th	335	139	–
6th	368	231	–
7th	478	233	–
8th	552	295	–
9th	576	299	–
10th	–	340	–

Test Match Averages: England v India 1990

England

Batting and Fielding	M	I	NO	HS	R	Avge	100	50	Ct/St
R.A. Smith	3	6	4	121*	361	180.50	2	2	1
G.A. Gooch	3	6	0	333	752	125.33	3	2	4
D.I. Gower	3	6	2	157*	291	72.75	1	–	–
M.A. Atherton	3	6	0	131	378	63.00	1	3	3
A.J. Lamb	3	6	0	139	364	60.66	2	1	2
R.C. Russell	3	3	1	35	59	29.50	–	–	11/1
J.E. Morris	3	5	2	32	71	23.66	–	–	3

Also batted: A.R.C. Fraser (3 matches), 1, 0; E.E. Hemmings (3 matches) 19, 51; C.C. Lewis (2 matches) 3 (4ct); D.E. Malcolm (3 matches) 13, 15*; N.F. Williams (1 match) 38.

Bowling	O	M	R	W	Avge	Best	5wI	10wM
A.R.C. Fraser	159.1	41	460	16	28.75	5-104	2	–
E.E. Hemmings	137.2	26	454	11	41.27	3-75	–	–
C.C. Lewis	65	8	281	5	56.20	2-26	–	–
D.E. Malcolm	110	16	436	7	62.28	2-65	–	–

Also bowled: M.A. Atherton 28-3-161-1; G.A. Gooch 18-4-70-1; N.F. Williams 41-5-148-2.

India

Batting and Fielding	M	I	NO	HS	R	Avge	100	50	Ct/St
M. Azharuddin	3	5	0	179	426	85.20	2	1	1
R.J. Shastri	3	5	0	187	336	67.20	2	–	2
S.R. Tendulkar	3	5	1	119*	245	61.25	1	1	3
Kapil Dev	3	5	1	110	220	55.00	1	1	–
S.V. Manjrekar	3	5	0	93	216	43.20	–	2	4
M. Prabhakar	3	5	1	67*	132	33.00	–	1	–
D.B. Vengsarkar	3	5	0	52	158	31.60	–	1	3
K.S. Moré	3	4	1	61*	91	30.33	–	1	8/-
N.D. Hirwani	3	4	3	15*	17	17.00	–	–	–
N.S. Sidhu	3	5	0	30	56	11.20	–	–	–

Also batted: A. Kumble (1 match) 2; S.K. Sharma (1 match) 0, 38; A.S. Wassan (1 match) 15.

Bowling	O	M	R	W	Avge	Best	5wI	10wM
Kapil Dev	128	23	445	7	63.57	2-66	–	–
N.D. Hirwani	212	41	586	9	65.11	4-174	–	–
M. Prabhakar	155	28	554	8	69.25	4-74	–	–

Also bowled: A. Kumble 60-10-170-3; S.K. Sharma 48-5-197-3; R.J. Shastri 95.5-6-341-2; A.S. Wassan 37-5-173-3.

Statistical Highlights of the Tests

1st Test, Lord's. (See p.119 for Gooch's individual records.) England recorded their highest total against India. Gooch and Lamb 3rd-wicket Stand of 308 highest for any England wicket against India. Lamb scored his 12th and highest Test hundred, his 2nd against India, equalling Gooch's feat of 4 hundreds at Lord's. Smith scored his 3rd Test hundred, his 1st against India. Gower played in a record 17th Test at Lord's. Shastri scored his 9th Test hundred, his 3rd against England. Azharuddin scored his 8th Test hundred, his 4th against England. It was the 22nd instance of both captains making hundreds in the same match. Kapil Dev scored 24 runs off Hemmings (006666) to save the follow-on, record number of successive sixes in a Test and equalling record for runs in 6-ball over. Fraser took 5 wickets for 2nd time. Lamb became Hirwani's 50th Test wicket in the 2nd innings. Atherton at 62* in the 2nd innings reached 500 Test runs in his 11th innings, and stand of 204 with Gooch in 2nd innings highest for England against India.

2nd Test, Old Trafford. Gooch's 12th Test hundred (5th against India), 4th England batsman to score hundreds in 3 successive Tests. Atherton's 2nd Test hundred. Gooch and Atherton 225 1st-wicket, beating their record for England against India, made in 1st Test. Azharuddin's 10th Test hundred (5th against England); also 3rd hundred in successive Tests. He scored 103* between lunch and tea on 3rd day. Prabhakar became Russell's 50th Test dismissal in just 16 Tests, and Fraser took 5 wickets for the 3rd time. Lamb's 13th Test hundred (3rd against India). Umpire Hampshire allowed an 8-ball over on Monday afternoon after break for rain had stopped the over with 4 balls bowled. Manjrekar (6*) reached 1,000 Test runs in 14th Test. Tendulkar, in 9th Test, scored his 1st hundred, at the age of 17 years and 112 days, second-youngest player to do so (Mushtaq Mohammad, 17 years 82 days, Pakistan v India, Delhi 1960-61). Match aggregate of 1,614 runs a record for a Test at Old Trafford.

3rd Test, Foster's Oval. India's highest total against England (553-8 dec at Kanput, 1984-85). Shastri's highest Test score, 10th hundred (4th against England). Kapil Dev and Gower both played their 109th Tests and both scored hundreds; Kapil Dev's 7th (2nd against England) and Gower's 16th (2nd against India). Gooch's 2nd-innings 88 left him with more records: 752 runs for the series, best-ever in a three-match series (Zaheer Abbas 583, Pakistan v India 1978-79); Test tally for 1990 season, 1,058 runs in 11 innings, Bradman 974 in 7 innings (1930). N.D. Hirwani bowled 59 consecutive overs in the second innings, from 3.05 p.m. Monday to 4.25 p.m. Tuesday, with only the scheduled breaks in play in which to rest. At the end of the match, Gooch stood 7th in England Test list, with 5,910 runs. Gower moved into 7th place on the world list, with 7,674 runs, passing M.C. Cowdrey (7,624) and C.H. Lloyd (7,515). Only G. Boycott (8,114) has more runs for England.

Milestones in Gooch's 333 and 123, England v India (Lord's)

1st innings, July 26, 27

35	30,000 career aggregate
74	1,000 Test runs v India (3rd England player)
85	1,210 runs in Tests at Lord's (beating Gower achieved in same match)
100	10th Test hundred, 1st player 4 Test hundreds at Lord's
197	Highest score in Test cricket (196 v Australia, Oval 1985)
200	8th 200 England v India
206	Highest score England v India at Lord's (205* Joe Hardstaff Jr 1946)
241	Highest score England at Lord's (W.R. Hammond 240 v Australia 1948)
247	Highest score England v India (G. Boycott 246, Headingley 1967)
255	Highest score any Test at Lord's (D.G. Bradman 254, 1930)
276	Highest first-class score (275 Essex v Kent, Chelmsford 1988)
281	Highest Test score v India (280* Javed Miandad, Hyderabad 1982-83)
286	Highest score by England captain (285* P.B.H. May v WI, Edgbaston 1957)
300	12th player 300 in Test, 5th England player
303	Passed 302 L.G. Rowe, WI v England, Bridgetown 1973-74
305	Passed 304 D.G. Bradman, Australia v England, Headingley 1934
308	Passed 307 R.M. Cowper, Australia v England, MCG 1965-66
311	Passed 310 J.H. Edrich, England v NZ, Headingley 1965 (highest score by England batsman since the war)
312	Passed 311 R.B. Simpson, Australia v England, Old Trafford 1964 (highest score by *any* Test captain)
317	Highest score any first-class match at Lord's (J.B. Hobbs 316* Surrey v Middlesex 1926)
326	Passed 325 A. Sandham, England v WI, Kingston 1929-30
333	6th highest score in all Tests; 3rd highest in all Tests for England

2nd innings, July 30

48	381 runs in one Test (G.S. Chappell 380, Australia v NZ, Wellington 1973-74)
71	404* runs in England home series against India (I.T. Botham 403, 1982)
97	1,356 runs v India (K.F. Barrington 1,355)
100	11th Test hundred; 1st player 5 Test hundreds at Lord's; 1st player 2 hundreds in match England v India, 1st player 300 & 100 in same first-class match; 9th instance captain 2 hundreds in same Test; 1st England player to score 2 hundreds in Test since D.C.S. Compton v Australia, Adelaide 1947-48
123	Aggregate for match 456; only Hanif Mohammad (499) has more runs in any first-class match

England v India, 1st Texaco Trophy International

India won by 6 wickets
Played at Headingley, Leeds, 18 July
Toss: India. Umpires: J.H. Hampshire and J.W. Holder
Man of the Match: A. Kumble (Adjudicator: G. Boycott)

England		Runs	Mins	Balls	6	4
G.A. Gooch*	c & b Shastri	45	89	75	–	–
M.A. Atherton	lbw b Prabhakar	7	27	18	–	–
D.I. Gower	b Kumble	50	116	93	–	3
A.J. Lamb	c Prabhakar b Kapil Dev	56	102	79	–	3
R.A. Smith	c Moré b Kumble	6	6	5	–	1
R.C. Russell†	c Manjrekar b Kapil Dev	14	26	20	–	–
P.A.J. DeFreitas	b Sharma	11	34	21	–	–
C.C. Lewis	lbw b Prabhakar	6	12	7	–	1
E.E. Hemmings	b Sharma	3	3	3	–	–
A.R.C. Fraser	not out	4	7	4	–	–
D.E. Malcolm	c Kapil Dev b Prabhakar	4	3	3	–	1
Extras	(B6, LB8, W9)	23				
	(54.3 overs; 221 minutes)	229				

India		Runs	Mins	Balls	6	4
W.V. Raman	c Atherton b DeFreitas	0	1	2	–	–
N.S. Sidhu	lbw b Lewis	39	100	70	–	5
S.V. Manjrekar	c Gower b Lewis	82	180	133	–	7
S.R. Tendulkar	b Malcolm	19	38	35	1	1
M. Azharuddin*	not out	55	80	50	–	5
R.J. Shastri	not out	23	35	29	–	4
K.S. Moré†	did not bat					
Kapil Dev	,,					
M. Prabhakar	,,					
S.K. Sharma	,,					
A. Kumble	,,					
Extras	(LB5, W9, NB1)	15				
	(53 overs; 217 minutes)	233-4				

India	O	M	R	W
Kapil Dev	11	1	49	2
Prabhakar	10.3	1	40	3
Sharma	11	1	57	2
Shastri	11	0	40	1
Kumble	11	2	29	2

England	O	M	R	W
DeFreitas	10	1	40	1
Malcolm	11	0	57	1
Fraser	11	3	37	0
Lewis	10	0	58	2
Hemmings	11	0	36	0

Fall of Wickets

Wkt	E	I
1st	22	1
2nd	86	76
3rd	134	115
4th	142	183
5th	186	–
6th	196	–
7th	211	–
8th	221	–
9th	224	–
10th	229	–

England v India, 2nd Texaco Trophy International

India won by 5 wickets
Played at Trent Bridge, Nottingham, 20 July
Toss: India. Umpires: M.J. Kitchen and D.R. Shepherd
Man of the Match: R.A. Smith (Adjudicator: R.B. Simpson)
Men of the Series: R.C. Russell (England) & M. Azharuddin (India)

England		Runs	Mins	Balls	6	4
G.A. Gooch*	b Prabhakar	7	13	15	–	1
M.A. Atherton	c Moré b Prabhakar	59	142	95	–	5
D.I. Gower	run out (Azharuddin/Moré)	25	35	30	–	6
A.J. Lamb	run out (Sidhu/Shastri)	3	24	18	–	–
R.A. Smith	b Shastri	103	117	105	–	11
R.C. Russell†	c Azharuddin b Kapil Dev	50	89	50	–	4
P.A.J. DeFreitas	c Vengsarkar b Sharma	1	8	4	–	–
C.C. Lewis	lbw b Prabhakar	7	16	10	–	–
G.C. Small	c Azharuddin b Kapil Dev	4	4	4	–	1
E.E. Hemmings	run out (Manjrekar/Kapil Dev)	0	1	0	–	–
A.R.C. Fraser	not out	0	1	0	–	–
Extras	(B1, LB12, W8, NB1)	22				
	(55 overs; 233 minutes)	**281**				

India		Runs	Mins	Balls	6	4
R.J. Shastri	c Atherton b Hemmings	33	82	57	–	3
N.S. Sidhu	b Small	23	38	27	–	3
S.V. Manjrekar	st Russell b Hemmings	59	114	93	–	4
D.B. Vengsarkar	b Lewis	54	91	63	2	3
M. Azharuddin*	not out	63	73	44	–	6
S.R. Tendulkar	b Fraser	31	31	26	–	2
Kapil Dev	not out	5	19	8	–	1
K.S. Moré†	did not bat					
M. Prabhakar	,,					
S.K. Sharma	,,					
A. Kumble	,,					
Extras	(LB5, W9)	14				
	(53 overs; 229 minutes)	**282-5**				

India	O	M	R	W
Kapil Dev	11	2	40	2
Prabhakar	11	0	58	3
Sharma	10	0	50	1
Shastri	11	0	52	1
Kumble	11	1	58	0
Tendulkar	1	0	10	0

England	O	M	R	W
Small	10	0	73	1
DeFreitas	11	0	59	0
Fraser	11	1	38	1
Hemmings	11	1	53	2
Lewis	10	0	54	1

Fall of Wickets

Wkt	E	I
1st	12	42
2nd	47	69
3rd	62	166
4th	173	186
5th	246	249
6th	254	–
7th	275	
8th	280	–
9th	281	–
10th	281	–

India Tour of England

Tests: Played 3; Won 0, Lost 1, Drawn 2
First-Class Matches: Played 13; Won 1, Lost 2, Drawn 10
All Matches: Played 18; Won 6, Lost 2, Drawn 10

First-Class Averages

Batting and Fielding	M	I	NO	HS	R	Avge	100	50	Ct/St
M. Azharuddin	9	11	1	179	770	77.00	3	3	3
R.J. Shastri	9	11	1	187	644	64.40	4	1	6
S.R. Tendulkar	11	19	4	119*	945	63.00	2	6	5
S.V. Manjrekar	11	17	3	158*	814	58.14	2	6	6
D.B. Vengsarkar	10	14	4	83*	576	57.60	–	6	4
W.V. Raman	8	15	2	127	623	47.92	1	7	6
N.S. Sidhu	9	17	3	142	639	45.64	2	4	1
N.R. Mongia	8	11	4	63*	269	38.42	–	2	9/3
Kapil Dev	9	12	2	110	377	37.70	1	2	3
S.K. Sharma	9	7	3	38	132	33.00	–	–	2
K.S. Moré	9	11	2	95	295	32.77	–	2	17/1
M. Prabhakar	10	14	3	76	296	26.90	–	2	4
S.L.V. Raju	6	6	2	40*	105	26.25	–	–	–
A.S. Wassan	9	3	1	24	47	23.50	–	–	–
A. Kumble	7	5	2	35*	63	21.00	–	–	1
N.D. Hirwani	9	5	3	15*	17	8.50	–	–	3

Bowling	O	M	R	W	Avge	Best	5wI	10wM
N.D. Hirwani	399.2	59	1280	31	41.29	5-117	1	–
A. Kumble	212	40	660	14	47.14	6-49	1	–
A.S. Wassan	207.3	24	886	18	49.22	6-89	1	–
Kapil Dev	246.4	59	744	13	57.23	2-28	–	–
S.L.V. Raju	182.3	41	528	9	58.66	4-73	–	–
M. Prabhakar	281	47	994	16	62.12	4-74	–	–
S.K. Sharma	229	36	873	13	67.15	2-53	–	–
R.J. Shastri	199.2	30	607	7	86.71	2-80	–	–

Also bowled: K.S. Moré 8-0-54-0; W.V. Raman 15-2-72-1; S.R. Tendulkar 79-12-268-3.

Results († One-Day Match)

† League Cricket Conference (Sunderland)	Won by 40 runs
Yorkshire (Headingley)	Drawn
Hampshire (Southampton)	Lost by 7 wickets
Kent (Canterbury)	Won by 7 wickets
Minor Counties (Trowbridge)	Drawn
† Scotland (Glasgow)	Won by 7 wickets
† Derbyshire (Derby)	Won by 2 wickets
† ENGLAND (Headingley)	Won by 6 wickets
† ENGLAND (Trent Bridge)	Won by 5 wickets
Leicestershire (Leicester)	Drawn
ENGLAND (Lord's)	Lost by 247 runs
Surrey (Foster's Oval)	Drawn
Gloucestershire (Bristol)	Drawn
ENGLAND (Old Trafford)	Drawn
TCCB Under-25 XI (Edgbaston)	Drawn
Glamorgan (Swansea)	Drawn
ENGLAND (Foster's Oval)	Drawn
Michael Parkinson's World XI (Scarborough)	Drawn

Hundreds (15)

4 – R.J. Shastri: 105 v Minor Counties (Trowbridge); 100 v England (First Test, Lord's); 133 v Glos (Bristol); 187 v England (Third Test, Foster's Oval).

3 – M. Azharuddin: 105 v Minor Counties (Trowbridge); 121 v England (First Test, Lord's); 179 v England (Second Test, Old Trafford).

2 – S.V. Manjrekar: 158* v Yorks (Headingley); 116 v TCCB Under-25 XI (Edgbaston).
    N.S. Sidhu: 142 v Glos (Bristol); 108* v TCCB Under-25 XI (Edgbaston).
    S.R. Tendulkar: 119* v England (Second Test, Old Trafford); 108 v M.H. Parkinson XI (Scarborough).

1 – Kapil Dev: 110 v England (Third Test, Foster's Oval).
    W.V. Raman: 127 v Surrey (Foster's Oval).

Sri Lanka in England

On a three-week tour of England at the end of the season, Sri Lanka were unbeaten in their six three-day matches against county sides, and lived up to their reputation as gifted stroke-players. But they lost their two limited-overs matches, to Surrey and Somerset.

Aravinda de Silva, fresh from his success in Australia and chosen as the *Daily Telegraph* Cricketer of the Year for Sri Lanka before they came to England (see p.31), demonstrated his fluent batting form at the county grounds. He scored more than 500 runs, and in the final match of the tour hit 221 not out against the Hampshire bowlers after Sri Lanka had followed on. He put on 263 for the fourth wicket with Hashan Tillekeratne (100).

Sri Lanka's sole victory, over Warwickshire, was their first against an English county – in 34 matches over five tours since 1979. Helped by an undefeated 109 from Tillekeratne, they declared at 327-4, 22 behind on first innings, and then swept Warwickshire out for 133. They reached their target of 156 with 8 wickets and 20 overs to spare.

First-Class Matches: Played 6; Won 1, Drawn 5
All Matches: Played 8; Won 1, Lost 2, Drawn 5

First-Class Averages

Batting and Fielding	M	I	NO	HS	R	Avge	100	50	Ct/St
P.A. De Silva	6	12	4	221*	563	70.37	1	3	10
M. Attapatu	6	8	4	74*	241	60.25	–	2	7
H.P. Tillekeratne	5	9	2	109*	349	49.85	2	–	7/2
R.S. Mahanama	6	10	0	114	494	49.40	2	2	10
S.T. Jayasuriya	6	9	2	105*	345	49.28	1	2	5
A.P. Gurusinha	3	6	3	58	138	46.00	–	1	–
U.C. Hathurasinghe	5	10	0	136	385	38.50	1	1	1
D.S.B.P. Kuruppu	5	10	1	56*	259	28.77	–	2	7/1
M.A.W. Madurasinghe	4	3	1	28*	43	21.50	–	–	1
G.F. Labrooy	4	6	0	69	121	20.16	–	1	1
P. Wickremasinghe	3	2	0	17	17	8.50	–	–	–

Also batted: C.P.H. Ramanayake (4 matches) 8*, 3*, 5*, 9*; K.I.W. Wijegunawardene (4 matches) 0 (6ct); P. Wijetunge (4 matches) 5* (2ct). F.S. Ahangama played in one match but did not bat.

Bowling	O	M	R	W	Avge	Best	5wI	10wM
A.P. Gurusinha	40	8	113	5	22.60	3-38	–	–
M.A.W. Madurasinghe	176.2	28	560	21	26.66	5-108	1	–
G.F. Labrooy	111	13	440	16	27.50	5-97	1	–
K.I.W. Wijegunawardene	87.3	13	318	9	35.33	2-30	–	–
P. Wijetunge	129.4	24	438	12	36.50	4-133	–	–
P. Wickremasinghe	79	17	251	6	41.83	3-95	–	–
C.P.H. Ramanayake	133	12	510	12	42.50	3-96	–	–

Also bowled: F.S. Ahangama 1.3-0-4-0; M. Attapatu 4-0-21-0; P.A. De Silva 25-3-81-2; U.C. Hathurasinghe 21.1-8-58-3; S.T. Jayasuriya 7-1-18-1.

Zimbabwe in England

As part of their preparation for the defence of the ICC Trophy in June, Zimbabwe made a two-week tour of England at the end of May, albeit without their captain and leading batsman David Houghton. They were comprehensively beaten by Essex and Sussex in limited-overs games, but drew their three three-day matches with other counties. They came close to victory against Gloucestershire. Ali Shah made 185 and then Traicos and Brandes got the county out for 206 after tea on the third day. Needing 106 to win, Zimbabwe ran out of time still requiring 17.

Zimbabwe Tour of England

First-Class Matches: Played 3; Drawn 3
All Matches: Played 5; Lost 2, Drawn 3

First-Class Averages

Batting and Fielding	M	I	NO	HS	R	Avge	100	50	Ct/St
A.H. Shah	3	3	0	185	215	71.66	1	–	–
J.P. Brent	2	4	2	34*	101	50.50	–	–	–
G. Bryant	2	3	0	69	109	36.33	–	1	1
C.M. Robertson	3	6	1	125	168	33.60	1	–	1
G.W. Flower	2	4	1	65	97	32.33	–	1	4
A.J. Pycroft	3	5	1	55	120	30.00	–	1	2
I.P. Butchart	3	5	1	71	115	28.75	–	1	–
W. James	3	6	1	52	143	28.60	–	1	4
E.A. Brandes	2	3	1	22	40	20.00	–	–	1
K.J. Arnott	1	2	0	2	2	1.00	–	–	–

Also batted: D.F. Dolphin (2 matches) 25; K.G. Duers (2 matches) 11*; E. Dube (2 matches) 1; M.P. Jarvis (1 match) 1*; A.J. Traicos (2 matches) 1 (5ct).

Bowling	O	M	R	W	Avge	Best	5wI	10wM
E.A. Brandes	49.2	12	165	7	23.57	4-35	–	–
A.H. Shah	75	19	193	5	38.60	2-46	–	–
A.J. Traicos	84	22	186	4	46.50	3-43	–	–
K.G. Duers	74	17	266	5	53.20	2-63	–	–

Also bowled: J.P. Brent 26-6-79-2; I.P. Butchart 41-7-156-2; D.F. Dolphin 39-10-134-1; E. Dube 25-4-107-0; G.W. Flower 29.5-4-101-3; M.P. Jarvis 30-7-101-2.

Pakistan U-19s in England

Engdand beat Pakistan 1-0 in a thrilling Under-19 series of 4-day 'Tests' sponsored by Bull Computers. After a draw at rain-hit Northampton, England won at Headingley thanks largely to Jeremy Hallett and Dominic Cork. They first shattered Pakistan's morale with a last-wicket stand of 79, and then bowled them out for 78. Cork, who took 8-91 in the match, was also the hero of the last 'Test'. Coming in as nightwatchman with England on 16-2 after following on, he stayed for more than five hours for 110 to earn a draw.

Cork's haul of 10 wickets in the 'Tests' at under 26 apiece was the best analysis of either side, and at 44.25 he was second to Crawley (257 runs at 64.25) in the England batting averages. Pakistan's captain and wicket-keeper Moin Khan averaged 57.66, but 16-year-old Zahid Fazal scored most runs for Pakistan (212 at 42.40) and chipped in with 2 wickets for 37 in short spells.

Pakistan drew the limited-overs series 1-1, and won their four other one-day games on tour. They were unbeaten in other games, winning four and drawing one.

England Under-19 team: W.M. Noon (capt, Northants), A.A.Barnett (Middx), K.A. Butler (Essex), D.G.Cork (Derbys), J.P. Crawley (Lancs), D.Gough (Yorks), P.A. Grayson (Yorks), J.C. Hallett (Somerset), P.C.L. Holloway (Warwicks), M. Keech (Middx), A.R. Roberts (Northants). Played in one-day internationals: R. Irani (Lancs), J.A. North (Sussex).

International Matches

18, 19(np), 20, 21 August at County Ground, Northampton. Match drawn. Toss: Pakistan PAKISTAN UNDER-19 298-8 dec (M. Jamshed 98, A. Rashid 76, N.A.Mughal 57) and 171-8 (Zahid Fazal 73). ENGLAND UNDER-19 352 (P.C.L. Holloway 96, J.P.Crawley 93; S. Hussain 4-66.

28, 29, 30 August at Headingley. ENGLAND UNDER-19 beat PAKISTAN UNDER-19 by 9 wickets. Toss: Pakistan. PAKISTAN UNDER-19 277 (Moin Khan 114*, Mohammad Shakeel 64; D. Gough 5-106, D.G. Cork 4-73) and 78 (J.C. Hallett 5-33, Cork 4-18). ENGLAND UNDER-19 325 (J.P. Crawley 84, J.C. Hallett 55*) and 34-1.

7, 8, 9, 10 September at County Ground, Taunton. Match drawn. Toss: Pakistan. PAKISTAN UNDER-19 561-5 dec (Shakeel Ahmed 190, Tariq Mehmood 106, Zahid Fazal 99, Mujahid Hussain 74, Moin Khan 52*). ENGLAND UNDER-19 364 (M. Keech 87) and 269-8 (D.G. Cork 110).

One-Day Internationals

8 August at Lord's. ENGLAND UNDER-19 beat PAKISTAN UNDER-19 by 76 runs. England Under-19 218-9 (55 overs) (K.A. Butler 77, W.M. Noon 51; Athar Laeeq 4-40). Pakistan Under-19 142 (42.2 overs) (D.G. Cork 4-24).

10 August at Foster's Oval. PAKISTAN UNDER-19 beat ENGLAND UNDER-19 by 23 runs. Pakistan Under-19 220-9 (55 overs) (Naseer Ahmed 77). England Under-19 197 (52.4 overs) (P.C.L. Holloway 60; Athar Laeeq 4-33).

1990
REST OF ENGLISH SEASON

First-Class Averages 1990

Batting (Qual: 8 inns, avge 10.00)	M	I	NO	HS	Runs	Avge	100s	50s
G.A. Gooch	18	30	3	333	2746	101.70	12	8
G.A. Hick	21	35	9	252*	2347	90.26	8	14
T.M. Moody	9	15	2	168	1163	89.46	7	1
A.N. Aymes	5	8	4	75*	317	79.25	–	3
M. Azharuddin	9	11	1	179	770	77.00	3	3
D.M. Ward	24	34	7	263	2072	76.74	7	3
M.E. Waugh	22	33	6	207*	2072	76.74	8	8
S.J. Cook	24	41	7	313*	2608	76.70	9	11
B.R. Hardie	12	17	7	125	728	72.80	2	4
M.A. Atherton	20	31	4	191	1924	71.25	7	12
P.A. De Silva	6	12	4	221*	563	70.37	1	3
N.H. Fairbrother	22	32	7	366	1740	69.60	4	9
D.J. Bicknell	15	23	4	186	1317	69.31	5	6
M.A. Crawley	11	14	3	105*	762	69.27	2	5
D.L. Haynes	23	39	5	255*	2346	69.00	8	7
R.A. Smith	18	30	8	181	1454	66.09	6	7
R.J. Shastri	9	11	1	187	644	64.40	4	1
R.J. Bailey	23	39	8	204*	1987	64.09	7	9
A.J. Lamb	17	29	4	235	1596	63.84	6	5
S.R. Tendulkar	11	19	4	119*	945	63.00	2	6
I.V.A. Richards	18	28	5	164*	1425	61.95	7	3
N.R. Taylor	22	37	5	204	1979	61.84	7	10
C.L. Smith	22	38	7	148	1886	60.83	4	12
R.J. Harden	24	31	7	104*	1460	60.83	3	12
M. Attapatu	6	8	4	74*	241	60.25	–	2
A.R. Butcher	23	41	5	151*	2116	58.77	6	15
C.J. Tavaré	24	32	4	219	1638	58.50	3	12
S.V. Manjrekar	11	17	3	158*	814	58.14	2	6
A.N. Hayhurst	22	35	8	170	1559	57.74	4	8
D.B. Vengsarkar	10	14	4	83*	576	57.60	–	6
M.J. Greatbatch	11	16	3	168*	744	57.23	2	4
J.P. Stephenson	25	41	8	202*	1887	57.18	4	13
M.W. Gatting	23	37	7	170*	1704	56.80	4	9
T.S. Curtis	22	39	8	197*	1731	55.83	4	7
G.D. Rose	24	29	11	97*	1000	55.55	–	8
H. Morris	25	46	5	160*	2276	55.51	10	10
I.A. Greig	24	29	6	291	1259	54.73	2	5
D.A. Reeve	25	38	12	202*	1412	54.30	3	5
B.C. Broad	22	43	2	227*	2226	54.29	9	3
J.E. Morris	21	33	6	157*	1459	54.03	6	6
K.R. Brown	24	36	8	200*	1505	53.75	5	8
M.D. Crowe	9	13	3	123*	537	53.70	1	5
G.D. Mendis	21	35	6	180	1551	53.48	4	8
A.H. Jones	10	16	3	121*	692	53.23	1	5
C.W.J. Athey	23	35	7	131	1474	52.64	3	9
R.I. Alikhan	11	16	2	138	726	51.85	2	4
W.M. ven der Merve	8	9	3	84	310	51.66	–	3
A.A. Metcalfe	23	44	4	194*	2047	51.17	6	7

England captain Graham Gooch displays the Cornhill Insurance trophy after the successful series against India. It was a season of triumph for Gooch, sandwiched between two broken fingers. He led England to victory against both touring sides, New Zealand and India. His personal achievements included leading the first class averages and runs scored – 2,746 at 101.70 – scoring 1,058 Test runs – the most in an English season – and hitting 333 against the Indians at Lord's – the sixth highest Test score ever.

England's depleted and inexperienced touring side to the West Indies were given little hope of avoiding another whitewash. In the event they shocked their opponents and the rest of the cricketing world by winning the first Test, and but for injuries to Gooch and Fraser might well have won or at least drawn the series.

LEFT: Devon Malcolm, whose 19 wickets in the series included 10 in the third Test, which West Indies saved only by some blatant time wasting.

BELOW: Allan Lamb on the way to his match-winning hundred in the first Test. Lamb was the leading scorer of either side, with 390 runs, and topped the Test averages with 55.71.

ABOVE: West Indies captain Desmond
Haynes – criticized for his dubious
tactics in the third Test – hits out at
Bridgetown in the fourth Test, in which
his return-to-form hundred shored up
the second innings. He went on to make
another century in the last Test and
clinch the series victory.

RIGHT: Curtly Ambrose celebrates the
downfall of Hussain at Bridgetown, one
of his six lbw victims in the match. His
8-45 in the second innings was the
turning point in the series.

Touring first, the New Zealanders were unlucky with the weather, and the first two Tests were inconclusive. England's bright summer began at Edgbaston when they won the third Test and with it the series.

RIGHT: Mike Atherton drives confidently at Trent Bridge in the first Test, on the way to 151, his first Test hundred. He grew in stature as the season progressed.

BELOW: Eddie Hemmings, 41, bowling at Edgbaston, where his 6-58 in the first innings proved a match-winning effort.

RIGHT: The Hadlee appeal, a familiar sight on cricket grounds all over the world, was last seen in the Test arena at Edgbaston. Knighted during the series, Sir Richard took his record Test haul to 431 wickets and topped the New Zealand averages with 16 at 24 apiece before retiring from the game.

The England-India Tests provided a feast of runs before England finally won the series 1-0.

RIGHT: Gooch in majestic action during his monumental 333 at Lord's in the first Test.

LEFT: Angus Fraser, also in action at Lord's, where his match haul of 8-143 helped England bowl India out twice and win by 247 runs.

RIGHT: At last there's a triumphant smile on David Gower's face, as he reaches a hundred at the Oval in the third Test. His innings of 157 not out made England safe after they had followed on. It also booked him a place on the plane to Australia.

BELOW: India captain Mohammad Azharuddin batting at Lord's, where his decision to put England in had the critics scoffing – but his magnificent hundred in 88 balls had them purring.

ABOVE: Worcestershire's last faint hope of saving the Benson & Hedges final is snuffed out as Lancashire's Philip DeFreitas bowls Ian Botham for an obdurate 38.

LEFT: Twenty years after his first winning final at Lord's, Lancashire captain David Hughes (left) holds the B & H trophy with all-rounder Mike Watkinson, who scored the only fifty of the match and took 2-37 to win the Gold Award.

RIGHT: In the NatWest Trophy final, Neil Fairbrother hit two 6's and nine 4's in a whirlwind 81 to put Lancashire on the way to their second one-day triumph.

BELOW: David Hughes clutches another trophy, with Man of the Match DeFreitas, whose 5-26 destroyed Northants.

ABOVE: Derbyshire won the Refuge Assurance League for the first time, although they lost the Cup final to Middlesex. The Derby squad for the final was: *Standing* (l-r): Simon Base, Bruce Roberts, Chris Adams, Tim O'Gorman, Martin Jean-Jacques, Adrian Kuiper, Steve Goldsmith. *Seated* (l-r): Devon Malcom, Geoff Miller, John Morris, Kim Barnett (capt.), Ole Mortensen, Peter Bowler.

LEFT: It was a summer of toil for bowlers and scorers, as the Oval scoreboard indicates – Lancashire's 863 in reply to Surrey's 707 was the highest total this century in a County Championship match.

RIGHT: Simon Hughes traps Bunting lbw and signals an innings win for Middlesex at Hove that gives them the Championship and consigns Sussex to bottom spot. Middlesex, with three wins in their last four matches, held off a late surge from Essex to win their 6th title in 15 years.

BELOW: Britannic Assurance County Champions Middlesex. *Back row* (l-r): P. Farbrace, M.A. Roseberry, J.C. Pooley, P.N. Weekes, K.R. Brown, A. Habib. *Middle row* (l-r): H. Sharp (scorer), D. Bennett (coach), M. Keetch, J.D. Carr, A.A. Barnett, J.R. Hemstock, I.J. Hutchinson, P.W.R. Tufnell, M.R. Ramprakash, J. Davis (physio), C.T. Radley (asst. coach), A. Jones (2nd XI scorer). *Front row* (l-r): S.P. Hughes, N.G. Cowans, P.R. Downton, J.E. Emburey, M.W. Gatting (capt.), R.O. Butcher, N.F. Williams, D.L. Haynes. *Inset:* A.R.C. Fraser.

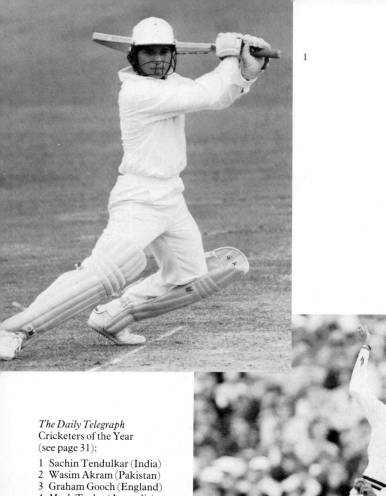

The Daily Telegraph
Cricketers of the Year
(see page 31):

1 Sachin Tendulkar (India)
2 Wasim Akram (Pakistan)
3 Graham Gooch (England)
4 Mark Taylor (Australia)
5 Adrian Kuiper (South Africa)
6 Curtly Ambrose (West Indies)
7 John Wright (New Zealand)
8 Arevinda de Silva (Sri Lanka)

3

4

5

6

7

8

England lost some much-loved old
cricketers during the year. (See
Obituary.)

ABOVE LEFT: Wicket-keeper
batsman Les Ames (Kent and
England).

ABOVE RIGHT: Sir George 'Gubby'
Allen (Middlesex and England), all-
rounder and leading administrator.

RIGHT: Cavalier batsman Colin
Milburn (Northants and England).

Another two England cricketers who died during the year were batsmen Sir Len Hutton (Yorkshire) and Joe Hardstaff Jr (Notts). They are pictured here in the famous Oval Test of 1938 as Hardstaff (right) congratulates his partner Hutton (centre) on passing the Test record of 334 set by the third man in the picture, Australia's Don Bradman.

ABOVE: In a season in which his mature performances established his position as opener for England and Lancashire, Mike Atherton receives the Young Cricketer of the Year award from Robin Marlar. BELOW: Two young cricketers who finished the season with high hopes when they were selected as the only uncapped players to tour Australia: spinner Phil Tufnell (left) of Middlesex and fast bowler Martin Bicknell (right) of Surrey.

Batting (contd)	M	I	NO	HS	Runs	Avge	100s	50s
K.M. Curran	23	33	8	144*	1267	50.68	3	5
J.G. Wright	9	15	2	121	653	50.23	1	5
K.J. Barnett	24	39	6	141	1648	49.93	5	9
N.E. Briers	24	44	4	176	1966	49.90	5	11
H.P. Tillekeratne	5	9	2	109*	349	49.85	2	–
R.S. Mahanama	6	10	0	114	494	49.40	2	2
P.M. Roebuck	18	28	5	201*	1134	49.30	2	6
S.T. Jayasuriya	6	9	2	105*	345	49.28	1	2
M.R. Benson	16	25	1	159	1171	48.79	5	5
A.J. Moles	24	46	8	224*	1854	48.78	4	10
P.J. Prichard	22	32	3	245	1407	48.51	5	4
M.R. Ramprakash	24	42	10	146*	1541	48.15	5	6
M.D. Moxon	22	40	6	218*	1633	48.02	3	7
W.V. Raman	8	15	2	127	623	47.92	1	7
G.R. Cowdrey	22	39	6	135	1576	47.75	3	8
T.C. Middleton	18	29	3	127	1238	47.61	5	5
D.J. Capel	18	29	6	123	1092	47.47	3	7
K.R. Rutherford	8	13	5	68*	376	47.00	–	1
P.W.G. Parker	15	25	4	107	985	46.90	2	6
D.I. Gower	20	32	5	157*	1263	46.77	3	3
G.R. Dilley	10	8	4	45*	185	46.25	–	–
G.S. Clinton	20	32	4	146	1292	46.14	1	8
K.P. Evans	15	25	9	100*	738	46.12	1	4
J.R. Ayling	9	11	3	62*	368	46.00	–	3
M.D. Marshall	18	24	3	117	962	45.80	2	6
T.J. Franklin	11	17	1	103	731	45.68	2	5
N.S. Sidhu	9	17	3	142	639	45.64	2	4
N. Shahid	19	29	7	125	1003	45.59	1	6
G.J. Lord	13	24	2	190	1003	45.59	3	5
M.A. Lynch	24	32	5	104	1227	45.44	1	9
N.J. Speak	6	9	0	138	409	45.44	1	3
J.J. Whitaker	24	45	6	124*	1767	45.30	4	8
R.E. Morris	9	12	1	96	498	45.27	–	6
J.J. Crowe	8	15	4	132	493	44.81	1	2
S.J. Rhodes	22	25	10	96	672	44.80	–	5
R.D.B. Croft	16	26	11	91*	672	44.80	–	4
P.A. Neale	21	32	10	122	976	44.36	2	3
P. Bainbridge	20	28	3	152	1107	44.28	2	5
G.D. Lloyd	14	20	2	96	796	44.22	–	8
A. Fordham	24	42	2	206*	1767	44.17	4	9
M.P. Maynard	23	41	7	125*	1501	44.14	2	11
M.J. Kilborn	6	8	1	95	309	44.14	–	2
P.E. Robinson	23	39	7	150*	1402	43.81	1	12
R.T. Robinson	23	45	5	220*	1747	43.67	4	8
T.E. Jesty	17	24	6	98	785	43.61	–	7
A.P. Wells	24	44	7	144*	1611	43.54	4	7
M.W. Priest	9	11	3	72	345	43.12	–	3
A.J. Stewart	17	29	6	100*	984	42.78	1	9
G.C. Holmes	10	15	4	125*	465	42.27	1	2
W.K. Hegg	21	22	6	100*	674	42.12	1	3
P.D. Bowler	22	39	5	210	1428	42.00	3	7
V.P. Terry	22	35	3	165	1332	41.62	5	4

Batting (contd)	M	I	NO	HS	Runs	Avge	100s	50s
N.J. Lenham	22	41	1	123	1663	41.57	4	9
N.A. Felton	22	39	2	122	1538	41.56	4	9
A.M. Brown	8	12	2	139*	413	41.30	1	1
N.G. Cowley	14	17	4	76	536	41.23	–	6
I. Smith	7	10	2	112*	328	41.00	1	2
C.S. Cowdrey	13	24	6	107*	733	40.72	3	2
T.J.E. O'Gorman	7	12	1	100	448	40.72	1	4
M.W. Alleyne	13	21	0	256	854	40.66	2	3
M.P. Speight	23	41	7	131	1375	40.44	2	11
M.A. Roseberry	24	44	4	135	1593	39.82	3	11
K. Sharp	9	13	5	53*	318	39.75	–	1
N.D. Burns	24	34	10	166	951	39.62	1	5
R.M. Ellison	15	19	7	81	473	39.41	–	3
G. Miller	14	14	8	47*	233	38.83	–	–
P.A.J. DeFreitas	18	20	3	102	660	38.82	2	2
M.P. Bicknell	21	16	8	50*	310	38.75	–	1
U.C. Hathurasinghe	5	10	0	136	385	38.50	1	1
M.R. Mongia	8	11	4	63*	269	38.42	–	2
D.B. D'Oliveira	23	35	2	155	1263	38.27	2	7
J.W. Lloyds	24	34	12	93	839	38.13	–	4
P. Johnson	23	43	3	165*	1518	37.95	3	9
R.C. Russell	17	23	2	120	794	37.80	2	3
Kapil Dev	9	12	2	110	377	37.70	1	2
M.V. Fleming	19	32	6	102	980	37.69	1	5
N. Hussain	16	23	3	197	752	37.60	1	2
T.J. Boon	24	45	4	138	1539	37.53	2	11
S.G. Hinks	24	43	0	234	1588	36.93	4	6
G.D. Hodgson	24	40	4	126	1320	36.66	2	10
D.W. Randall	15	28	1	178	987	36.55	2	5
P.A. Grayson	5	8	4	44*	145	36.25	–	–
M. Watkinson	19	23	2	138	754	35.90	1	4
M.C.J. Nicholas	23	35	10	104	895	35.80	1	5
B. Roberts	24	38	7	124*	1108	35.74	2	4
P.J. Newport	21	18	6	98	424	35.33	–	3
I.T. Botham	13	18	1	113	595	35.00	1	4
G.W. Humpage	13	22	4	74	628	34.88	–	5
J.D.R. Benson	18	27	6	106	725	34.52	1	3
S.P. James	16	31	2	131*	1000	34.48	4	5
I.P. Butcher	12	19	4	102	513	34.20	1	2
C.S. Pickles	16	22	8	57*	478	34.14	–	3
D.R. Pringle	17	15	2	84	443	34.07	–	3
M. Newell	15	27	2	112	851	34.04	1	6
P. Willey	22	40	6	177	1150	33.82	2	5
J.G. Bracewell	8	8	3	40*	169	33.80	–	–
S.A. Marsh	24	35	8	114*	911	33.74	1	5
W.K.M. Benjamin	12	15	2	101*	437	33.61	1	4
A.I.C. Dodemaide	24	38	8	112	1001	33.36	2	4
P.A. Cottey	20	35	5	156	1001	33.36	3	4
C.M. Wells	20	33	5	113*	933	33.32	2	4
R.K. Illingworth	23	22	6	117	532	33.25	1	3
C.C. Lewis	17	26	5	189*	697	33.19	1	2
R.C.J. Williams	8	8	4	50*	132	33.00	–	1

Batting (contd)	M	I	NO	HS	Runs	Avge	100s	50s
J.J.E. Hardy	9	16	5	91	361	32.81	–	1
P.W. Romaines	7	11	2	95	295	32.77	–	2
K.S. Moré	9	11	2	95	295	32.77	–	2
L. Potter	23	38	5	109*	1080	32.72	1	7
J.W. Hall	20	37	2	125	1140	32.57	2	5
P.A. Smith	12	20	4	117	520	32.50	1	3
G. Fowler	21	35	6	126	938	32.34	2	2
T.R. Ward	15	28	1	175	863	31.96	2	5
A.L. Penberthy	12	17	3	101*	435	31.07	1	3
C.J. Adams	23	34	4	111*	932	31.06	2	5
S.A. Kellett	16	28	3	75*	774	30.96	–	6
N.M.K. Smith	10	14	2	83*	370	30.83	–	1
P.N. Hepworth	4	8	2	55*	185	30.83	–	1
I.D. Austin	13	15	6	58	276	30.66	–	1
P.D. Lunn	8	10	4	49*	184	30.66	–	–
M. Saxelby	8	15	4	73	335	30.45	–	2
R.J. Blakey	25	43	9	111	1033	30.38	1	6
B.T.P. Donelan	11	13	6	53	211	30.14	–	1
D.J.R. Martindale	17	28	3	138	751	30.04	2	2
D.P. Ostler	11	19	2	71	510	30.00	–	5
D. Ripley	21	28	6	109*	656	29.81	1	2
M.A. Garnham	24	28	7	84*	615	29.28	–	2
M.A. Feltham	15	16	3	101	379	29.15	1	2
R.J. Maru	25	20	2	59	520	28.88	–	3
P. Bent	7	12	0	79	346	28.83	–	2
F.D. Stephenson	20	35	7	121	807	28.82	1	4
D.S.B.P. Kuruppu	5	10	1	56*	259	28.77	–	2
D. Byas	19	29	4	83	704	28.16	–	5
J.E. Emburey	23	32	7	111*	702	28.08	1	2
W. Larkins	15	25	0	207	701	28.04	2	2
Waqar Younis	14	9	7	14	56	28.00	–	–
J.D. Ratcliffe	16	31	3	81*	780	27.85	–	3
Asif Din	22	39	4	100*	974	27.82	1	5
I.R. Bishop	13	16	4	103*	333	27.75	1	–
G.P. Thorpe	18	28	6	86	608	27.63	–	3
P.A. Nixon	19	23	8	46	411	27.40	–	–
C.A. Walsh	20	20	3	63*	464	27.29	–	3
R.G. Williams	17	26	5	96	566	26.95	–	4
M. Prabhakar	10	14	3	76	296	26.90	–	2
J.E. Benjamin	15	14	7	41	188	26.85	–	–
R.G. Twose	6	10	1	64*	241	26.77	–	3
P.R. Downton	16	24	2	63	587	26.68	–	4
N.A. Foster	22	22	2	101	530	26.50	1	2
G. Cook	9	12	1	87	287	26.09	–	1
A.J. Wright	23	38	3	112	911	26.02	1	5
P. Carrick	18	22	2	64	515	25.75	–	3
K.T. Medlycott	23	25	9	44	410	25.62	–	–
N.A. Mallender	20	10	3	87*	177	25.28	–	1
D.M. Smith	9	16	2	71	353	25.21	–	2
A.N. Jones	22	9	5	41	100	25.00	–	–
T.A. Lloyd	15	27	1	101	646	24.84	1	4
G.J. Turner	9	12	0	59	298	24.83	–	2

Batting (contd)	M	I	NO	HS	Runs	Avge	100s	50s
C.A. Connor	22	10	4	46	148	24.66	–	–
A.I. Kallicharran	7	10	1	72	221	24.55	–	2
I.D.K. Salisbury	20	23	10	68	313	24.07	–	1
A.P. Kuiper	12	17	0	68	407	23.94	–	2
D.P. Hughes	18	17	7	57	237	23.70	–	1
I.J. Gould	8	12	2	73	235	23.50	–	2
V.J. Wells	8	15	0	58	352	23.46	–	2
S.M. McEwan	15	12	5	54	164	23.42	–	1
K.J. Piper	16	21	1	111	461	23.05	1	1
M.J. Lowrey	10	18	2	72	363	22.68	–	2
E.E. Hemmings	17	20	5	83	333	22.20	–	2
R. Heap	10	19	2	63	376	22.11	–	2
P.S. De Villiers	12	15	3	37	264	22.00	–	–
P.C.R. Tufnell	23	22	9	37	283	21.76	–	–
P. Moores	25	36	4	106*	694	21.68	1	2
N.F. Williams	21	24	3	55*	448	21.33	–	2
P. Pollard	7	13	0	72	277	21.30	–	1
P. Farbrace	8	8	2	79	124	20.66	–	1
M.J. Cann	6	10	0	64	206	20.60	–	2
R.A. Pick	17	16	6	35	204	20.40	–	–
B.N. French	22	34	9	105*	506	20.24	1	–
D.H. Shufflebotham	8	9	3	29	121	20.16	–	–
J.C.M. Atkinson	11	21	2	72	374	19.68	–	2
R.J. Parks	20	21	10	36*	216	19.63	–	–
S.J. Base	13	13	2	58	215	19.54	–	2
A.R.C. Fraser	15	13	2	97	214	19.45	–	1
P.-J. Bakker	16	9	4	20	95	19.00	–	–
R.J. Turner	9	16	0	38	302	18.87	–	–
A.C.S. Pigott	21	29	5	64*	451	18.79	–	4
S.R. Lampitt	23	24	5	45*	356	18.73	–	–
I.G. Swallow	23	17	7	32	187	18.70	–	–
K.M. Krikken	22	29	2	77*	488	18.07	–	2
R.J. Scott	6	10	2	71	144	18.00	–	1
G.B.A. Dyer	4	8	2	23	107	17.83	–	–
P.W. Jarvis	15	16	4	43*	212	17.66	–	–
J.D. Robinson	8	10	0	72	175	17.50	–	1
R.P. Davis	24	32	3	59	504	17.37	–	2
P.A. Booth	10	16	2	60	240	17.14	–	2
N.V. Radford	12	8	1	43*	118	16.85	–	–
S.C. Goldsmith	12	17	1	51	267	16.68	–	1
J.D. Fitton	15	13	5	25*	133	16.62	–	–
R.P. Lefebvre	17	16	3	53	214	16.46	–	1
G.C. Small	15	22	4	55	296	16.44	–	1
A. Dale	9	14	0	92	229	16.35	–	1
M.P. Metson	23	27	5	50	352	16.00	–	1
H.A.G. Anthony	6	8	0	39	127	15.87	–	–
C.E.L. Ambrose	15	18	5	55*	203	15.61	–	1
P.J. Hartley	17	15	1	75	218	15.57	–	1
N.M. Kendrick	13	12	4	52*	124	15.50	–	1
M.C. Ilott	9	10	2	42*	123	15.37	–	–
J.G. Thomas	12	13	3	48	152	15.20	–	–
M.M. Patel	9	12	5	41*	104	14.85	–	–

Batting (contd)

	M	I	NO	HS	Runs	Avge	100s	50s
M.J. Morris	10	17	3	45	206	14.71	–	–
D.A. Hagan	9	12	0	47	175	14.58	–	–
A.R.K. Pierson	11	9	5	16*	57	14.25	–	–
C. White	10	11	2	38	127	14.11	–	–
M. Jean-Jacques	12	13	5	25	107	13.37	–	–
S.J.W. Andrew	18	16	7	35	119	13.22	–	–
A.P. Igglesden	14	17	9	24	105	13.12	–	–
N.G.B. Cook	19	19	8	30	143	13.00	–	–
N.G. Cowans	18	17	7	46*	127	12.70	–	–
D.J.M. Kelleher	5	8	0	44	101	12.62	–	–
Wasim Akram	8	11	0	32	135	12.27	–	–
J.P. Agnew	22	26	5	46*	257	12.23	–	–
D.A. Graveney	13	13	4	46*	107	11.88	–	–
K.E. Cooper	21	26	6	35*	227	11.35	–	–
P.S. Gerrans	9	9	0	39	102	11.33	–	–
G.J. Parsons	10	13	3	20	112	11.20	–	–
J.H. Childs	23	16	5	26	123	11.18	–	–
D. Gough	14	17	6	24	123	11.18	–	–
T.A. Merrick	7	8	2	35	66	11.00	–	–
S.L. Watkin	24	25	8	25*	187	11.00	–	–
R.A. Bunting	15	13	5	24*	85	10.62	–	–
M.J. Weston	6	10	1	38*	90	10.00	–	–
O.H. Mortensen	12	11	9	5*	20	10.00	–	–

Bowling

(Qual: 10 wkts in 10 inns)	O	M	R	W	Avge	Best	5wI	10wM
I.R. Bishop	407.3	92	1124	59	19.05	6-71	3	–
M.D. Marshall	554.2	141	1381	72	19.18	7-47	4	2
D.J. Millns	206.4	36	662	31	21.35	6-63	2	–
O.H. Mortensen	316.2	91	785	35	22.42	4-22	–	–
C.E.L. Ambrose	503.4	127	1413	61	23.16	7-89	5	1
Waqar Younis	423	70	1357	57	23.80	7-73	3	1
M.W. Alleyne	112	29	391	16	24.43	3-23	–	–
P.A. Smith	148.5	34	497	20	24.85	5-48	1	–
N.A. Foster	819.2	175	2502	94	26.61	6-32	6	1
A.R.C. Fraser	596	144	1533	57	26.89	6-30	4	–
M.P. Bicknell	671.1	157	1827	67	27.26	5-34	1	–
G.J. Parsons	304.5	77	963	35	27.51	6-75	2	–
M.C. Snedden	231.5	56	633	23	27.52	5-63	1	–
J.E. Benjamin	388.3	68	1205	43	28.02	5-29	4	–
C.A. Walsh	611.1	107	2022	72	28.08	8-58	3	1
R.K. Illingworth	875.5	280	2122	75	28.29	5-59	1	–
D.J. Capel	234	51	711	25	28.44	5-74	1	–
D.A. Reeve	377.4	110	940	33	28.48	4-42	–	–
T.A. Merrick	184.3	45	488	17	28.70	4-66	–	–
M.A. Feltham	349.4	61	1150	40	28.75	6-53	2	–
T.A. Munton	829.1	199	2254	78	28.89	5-33	2	–
K.J. Barnett	293.3	55	757	26	29.11	4-28	–	–
D.R. Pringle	358.3	90	994	34	29.23	5-66	1	–
I.T. Botham	194.4	38	614	21	29.23	4-65	–	–
N.F. Williams	530.1	98	1618	54	29.96	7-61	2	–

Bowling (contd)	O	M	R	W	Avge	Best	5wI	10wM
C.C. Lewis	536.2	102	1697	56	30.30	6-55	2	1
S. Bastien	317.1	57	1187	39	30.43	6-75	2	–
K.M. Curran	598.3	111	1961	64	30.64	5-63	1	–
W.K.M. Benjamin	284.3	63	858	28	30.64	5-73	2	–
M.A. Atherton	433.3	103	1398	45	31.06	6-78	3	–
N.A. Mallender	544.2	116	1585	51	31.07	5-46	2	–
S.M. McEwan	375.2	75	1189	38	31.28	3-31	–	–
P.J. Newport	626.2	117	2001	63	31.76	6-54	4	–
N.G. Cowans	460	124	1247	39	31.97	5-67	1	–
J.E. Emburey	942.3	272	1957	61	32.08	5-32	2	–
G.A. Hick	208.5	41	645	20	32.25	5-37	1	–
T.D. Topley	223	53	713	22	32.40	4-67	–	–
D.E. Malcolm	518.2	99	1688	52	32.46	5-46	2	–
R.A. Pick	494.5	83	1657	51	32.49	7-128	1	1
S.R. Lampitt	565.3	98	1889	58	32.56	5-34	2	–
A.P. Kuiper	125.3	29	393	12	32.75	4-69	–	–
J.G. Bracewell	383.3	102	1120	34	32.94	7-120	2	1
M.C. Ilott	322.1	65	1036	31	33.41	5-34	2	–
M. Watkinson	508.2	122	1578	47	33.57	5-65	3	–
G.R. Dilley	224.2	30	818	24	34.08	5-62	2	–
N.G.B. Cook	527.1	167	1364	40	34.10	5-44	2	–
D.V. Lawrence	496.3	53	1979	58	34.12	5-51	2	–
P. Carrick	601	173	1570	46	34.13	5-49	3	–
P.J. Hartley	491	80	1781	52	34.25	6-57	2	–
M. Frost	557.1	74	2047	59	34.69	5-40	2	1
B.P. Patterson	282.4	45	1015	29	35.00	4-52	–	–
A.H. Gray	239.5	43	666	19	35.05	4-83	–	–
P.C.R. Tufnell	1046.5	281	2635	74	35.60	6-79	2	–
S.D. Fletcher	292.5	59	1035	29	35.68	5-94	1	–
P.M. Such	272.4	67	715	20	35.75	3-34	–	–
A.P. Igglesden	326	47	1150	32	35.93	4-79	–	–
A.L. Penberthy	207.4	29	791	22	35.95	4-91	–	–
P.A.J. DeFreitas	489.3	109	1440	40	36.00	6-39	2	–
E.E. Hemmings	688.2	197	1844	51	36.15	6-58	2	–
K.P. Evans	356	78	1232	34	36.23	4-50	–	–
R.J. Maru	852.1	219	2420	66	36.66	6-97	2	–
A.N. Jones	572.4	92	2055	56	36.69	6-75	2	–
G.D. Rose	571.4	99	1951	53	36.81	5-52	1	–
A.C.S. Pigott	541	94	1997	54	36.98	5-52	3	–
D. Gough	279.4	49	1037	28	37.03	4-68	–	–
G.C. Small	425.4	105	1190	32	37.18	6-94	2	–
J.P. Agnew	612	108	2196	59	37.22	5-54	5	–
G. Miller	461	114	1308	35	37.37	6-45	1	–
M.A. Crawley	224.5	38	750	20	37.50	6-92	1	–
A.A. Donald	391	89	1089	29	37.55	3-28	–	–
S.N. Barnes	207	45	602	16	37.62	4-51	–	–
P.W. Jarvis	405.2	68	1393	37	37.64	4-53	–	–
A.D. Mullally	487.2	117	1446	38	38.05	4-59	–	–
C.A. Connor	510.1	88	1791	47	38.10	5-96	1	–
D.P. Hughes	280.4	61	918	24	38.25	4-25	–	–
D.A. Graveney	485.4	137	1189	31	38.35	5-45	3	1

Bowling (contd)	O	M	R	W	Avge	Best	5wI	10wM
A.R.K. Pierson	302.4	55	965	25	38.60	5-101	1	–
R.G. Williams	432.3	119	1204	31	38.83	4-94	–	–
F.D. Stephenson	610.4	94	2098	54	38.85	6-84	2	–
P.-J. Bakker	436.2	90	1439	37	38.89	5-101	1	–
R.P. Davis	905.1	221	2844	73	38.95	6-40	5	1
S.P. Hughes	386.2	73	1287	33	39.00	5-101	1	–
K.T. Medlycott	748.5	170	2382	61	39.04	7-92	3	–
K.J. Shine	156.4	30	550	14	39.28	4-52	–	–
T.M. Tremlett	120.5	30	393	10	39.30	3-33	–	–
S.L. Watkin	796.1	137	2712	69	39.30	5-100	1	–
P.J. Martin	275.3	52	868	22	39.45	4-68	–	–
P.S. De Villiers	304.5	58	992	25	39.68	6-70	1	–
Wasim Akram	204	44	640	16	40.00	3-76	–	–
S.J. Base	414.3	68	1402	35	40.05	6-105	2	–
G.J.F. Ferris	138.2	29	482	12	40.16	4-44	–	–
A.I.C. Dodemaide	763.1	130	2457	61	40.27	6-106	1	–
A.E. Warner	393.3	67	1330	33	40.30	3-56	–	–
J.G. Thomas	305.2	51	1171	29	40.37	7-75	1	–
P.J.W. Allott	266	77	730	18	40.55	4-23	–	–
K.E. Cooper	703.4	153	2203	54	40.79	5-56	3	–
S.D. Udal	233.3	46	900	22	40.90	4-139	–	–
S.J.W. Andrew	503	75	1897	46	41.23	5-55	1	–
N.D. Hirwani	399.2	59	1280	31	41.29	5-117	1	–
R.P. Lefebvre	506.1	137	1281	31	41.32	5-30	1	–
C.S. Pickles	325.1	72	1163	28	41.53	3-56	–	–
M.M. Patel	297.5	72	836	20	41.80	6-57	2	1
D.K. Morrison	234.4	36	889	21	42.33	4-64	–	–
M. Jean-Jacques	300	42	1106	25	44.24	6-60	1	–
A.J. Murphy	404.2	76	1367	30	45.56	5-67	2	–
J.A. Afford	688	209	1944	42	46.28	4-137	–	–
C. White	159	23	608	13	46.76	5-74	1	–
P. Bainbridge	162.4	30	515	11	46.81	3-23	–	–
A. Kumble	212	40	660	14	47.14	6-49	1	–
A.J. Buzza	287	47	1086	23	47.21	4-87	–	–
M.A. Robinson	559.1	104	1889	40	47.22	3-47	–	–
P. Willey	421.4	119	1091	23	47.43	2-7	–	–
R.D.B. Croft	397.1	83	1335	28	47.67	3-10	–	–
N.M. Kendrick	348	66	1194	25	47.76	4-110	–	–
M.J. Lowrey	151.2	33	483	10	48.30	2-13	–	–
S.J. Dennis	322	61	1071	22	48.68	5-76	1	–
M.V. Fleming	394.5	94	1072	22	48.72	3-65	–	–
P.A. Booth	250.5	75	636	13	48.92	4-55	–	–
A.S. Wassan	207.3	24	886	18	49.22	6-89	1	–
I.D.K. Salisbury	601.1	108	2075	42	49.40	5-32	2	–
B.T.P. Donelan	304.4	56	1000	20	50.00	3-79	–	–
R.A. Bunting	360	61	1314	26	50.53	2-26	–	–
R.M. Ellison	291.5	51	963	19	50.68	4-76	–	–
J.R. Ayling	171.2	46	572	11	52.00	2-48	–	–
P.S. Gerrans	208	40	695	13	53.46	3-86	–	–
R.J. Bailey	168.2	29	604	11	54.90	3-82	–	–
I.D. Austin	245	76	662	12	55.16	3-42	–	–

Bowling (contd)	O	M	R	W	Avge	Best	5wI	10wM
J.W. Lloyds	382.5	59	1429	25	57.16	4-11	–	–
Kapil Dev	246.4	59	744	13	57.23	2-28	–	–
C. Penn	186	35	636	11	57.81	3-45	–	–
J.H. Childs	655.5	212	1590	27	58.88	4-56	–	–
J.D. Batty	195	29	722	12	60.16	4-76	–	–
M. Prabhakar	281	47	994	16	62.12	4-74	–	–
W.W. Davis	237.5	28	812	13	62.46	3-28	–	–
R.A. Pyman	308.4	81	938	15	62.53	2-29	–	–
Asif Din	159.1	30	635	10	63.50	3-17	–	–
R.H.J. Jenkins	281.4	41	959	15	63.93	5-100	1	–
I.G. Swallow	689.1	161	2174	34	63.94	3-88	–	–
A.N. Hayhurst	321.2	50	1087	17	63.94	3-58	–	–
M.E. Waugh	191	33	771	12	64.25	5-37	1	–
M.W. Priest	312.4	90	907	14	64.78	3-35	–	–
I.A. Greig	216.1	21	858	13	66.00	3-60	–	–
N.V. Radford	302	49	1195	18	66.38	4-55	–	–
S.K. Sharma	229	36	873	13	67.15	2-53	–	–
C.M. Wells	374	68	1237	17	72.76	3-48	–	–
N.G. Cowley	316.3	64	900	12	75.00	3-84	–	–
G.J. Turner	212.2	39	819	10	81.90	3-100	–	–
J.D. Fitton	454.4	91	1447	14	103.35	3-69	–	–

The following bowlers took 10 wickets but bowled in fewer than 10 innings:

	O	M	R	W	Avge	Best	5wI	10wM
V.J. Wells	85	19	257	12	21.41	5-43	1	–
Sir Richard Hadlee	201.5	39	586	24	24.41	5-27	2	–
M.A.W. Madurasinghe	176.2	28	560	21	26.66	5-108	1	–
G.F. Labrooy	111	13	440	16	27.50	5-97	1	–
J.P. Millmow	105	14	391	11	35.54	3-66	–	–
P. Wijetunge	129.4	24	438	12	36.50	4-133	–	–
H.A.G. Anthony	132.4	32	466	12	38.83	3-95	–	–
C.P.H. Ramanayake	133	12	510	12	42.50	3-96	–	–
C. Pringle	149	32	483	10	48.30	2-49	–	–

Fielding Statistics (Qual: 20 dismissals)

68 S.J. Rhodes (60c, 8s)
63 K.M. Krikken (60c, 3s)
63 P.M. Moores (53c, 10s)
58 C.P. Metson
57 B.N. French (47c, 10s)
54 S.A. Marsh (49c, 5s)
54 R.J. Blakey (45c, 9s)
53 R.J. Parks (49c, 4s)
51 W.K. Hegg (49c, 2s)
50 P.A. Nixon (49c, 1s)
50 M.A. Garnham (48c, 2s)
47 R.C. Russell (46c, 1s)
45 P.R. Downton (42c, 3s)
44 N.D. Burns (43c, 1s)

43 K.J. Piper (39c, 4s)
35 D.M. Ward (32c, 3s)
34 D. Ripley (28c, 6s)
33 D.B. D'Oliveira
33 J.E. Emburey
31 R.C.J. Williams (27c, 4s)
30 K.R. Brown
30 G.W. Humpage
30 M.A. Lynch
30 R.J. Maru
27 R.P. Davis
26 G.A. Hick
26 D.A. Reeve
25 C.J. Adams

24 M.A. Atherton
24 A.J. Stewart
24 V.P. Terry
23 L. Potter
23 B. Roberts
23 M.A. Roseberry
23 A.J. Wright
22 A. Fordham
22 N. Shahid
21 D. Byas
20 N.H. Fairbrother
20 M.W. Gatting
20 P.E. Robinson

Benson & Hedges Cup

Lancashire won the Benson & Hedges Cup on a lovely day at Lord's in July, beating Worcestershire easily by 68 runs. Despite their many successes in the earlier days of limited-overs cricket, they had won this competition only once before, in 1984, compared with their four successes in the Gillette/NatWest tournaments and their three wins in the John Player/Refuge Assurance Sunday League.

Worcestershire had been dogged by injuries, and though they won the toss and put Lancashire in, there were few moments after Atherton and Watkinson began repairing a start of 47 for 3 when Lancashire did not look in control. Mike Watkinson made the only 50 of the match, and with his two early wickets was a worthy winner of the Gold Award. So would the ever more formidable all-rounder Wasim Akram have been.

Many will have been delighted by this latest success of the Lancashire captain David Hughes, who first played in a winning side in a Lord's final in 1970 and now, aged 43, handled Lancashire's affairs with a happy touch. He had a strong hand of bowlers on a pitch that would reward those who bowled straight.

The earlier rounds had had less than usual opposition from the weather, though the Combined Universities needed two days to beat Yorkshire. A match between Lancashire and Hampshire, which was badly affected by rain, kept the umpires busy interpreting the rule book. The first attempt was abandoned after Lancashire had made 352 for 6 and taken a Hampshire wicket. The second, scheduled for 18 overs a side, was being won for Hampshire by Chris Smith and David Gower when further rain produced the more equitable result of a draw.

Middlesex and Essex had looked the strongest opponents for Lancashire, but both were knocked out in the quarter-finals. Somerset, who had lost only narrowly to Middlesex in their group, now beat them at Taunton when Middlesex went rather too boldly about making 184. Essex were well beaten at Chelmsford by Nottinghamshire.

In the semi-final, Curtis, Weston, and Hick made 232 for 1 to beat Notts at Trent Bridge. But Lancashire's victory over Somerset at Old Trafford with 10 overs to spare left little doubt that they were again a major force in English limited-overs cricket – and perhaps more.

Zonal Results

Group A	P	W	L	NR	Pts
WORCESTERSHIRE	4	3	1	0	6
GLAMORGAN	4	3	1	0	6
Kent	4	2	1	1	5
Warwickshire	4	1	3	0	2
Gloucestershire	4	0	3	1	1

Group C	P	W	L	NR	Pts
LANCASHIRE	4	3	0	1	7
SURREY	4	2	2	0	4
Yorkshire	4	2	2	0	4
Hampshire	4	1	2	1	3
Combined Universities	4	1	3	0	2

Group B	P	W	L	NR	Pts
SOMERSET	4	3	1	0	6
MIDDLESEX	4	3	1	0	6
Sussex	4	2	2	0	4
Derbyshire	4	2	2	0	4
Minor Counties	4	0	4	0	0

Group D	P	W	L	NR	Pts
ESSEX	4	3	0	1	7
NOTTINGHAMSHIRE	4	3	1	0	6
Leicestershire	4	1	2	1	3
Scotland	4	1	3	0	2
Northamptonshire	4	1	3	0	2

Note: Where two or more teams have equal points, their positions are determined by runs per 100 balls (runs scored 100, divided by balls faced) in all zonal rounds. Winners of each match receive £750.

Final Rounds

Quarter-Finals 30 May	Semi-Finals 13 June	Final 14 July
Lancashire† Surrey (£3,000)	Lancashire†	
Somerset† Middlesex (£3,000)	Somerset (£6,000)	Lancashire
Nottinghamshire Essex † (£3,000)	Nottinghamshire† (£6,000)	LANCASHIRE (£24,000)
Glamorgan (£3,000) Worcestershire †	Worcestershire	Worcestershire (£12,000)

† Home team. Prize money in brackets.

Benson & Hedges Cup Winners

1972	Leicestershire	1979	Essex	1985	Leicestershire
1973	Kent	1980	Northamptonshire	1986	Middlesex
1974	Surrey	1981	Somerset	1987	Yorkshire
1975	Leicestershire	1982	Somerset	1988	Hampshire
1976	Kent	1983	Middlesex	1989	Nottinghamshire
1977	Gloucestershire	1984	Lancashire	1990	Lancashire
1978	Kent				

Lancashire v Worcestershire
1990 Benson & Hedges Cup Final

Lancashire won by 69 runs
Played at Lord's, 14 July
Toss: Worcestershire. Umpires: J.H. Hampshire and N.T. Plews
Gold Award Winner: M. Watkinson (Adjudicator: R.B. Simpson)

Lancashire		Runs	Mins	Balls	6	4
G.D. Mendis	c Neale b Botham	19	35	31	–	2
G. Fowler	c Neale b Newport	11	23	17	–	2
M.A. Atherton	run out (Lampitt)	40	124	105	–	1
N.H. Fairbrother	b Lampitt	11	25	19	–	2
M. Watkinson	c & b Botham	50	88	79	–	7
Wasim Akram	c Radford b Newport	28	32	21	2	1
P.A.J. DeFreitas	b Lampitt	28	35	30	–	2
I.D. Austin	run out (Rhodes)	17	19	12	–	2
W.K. Hegg†	not out	31	18	17	1	3
D.P. Hughes*	not out	1	3	2	–	–
P.J.W. Allott	did not bat					
Extras	(LB4, NB1)	5				
	(55 overs; 209 minutes)	**241-8**				

Worcestershire		Runs	Mins	Balls	6	4
T.S. Curtis	c Hegg b Akram	16	52	52	–	1
M.J. Weston	b Watkinson	19	76	43	–	2
G.A. Hick	c Hegg b Akram	1	17	12	–	–
D.B. D'Oliveira	b Watkinson	23	49	45	–	1
I.T. Botham	b DeFreitas	38	93	73	–	3
P.A. Neale*	c Hegg b Austin	0	4	5	–	–
S.J. Rhodes†	lbw b Allott	5	34	21	–	–
N.V. Radford	not out	26	56	40	–	1
R.K. Illingworth	lbw b DeFreitas	16	30	21	–	–
P.J. Newport	b Akram	3	10	12	–	–
S.R. Lampitt	b Austin	4	5	6	–	1
Extras	(LB9, W8, NB4)	21				
	(54 overs; 222 minutes)	**172**				

Worcestershire	O	M	R	W
Newport	11	1	47	2
Botham	11	0	49	2
Lampitt	11	3	43	2
Radford	8	1	41	0
Illingworth	11	0	41	0
Hick	3	0	16	0

Lancashire	O	M	R	W
Allott	10	1	22	1
DeFreitas	11	2	30	2
Wasim Akram	11	0	30	3
Watkinson	11	0	37	2
Austin	11	1	44	2

Fall of Wickets

Wkt	La	Wo
1st	25	27
2nd	33	37
3rd	47	41
4th	135	82
5th	136	87
6th	191	112
7th	199	114
8th	231	154
9th	–	164
10th	–	172

NatWest Bank Trophy

Judged by their unhindered progress through the four rounds leading to the final, in which they outclassed Northamptonshire, there was no question that Lancashire were outstanding in this competition. But there must be a great deal of sympathy for the runners-up, whose appearance in the final was a crumb of comfort in an otherwise disastrous season.

It was a depressingly poor final, 14 overs and two balls being left when Lancashire fulfilled their modest requirement of 172 runs. The issue truly was decided within the first hour, when Northants, put in, were 39 for five. Northants were virtually shoved out of contention when Allan Lamb lost the toss for the fifth time in the competition. It is no coincidence that the beaten side in the last five finals was the one batting first.

The disadvantage was the greater this time, for the pitch was palpably damp. DeFreitas used it remorselessly, and took five wickets in the eight overs of his first spell. Not only had he raised the prospect of a Lancashire win, but ensured for himself the Man of the Match award. Lancashire continued to enjoy the rub of the green, in that two Northants batsmen who promised a substantial revival, Ambrose and Capel, were both run out when non-strikers by the bowler deflecting the ball onto the stumps.

But Northants also brought ill luck on themselves later, in the field. They dislodged the redoubtable Lancashire openers, Mendis and Fowler, for only 28 runs, but then allowed two lives to the devastating Fairbrother while he was making the first six of his 81 runs, scored off only 68 balls.

Curiously, the one clash in the first round between two first-class counties featured the only two who have never reached the final – Hampshire and Leicestershire. It was a real humdinger, Hampshire winning by one run. Minor County opposition was swamped. The only one to achieve a margin at all respectable – 34 runs – was Dorset, against Glamorgan. This was despite Viv Richards scoring 118. Poor Devon took a fearful drubbing from Somerset's all-rounder Graham Rose, who hit seven sixes and ten fours in reaching his hundred off only 36 balls. Given such impetus, Somerset soared away to a monumental total of 413, which was the forerunner of the biggest margin of victory in limited-overs cricket – 346 runs.

The second round saw the exit of the holders, Warwickshire, comprehensively beaten by 10 wickets, at Headingley, by Yorkshire. Hampshire were again involved in a cliffhanger, against Essex, for whom Gooch made 144. The match finished with scores level at 307 and it was Hampshire's loss of five wickets to Essex's six that gained them entry into the quarter-finals.

At this stage, however, Hampshire, thanks to Malcolm Marshall, were spared the agony they had endured at Leicester and Chelmsford. He fairly savaged Yorkshire (4 for 17) when they replied to a score of 229. Much against form in the County Championship, Northants put out Worcestershire. It took a typical Botham spectacular, 86 off 80 balls, to narrow the margin to a mere four runs. Robinson was due credit for keeping a calm head in bowling the final over, from which Worcestershire needed nine runs.

Come the semi-finals, Hampshire were involved in another last-ball finish, against Northamptonshire, who would have won more comfortably had they not twice dropped Marshall, at 28 and 46, and Gower, just after he had passed his 50. Coming together at 55 for three in reply to Northants' 284, they put on 141 in 20 overs.

The other semi-final, at Old Trafford, was stretched by rain over three days. A two-hour break on the first was detrimental to Middlesex, in that Gatting got out immediately after the resumption. A superb 149 not out by Haynes gave Middlesex, who added 97 from their last 11 overs, a challenging total of 296, but they did not bowl well enough in its defence. Moreover, Mendis, who batted through the Lancashire innings for 121, was dropped at 15. Fairbrother and Watkinson imposed such authority that Lancashire were home with 4.1 overs to spare – very worthy finalists.

Gillette Cup Winners

1963	Sussex	1969	Yorkshire	1975	Lancashire
1964	Sussex	1970	Lancashire	1976	Northamptonshire
1965	Yorkshire	1971	Lancashire	1977	Middlesex
1966	Warwickshire	1972	Lancashire	1978	Sussex
1967	Kent	1973	Gloucestershire	1979	Somerset
1968	Warwickshire	1974	Kent	1980	Middlesex

NatWest Bank Trophy Winners

1981	Derbyshire	1985	Essex	1988	Middlesex
1982	Surrey	1986	Sussex	1989	Warwickshire
1983	Somerset	1987	Notts	1990	Lancashire
1984	Middlesex				

1990 Tournament

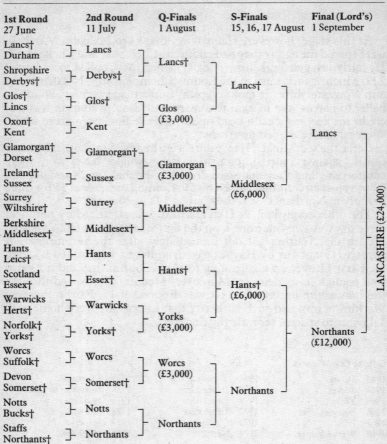

1st Round 27 June	2nd Round 11 July	Q-Finals 1 August	S-Finals 15, 16, 17 August	Final (Lord's) 1 September
Lancs† Durham	Lancs	Lancs†		
Shropshire Derbys†	Derbys†		Lancs†	
Glos† Lincs	Glos†	Glos (£3,000)		Lancs
Oxon† Kent	Kent			
Glamorgan† Dorset	Glamorgan†	Glamorgan (£3,000)		
Ireland† Sussex	Sussex		Middlesex (£6,000)	
Surrey Wiltshire†	Surrey	Middlesex†		
Berkshire Middlesex†	Middlesex†			
Hants Leics†	Hants	Hants†		
Scotland Essex†	Essex†		Hants† (£6,000)	
Warwicks Herts†	Warwicks	Yorks (£3,000)		Northants (£12,000)
Norfolk† Yorks†	Yorks†			
Worcs Suffolk†	Worcs	Worcs (£3,000)		
Devon Somerset†	Somerset†		Northants	
Notts Bucks†	Notts	Northants		
Staffs Northants†	Northants			

LANCASHIRE (£24,000)

†Home team.
Amounts in parentheses are prize money won by that county.

Lancashire v Northamptonshire, 1990 NatWest Bank Trophy Final

Lancashire won by 7 wickets
Played at Lord's, 1 September
Toss: Lancashire. Umpires: J.W. Holder and D.R. Shepherd
Man of the Match: P.A.J. DeFreitas (Adjudicator: F.S.Trueman)

Northamptonshire		Runs	Mins	Balls	6	4
A. Fordham	lbw b DeFreitas	5	24	15	–	1
N.A. Felton	c Allott b DeFreitas	4	6	4	–	1
W. Larkins	C. Hegg b DeFreitas	7	25	24	–	–
A.J. Lamb*	lbw b DeFreitas	8	33	17	–	1
R.J. Bailey	c Hegg b DeFreitas	7	17	15	–	1
D.J. Capel	run out (via Allott, bowler)	36	152	100	–	5
R.G. Williams	b Watkinson	9	22	14	–	2
D. Ripley†	b Watkinson	13	64	60	–	2
C.E.L. Ambrose	run out (via Akram, bowler)	48	90	94	–	5
N.G.B. Cook	b Austin	9	39	17	–	–
M.A. Robinson	not out	3	4	3	–	–
Extras	(B1, LB10, W9, NB2)	22				
	(60 overs; 247 minutes)	**171**				

Lancashire		Runs	Mins	Balls	6	4
G.D. Mendis	c Ripley b Capel	14	63	62	–	–
G. Fowler	c Cook b Robinson	7	36	26	–	–
M.A. Atherton	not out	38	133	103	–	5
N.H. Fairbrother	c Ambrose b Williams	81	89	68	2	9
M. Watkinson	not out	24	15	18	2	2
D.P. Hughes*	did not bat					
Wasim Akram	"					
P.A.J. DeFreitas	"					
W.K. Hegg†	"					
I.D. Austin	"					
P.J.W. Allott	"					
Extras	(LB4, W2, NB3)	9				
	(45.4 overs; 171 minutes)	**173-3**				

Lancashire	O	M	R	W
Allott	12	3	29	0
DeFreitas	12	5	26	5
Akram	12	0	35	0
Watkinson	12	1	29	2
Austin	12	4	41	1

Northamptonshire	O	M	R	W
Ambrose	10	1	23	0
Robinson	9	2	26	1
Cook	10.4	2	50	0
Capel	9	0	44	1
Williams	7	0	26	1

Fall of Wickets

Wkt	Nh	La
1st	8	16
2nd	19	28
3rd	20	142
4th	38	–
5th	39	–
6th	56	–
7th	87	–
8th	126	–
9th	166	–
10th	171	–

Refuge Assurance League & Cup

Until the last round of matches, played on a delightful, cloudless Sunday in August, the Refuge title could have gone to any one of three counties – Middlesex, who were irresistible in their early matches, Derbyshire, who also showed their potential from the initial stages, and Lancashire, who, after losing their opening fixture to none other than Middlesex, had a run of wins that was halted by the only abandoned match of that day, against Sussex, whom they would have been fancied to beat.

On the final day, Derbyshire were home to Essex, who, despite Graham Gooch's unstoppable flow of runs, had a poor season in terms of one-day cricket. But they could never be underestimated. Middlesex were away at Scarborough to Yorkshire, who had struck a rich vein of form after the halfway mark. Lancashire were at home to Warwickshire, lowly placed in the table, but quite capable of staging an upset.

The dice were loaded against Middlesex by a quirk of the weather – unusual for the golden summer of 1990 – which forced an abandonment of their match against their keen rivals, Derbyshire, on the penultimate Sunday. When rain struck decisively, Middlesex were handily placed to win a contest that had been reduced to a 14-overs slog.

Even their two-points lead at the top was a comfortable cushion for Derbyshire as the front-runners approached the grandstand. A final day of widespread rain would have sufficed for them. But in the light of simultaneous events at Old Trafford, Derbyshire had to beat Essex, who were without three of their stalwarts, Gooch, Pringle, and Foster.

Still, Derbyshire must have been apprehensive, for they had not won against Essex in any competition since 1982. But they laid the bogey all right, and that despite missing five chances, three of them grassed by Adrian Kuiper. But the South African atoned for these lapses as well as his profligacy as a bowler with a match-winning innings of 56 – reaching his 50 off only 31 balls. Kuiper turned the hopeless position of Derbyshire wanting 106 from the last 13 overs into a dramatic victory, achieved with three balls to spare.

Second-placed Lancashire did all they could have done on the final day to retain their title. They beat Warwickshire convincingly by 46 runs in a match of no batting heroics, but a worthy bowling performance from Mike Watkinson, who took five for 49. However, quite a while before Watkinson dealt the decisive blow, news had arrived of Derbyshire's triumph. It silenced a roaring, tumultuous crowd of 10,000.

Middlesex's challenge ended in galling anticlimax. Without Gatting, who had strained a hamstring, and Fraser and Williams, who were on Test duty, they were fairly routed by Yorkshire, who posed them with their record score of 271. Winning for the eighth time in their last 11 matches, Yorkshire, struggling to lift themselves off the bottom of the table at one stage, finished sixth. Conversely, Kent, who were at the top, or nearabouts, until the halfway mark, with only one loss in their first eight matches, never won again and finished 10th.

If Middlesex's strongest-ever bid for the Sunday title failed, they proved their potential over the 40-overs distance by winning the Refuge Assurance Cup, fought for by the league's top four teams. To do so, they beat the runners-up, Lancashire, quite comprehensively on their own heath, in the semi-finals, and the champions, Derbyshire, just as emphatically in the Edgbaston final.

Refuge Assurance Cup Semi-finals

5 September, Derby. DERBYSHIRE beat NOTTINGHAMSHIRE by 22 runs. Toss: Nottinghamshire. Derbyshire 255-4 (40 overs) (K.J. Barnett 83, A.P. Kuiper 74, P.D. Bowler 59). Nottinghamshire 233-8 (40 overs) (R.T. Robinson 96, K.P. Evans 55*). Award: R.T.Robinson (96 & 1ct).

5 September, Old Trafford. MIDDLESEX beat LANCASHIRE by 45 runs. Toss: Lancashire. Middlesex 272-6 (40 overs) (M.A. Roseberry 86, D.L. Haynes 72, K.R. Brown 48*). Lancashire 227-7 (40 overs) (G.D. Lloyd 65, N.H. Fairbrother 56; J.E. Emburey 8-1-39-4). Award: M.A. Roseberry (86).

Final

16 September, Edgbaston. MIDDLESEX beat DERBYSHIRE by 5 wickets. Toss: Middlesex. Derbyshire 197-7 (40 overs) (J.E. Morris 46, K.J. Barnett 42). Middlesex 201-5 (39.4 overs) (D.L. Haynes 49, M.W. Gatting 44, K.R. Brown 40). Award: P.R. Downton (34*).

Awards: Middlesex won £6,000 and the Refuge Assurance Cup. Derbyshire won £3,000. Nottinghamshire and Lancashire won £1,500 each.

Final Table	P	W	L	T	NR	Pts	Away Wins	Runs/ 100B
1 DERBYSHIRE (5)	16	12	3	0	1	50	6	87.354
2 Lancashire (1)	16	11	3	0	2	48	7	100.186
3 Middlesex (9)	16	10	5	0	1	42	5	95.400
4 Nottinghamshire (4)	16	10	5	0	1	42	4	89.312
5 Hampshire (6)	16	9	5	0	2	40	4	88.827
6 Yorkshire (11)	16	9	6	0	1	38	4	83.607
7 Surrey (6)	16	9	6	0	1	38	3	90.393
8 Somerset (10)	16	8	8	0	0	32	4	91.254
9 Gloucestershire (16)	16	7	7	0	2	32	2	87.807
10 Worcestershire (2)	16	7	8	0	1	30	4	84.964
11 Kent (11)	16	7	8	0	1	30	3	85.949
12 Essex (3)	16	6	9	0	1	26	3	90.560
13 Sussex (11)	16	5	9	0	2	24	2	85.906
14 Warwickshire (14)	16	5	10	0	1	22	2	90.694
15 Glamorgan (16)	16	4	11	0	1	18	2	84.208
16 Leicestershire (14)	16	4	11	0	1	18	1	76.590
17 Northamptonshire (6)	16	3	12	0	1	14	1	86.406

The final positions for teams finishing with equal points are decided by (a) most wins, (b) most away wins, (c) runs per 100 balls. The first four teams qualified for the Refuge Assurance Cup. 1989 positions are shown in brackets.

Sunday League Winners

1969	Lancashire	1977	Leicestershire	1985	Essex
1970	Lancashire	1978	Hampshire	1986	Hampshire
1971	Worcestershire	1979	Somerset	1987	Worcestershire
1972	Kent	1980	Warwickshire	1988	Worcestershire
1973	Kent	1981	Essex	1989	Lancashire
1974	Leicestershire	1982	Sussex	1990	Derbyshire
1975	Hampshire	1983	Yorkshire		
1976	Kent	1984	Essex		

1990 Awards

£24,000 and League Trophy to champions DERBYSHIRE; £12,000 to runners-up Lancashire; £6,000 to third-placing Middlesex; £3,000 to fourth-placing Nottinghamshire; £275 to the winner of each match (shared in the event of 'no result' or tie). £300 to G.D. Rose, 148 Somerset v Glamorgan at Neath on 22 July, for the highest individual innings of the season; £300 each to P.W. Jarvis, 5-18 Yorkshire v Derbyshire at Headingley on 13 May, and D.V. Lawrence, 5-18 Gloucestershire v Somerset at Bristol on 3 June, the best individual bowling performances of the season.

Oxford and Cambridge

Even in a summer of heat and hosepipe bans, the Varsity match was not spared by rain. For the fourth consecutive year, no conclusion was reached, despite a contrived effort to settle the argument by the forfeiture of two innings. Cambridge were left 3½ hours to score 270 runs, at just under 4.5 runs an over, but they decided to shut up shop after the loss of four wickets.

Oxford went through eight matches against the counties without a loss, and only once were they got out for less than 200. But they found dismissing the opposition no easier than in the past, and that despite the presence in their attack of van der Merwe, a swiftish bowler who came up with the background of having played Currie Cup cricket in his native South Africa. The only instance of any Oxford bowler taking five wickets or more in an innings was Mark Crawley's six for 92, at a steady medium pace, against Glamorgan. Crawley, in his last year, was spared injuries for once and topped the 'Oxbridge' averages in both bowling and batting. He made two hundreds and 91 not out against his own county, Lancashire.

Oxford's improved performance must be attributed to the engagement of a full-time coach for the first time in many seasons. The choice, too, was excellent – Les Lenham, a National Coach.

Cambridge were again coached by Graham Saville, who has had considerable success at Fenner's over the last five years. But he had to cope with a significant turnover of players from the year before. The Light Blues were beaten four times. Against that, they pulled off a splendid win against Sussex in a run chase at Hove, on the eve of the Varsity match.

This win was a triumph for Stephen James, who scored 61 and 102, his fourth century. He made his top score, 131 not out, for the Combined Universities against New Zealand, inflicting on the tourists their only defeat apart from the loss of the third Test. This win was the first against a visiting team by either university or a combined side since Cambridge beat the Pakistanis in 1971. It was a highly meritorious win, Oxbridge chasing 263 in just over four hours on a pitch giving copious help to the spin of John Bracewell. Russell Morris, the Oxford captain, also played a major role, scoring 53 and helping James lay a foundation to the innings. Both had distinguished themselves in the first innings as well, James with 67 and Morris 75.

Between them, Oxbridge had five representatives in the Combined Universities side for the Benson & Hedges Cup. The undergraduates finished bottom of their group, but beat Yorkshire and gave the ultimate champions, Lancashire, the closest run they had right through the competition.

D.J. RUTNAGUR

Oxford University v Cambridge University 1990

Match Drawn
Played at Lord's, 4(np), 5, 6 July
Toss: Cambridge University. Umpires D.J. Constant and K.E. Palmer

Oxford University

D.A. Hagan	c James b Jenkins	8
R.E. Morris*	c Turner b Jenkins	21
P.D. Lunn	b Shufflebotham	35
G.J. Turner	c Jenkins b Shufflebotham	36
M.A. Crawley	c Johnson b Buzza	55
D.M. Curtis	run out	27
W. Van der Merwe	st Turner b Buzza	50
P.S. Gerrans	c James b Shufflebotham	16
S.D. Weale	not out	4
I.M. Henderson	not out	0
R.W.D. Trevelyan†	did not bat	
Extras	(B3, LB12, NB2)	17
	(8 wkts dec)	**269**

Oxford 2nd innings forfeited, Cambridge 1st innings forfeited

Cambridge University

S.P. James	c Hagan b Crawley	56
R. Heap	b Crawley	37
R.J. Turner†	run out	7
J.C.M. Atkinson*	b Crawley	7
M.J. Lowrey	not out	18
M.J. Morris	not out	9
R.A. Pyman	did not bat	
D.H. Shufflebotham	„	
R.H.J. Jenkins	„	
A.J. Buzza	„	
S.W. Johnson	„	
Extras	(B3, LB7, NB2)	12
	(4 wkts)	**146**

Cambridge U.	O	M	R	W
Johnson	16	1	48	0
Jenkins	20	2	68	2
Pyman	18	7	63	0
Shufflebotham	19	5	60	3
Buzza	8	1	15	2

Oxford U.	O	M	R	W
Van der Merwe	14	2	23	0
Henderson	5	0	21	0
Gerrans	13	0	37	0
Crawley	17	4	46	3
Lunn	2	1	9	0

Fall of Wickets

	OU	CU
Wkt	1st	2nd
1st	13	87
2nd	41	110
3rd	95	111
4th	108	118
5th	175	—
6th	238	—
7th	263	—
8th	265	—
9th	—	—
10th	—	—

Cambridge University

Results: Played 10; Won 1, Lost 4, Drawn 5

First-Class Averages

Batting	M	I	NO	HS	R	Avge
S.P. James†‡	11	21	2	131*	921	48.47
J. Arscott	2	4	1	43*	75	25.00
M.J. Lowrey†	10	18	2	72	363	22.68
R. Heap†	10	19	2	63	376	22.11
D.H. Shufflebotham†	8	9	3	29	121	20.16
J.C.M. Atkinson†‡	11	21	2	72	374	19.68
R.J. Turner†‡	9	16	0	38	302	18.87
G.B.A. Dyer	4	8	2	23	107	17.83
S.W. Johnson†	6	6	4	14*	35	17.50
M.J. Morris†	10	17	3	45	206	14.71
R.H.J. Jenkins†	9	12	5	19*	58	8.28
R.A. Pyman†	10	14	2	23*	98	8.16
A.J. Buzza†‡	10	12	3	21	49	5.44
A.M. Hooper	2	3	0	5	5	1.66

Also batted: G. Hutchinson (2 matches) 29, 2; G.A. Pointer (1 match) 7, 9.

Hundreds (4)

4 S.P. James: 116 v Glos (Cambridge); 104* v Notts (Cambridge); 102 v Sussex (Hove); 131* Combined Universities v New Zealand (Cambridge).

Bowling	O	M	R	W	Avge	Best
Buzza	287	47	1086	23	47.21	4-87
Lowrey	151.2	33	483	10	48.30	2-13
Pyman	308.4	81	938	15	62.53	2-29
Jenkins	281.4	41	959	15	63.93	5-100
Shufflebotham	139	20	538	6	89.66	3-60

Also bowled: Atkinson 23-3-101-1; Johnson 113-14-452-3; Pointer 17-3-67-0.

Fielding

12 Turner (8ct/4st); 7 James, Atkinson; 4 Morris; 3 Buzza, Heap; 2 Arscott (2st), Johnson, Pyman; 1 Hooper, Jenkins, Lowrey, Shufflebotham.

Oxford University

Results: Played 9; Drawn 9

First-Class Averages

Batting	M	I	NO	HS	R	Avge
M.A. Crawley†‡	10	12	3	105*	672	74.66
W. Van der Merwe†‡	8	9	3	84	310	51.66
I.M. Henderson†	6	4	3	44	46	46.00
R.E. Morris†‡	9	12	1	96	498	45.27
M.J. Kilborn‡	6	8	1	95	309	44.14
P.D. Lunn†	8	10	4	44*	184	30.66
G.J. Turner†‡	9	12	0	59	298	24.83
M.D. Curtis†	4	4	0	43	89	22.25
H.R. Davies	4	4	2	24	36	18.00
D.A. Hagan†	9	12	0	47	175	14.58
S.D. Weale†	5	4	2	13	24	12.00
P.S. Gerrans†‡	9	9	0	39	102	11.33
M.J. Russell	4	3	0	4	10	3.33

Also batted: S.A. Almaer (1 match) 4 (2ct); S. Chauhan (3 matches) 25, 4; J.E. McGrady (6 matches) 14, 1 (2st); R.W.D. Trevelyan† (3 matches) 0 (2ct); A. Winchester (1 match) 0*.

Hundreds (2)

2 M.A. Crawley: 103* v Glamorgan (Cambridge); 105* v Leics (Cambridge).

Bowling	O	M	R	W	Avge	Best
Crawley	210.5	35	725	20	36.25	6-92
Gerrans	208	40	695	13	53.46	3-86
Henderson	105.2	9	469	6	78.16	3-102
Turner	212.2	39	819	10	81.90	3-100

Also bowled: Chauhan 15-1-58-1; M.D. Curtis 1-0-8-0; Davies 54-6-261-3; Lunn 23-4-92-2; Van der Merwe 131-27-399-3; Weale 50-8-251-1; Winchester 13-0-81-0.

Fielding

9 Crawley; 6 Van der Merwe; 5 Kilborn, Turner; 4 Gerrans, 2 Hagan, Henderson; 1 Morris, Russell.

---

* not out; † Blue 1990; ‡Combined Universities v New Zealand at Cambridge, June 27-29 (Comb. Univ. won by 2 wickets).

Second XI Competition

Sussex won the Rapid Cricketline Championship with plenty to spare, suggesting that a phoenix could rise from the ashes of first-team failure in a few years' time, if not in 1991. They might have finished bottom of the Britannic Assurance Championship, but this was definitely their year in second-team cricket. Coached by Ian Waring, they put themselves in the happy position of not requiring declarations by their opponents to force victories – none of their nine wins needed help in this way and, indeed, they almost beat Worcestershire in one day at Hove with the other two days rained off.

Their success was achieved by a young side with a nucleus of home-grown players. Bowling was the main strength, Andy Clarke's leg-spin leading the way with 42 wickets, followed by 40 wickets from Brad Donelan, the promising off-spinner. Philip Threlfall, at the age of 21, lived up to his reputation as one of the fastest white bowlers in professional cricket, but he remained susceptible to injury. John North, an 18-year-old from Chichester, made progress with his fast-medium bowling and batting, which has stamped him as a classy all-rounder of the future.

Graham Burnett, a New Zealander on a scholarship, provided the backbone of the batting. His 1,432 runs (average 57.28) proved to be the highest aggregate in the championship and he recorded two double centuries.

Robin Hanley, aged 21, hit 992 runs in only 12 matches, including a hundred in 66 minutes in the first morning of the match against Essex at Hove. Keith Greenfield's 840 runs at an average of 52.4 was also an impressive return.

Glamorgan climbed to second place mainly through experienced players such as Simon Dennis and Steve Barwick with the ball and John Derrick with the bat. They provided stability for young fringe first-teamers such as Anthony Cottee, Steve James, Robert Croft, Mike Cann, and Steve Bastien. James, with 342 runs in five games after coming down from Cambridge University, and David Hemp, 19, a student at West Glamorgan Institute, were especially impressive. Croft, James, Hemp, Adrian Dale, and Adrian Shaw, the England Under-19 wicket-keeper, benefited from the ASW-sponsored Glamorgan youth scheme, in its third year, which was set up to develop Welsh youngsters for county cricket.

Though there were no restrictions on the size of the ball's seam, as in first-team games, there were still a high number of drawn games on the pale strips around the circuit, with Leicestershire drawing 15 of their 16 games to finish above Yorkshire in bottom place.

The Bain Clarkson Trophy was won by Lancashire, at Old Trafford, to be placed in the silverware cabinet alongside the Benson & Hedges Cup and NatWest Trophy won by the first team.

CHARLES RANDALL

Rapid Cricketline 2nd XI Championship 1990

Final Table

	P	W	L	D	Bonus pts Bt	Bl	Pts
1 SUSSEX (14)	16	9	1	6	45	39	228
2 Glamorgan (10)	16	7	3	6	34	56	202
3 Surrey (16)	16	5	1	9	40	54	182†
4 Nottinghamshire (7)	16	6	4	6	32	53	181
5 Kent (3)	16	5	2	9	43	46	169
6 Middlesex (1)	16	4	3	9	45	43	152
7 Warwickshire (2)	16	4	3	9	39	46	149
8 Lancashire (15)	16	3	5	8	43	48	139
9 Essex (12)	16	3	3	10	39	49	136
10 Worcestershire (17)	16	2	3	10	43	51	134†
11 Hampshire (6)	16	2	5	9	45	44	129
12 Northamptonshire (5)	16	3	4	9	40	35	123
13 Derbyshire (4)	16	2	8	6	33	44	109
14 Gloucestershire (11)	16	2	5	9	33	36	101
15 Somerset (13)	16	1	2	13	41	40	97
16 Leicestershire (8)	16	0	1	15	43	47	90
17 Yorkshire (9)	16	1	6	9	33	40	89

†Includes 8 pts for tie. 1989 positions in brackets.

Bain Clarkson Trophy 1990

North Zone	P	W	L	NR	Pts
LANCASHIRE	10	7	1	2	16
Yorkshire	10	6	4	–	12
Northamptonshire	10	5	5	–	10
Nottinghamshire	10	4	5	1	9
Leicestershire	10	4	5	1	9
Derbyshire	10	1	7	2	4

South-West Zone	P	W	L	NR	Pts
SOMERSET	8	5	1	2	12
WARWICKSHIRE*	8	5	2	1	11
Worcestershire	8	3	4	1	7
Glamorgan	8	3	4	1	7
Gloucestershire	8	1	6	1	3

*Warwickshire qualified for semi-finals on run-rate.

South-East Zone	P	W	L	NR	Pts
SURREY	10	7	2	1	15
Sussex	10	6	3	1	13
Kent	10	5	4	1	11
Hampshire	10	4	6	–	8
Middlesex	10	4	6	–	8
Essex	10	2	7	1	5

Semi-finals

13 August, Guildford. SOMERSET beat SURREY by 27 runs. Somerset 264-7 (W.J. Pringle 122*). Surrey 237 (R. Alikhan 65).

14 August, Liverpool. LANCASHIRE beat WARWICKSHIRE by 8 wickets. Warwickshire 159 (J.D. Fitton 4-42). Lancashire 160-2 (T.M. Orrell 71*).

Final

3 September, Old Trafford. LANCASHIRE beat SOMERSET by 8 wickets. Somerset 201-7 (55 overs) (A.N. Hayhurst 64, R.J. Bartlett 71). Lancashire 202-2 (51.4 overs) (J.P.Crawley 85*, M.A. Crawley 54*).

Minor Counties

The season's domestic honours went to Herts, who achieved their fourth Championship title, and Bucks, who took the Holt Cup for the first time.

The representative Minor Counties XI proved themselves no exception to the general rule in a season of high scoring. They scored their highest ever total in the Benson & Hedges Cup, 273 for two against Sussex at Marlow, where opener Malcolm Roberts made 121 to win the gold award, but Sussex won easily in the end. At Trowbridge, Minor Counties produced an opening stand of 178 against the Indian tourists, with Durham's Gary Brown (brother of Middlesex's Keith) achieving a maiden first-class hundred and Roberts hitting 85. In the second innings, Brown helped stave off defeat and was only 11 runs short of a second hundred when time ran out.

Minor Counties Championship 1990

E. Division	P	W	L	D	NR	Bonus Pts	Total Pts
Herts*	9	3	2	4	0	34	77
Lincs*	9	2	2	5	0	36	68
Staffs*	9	3	1	4	1	24	65
Beds*	9	3	1	4	1	22	63
Durham*	9	1	0	8	0	33	63
Norfolk*	9	2	1	6	0	33	61
Cambs*	9	1	2	6	0	31	57
Suffolk	9	2	3	4	0	24	53
C'berland	9	0	2	7	0	30	48
N'berland	9	0	3	6	0	23	34

W. Division	P	W	L	D	NR	Bonus Pts	Total Pts
Berkshire*	9	3	1	5	0	26	69
Oxon*	9	2	1	6	0	26	63
Shrops*	9	2	0	7	0	25	60
Bucks*	9	2	0	7	0	25	60
Dorset*	9	2	3	4	0	27	57
Devon*	9	0	1	8	0	32	57
Wilts*	9	1	3	4	1	24	53
Wales	9	1	2	6	0	28	46
Cheshire	9	1	0	7	1	16	40
Cornwall	9	1	4	4	0	17	33

Qualified for the 1991 NatWest Bank Trophy

Leading Averages

Batting	I	NO	HS	Runs	Avge
J. Abrahams	13	4	113*	765	85.00
M.R. Davies	15	7	114*	628	78.50
A. Needham	13	2	130*	750	68.18
P. Burn	13	4	105	582	64.67
M.G. Lickley	16	3	122*	838	64.46
A.S. Patel	12	4	103*	512	64.00
D.R. Turner	17	3	125*	887	63.36
S.N.V. Waterton	17	3	123*	883	63.07
G.W. Ecclestone	10	2	111	487	60.88
G.K. Brown	11	4	110*	417	59.57

Bowling	O	M	R	W	Avge
A.S. Patel	119.5	35	318	21	15.14
D. Surridge	224.4	69	488	29	16.83
S. Turner	286.5	79	727	40	18.17
A.C. Jelfs	158.5	36	488	25	19.52
P.J. Kippax	220.4	75	531	26	20.42
N.R. Taylor	165	39	497	24	20.71
A. Greasley	140.1	32	471	22	21.41
I.L. Pont	150.5	26	569	26	21.88
G. Edmunds	270.4	68	807	36	22.42
J.H. Shackleton	290.3	78	759	33	23.00

Holt Cup Knock-out Competition

Final: At Lord's, 20 August. BUCKS beat LINCOLNSHIRE by 16 runs (55 overs). Bucks 227-7 (Atkins 97 not out, Harwood 52; Love 4-44). Lincolnshire 211-9 (Love 47, Illingworth 31; Barry 3-39).

Minor Counties Championship Play-off
Hertfordshire v Berkshire

Hertfordshire won by 7 wickets
Played at Wardown Park, Luton, 9 September 1990 (55 overs)
Toss: Hertfordshire. Umpires: P. Adams & T.V. Wilkins.

Berkshire

M.G. Lickley	c Ligertwood b Merry	15
G.E. Loveday	c Ligertwood b Smith	42
G.T. Headley	not out	50
D.J.M. Mercer	c & b Smith	0
M.L. Simmons*	run out	6
P. Oxley	c MacLaurin b Surridge	31
T.P. Dodd	not out	3
M.G. Stear	did not bat	
M.E. Stevens†	,,	
J.H. Jones	,,	
P.J. Lewington	,,	
Extras		24
(55 overs, 5 wkts)		**171**

Hertfordshire

N.P.G. Wright	c Stevens b Jones	45
J.D. Carr	c Simmons b Jones	16
A. Needham	c Oxley b Lewington	29
N.R.C. MacLaurin	not out	52
B.G. Evans	not out	18
D.G. Ligertwood†	did not bat	
D.M. Smith	,,	
E.P. Neal	,,	
W.G Merry	,,	
D. Surridge*	,,	
G.A.R. Harris	,,	
Extras		12
(52.5 overs, 3 wkts)		**172**

Hertfordshire	O	M	R	W
Harris	10	1	36	0
Merry	11	2	36	1
Neal	2	0	12	0
Surridge	10	1	31	1
Needham	11	3	24	0
Smith	11	3	15	2

Berkshire	O	M	R	W
Jones	10.5	3	35	2
Headley	5	3	10	0
Stear	10	2	31	0
Dodd	7	1	30	0
Lewington	11	3	30	1
Oxley	9	0	27	0

Fall of Wickets

Wkt	B	H
1st	25	23
2nd	88	81
3rd	88	118
4th	97	–
5th	167	–
6th	–	–
7th	–	–
8th	–	–
9th	–	–
10th	–	–

Schools and Youth Cricket

Examination demands and a shortened summer term restricted midweek inter-school fixtures, but in mid-May Cheltenham went to St Edward's, Oxford, and returned with a good victory by eight wickets. Green, quickish left-arm, took 7 for 43. Cheltenham have the makings of a strong side again. In a batsman's season, Kennis of Tiffin became the first to score 1,000 runs for the Surrey school. Parsons set a record for Richard Huish College, Taunton, scoring three centuries in an aggregate of 834. Richard Huish, too, became the first state school to win the Barclay's Under-17 Cup, beating Durham in a tense final. Against Tiffin, John Fisher School, Purley, scored 307 for 7 and won by 3 wickets.

Eton beat Harrow in an exciting finish to the 155th match between the schools at Lord's on 9 June, winning by seven wickets with four balls of the final over remaining. This ended a succession of drawn games and was only the third such result since 1976. Eton have now won 51, Harrow 44, and 60 have been drawn. Chetwood, Eton's captain, put Harrow in, relying on his own off-spin and Whittington's left-armers to achieve a breakthrough. Chetwood was injured while fielding, and bowled only 10 overs. But Jonathan Whittington, who won the *Daily Telegraph* schools Under-19 bowling award (see page 32), took 3 for 78 in 25 overs of controlled left-arm spin. Harrow declared at 219-8 after 76 overs, leaving Eton with some 28 overs fewer to reach the target. With two hours left they needed 195, but, after a sound 50 from Eastwood, Sellar and Hagen added 70 in rapid time. Hagen and Strickland then saw Eton home, the latter hitting Pool for six runs off the first two balls of the last over.

9 June at Lord's. ETON beat HARROW by 7 wickets. Toss: Eton. Harrow 219-8 (Holyoake 47, Hewens 43, Guillebaud 34; Lewis 3-50, Whittington 3-78). Eton 221-3 (Sellar 57, Eastwood 53, Hagen 53*).

This year, the fifth MCC Schools Festival was held in mid-July at Oxford and then at Lord's. In the first two trial matches Southern Schools beat HMC "Rest" by three wickets and ESCA North had the better of a two-day drawn game with ESCA south. In the next trial, with teams selected regardless of school background, Graeme Archer of Stafford CFE hit a brilliant 159 for N. Gibbs' side on St Edmund's ground, and on neighbouring Keble College ground Wasim Khan hit a forcing 88 for his own team, who drew with one led by A. Richards. In the final trial, at Christ Church ground, Oxford, MCC East strode to easy victory against MCC West. Declaring at 267 for 7, East then bowled West out for 194. The most impressive batsman on display was Tim Walton of Leeds GS, with a fine 88 for East.

Richards of Forest School, Snaresbrook, was appointed captain of the following MCC Schools side to play the traditional three one-day matches at Lord's on 18, 19, and 20 July: W. Khan (Josiah Mason SFC), G. Archer (Stafford CFE), D. Fulton (Judd School); J. Laney (St. John's, Marlborough), T. Walton (Leeds GS), R. Murray (Brigshaw School), A. Richards (Forest), S. Laudat (Oxford CFE), M. Khan (Aylesbury CFE), P. Weston (Durham), J. Hodgson (Ranelagh), J. Snape (Denstone).

It was Walton of Leeds, with a rapid unbeaten 64, who gave MCC Schools victory by two wickets over the 'parent' club at Lord's on 18 July. MCC, put in first, declared at 206 for 4, Goldsmith of Chobham hitting 103; Hodgson took 3 for 65. Schools quickly lost Archer, but Wasim Khan (73) and Fulton (39) added 94 for the second wicket. Schools then fell from 120-2 to 205-8 with only Walton to lead the fight-back; this he duly did.

On 19 July MCC Schools fell 35 runs short of beating National Association of Young Cricketers, who had declared at 215-6. Wasim Khan was again in form, but his 61 was not enough to take Schools beyond 181-6 in 48 overs. On the last day at Lord's, though, a National Cricket Association Young Cricketers side, drawn from MCC Schools and NAYC, bowled out Combined Services for 231 and proceeded to win by 8 wickets. Wasim (80) and Williams (75) opened with 154. From 166-2, Walton (67) and Simmonite saw NCA to 233-2 without any trouble.

The fifth Esso/NAYC Under-19 Festivals took place at Oxford and Cambridge venues from 13 to 18 August, with the young hopefuls of 32 counties taking part, Gloucestershire and Buckinghamshire joining in for the first time. In the 60-overs tournament, there is no restriction on the number of overs by any one bowler, and the spinners, for once, have the chance to exploit their skills.

In the Oxford section, Warwickshire, winners for the two previous years, lost in the semi-final to Hertfordshire by 3 runs, rather misjudging the overs schedule. Essex beat Surrey by 38 runs at Cambridge. Predictably, Essex won the final at Christ Church ground, beating the minor county by 92 runs. They made 251 for 8 from their 60 overs and then bowled Hertfordshire out for 159 in the 57th over.

Esso/NAYC Under-19 County Final (60 overs). ESSEX beat HERTS by 92 runs. Christ Church, Oxford, 18 August. Essex 251-8 (60 overs) (Churchill 55, Bate 50, Robinson 34). Herts 159 (56.3 overs) (Beynon 39, Yeabsley 30; Ranawat 4-59, Carpenter 3-18).

JOHN FOGG

Village and Club Cricket

After two years of washed-out finals – replayed elsewhere – superb weather at Lord's gave the 'grass roots' champions their due reward for striving all season, and the large crowds, admittedly partisan, saw some excellent cricket.

In the Cockspur Cup, Blackpool beat Cheam by three wickets, thanks mainly to a heroic unbeaten 86 by Tony Hesketh. Cheam chose to bat first and made steady progress in the morning. Mark Butcher, elder son of Glamorgan's captain, signalled lunch with a straight six to the Nursery End, but in the necessary acceleration after lunch he holed out to Sanders in the covers going for another big hit. Their captain, Falconer, made Cheam's top score with 53 but had little support, and Cheam had to settle for 193 for 8 from their 45 overs.

Blackpool started badly, losing both openers for 10, and at one stage were 95 for 5. But Hesketh, coming in after the fall of the first wicket, did not allow Blackpool to get too far behind the asking rate and clinched victory with boundaries off the first two balls of the final over. Blackpool received £1,250, plus a trip to Barbados; Cheam got £750.

The Cockspur Cup (45 overs). Lord's, 24 August. Toss: Cheam. Cheam 193-8 (R.J. Falconer 53, A.W. Smith 35). Blackpool 194-7 (44.2 overs) (A. Hesketh 86 not out). **Blackpool won by 3 wickets.**

Kevin Iles, captain of Wiltshire's Goatacre, played one of the best innings seen at Lord's for many a season and led his side to victory by 50 runs over Dunstall from Staffordshire in the final of the National Village Championship. Iles made a superb 123, his 100 taking only 45 minutes. This was no slogging innings but one of perfect timing and control. It included seven sixes and six fours, and was the first century made in a final since *The Cricketer* launched this unique competition in 1972.

Goatacre's 267 for five from 40 overs was also a record for the final. The rate required was beyond Dunstall's capacity, but Phillip Wallbank, their captain, made a resolute 51.

Goatacre, also champions in 1988, received £400 and the trophy from the President of MCC. Dunstall got £250. The 484 runs scored from 80 overs was also a competition final record.

National Village Championship Final (40 overs). Lord's, 25 August. Toss: Goatacre. Goatacre 267-5 (K.M. Iles 123, J.B.Turner 53; D.K. Shipton 3-83). Dunstall 217-8 (P.M. Wallbank 51, G.M. Shilton 35, A. Ali 31 not out; J. Angell 4-18). **Goatacre won by 50 runs.**

JOHN FOGG

Women's Cricket

England's strength in Europe was emphasized once again when they comfortably retained the European Cup, beating Ireland in the final by 65 runs at Great Oakley Cricket Club, Northamptonshire, in July. Their convincing victories against the Netherlands, Denmark, and Ireland *en route* to a place in the final was an indication of their greater all-round preparation and superior experience. Ireland won their other two matches to finish second in the preliminary group.

Opener Wendy Watson from the East Midlands was England's most successful batsman, scoring 229 runs for just one dismissal. Her aggregate included a fine unbeaten 107 in the final. Her entertaining third-wicket partnership with her county team-mate Karen Smithies, who hit a rapid 41, enabled England to reach 224 for 3 off their 55 overs and set Ireland a target that was always going to be beyond their reach. Tight bowling by Clare Taylor (2-7), Janet Aspinall (2-34), and Smithies (2-17) restricted the Irish to 159 for 8.

In order to give some promising young players a chance to sample the international scene, the England selectors named Karen Smithies to captain an England team on a two-match tour of Ireland in August. A bold selection was that of the Sussex medium-pace bowler Sarah Jane Cook, who is completely deaf and dumb. The English easily beat Ireland in the two games, which were played in Dublin.

The County Championships were played over five days at various college pitches around Cambridge. East Midlands and Yorkshire both won their groups with a 100% record, and East Midlands then beat Yorkshire in the final by 4 runs to retain the trophy. The East Midlands batted first and although they lost their legendary opener, Enid Bakewell, cheaply, a profitable partnership between Wendy Watson (44) and Jane Smit (50) and some powerful batting at the close by Karen Smithies (33), Kim Robertson, and Jo Chamberlain helped them accumulate 200-5 after their 55 overs. In reply, Yorkshire did not make a great start, and after losing their two openers early on, their talented young international Debbie Maybury (45) made some progress. But the asking rate slowly crept up to around 6 an over in the latter stages, and despite a fighting 57 not out from Sue Metcalfe, they narrowly failed to reach the target.

The North regained the Territorial Trophy when they won all their matches in the three-day tournament held in Oxford over the August Bank Holiday weekend. The South took full advantage of a batting collapse by the holders, the Mid West, to edge them into third spot.

On the club scene, Wakefield completed another splendid season when they beat the London club Gunnersbury to retain their National Club's title at the Maori Club in Surrey. They followed up this triumph with a competent seven-wicket defeat of Riverside, from Middlesex, in the final of the National League. Playing without the injured England all-rounder Carole Hodges in the club final, Wakefield owed much of their success to an attacking 77 scored off 69 deliveries by Janet Aspinall, and some fine pace bowling by Joanne Pitcher and Sally Stevenson, who each took three wickets.

CATHY HARRIS

European Cup

ENGLAND beat THE NETHERLANDS by 8 wickets. Netherlands 57 (33 overs) (Barrs 3-1). England 58-2 (19.5 overs).

ENGLAND beat DENMARK by 206 runs. England 270 (54 overs) (Powell 98*, Maybury 56). Denmark 64 (24.3 overs) (Smith 5-15).

ENGLAND beat IRELAND by 9 wickets. Ireland 169 (52 overs) (Aspinall 4-35). England 170-1 (41.4 overs) (Watson 93*).

Qualifying group	P	W	L	Pts
ENGLAND	3	3	0	6
IRELAND	3	2	1	4
The Netherlands	3	1	2	2
Denmark	3	0	3	0

Final

ENGLAND beat IRELAND by 65 runs. England 224-3 (55 overs) (Watson 107*, Smithies 41). Ireland 159-8 (55 overs).

England Tour to Ireland

ENGLAND beat IRELAND by 62 runs. England 156-9 (55 overs). Ireland 94.

ENGLAND beat IRELAND by 10 wickets. Ireland 79. England 84-0.

County Championship

Group 1	W	L	Pts	Group 2	W	L	Pts
E. Midlands	5	0	108.5	Yorkshire	5	0	107
Middlesex	4	1	87	Surrey	4	1	87.5
East Anglia	2	3	57.5	Kent	3	2	75.5
Thames Valley	2	3	54	Lancs/Cheshire	2	3	61.5
B. Daniels' XI	1	4	39	A. Woods' XI	1	4	39.5
West	1	4	37	Sussex	0	5	20.5

Final

1 September, at Shepperton CC. EAST MIDLANDS beat YORKSHIRE by 4 runs. East Midlands 200-5 (55 overs) (Smit 50, Watson 44). Yorkshire 196 (54.4 overs) (Metcalfe 57*, Maybury 45).

National Club Knock-out Final

1 September at Maori Club, Surrey. WAKEFIELD beat GUNNERSBURY by 80 runs. Wakefield 172-9 (40 overs) (Aspinall 77). Gunnersbury 92 (Stevenson 3-10).

National League Final

At Collingham and Linton Club. WAKEFIELD beat RIVERSIDE by 7 wickets. Riverside 134-7 (40 overs) (Heggs 44; Aspinall 3-30) Wakefield 135-3 (33.1 overs) (Hodges 55, Burnley 52).

Trial Matches

At Denstone College, Nr Uttoxeter. JUNIOR ENGLAND beat YOUNG ENGLAND by 83 runs. Junior England 183-7 (55 overs) (Maybury 98; Jones 4-31). Young England 100 (50 overs).

At Mitchell's & Butlers CG. J. POWELL'S XI drew with K. SMITHIES' XI. Powell's XI 206-3 dec (Powell 100*, Metcalfe 41*). Smithies' XI 199-8 (Hodges 89, Smithies 40).

1989-90

OVERSEAS CRICKET

Pakistan v India

This, the tenth rubber between the two neighbouring countries, was one of the less distinguished, and all four Tests were drawn. It was remarkable, however, in being free from controversial incidents and being played in a spirit of cordiality not typical of past encounters between the deadly rivals.

The main reason for the wholesome atmosphere was that the series was supervised, at the insistence of the Pakistanis, by 'third country' (a euphemism for 'neutral') umpires. The success of the experiment should not, however, be attributed to the 'neutrality' of the umpires, J.W. Holder and J.H. Hampshire (both English), but to their competence and professionalism. They were relaxed and yet firm.

India's tour party contained many new names, including the 16-year-old Sachin Tendulkar, and was conspicuously short of experience in both departments. They did well to come out of the series unscathed. Perhaps they never aspired to anything more than avoiding defeat. Man for man, Pakistan were clearly superior. For their inability to prove it, there were two reasons. Firstly, the pitches were unresponsive. More significant, their slip catching disastrously poor. Once India, 85 for 6 at one stage and in dire peril of following on, saved the first Test, they batted with increasing confidence.

The mainstay of their batting was Sanjay Manjrekar, who aggregated 569 runs, including a double century. Azharuddin's 109 in the second Test was a watershed in the career of the present Indian captain, who was not an automatic choice at the start of the series but got in the side because Raman Lamba was injured.

The pressure on India's middle order was the greater for the total eclipse of their captain and opening batsman Srikkanth, whom Wasim Akram dismissed at will six times in seven innings. But Sachin Tendulkar was undaunted by either the charged atmosphere of Test cricket or the mighty reputations of the bowlers in opposition. Confident, if sometimes impetuous, he totalled 215 in six innings.

Kapil Dev, despite a troubled knee and advancing years, and Manoj Prabhakar, who made a marked advance during the series, bore the main burden of the bowling.

Pakistan scored runs effortlessly and in abundance. Only in the last Test did they fail to total 300. Except Rameez Raja – and even he averaged over 40 – all their main batsmen scored hundreds. Javed Miandad, by his own standards, however had a moderate series. Always a heavy scorer against India, his one century on a dead pitch at Lahore was in celebration of his hundredth Test. As for the Pakistan bowling, Imran made heavy demands on Wasim Akram, who distinguished himself by taking 18 wickets in the series.

Pakistan v India 1989-90 1st Test

Match Drawn
Played at National Stadium, Karachi, 15, 16, 17, 19, 20 November
Toss: India. Umpires: J.H. Hampshire and J.W. Holder
Debuts: Pakistan – Shahid Saeed, Waqar Younis. India – S.A. Ankola, S.R. Tendulkar

Pakistan

Aamer Malik	c Azharuddin b Kapil Dev	0	c Manjrekar b Kapil Dev	15
Rameez Raja	c Shastri b Prabhakar	44	b Prabhakar	2
Shoaib Mohammad	c Azharuddin b Kapil Dev	67	lbw b Kapil Dev	95
Javed Miandad	c Azharuddin b Kapil Dev	78	b Kapil Dev	36
Salim Malik	c Azharuddin b Ankola	36	(6) not out	102
Imran Khan*	not out	109	(7) not out	28
Shahid Saeed	c Moré b Kapil Dev	12		
Salim Yousuf†	c Moré b Prabhakar	36	(5) c Moré b Ankola	4
Wasim Akram	c Azharuddin b Prabhakar	0		
Abdul Qadir	c Moré b Prabhakar	4		
Waqar Younis	c Moré b Prabhakar	0		
Extras	(B4, LB9, W3, NB7)	23	(B3, LB11, NB9)	23
		409	(5 wkts dec)	**305**

India

K. Srikkanth*	lbw b Akram	4	lbw b Akram	31
N.S. Sidhu	b Akram	0	c Rameez b Imran	85
S.V. Manjrekar	c Yousuf b Younis	3	not out	113
M. Azharuddin	lbw b Imran	35	c Aamer b Qadir	35
M. Prabhakar	b Younis	9		
S.R. Tendulkar	b Younis	15		
R.J. Shastri	c Imran b Qadir	45	(5) not out	22
Kapil Dev	c Miandad b Younis	55		
K.S. Moré†	not out	58		
Arshad Ayub	lbw b Akram	1		
S.A. Ankola	b Akram	6		
Extras	(B5, LB10, W5, NB11)	31	(B9, LB4, W1, NB3)	17
		262	(3 wkts)	**303**

India	O	M	R	W	O	M	R	W
Kapil Dev	24	5	69	4	36	15	82	3
Prabhakar	34.5	6	104	5	30	4	107	1
Ankola	19	1	93	1	11	6	35	1
Shastri	10	1	37	0	5	0	15	0
Arshad Ayub	27	3	81	0	10	1	37	0
Srikkanth	1	0	2	0				
Tendulkar	1	0	10	0	4	0	15	0

Pakistan	O	M	R	W	O	M	R	W
Wasim Akram	26.2	4	83	4	25	7	68	1
Waqar Younis	19	1	80	4	2	0	11	0
Imran Khan	15	4	44	1	28	10	56	1
Shahid Saeed	2	0	7	0	13	0	36	0
Abdul Qadir	10	1	33	1	28	3	119	1

Fall of Wickets

Wkt	P 1st	I 1st	P 2nd	I 2nd
1st	4	1	2	43
2nd	83	13	24	178
3rd	158	13	92	256
4th	233	41	109	–
5th	271	73	250	–
6th	307	85	–	–
7th	398	163	–	–
8th	398	220	–	–
9th	409	241	–	–
10th	409	262	–	–

Pakistan v India 1989-90 2nd Test

Match Drawn
Played at Iqbal Stadium, Faisalabad, 23, 24, 25, 27, 28 November
Toss: Pakistan. Umpires: J.H. Hampshire and J.W. Holder
Debuts: Pakistan – Nadeem Abbasi, Naved Anjum.   India – V. Razdan

India

K. Srikkanth*	lbw b Akram	36	b Akram	13
N.S. Sidhu	c Abbasi b Akram	20	run out (Salim Malik)	51
S.V. Manjrekar	c Salim Malik b Anjum	76	lbw b Anjum	83
M. Azharuddin	lbw b Akram	0	b Anjum	109
R.J. Shastri	c Abbasi b Jaffer	11	c Abbasi b Akram	5
S.R. Tendulkar	lbw b Imran	59	run out (Akram)	8
M. Prabhakar	not out	24	not out	54
Kapil Dev	lbw b Anjum	0	c Rameez b Qadir	49
K.S. Moré†	lbw b Imran	4	not out	2
Maninder Singh	c Rameez b Imran	3		
V. Razdan	c sub (Ijaz Ahmed) b Imran	0		
Extras	(B2, LB16, W15, NB22)	55	(B7, LB7, W7, NB3)	24
		288	(7 wkts)	**398**

Pakistan

Aamer Malik	c & b Prabhakar	117
Rameez Raja	c Srikkanth b Prabhakar	58
Shoaib Mohammad	lbw b Kapil Dev	24
Javed Miandad	lbw b Prabhakar	13
Salim Malik	lbw b Prabhakar	63
Imran Khan*	c Azharuddin b Prabhakar	34
Naved Anjum	c Moré b Kapil Dev	12
Nadeem Abbasi	c Moré b Kapil Dev	36
Wasim Akram	c Tendulkar b Prabhakar	28
Abdul Qadir	not out	5
Salim Jaffer	not out	0
Extras	(B2, LB9, W8, NB14)	33
	(9 wkts dec)	**423**

Pakistan	O	M	R	W	O	M	R	W
Imran Khan	26.1	7	45	4	27	5	100	0
Wasim Akram	38	4	107	3	31	6	86	2
Salim Jaffer	17	4	54	1				
Naved Anjum	29	6	57	2	22	4	92	2
Abdul Qadir	3	1	7	0	31	3	90	1
S. Mohammad					3	0	7	0
Aamer Malik					2	0	9	0

India	O	M	R	W
Kapil Dev	45	11	106	3
Prabhakar	42.3	4	132	6
Razdan	13	1	62	0
Maninder Singh	21	4	70	0
Shastri	9	0	29	0
Srikkanth	2	0	13	0

Fall of Wickets

	I	P	I
Wkt	1st	1st	2nd
1st	68	105	33
2nd	74	157	91
3rd	85	193	249
4th	101	289	258
5th	244	307	274
6th	252	331	290
7th	253	368	385
8th	278	409	–
9th	284	419	–
10th	288	423	–

Pakistan v India 1989-90 3rd Test

Match Drawn
Played at Gaddafi Stadium, Lahore, 1, 2, 3, 5, 6 December
Toss: India. Umpires: J.H. Hampshire and J. W. Holder
Debuts: Pakistan – Akram Raza, Shahid Mahboob

India

K. Srikkanth*	b Akram	0
N.S. Sidhu	lbw b Imran	4
S.V. Manjrekar	run out (Qadir/Abbasi)	218
M. Azharuddin	c Abbasi b Mahboob	77
R.J. Shastri	c Miandad b Mahboob	61
M. Prabhakar	run out	
	(Rameez/Abbasi)	45
S.R. Tendulkar	b Qadir	41
Kapil Dev	b Qadir	1
K.S. Moré†	not out	26
Arshad Ayub	c sub (Ijaz Ahmed)	
	b Qadir	10
Maninder Singh	c Raza b Imran	0
Extras	(B4, LB19, W1, NB2)	26
		509

Pakistan

Aamer Malik	c sub (W.V. Raman)	
	b Maninder	113
Rameez Raja	c Moré b Prabhakar	63
Salim Malik	c Manjrekar b Maninder	55
Javed Miandad	b Shastri	145
Shoaib Mohammad	not out	203
Imran Khan*	c Manjrekar b Shastri	66
Abdul Qadir	not out	39
Wasim Akram	did not bat	
Akram Raza	"	
Nadeem Abbasi†	"	
Shahid Mahboob	"	
Extras	(B3, LB4, NB8)	15
	(5 wkts dec)	**699**

Pakistan	O	M	R	W
Imran Khan	50.2	13	130	2
Wasim Akram	24	6	65	1
Shahid Mahboob	49	12	131	2
Akram Raza	18	3	59	0
Abdul Qadir	35	8	97	3
Salim Malik	1	0	2	0
Aamer Malik	1	0	3	0

India	O	M	R	W
Kapil Dev	28	2	77	0
Prabhakar	34	2	107	1
Maninder Singh	61	7	191	2
Arshad Ayub	49	4	182	0
Srikkanth	3	0	18	0
Shastri	26.4	2	105	2
Moré	2	0	12	0

Fall of Wickets

	I	P
Wkt	1st	1st
1st	1	100
2nd	5	223
3rd	154	248
4th	340	494
5th	375	628
6th	466	–
7th	466	–
8th	469	–
9th	508	–
10th	509	–

Pakistan v India 1989-90 4th Test

Match Drawn
Played at Jinnah Park, Sialkot, 9, 10, 11, 13, 14 December
Toss: Pakistan. Umpires: J.H. Hampshire and J.W. Holder
Debuts: nil

India

K. Srikkanth*	lbw b Akram	10	c Akram b Imran		3
N.S. Sidhu	c Rameez b Akram	12	c Imran b Zakir		97
S.V. Manjrekar	lbw b Younis	72	lbw b Imran		4
M. Azharuddin	run out (Shoaib/Younis)	52	c Shoaib b Akram		4
R.J. Shastri	c & b Imran	20	lbw b Akram		0
S.R. Tendulkar	lbw b Akram	35	c Abbasi b Imran		57
Kapil Dev	b Akram	27	lbw b Razdan		27
M. Prabhakar	c Shoaib b Imran	25	not out		11
K.S. Moré†	c Zakir b Younis	15	not out		17
Maninder Singh	c Abbasi b Akram	8			
V. Razdan	not out	6			
Extras	(B6, LB14, W8, NB14)	42	(B5, LB7, NB2)		14
		324	(7 wkts)		**234**

Pakistan

Aamer Malik	lbw b Prabhakar	9
Rameez Raja	b Razdan	56
Shoaib Mohammad	b Razdan	23
Javed Miandad	c Moré b Kapil Dev	7
Salim Malik*	c Shastri b Razdan	34
Imran Khan*	c Moré b Prabhakar	25
Nadeem Abbasi†	b Prabhakar	10
Wasim Akram	b Razdan	30
Abdul Qadir	c Azharuddin b Razdan	7
Zakir Khan	not out	9
Waqar Younis	c Moré b Kapil Dev	4
Extras	(B7, LB24, W1, NB4)	36
		250

Pakistan	O	M	R	W	O	M	R	W
Wasim Akram	28.2	6	101	5	32	17	41	2
Waqar Younis	21	2	83	2	16	0	63	0
Zakir Khan	16	3	59	0	13	0	50	2
Imran Khan	17	3	61	2	22	4	68	3
Abdul Qadir	2	2	0	0				
S. Mohammad					1	1	0	0

India	O	M	R	W
Kapil Dev	35.4	17	44	2
Prabhakar	40	10	92	3
Razdan	27	5	79	5
Maninder Singh	1	0	4	0

Fall of Wickets

	I	P	I
Wkt	1st	1st	2nd
1st	20	11	10
2nd	39	76	33
3rd	167	87	38
4th	181	133	38
5th	225	170	139
6th	251	185	198
7th	270	194	207
8th	296	222	–
9th	314	243	–
10th	324	250	–

Test Match Averages: Pakistan v India 1989-90

Pakistan

Batting and Fielding	M	I	NO	HS	R	Avge	100	50	Ct/St
Shoaib Mohammad	4	5	1	203*	412	103.00	1	2	2
Imran Khan	4	5	2	109*	262	87.33	1	1	3
Salim Malik	4	5	1	102*	290	72.50	1	2	1
Javed Miandad	4	5	0	145	279	55.80	1	1	2
Aamer Malik	4	5	0	117	254	50.80	2	–	1
Ramiz Raja	4	5	0	63	223	44.60	–	3	4
Abdul Qadir	4	4	2	39*	55	27.50	–	–	–
Nadeem Abbasi	3	2	0	36	46	23.00	–	–	6/-
Wasim Akram	4	3	0	30	58	19.33	–	–	1

Also batted: Naved Anjum (1 match) 12; Salim Jaffer (1 match) 0*; Salim Yousuf (1 match) 36, 4 (1ct); Shahid Saeed (1 match) 12; Waqar Younis (2 matches) 0, 4; Zakir Khan (1 match) 9* (1ct).
Akram Raza (1ct) and Shahid Mahboob played in one match but did not bat.

Bowling	O	M	R	W	Avge	Best	5wI	10wM
Wasim Akram	204.4	50	551	18	30.61	5-101	1	–
Imran Khan	185.3	46	504	13	38.76	4-45	–	–
Waqar Younis	58	3	237	6	39.50	4-80	–	–
Abdul Qadir	109	18	346	6	57.66	3-97	–	–

Also bowled: Aamer Malik 3-0-12-0; Akram Raza 18-3-58-0; Naved Anjum 51-10-149-4; Salim Jaffer 17-4-54-1; Salim Malik 1-0-2-0; Shahid Mahboob 49-12-131-2; Shahid Saeed 15-0-43-0; Shoaib Mohammad 4-1-7-0; Zakir Khan 29-3-109-2.

India

Batting and Fielding	M	I	NO	HS	R	Avge	100	50	Ct/St
S.V. Manjrekar	4	7	1	218	569	94.83	2	3	3
K.S. Moré	4	6	4	58*	122	61.00	–	1	11/-
M. Prabhakar	4	6	3	54*	168	56.00	–	1	1
M. Azharuddin	4	7	0	109	312	44.57	1	2	7
N.S. Sidhu	4	7	0	97	269	38.42	–	3	–
S.R. Tendulkar	4	6	0	59	215	35.83	–	2	1
R.J. Shastri	4	7	1	61	164	27.33	–	1	2
Kapil Dev	4	6	0	55	159	26.50	–	1	–
K. Srikkanth	4	7	0	36	97	13.85	–	–	1
Maninder Singh	3	3	0	8	11	3.66	–	–	–

Also batted: S.A. Ankola (1 match) 6; Arshad Ayub (2 matches) 1, 10; V. Razdan (2 matches) 0, 6*.

Bowling	O	M	R	W	Avge	Best	5wI	10wM
V. Razdan	40	6	141	5	28.20	5-79	1	–
Kapil Dev	168.4	50	378	12	31.50	4-69	–	–
M. Prabhakar	181.2	26	542	16	33.87	6-132	2	–

Also bowled: S.A. Ankola 30-7-128-2; Arshad Ayub 86-8-300-0; Maninder Singh 83-11-265-2; K.S. Moré 2-0-12-0; R.J. Shastri 50.4-3-186-2; K. Srikkanth 6-0-33-0; S.R. Tendulkar 5-0-25-0.

Statistical Highlights of the Tests

1st Test, Karachi. Neutral umpires were used for the second Test series (P.D. Reporter & V.K. Ramaswamy of India stood in two Tests, Pakistan v West Indies 1986-87). Kapil Dev became the 9th player (3rd Indian) to play 100 Tests. He became the 4th bowler with 350 Test wickets. Imran Khan scored his 5th Test hundred, his 3rd against India. Prabhakar took 5 wickets for the 1st time. Azharuddin equalled the world record with 5 catches in the 1st innings. Salim Malik scored his 7th Test hundred, his 2nd against Pakistan. Manjrekar scored his 2nd Test hundred. Sidhu and Manjrekar added 135 for the 2nd wicket in the 2nd innings, a record for India against Pakistan. Tendulkar made his debut aged 16 years and 205 days, the youngest Indian and the third-youngest in history.

2nd Test, Faisalabad. Tendulkar (16 years 214 days) is the youngest player to score a Test 50. Aamer Malik scored his 1st Test hundred. Prabhakar took 5 wickets for the 2nd time, his best Test return. Azharuddin scored his 7th Test hundred, his 3rd against Pakistan. At 18* he reached 2,000 Test runs. Moré took his 50th Test catch when he helped Kapil Dev to dismiss Naved Anjum for his 356th wicket (past D.K. Lillee).

3rd Test, Lahore. Javed Miandad became the 10th player to play 100 Tests. He scored his 22nd Test hundred, his 5th against India. He thus became the 2nd player (Cowdrey) to score 100 in his 100th Test. At 76* he reached 7,625 runs, passing Cowdrey to stand 6th in the list of leading batsmen. Manjrekar scored his 3rd Test hundred, his highest score and the highest by either side in Pakistan/India Tests. Aamer Malik scored his 2nd Test hundred. Shoaib scored his 4th Test hundred, his 2nd against India. He and his father provide the first instance of father and son with a Test 200. Abdul Qadir at 24* reached 1,000 Test runs to become the 4th Pakistan player with 1,000 runs and 100 wickets. He is only the 2nd with 1,000 and 200 wickets. Shastri (45*) became the 6th Indian with 3,000 Test runs. Manjrekar and Shastri put on 186 for a new 4th-wicket record for India against Pakistan. Each side made its highest score against the other.

4th Test, Sialkot. India made the highest total in a Test at Sialkot. Sidhu made the highest individual score at Sialkot. Imran Khan became the 5th bowler to take 350 Test wickets, when he dismissed Shastri. Wasim Akram took 5 wickets for the 5th time, 2nd against India. Razdan took 5 wickets for the first time.

One-day Internationals

16 December at Arbab Niaz Stadium, Peshawar. Match abandoned without a ball being bowled.

18 December at Municipal Stadium, Gujranwala. PAKISTAN beat INDIA by 7 runs. Toss: India. Pakistan 87-9 (16 overs) (Saeed Anwar 42*). India 80-9 (16 overs). Award: Saeed Anwar (42*).

20 December at National Stadium, Karachi. MATCH ABANDONED (crowd trouble). Toss: India. Pakistan 28-3 (14.3 overs).

22 December at Gaddafi Stadium, Lahore. PAKISTAN beat INDIA by 38 runs. Toss: India. Pakistan 150-8 (37 overs). India 112 (30.2 overs). Award: Aaqib Javed (8-1-28-3).

India Tour of Pakistan 1989-90

First-Class Matches: Played 5; Drawn 5
All Matches: Played 9; Lost 2, Drawn 5, Abandoned 2

First-Class Averages

Batting and Fielding	M	I	NO	HS	R	Avge	100	50	Ct/St
S.V. Manjrekar	5	8	1	218	581	83.00	2	3	3
M. Prabhakar	4	6	3	54*	168	56.00	–	1	1
K.S. Moré	5	7	4	58*	147	49.00	–	1	13/-
M. Azharuddin	5	8	0	109	323	40.37	1	2	8
N.S. Sidhu	4	7	0	97	269	38.42	–	3	–
S.R. Tendulkar	5	7	0	59	262	37.42	–	2	2
R.J. Shastri	5	8	2	61	223	37.16	–	2	2
Kapil Dev	4	6	0	55	159	26.50	–	1	–
K. Srikkanth	5	8	0	36	119	14.87	–	–	1
Maninder Singh	4	4	0	8	15	3.75	–	–	1
V. Razdan	3	3	1	6*	6	3.00	–	–	1

Also batted: S.A. Ankola (2 matches) 8, 6; Arshad Ayub (2 matches) 1, 10; R. Lamba (1 match) 62; W.V. Raman (1 match) 1.

Bowling	O	M	R	W	Avge	Best	5wI	10wM
S.A. Ankola	56	8	251	10	25.10	6-77	1	–
V. Razdan	64	12	270	9	30.00	5-79	1	–
Kapil Dev	168.4	50	378	12	31.50	4-69	–	–
M. Prabhakar	181.2	26	542	16	33.87	6-132	2	–

Also bowled: Arshad Ayub 86-8-300-0; Maninder Singh 118-17-385-3; K.S. Moré 2-0-12-0; W.V. Raman 14-1-68-0; R.J. Shastri 67.4-12-219-3; K. Srikkanth 9-0-40-0; S.R. Tendulkar 11-0-56-0.

Australia v New Zealand

This, a one-off Test, will always be remembered as Mark Greatbatch's match. The tall, solidly built, blond, moustachioed left-hander, in only his seventh Test and two weeks short of his 26th birthday, defied Australia's four fast bowlers for 14½ hours, including almost 11 hours in New Zealand's second innings, to force an improbable draw. Greatbatch's heroic 146 not out, after his top-scoring 76 in the first innings, claimed a proud, permanent place on New Zealand cricket's honour roll.

On a Perth pitch that was not quite as quick or as bouncy as normal, Australia went into the match still high on the euphoria of their 4-0 Ashes triumph in England, but without vice-captain Geoff Marsh, whose left big toe had been broken by a Carl Rackemann 'sandshoe crusher' at net practice two days before the start. But New Zealand were severely underdone and undermanned, having played only three warm-up games and without Richard Hadlee, who had stayed in Christchurch because of a ruptured Achilles tendon, and late casualties John Bracewell and Andrew Jones.

Australia responded to John Wright's generosity in sending them in to bat by amassing 521 for 9 declared – the ninth consecutive Test in which they had passed 400. David Boon's belligerent 200, Dean Jones's exhilarating 99, and debutant Tom Moody's careful 61 exposed the inadeqacies of the New Zealand attack.

After following on 290 behind, New Zealand started the last day at 168 for 4, with the second new ball due after six more overs, and finished at 322 for 7 (32 ahead). Greatbatch added 77 of the 154. He and Martin Snedden (33 not out) shared a remarkable unbeaten eighth-wicket stand of 88 in 202 minutes. The Australians ruined their victory chances by dropping three catches in the last session – Greatbatch at 124 and Snedden at 21 and 33.

Disappointingly and surprisingly, the five-day crowd figure just failed to reach 30,000, raising further doubts about Perth's automatic entitlement to a Test every season.

Statistical Highlights of the Test

Boon scored his 8th Test hundred, his 2nd against New Zealand and his highest score in 78 innings. At 148* he reached 3,000 Test runs. It was the 1st 200 in Tests at WACA. In the second innings Greatbatch scored his 2nd Test hundred, becoming only the 3rd player after O.G. Smith and C.H. Lloyd of West Indies to make hundreds against both Australia and England on debut. It was the slowest Test hundred in Tests in Australia (462 min) and was for a few days the slowest first-class hundred in Australia (overtaken by G.J. Shipperd of Tasmania).

Australia v New Zealand 1989-90

Match Drawn
Played at W.A.C.A. Ground, Perth, 24, 25, 26, 27, 28 November
Toss: New Zealand. Umpires: R.J. Evans and P.J. McConnell
Debuts: Australia – T.M. Moody.   New Zealand – C.L. Cairns

Australia

M.A. Taylor	c Wright b Morrison	9
D.C. Boon	c Wright b Snedden	200
T.M. Moody	c Smith b Snedden	61
A.R. Border*	b Morrison	50
D.M. Jones	lbw b Morrison	99
S.R. Waugh	c Greatbatch b Snedden	17
I.A. Healy†	c J.J. Crowe b Patel	28
M.G. Hughes	c Wright b Snedden	16
G.F. Lawson	b Morrison	1
C.G. Rackemann	not out	15
T.M. Alderman	did not bat	
Extras	(B1, LB9, W2, NB13)	25
	(9 wkts dec)	**521**

New Zealand

J.G. Wright*	b Rackemann	34	c Border b Lawson		3
R.H. Vance	b Alderman	4	c Alderman b Rackemann		8
M.J. Greatbatch	c Healy b Hughes	76	not out		146
M.D. Crowe	lbw b Alderman	62	c Taylor b Moody		30
D.N. Patel	c Boon b Hughes	0	lbw b Alderman		7
J.J. Crowe	c Healy b Rackemann	7	lbw b Hughes		49
I.D.S. Smith†	c Lawson b Hughes	11	c Border b Hughes		0
C.L. Cairns	c Healy b Hughes	1	lbw b Hughes		28
M.C. Snedden	not out	13	not out		33
D.M. Morrison	c Border b Lawson	3			
W. Watson	lbw b Alderman	4			
Extras	(B1, LB6, W4, NB5)	16	(LB14, NB4)		18
		231	(7 wkts)		**322**

New Zealand	O	M	R	W
Morrison	39.1	8	145	4
Cairns	12	2	60	0
Snedden	42	10	108	4
Watson	37	7	118	0
Patel	28	5	80	1

Australia	O	M	R	W	O	M	R	W
Alderman	25.4	7	73	3	32	14	59	1
Lawson	22	5	54	1	38	12	88	1
Rackemann	20	4	39	2	31	21	23	1
Hughes	20	7	51	4	36	8	92	3
Moody	4	1	6	0	17	6	23	1
Border	1	0	1	0	5	2	17	0
Jones					3	2	6	0

Fall of Wickets

Wkt	A 1st	NZ 1st	NZ 2nd
1st	28	28	11
2nd	177	84	11
3rd	316	173	79
4th	361	178	107
5th	395	191	189
6th	449	204	189
7th	489	206	234
8th	490	212	–
9th	521	226	–
10th	–	231	–

Australia v Sri Lanka

A first innings lead and an honourable draw in Brisbane, and a defeat with only half an hour left in Hobart – thus, as Allan Border said, Sri Lanka could be proud of their performances in only their third and fourth Tests against Australia and their first Test appearances for 16 months.

Only two weeks before the Brisbane Test, there was widespread pity for the 'poor little Sri Lankans' when they had lost to Victoria by an innings. Victorian captain Simon O'Donnell had said: 'I shudder to think what the Australia Test side will do to them.'

In the event, Sri Lanka more than played their part in two high-quality Tests, and won much-deserved respect and admiration from their Australian opponents, appreciative crowds, and TV audiences of millions. They took a shock 51-run first-innings lead in Brisbane, thanks largely to persistent opening bowler Graeme Labrooy's five-wicket haul and pocket dynamo Aravinda de Silva's marvellous five-hour 167. Australia were left with no other course than to bat out the last eight hours, with opener Mark Taylor's 164 making him the first batsman to pass 1,000 runs in his first year of Test cricket.

De Silva won his second Man of the Match award and the Man of the Series award by again caning the Australians for 75 and 72 in Hobart, where Sri Lanka, having trailed by only 8 on first innings, were set 522 for an unlikely victory and finally succumbed for 348. Complaints about the standard of umpiring and accusations of racist abuse (strenuously denied by the Australians) somewhat soured the otherwise sweet success of Tasmania's first Test and reflected the Sri Lankans' frustration – and inexperience – at this level.

Statistical Highlights of the Tests

1st Test, Brisbane. Moody scored his 1st Test hundred, and shared record 3rd wkt (A v SL) 158 with Border. Australia were dismissed for under 400 in 1st innings after 9 Tests with scores of 400. Aravinda De Silva scored 3rd Test 100, the 1st and highest 100 for SL v A, and shared record 7th-wkt (SL v A) 144 with Ravi Ratnayeke. Taylor scored his 3rd Test 100, highest score A v SL and his 1st in Australia, at 76* reaching 1,000 Test runs in calendar year. He and Waugh put on record 149 for 4th wicket (A v SL).

2nd Test, Hobart. Hobart became the 62nd Test venue. Rumesh Ratnayake took 5 wkts for 3rd time, with match figures (8-189) best for SL v A. Taylor scored his 4th Test hundred, the 1st in a Hobart Test. Hughes took 5 wkts for 4th time, with new record match figures (8-156). Jones scored his 7th Test 100 and Waugh his 3rd (1st in Australia). They put on record 260* for 6th wicket against Sri Lanka. Border took his 123rd catch (Ratnayake) and went ahead of G.S. Chappell's record 122.

Australia v Sri Lanka 1989-90 1st Test

Match Drawn
Played at Woolloongabba, Brisbane, 8, 9, 10, 11, 12 December
Toss: Sri Lanka. Umpires: A.R. Crafter and C.D. Timmins
Debuts: Sri Lanka – D. Ranatunga, A.G.D. Wickremasinghe

Australia

D.C. Boon	c Samarasekera b Labrooy	0	(2) lbw b Ramanayake		26
M.A. Taylor	c Wickremasinghe b Ramanayake	0	(1) lbw b Ramanayake		164
T.M. Moody	c Wickremasinghe b Labrooy	106	c A. Ranatunga b E.A.R. De Silva		30
A.R. Border*	c A. Ranatunga b Labrooy	56			
D.M. Jones	lbw b Labrooy	15	(4) c Ramanayake b P.A. De Silva		23
S.R. Waugh	c A. Ranatunga b Ramanayake	60	(5) b Gurusinha		57
I.A. Healy†	lbw b Gurusinha	21	(6) not out		26
M.G. Hughes	run out (Gurusinha/Wickremasinghe)	25	not out		23
G.F. Lawson	c Wickremasinghe b Labrooy	22			
C.G. Rackemann	not out	5	(7) b Gurusinha		0
T.M. Alderman	c P.A. De Silva b Gurusinha	18			
Extras	(B1, LB8, NB21)	30	(B5, LB4, NB17)		26
		367	(6 wkts)		**375**

Sri Lanka

R.S. Mahanama	lbw b Alderman	5
D. Ranatunga	c Waugh b Lawson	40
A.P. Gurusinha	c Healy b Rackemann	43
E.A.R. De Silva	b Alderman	22
P.A. De Silva	c Lawson b Rackemann	167
A. Ranatunga*	lbw b Hughes	25
M.A.R. Samarasekera	c Moody b Rackemann	18
J.R. Ratnayeke	lbw b Hughes	56
A.G.D. Wickremasinghe†	c Boon b Hughes	2
G.F. Labrooy	lbw b Alderman	1
C.P.H. Ramanayake	not out	10
Extras	(LB23, W2, NB4)	29
		418

Sri Lanka	O	M	R	W	O	M	R	W
Ratnayeke	8.5	1	17	0				
Labrooy	31.1	5	133	5	24	4	69	0
Ramanayake	26	2	101	2	28	3	81	2
A. Ranatunga	13	1	49	0	6	0	25	0
E.A.R. De Silva	8	1	21	0	39	8	112	1
Gurusinha	8.3	1	37	2	10	3	31	2
P.A. De Silva					15	2	45	1
Mahanama					1	0	3	0

Australia	O	M	R	W
Alderman	40	13	81	3
Lawson	33	10	51	1
Rackemann	30.3	6	88	3
Hughes	39	8	123	3
Moody	16	8	15	0
Border	7	0	36	0
Jones	1	0	1	0

Fall of Wickets

Wkt	A 1st	SL 1st	A 2nd
1st	1	10	60
2nd	27	80	124
3rd	185	114	167
4th	197	148	316
5th	210	201	324
6th	247	238	324
7th	295	382	–
8th	339	386	–
9th	339	391	–
10th	367	418	–

Australia v Sri Lanka 1989-90 2nd Test

Australia won by 173 runs
Played at Bellerive Oval, Hobart, 16, 17, 18, 19, 20 December
Toss: Sri Lanka. Umpires: L.J. King and S.G. Randell
Debuts: Sri Lanka – H.P. Tillekeratne

Australia

D.C. Boon	c Mahanama b Ratnayake	41	(2) c Ratnayake b Labrooy		0
M.A. Taylor	c Tillekeratne b Ratnayake	23	(1) c Gurusinha b P.A. De Silva		108
T.M. Moody	c Gurusinha b Ratnayake	6	c Tillekeratne b Ratnayake		5
A.R. Border*	c E.A.R. De Silva b Ratnayeke	24	(5) b P.A. De Silva		85
D.M. Jones	c Tillekeratne b Ratnayake	3	(6) not out		118
S.R. Waugh	c Tillekeratne b Labrooy	16	(7) not out		134
P.R. Sleep	not out	47			
I.A. Healy†	c Tillekeratne b Gurusinha	17			
M.G. Hughes	b E.A.R. De Silva	27	(4) c Gurusinha b Ratnayake		30
G.D. Campbell	c Mahanama b Ratnayake	6			
T.M. Alderman	b Ratnayake	0			
Extras	(LB7, W1, NB6)	14	(B2, LB5, W4, NB22)		33
		224	(5 wkts dec)		**513**

Sri Lanka

R.S. Mahanama	c Healy b Sleep	85	lbw b Campbell		5
D. Ranatunga	c Moody b Alderman	2	c Healy b Hughes		45
A.P. Gurusinha	c Taylor b Alderman	0	c sub (R.J. Tucker) b Hughes		20
E.A.R. De Silva	c Border b Campbell	2	(8) b Campbell		50
P.A. De Silva	lbw b Campbell	75	(4) c Campbell b Sleep		72
A. Ranatunga*	c Moody b Sleep	21	(5) c Jones b Hughes		38
H.P. Tillekeratne†	c Taylor b Sleep	0	(6) c Waugh b Sleep		6
J.R. Ratnayeke	c Taylor b Hughes	9	(7) c Healy b Campbell		75
G.F. Labrooy	b Hughes	11	b Hughes		5
C.P. Ramanayake	not out	4	not out		2
R.J. Ratnayake	c Border b Hughes	0	lbw b Hughes		5
Extras	(LB4, NB3)	7	(B9, LB12, NB4)		25
		216			**348**

Sri Lanka	O	M	R	W	O	M	R	W
Ratnayeke	15	2	39	1	19	1	86	0
Labrooy	19	3	61	1	22	3	100	1
Ratnayake	19.4	2	66	6	35	5	123	2
Ramanayake	4	0	21	0	10	0	49	0
Gurusinha	6	0	20	1				
E.A.R. De Silva	9	6	10	1	21	2	83	0
P.A. De Silva					18	1	65	2

Australia	O	M	R	W	O	M	R	W
Alderman	23	2	71	2	30	12	48	0
Campbell	23	9	41	2	33	8	102	3
Hughes	21.4	6	68	3	31.4	8	88	5
Sleep	10	4	26	3	36	16	73	2
Waugh	6	3	6	0				
Moody					2	0	9	0
Jones					4	2	5	0
Border					5	4	2	0

Fall of Wickets

	A	SL	A	SL
Wkt	1st	1st	2nd	2nd
1st	50	11	1	6
2nd	68	15	10	53
3rd	83	18	77	94
4th	89	146	240	187
5th	112	188	253	187
6th	123	192	–	208
7th	166	193	–	332
8th	207	201	–	337
9th	224	216	–	337
10th	224	216	–	348

Test Match Averages: Australia v Sri Lanka 1989-90

Australia

Batting and Fielding	M	I	NO	HS	R	Avge	100	50	Ct/St
S.R. Waugh	2	4	1	134*	267	89.00	1	2	2
M.A. Taylor	2	4	0	164	304	76.00	2	–	3
A.R. Border	2	3	0	85	165	55.00	–	2	2
D.M. Jones	2	4	1	118*	159	53.00	1	–	1
T.M. Moody	2	4	0	106	147	36.75	1	–	3
M.G. Hughes	2	4	1	30	105	35.00	–	–	–
I.A. Healy	2	3	1	26*	64	32.00	–	–	4/–
D.C. Boon	2	4	0	41	67	16.75	–	–	1

Also batted: T.M. Alderman (2 matches) 18, 0; G.D. Campbell (1 match) 6 (1ct);
G.F. Lawson (1 match) 22 (1ct); C.G. Rackemann (1 match) 5*, 0; P.R. Sleep (1 match) 47*.

Bowling	O	M	R	W	Avge	Best	5wI	10wM
P.R. Sleep	46	20	99	5	19.80	3-26	–	–
M.H. Hughes	92.2	22	279	11	25.36	5-88	1	–
G.D. Campbell	56	17	143	5	28.60	3-102	–	–
T.M. Alderman	93	27	200	5	40.00	3-81	–	–

Also bowled: A.R. Border 12-4-38-0; D.M. Jones 5-2-6-0; G.F. Lawson 33-10-51-1;
T.M. Moody 18-8-24-0; C.G. Rackemann 30.3-6-88-3; S.R. Waugh 6-3-6-0.

Sri Lanka

Batting and Fielding	M	I	NO	HS	R	Avge	100	50	Ct/St
P.A. De Silva	2	3	0	167	314	104.66	1	2	1
J.R. Ratnayeke	2	3	0	75	140	46.66	–	2	–
R.S. Mahanama	2	3	0	85	95	31.66	–	1	2
D. Ranatunga	2	3	0	45	87	29.00	–	–	–
A. Ranatunga	2	3	0	38	84	28.00	–	–	3
E.A.R. De Silva	2	3	0	50	74	24.66	–	1	1
A.P. Gurusinha	2	3	0	43	63	21.00	–	–	3
G.F. Labrooy	2	3	0	11	17	5.66	–	–	–

Also batted: C.P. Ramanayake (2 matches) 10*, 4*, 2* (1ct); R.J. Ratnayake (1 match) 0, 5
(1ct); M.A.R. Samarasekera (1 match) 18 (1 ct); H.P. Tillekeratne (1 match) 0, 6 (5 ct);
A.G.D. Wickremasinghe (1 match) 2 (3ct).

Bowling	O	M	R	W	Avge	Best	5wI	10wM
A.P. Gurusinha	24.3	4	88	5	17.60	2-31	–	–
R.J. Ratnayake	54.4	7	189	8	23.62	6-66	1	–
G.F. Labrooy	96.1	15	363	7	51.85	5-133	1	–

Also bowled: E.A.R. De Silva 77-17-226-2; P.A. De Silva 33-3-110-3; R.S. Mahanama
1-0-3-0; C.P. Ramanayake 68-5-252-4; A. Ranatunga 19-1-74-0; J.R. Ratnayeke
42.5-4-142-1.

Australia v Pakistan

An Australian win by 92 runs, with just 22 minutes to spare, on a sporting Melbourne pitch ... an enthralling draw on an Adelaide 'belter' ... and a rain-ruined draw in Sydney where only 11 hours and 19 minutes of play was possible in six days. So Australia beat Pakistan 1-0 and extended their unbeaten sequence to 14 Tests (seven wins, seven draws) since they had lost to the West Indies in Melbourne in late December 1988. This left Allan Border one short of equalling Don Bradman's Australian captaincy record of 15 consecutive Tests without defeat. However, within six weeks of the Sydney Test against Pakistan, Border was to be denied a share of the record when Australia lost to New Zealand at Wellington.

Pakistan captain Imran Kahn had hailed his team's series with Australia as the one to decide the No. 2 ranking in world cricket – after the West Indies. Later, after what he said was 'definitely' his last tour of Australia, Imran, 37, blamed Pakistan's 'top-order batting and fielding' for their failure to win. 'The Australians showed us how inadequate we were in our catching,' he said. 'They took their catches. But, time and again, we let Australia off the hook by dropping vital catches. And Mark Taylor, of all the batsmen, really showed the temperament required of a top-order batsman. This is where we went wrong. Our top order just didn't function, I was very disappointed. I felt we had a better all-round team and that Australia basically had three fast bowlers (Merv Hughes, Terry Alderman, and Carl Rackemann) who did all the damage.' Imran said Australia's attack was 'quite stereotyped' and they needed a spinner to have a chance of beating the West Indies in the Caribbean from February to May 1991.

In addition, Pakistan were plagued by injury problems. Spinner Abdul Qadir was a shock withdrawal from the tour two days before the first test, giving as his reasons a bruised right ring finger and lack of form. Pakistan's 'Big Three' – fast-bowling all-rounders Imran (hamstring) and Wasim Akram (chronic groin trouble) and ace batsman Javed Miandad (back) – carried injuries throughout the series, and several other players were often unfit.

Akram's explosive left-arm quick bowling and hefty left-hand batting were a revelation to Australian audiences. He was the leading wicket-taker in the series and, in the second Test, scored 52 in 1½ hours and 123 in four hours in a memorable sixth-wicket partnership of 191 with Imran, who, typically, fought defiantly for eight hours for a superb 136. Akram, only 23, won the Man of the Match award in the first two Tests and was the Man of the Series.

Inevitably, the Pakistanis were not satisfied with the umpiring, mainly in Melbourne, where Peter McConnell and Rick Evans gave 11 lbw decisions – eight against them (six in their second innings, including five to Alderman).

Australia v Pakistan 1989-90 1st Test

Australia won by 92 runs
Played at Melbourne Cricket Ground, 12, 13, 14, 15, 16 January
Toss: Pakistan. Umpires: R.J. Evans and P.J. McConnell
Debuts: nil

Australia

G.R. Marsh	c Yousuf b Akram	30	(2) c Akram b Aaqib	24
M.A. Taylor	c Aaqib b Imran	52	(1) c Aamer b Tausif	101
D.C. Boon	lbw b Akram	0	run out (Wasim Akram/ Yousuf	21
A.R. Border*	c Miandad b Akram	24	not out	62
D.M. Jones	c Younis b Imran	0	lbw b Akram	10
S.R. Waugh	c Yousuf b Aaqib	20	c Yousuf b Akram	3
P.R. Sleep	lbw b Akram	23	b Akram	0
I.A. Healy†	c Shoaib b Aaqib	48	c Ijaz b Akram	25
M.G. Hughes	c Mansoor b Akram	8	c Mansoor b Akram	32
T.M. Alderman	c Aamer b Akram	0	not out	1
C.G. Rackemann	not out	0		
Extras	(LB9, NB9)	18	(B2, LB10, W1, NB20)	33
		223	(8 wkts dec)	**312**

Pakistan

Aamer Malik	lbw b Alderman	7	c Taylor b Hughes	0
Shoaib Mohammad	c Healy b Alderman	6	(3) c Boon b Hughes	10
Mansoor Akhtar	c Taylor b Rackemann	5	(2) lbw b Alderman	14
Javed Miandad	c Healy b Alderman	3	lbw b Waugh	65
Ijaz Ahmed	c Taylor b Hughes	19	c Marsh b Hughes	121
Imran Khan*	c Alderman b Rackemann	3	lbw b Alderman	45
Salim Yousuf†	c Taylor b Hughes	16	lbw b Alderman	38
Wasim Akram	c Healy b Hughes	6	c Taylor b Sleep	6
Tausif Ahmed	not out	9	not out	14
Waqar Younis	lbw b Sleep	18	lbw b Alderman	4
Aaqib Javed	c Healy b Rackemann	0	lbw b Alderman	0
Extras	(B1, LB4, NB10)	15	(B1, LB7, W2, NB9)	19
		107		**336**

Pakistan	O	M	R	W	O	M	R	W
Imran Khan	18	6	53	2	8	2	21	0
Wasim Akram	30	9	62	6	41.4	12	98	5
Aaqib Javed	22.1	7	47	2	21	1	55	1
Waqar Younis	12	3	27	0	22	4	68	0
Tausif Ahmed	8	1	25	0	16	3	58	1

Australia	O	M	R	W	O	M	R	W
Alderman	19	6	30	3	33.5	6	105	5
Rackemann	21.5	8	32	3	38	13	67	0
Hughes	17	7	34	3	42	14	79	3
Sleep	8	5	6	1	21	7	64	1
Waugh					3	0	13	1

Fall of Wickets

Wkt	A 1st	P 1st	A 2nd	P 2nd
1st	90	12	73	4
2nd	90	20	116	23
3rd	98	20	204	31
4th	98	44	216	134
5th	131	44	220	218
6th	148	65	220	291
7th	201	71	260	303
8th	223	71	305	328
9th	223	106	–	333
10th	223	107	–	336

Australia v Pakistan 1989-90 2nd Test

Match Drawn
Played at Adelaide Oval, 19, 20, 21, 22, 23 January
Toss: Pakistan. Umpires: A.R. Crafter and L.J. King
Debuts: Pakistan – Mushtaq Ahmed

Pakistan

Shoaib Mohammad	lbw b Hughes	43		c Healy b Hughes	0
Rameez Raja	c P.L. Taylor			c Waugh b Hughes	2
	b Campbell	9			
Salim Yousuf†	lbw b Rackemann	38		c M.A. Taylor b Hughes	1
Javed Miandad	c Healy b Campbell	52	(6)	c P.L. Taylor b Hughes	21
Ijaz Ahmed	c Marsh b Border	28	(4)	c P.L.Taylor b Hughes	4
Salim Malik*	c Healy b Hughes	11	(8)	not out	65
Imran Khan*	c Healy b Rackemann	13	(5)	b P.L. Taylor	136
Wasim Akram	c Border b Campbell	52	(7)	b Campbell	123
Tausif Ahmed	c Healy b Rackemann	0		c Healy b Rackemann	18
Mushtaq Ahmed	c Healy b Rackemann	0		b P.L. Taylor	4
Waqar Younis	not out	1			
Extras	(B4, LB4, W1, NB1)	10		(B4, LB5, W1, NB3)	13
		257		(9 wkts dec)	387

Australia

G.R. Marsh	c Yousuf b Akram	13			
M.A. Taylor	lbw b Imran	77	(1)	c sub (Saeed Anwar)	
				b Mushtaq	59
D.C. Boon	lbw b Akram	29	(2)	c Rameez b Akram	5
A.R. Border*	b Younis	13	(3)	c Yousuf b Younis	8
D.M. Jones	c Akram b Imran	116	(4)	not out	121
S.R. Waugh	lbw b Akram	17	(5)	b Tausif	4
I.A. Healy†	c sub (Maqsood Rana)		(6)	c sub (Aamer Malik)	
	b Younis	12		b Tausif	27
P.L. Taylor	run out (Imran/Yousuf)	33	(7)	c Shoaib b Tausif	1
M.G. Hughes	not out	6	(8)	not out	2
G.D. Campbell	lbw b Akram	0			
C.G. Rackemann	b Akram	0			
Extras	(LB12, NB13)	25		(LB3, NB3)	6
		341		(6 wkts)	233

Australia	O	M	R	W	O	M	R	W
Hughes	18	5	63	2	32	9	111	5
Campbell	21.3	2	79	3	29	5	83	1
Rackemann	21	3	40	4	37	11	85	1
P.L. Taylor	12	0	57	0	41.5	13	94	2
Border	4	0	10	1	4	0	5	0

Pakistan	O	M	R	W	O	M	R	W
Wasim Akram	43	10	100	5	11	3	29	1
Waqar Younis	26	4	66	2	14	4	42	1
Mushtaq Ahmed	23	4	69	0	25	5	72	1
Imran Khan	27	6	61	2				
Tausif Ahmed	14	1	33	0	32	6	80	3
S. Mohammad					1	0	7	0

Fall of Wickets

Wkt	P 1st	A 1st	P 2nd	A 2nd
1st	27	82	0	9
2nd	91	113	2	33
3rd	95	156	7	106
4th	166	188	22	129
5th	187	216	90	213
6th	187	328	281	229
7th	241	328	316	–
8th	251	341	380	–
9th	251	341	387	–
10th	257	341	–	–

Australia v Pakistan 1989-90 3rd Test

Match Drawn
Played at Sydney Cricket Ground, 3(np), 4(np), 5, 6, 7(np), 8 February
Toss: Australia. Umpires: A.R. Crafter and P.J. McConnell
Debuts: Pakistan – Nadeem Ghauri

Pakistan

Aamer Malik	c Healy b Alderman	7
Rameez Raja	c & b Hughes	0
Shoaib Mohammad	lbw b Alderman	9
Javed Miandad	c Jones b Hughes	49
Ijaz Ahmed	c M.A. Taylor b Rackemann	8
Imran Khan*	not out	82
Wasim Akram	c M.A. Taylor b Alderman	10
Salim Yousuf†	c Jones b Rackemann	6
Tausif Ahmed	b Alderman	0
Waqar Younis	c Veletta b Hughes	16
Nadeem Ghauri	b Alderman	0
Extras	(B1, LB7, NB4)	12
		199

Australia

M.A. Taylor	not out	101
M.R.J. Veletta	lbw b Younis	9
T.M. Moody	c Aamer b Tausif	26
A.R. Border*	not out	27
D.M. Jones	did not bat	
S.R. Waugh	,,	
I.A. Healy†	,,	
P.L. Taylor	,,	
M.G. Hughes	,,	
T.M. Alderman	,,	
C.G. Rackemann	,,	
Extras	(B4, LB5, NB4)	13
	(2 wkts)	**176**

Australia	O	M	R	W
Alderman	33.5	10	65	5
Hughes	31	16	70	3
Rackemann	22	8	33	2
P.L. Taylor	8	1	23	0

Pakistan	O	M	R	W
Wasim Akram	10	3	29	0
Imran Khan	17	2	32	0
Tausif Ahmed	19	3	62	1
Nadeem Ghauri	8	1	20	0
Waqar Younis	9	4	21	1
Ijaz Ahmed	2	0	3	0

Fall of Wickets

Wkt	P 1st	A 1st
1st	2	33
2nd	15	106
3rd	20	–
4th	51	–
5th	106	–
6th	128	–
7th	154	–
8th	160	–
9th	191	–
10th	199	–

Test Match Averages: Australia v Pakistan 1989-90

Australia

Batting and Fielding	M	I	NO	HS	R	Avge	100	50	Ct/St
M.A. Taylor	3	5	1	101*	390	97.50	2	3	8
D.M. Jones	3	4	1	121*	247	82.33	2	–	2
A.R. Border	3	5	2	62*	134	44.66	–	1	1
I.A. Healy	3	4	0	48	112	28.00	–	–	12/-
M.G. Hughes	3	4	2	32	48	24.00	–	–	1
G.R. Marsh	2	3	0	30	67	22.33	–	–	2
D.C. Boon	2	4	0	29	55	13.75	–	–	1
S.R. Waugh	3	4	0	20	44	11.00	–	–	1

Also batted: T.M. Alderman (2 matches) 0, 1* (1 ct); G.D. Campbell (1 match) 0; T.M. Moody (1 match) 26; C.G. Rackemann (3 matches) 0*; P.R. Sleep (1 match) 23, 0; P.L. Taylor (2 matches) 33, 1 (3ct); M.R. Veletta (1 match) 9 (1ct).

Bowling	O	M	R	W	Avge	Best	5wI	10wM
T.M. Alderman	86.4	22	200	13	15.38	5-65	2	–
M.H. Hughes	140	51	357	16	22.31	5-111	1	–
C.G. Rackemann	139.5	43	257	10	25.70	4-40	–	–

Also bowled: A.R. Border 8-0-15-1; G.D. Campbell 50.3-7-162-4; P.R. Sleep 29-12-70-2; P.L. Taylor 61.5-14-174-2; S.R. Waugh 3-0-13-1.

Pakistan

Batting and Fielding	M	I	NO	HS	R	Avge	100	50	Ct/St
Imran Khan	3	5	1	136	279	69.75	1	1	–
Wasim Akram	3	5	0	123	197	39.40	1	1	2
Javed Miandad	3	5	0	65	190	38.00	–	2	1
Ijaz Ahmed	3	5	0	121	180	36.00	1	–	1
Salim Yousuf	3	5	0	38	99	19.80	–	–	6/-
Tausif Ahmed	3	5	2	18	41	13.66	–	–	–
Shoaib Mohammad	3	5	0	43	68	13.60	–	–	2
Waqar Younis	3	4	1	18	39	13.00	–	–	–
Aamer Malik	2	3	0	7	14	4.66	–	–	3
Ramiz Raja	2	3	0	9	11	3.66	–	–	1

Also batted: Aaqib Javed (1 match) 0, 0 (1ct); Mansoor Akhtar (1 match) 5, 14 (2ct); Mushtaq Ahmed (1 match) 0, 4; Nadeem Ghauri (1 match) 0; Salim Malik (1 match) 11, 65*.

Bowling	O	M	R	W	Avge	Best	5wI	10wM
Wasim Akram	135.4	37	318	17	18.70	6-62	3	1
Imran Khan	70	16	167	4	41.75	2-53	–	–
Tausif Ahmed	89	14	258	5	51.60	3-80	–	–
Waqar Younis	83	19	224	4	56.00	2-66	–	–

Also bowled: Aaqib Javed 43.1-8-102-3; Ijaz Ahmed 2-0-3-0; Mushtaq Ahmed 48-9-141-1; Nadeem Ghauri 8-1-20-0; Shoaib Mohammad 1-0-7-0.

Statistical Highlights of the Tests

1st Test, Melbourne. Border captained Australia for a record 49th time, beating G.S. Chappell (48). Wasim Akram took 5 wickets for 6th/7th time, the 1st innings being his best innings return. His match figures were also his best, being his 2nd 10 wickets/match. Alderman was his 100th Test wicket in his 30th Test. Taylor scored his 5th Test hundred, his 1st against Pakistan and his third in successive matches. He has now scored 100 on debut against England, Sri Lanka, and Pakistan. Ijaz scored his 2nd Test hundred, also against Australia. Alderman took 5 wickets for 12th time, the 1st against Pakistan. The last wicket fell with just 22 minutes remaining.

2nd Test, Adelaide. Jones scored his 8th/9th Test hundreds, his 1st/2nd against Pakistan. It was the 12th instance (10th player) for Australia and their 3rd instance against Pakistan. Healy took 5 dismissals for 1st time, to give him 50 in Tests. Wasim Akram took 5 wickets for 8th time, his 3rd against Australia. He followed this with his highest first-class score, his 1st Test hundred. Together with Imran, making his highest Test score, he added a record 191 for 6th wicket against Australia. Imran's 6th Test hundred was his 1st against Australia. Taylor brought his aggregate in the year since his 1st Test innings on 27th January 1989 to 1,508 runs, including 5 hundreds and 8 fifties.

3rd Test, Sydney. An extra day was added after the first two were washed out, but the fifth day was also lost, leaving just over 11 hours' play during the 6-day match. Javed Miandad on 8* reached 7,850 runs and went past I.V.A. Richards. Alderman took 5 wickets for 13th time, his 2nd against Pakistan. Taylor scored his 6th Test hundred, his 2nd against Pakistan.

Pakistan tour of Australia 1989-90

First-Class Matches: Played 6; Won 0, Lost 3, Drawn 3
All Matches: Played 17; Won 5, Lost 9, Drawn 3

First-Class Averages

Batting and Fielding	M	I	NO	HS	R	Avge	100	50	Ct/St
Javed Miandad	4	7	1	77	322	53.66	–	4	1
Imran Khan	4	7	1	136	320	53.33	1	1	1
Wasim Akram	3	5	0	123	197	39.40	1	1	2
Ijaz Ahmed	6	11	0	121	349	31.72	1	–	6
Salim Yousuf	6	11	2	78	265	29.44	–	1	12/-
Saeed Anwar	3	6	0	44*	131	21.83	–	–	4
Mansoor Akhtar	3	6	0	74	127	21.16	–	1	2
Shoaib Mohammad	6	11	0	52	219	19.90	–	1	3
Tausif Ahmed	4	7	2	36	99	19.80	–	–	–
Abdul Qadir	2	3	0	51	51	17.00	–	1	1
Mushtaq Ahmed	2	4	0	32	51	12.75	–	–	2
Aamer Malik	5	9	0	53	113	12.55	–	1	5
Waqar Younis	6	9	2	23	81	11.57	–	–	–
Nadeem Ghauri	3	5	1	19	20	5.00	–	–	1
Ramiz Raja	3	5	0	9	24	4.80	–	–	1
Aaqib Javed	4	7	2	9*	10	2.00	–	–	2

Also batted: Maqsood Rana (1 match) 0, 7 (1ct); Salim Malik (1 match) 11,65*.

Bowling	O	M	R	W	Avge	Best	5wI	10wM
Wasim Akram	135.4	37	318	17	18.70	6-62	3	1
Nadeem Ghauri	76	21	194	7	27.71	4-59	–	–
Tausif Ahmed	131.5	26	358	10	35.80	5-42	1	–
Aaqib Javed	121.1	30	327	9	36.33	2-47	–	–
Mushtaq Ahmed	74	18	212	5	42.40	2-17	–	–
Waqar Younis	157	26	496	10	49.60	3-84	–	–
Imran Khan	104	22	247	4	61.75	2-53	–	–

Also bowled: Aamer Malik 14-1-57-2; Abdul Qadir 53.2-8-181-3; Ijaz Ahmed 2-0-3-0; Maqsood Rana 15-2-57-2; Saeed Anwar 14.5-1-35-2; Shoaib Mohammad 5-1-26-0.

New Zealand v India

The three-match series, which New Zealand won 1-0, was a splendid advertisement for cricket and will also be remembered as the occasion when Richard Hadlee took his 400th Test wicket.

Hadlee, 38, having had surgery on his Achilles tendon not long before, was not expected to play in the first Test on his home ground, Christchurch's Lancaster Park. But closer to its start, Willie Watson injured himself and Hadlee, after finding himself bowling well in the nets, was persuaded to fill the breach. New Zealand won the toss and put up a huge score of 459, their innings stretching past tea on the second day. Its main pillar was 185 by John Wright, who batted for 554 minutes. By the end of the second day, India had lost three wickets, all taken by Hadlee, who now needed only one more for his 400. Failing to get it in his first spell next morning, he had to wait until the second innings because Morrison and Snedden ran through the rest of the Indian batting.

To add to India's misery in being bowled out on a good pitch for a meagre 164, Sidhu had sustained a fracture in his finger while making a gritty 51 and was ruled out from playing again on the tour. The experienced Vengsarkar was hurriedly sent for as a replacement.

Prabhakar, promoted to open the innings when India followed on, did his bit and with Raman put on 80 for the first wicket. The stand was broken by Morrison, and Hadlee was brought on fresh to bowl at the new batsman, Manjrekar, bowling him fourth delivery for the historic wicket.

The depressing prospect of defeat did not stop the Indians participating in the jubilation that Hadlee's feat sparked off. Always an extrovert, Bishen Bedi, India's coach, ran out to congratulate Hadlee and the new batsman, skipper Azharuddin, warmly shook his hand on his way to the wicket. Hadlee took three more wickets to hasten India's rout. New Zealand winning by 10 wickets with a day to spare.

Rain played havoc with the second Test at Napier. Although the pitch was slow in the extreme, India's innings – a solid 95 from Prabhakar notwithstanding – was faltering until Tendulkar made 88, an indiscreet shot preventing his becoming cricket's youngest Test century maker. John Wright notched up another hundred before the weather intervened.

The third Test, at Auckland, was also marred by rain, but both sides played some magnificent and exciting cricket before it struck. Put in on a lively pitch, New Zealand were 85 for 6 at one stage, with Wasson playing havoc. But they came back strongly to total 391, thanks to a lusty 87 from Hadlee and a swashbuckling 173 in only 136 balls from Ian Smith. India's shaky start was rectified by a superb 192 in 259 balls by Azharuddin. A Test up, New Zealand needed no more than a draw to clinch the series, and 170 from Jones and 113 by Martin Crowe, who had a poor series otherwise, ensured it long before the rain arrived on the final day.

New Zealand v India 1989-90 1st Test

New Zealand won by 10 wickets
Played at Lancaster Park, Christchurch, 2, 3, 4, 5 February
Toss: New Zealand. Umpires: R.S. Dunne and S.J. Woodward
Debuts: India – S.L. Venkatapathy Raju, A.S. Wassan

New Zealand

T.J. Franklin	c Prabhakar b Kapil Dev	20		
J.G. Wright*	b Raju	185		
A.H. Jones	c Raju b Hirwani	52		
M.D. Crowe	lbw b Raju	24		
M.J. Greatbach	b Wassan	46		
K.R. Rutherford	b Kapil Dev	69		
J.G. Bracewell	b Hirwani	0		
I.D.S. Smith†	lbw b Raju	9		
R.J. Hadlee	c Hirwani b Prabhakar	28		
M.C. Snedden	lbw b Kapil Dev	3	(1) not out	1
D.K. Morrison	not out	1	(2) not out	1
Extras	(B3, LB12, NB7)	22		
		459	(0 wkt)	**2**

India

W.V. Raman	lbw b Hadlee	0	c Jones b Morrison	96
N.S. Sidhu	lbw b Morrison	51	absent injured	
S.V. Manjrekar	c Jones b Hadlee	5	b Hadlee	4
M. Azharuddin*	lbw b Hadlee	48	b Bracewell	30
S.L. Venkatapathy Raju	c Crowe b Snedden	31	(8) c Smith b Snedden	21
S.R. Tendulkar	c Smith b Morrison	0	c Smith b Bracewell	24
M. Prabhakar	c Smith b Snedden	1	(2) b Snedden	40
Kapil Dev	c Snedden b Morrison	4	(7) lbw b Hadlee	25
K.S. Moré†	c Smith b Morrison	1	(5) b Hadlee	11
A.S. Wassan	c Smith b Morrison	2	(9) not out	24
N.D. Hirwani	not out	1	(10) c Bracewell b Hadlee	0
Extras	(B5, LB5, NB10)	20	(B6, LB2, NB13)	21
		164		**296**

India	O	M	R	W	O	M	R	W
Kapil Dev	28.3	4	89	3				
Prabhakar	38	8	114	1	0.5	0	2	0
Raju	35	12	86	3				
Wassan	25	3	95	1				
Hirwani	29	9	60	2				

New Zealand	O	M	R	W	O	M	R	W
Hadlee	14	1	45	3	22.5	3	69	4
Morrison	16	2	75	5	19	0	94	1
Bracewell	3	0	14	0	20	3	45	2
Snedden	12.5	4	20	2	25	5	59	2
Rutherford					5	0	21	0

Fall of Wickets

Wkt	NZ 1st	I 1st	I 2nd	NZ 2nd
1st	26	0	80	–
2nd	131	27	85	–
3rd	182	88	135	–
4th	307	146	160	–
5th	374	146	206	–
6th	375	148	242	–
7th	394	153	254	–
8th	448	158	289	–
9th	454	161	296	–
10th	459	164	–	–

New Zealand v India 1989-90 2nd Test

Match drawn
Played at McLean Park, Napier, 9(np), 10, 11, 12, 13(np) February
Toss: India. Umpires: B.L. Aldridge and S.J. Woodward
Debuts: nil

India

W.V. Raman	lbw b Hadlee	0
M. Prabhakar	c Smith b Hadlee	95
S.V. Manjrekar	c Smith b Morrison	42
M. Azharuddin*	b Morrison	33
D.B. Vengsarkar	c Smith b Morrison	0
S.R. Tendulkar	c Wright b Morrison	88
Kapil Dev	lbw b Hadlee	4
K.S. Moré†	c Franklin b Snedden	73
S.L. Venkatapathy Raju	not out	3
A.S. Wassan	b Morrison	0
N.D. Hirwani	not out	1
Extras	(LB5, NB14)	19
	(9 wkts dec)	**358**

New Zealand

T.J. Franklin	c Kapil Dev b Wassan	50
J.G. Wright*	not out	113
A.H. Jones	not out	4
M.D. Crowe	did not bat	
M.J. Greatbatch	,,	
K.R. Rutherford	,,	
I.D.S. Smith†	,,	
R.J. Hadlee	,,	
J.G. Bracewell	,,	
M.C. Snedden	,,	
D.K. Morrison	,,	
Extras	(B5, LB3, W1, NB2)	11
	(1 wkt)	**178**

New Zealand	O	M	R	W
Hadlee	35	11	73	3
Morrison	38	8	98	5
Snedden	42	10	104	1
Bracewell	22	2	50	0
Rutherford	9	0	28	0

India	O	M	R	W
Prabhakar	13	3	25	0
Kapil Dev	14	4	30	0
Wassan	15	2	48	1
Hirwani	18	7	40	0
Raju	11	4	27	0

Fall of Wickets

	I	NZ
Wkt	1st	1st
1st	0	149
2nd	92	–
3rd	150	–
4th	152	–
5th	210	–
6th	218	–
7th	346	–
8th	356	–
9th	356	–
10th	–	–

New Zealand v India 1989-90 3rd Test

Match Drawn
Played at Eden Park, Auckland, 22, 23, 24, 25, 26 February
Toss: India. Umpires: B.L. Aldridge and R.S. Dunne
Debuts: New Zealand – S.A. Thomson.   India – Gursharan Singh

New Zealand

T.J. Franklin	c Tendulkar b Wassan	4	lbw b Prabhakar	2
J.G. Wright*	c Gursharan b Kapil Dev	3	c Wassan b Hirwani	74
A.H. Jones	c Moré b Prabhakar	19	not out	170
M.D. Crowe	c Moré b Wassan	24	lbw b Hirwani	113
M.J. Greatbatch	b Wassan	4	c Gursharan b Wassan	43
K.R. Rutherford	c Prabhakar b Wassan	20	c Moré b Hirwani	8
S.A. Thomson	c Moré b Kapil Dev	22	not out	43
R.J. Hadlee	b Hirwani	87		
I.D.S. Smith†	lbw b Prabhakar	173		
M.C. Snedden	c Moré b Prabhakar	22		
D.K. Morrison	not out	0		
Extras	(LB9, NB4)	13	(B4, LB14, NB12)	30
		391	(5 wkts dec)	**483**

India

W.V. Raman	c Franklin b Hadlee	8	not out	72
M. Prabhakar	lbw b Snedden	36	not out	63
S.V. Manjrekar	b Morrison	16		
D.B. Vengsarkar	c Smith b Morrison	47		
M. Azharuddin*	c Rutherford b Thomson	192		
S.R. Tendulkar	c Smith b Morrison	5		
Gursharan Singh	c & b Thomson	18		
Kapil Dev	c Jones b Hadlee	22		
K.S. Moré†	lbw b Morrison	50		
A.S. Wassan	b Morrison	53		
N.D. Hirwani	not out	0		
Extras	(B1, LB11, W1, NB22)	35	(LB9, NB5)	14
		482	(0 wkt)	**149**

India	O	M	R	W	O	M	R	W
Kapil Dev	29.2	6	85	2	31	4	101	0
Prabhakar	29.2	3	123	3	38	6	118	1
Wassan	16.4	1	108	4	25	5	80	1
Hirwani	17	1	66	1	46	11	143	3
Raman					19	10	23	0

New Zealand	O	M	R	W	O	M	R	W
Hadlee	30	8	123	2	4	1	9	0
Morrison	30	3	145	5	7	1	34	0
Snedden	26	4	110	1	12	1	29	0
Thomson	18.3	3	92	2	9	1	30	0
Jones					9	1	28	0
Rutherford					3	0	10	0
Greatbatch					1	1	0	0

Fall of Wickets

	NZ	I	NZ	I
Wkt	1st	1st	2nd	2nd
1st	8	15	7	–
2nd	29	65	155	–
3rd	29	71	334	–
4th	51	215	396	–
5th	64	223	406	–
6th	85	263	–	–
7th	131	308	–	–
8th	234	396	–	–
9th	370	482	–	–
10th	391	482	–	–

Test Match Averages: New Zealand v India 1989-90

New Zealand

Batting and Fielding	M	I	NO	HS	R	Avge	100	50	Ct/St
J.G. Wright	3	4	1	185	375	125.00	2	1	1
A.H. Jones	3	4	2	170*	245	122.50	1	1	3
I.D.S. Smith	3	2	0	173	182	91.00	1	–	11
M.D. Crowe	3	3	0	113	161	53.66	1	–	1
K.R. Rutherford	3	3	0	69	97	32.33	–	1	1
M.J. Greatbatch	3	3	0	46	93	31.00	–	–	–
T.J. Franklin	3	4	0	50	76	19.00	–	1	2
M.C. Snedden	3	3	1	22	26	13.00	–	–	1

Also batted: J.G. Bracewell (2 matches) 0 (1ct); R.J. Hadlee (3 matches) 28, 87;
D.K. Morrison (3 matches) 1*, 1*, 0*; S.A. Thomson (1 match) 22, 43* (1ct).

Bowling	O	M	R	W	Avge	Best	5wI	10wM
R.J. Hadlee	105.5	24	319	12	26.58	4-69	–	–
D.K. Morrison	110	14	446	16	27.87	5-75	3	–
M.C. Snedden	117.5	24	322	6	53.66	2-20	–	–

Also bowled: J.G. Bracewell 45-5-109-2; M.J. Greatbatch 1-1-0-0; A.H. Jones 9-1-28-0;
K.R. Rutherford 17-0-59-0; S.A. Thomson 27.3-4-122-2.

India

Batting and Fielding	M	I	NO	HS	R	Avge	100	50	Ct/St
M. Azharuddin	3	4	0	192	303	75.75	1	–	–
M. Prabhakar	3	5	1	95	235	58.75	–	2	2
W.V. Raman	3	5	1	96	176	44.00	–	2	–
K.S. Moré	3	4	0	73	135	33.75	–	2	5/-
S.R. Tendulkar	3	4	0	88	117	29.25	–	1	1
S. Venkatapathy Raju	2	3	1	31	55	27.50	–	–	1
A. Wassan	3	4	1	53	79	26.33	–	1	1
S.V. Manjrekar	3	4	0	42	67	16.75	–	–	–
Kapil Dev	3	4	0	25	55	13.75	–	–	1
N.D. Hirwani	3	4	3	1*	2	2.00	–	–	1

Also batted: Gursharan Singh (1 match) 18 (2ct); N.S. Sidhu (1 match) 51; D.B. Vengsarkar
(2 matches) 0, 47.

Bowling	O	M	R	W	Avge	Best	5wI	10wM
A. Wassan	81.4	11	331	7	47.28	4-108	–	–
N.D. Hirwani	110	28	309	6	51.50	3-143	–	–
Kapil Dev	102.5	18	305	5	61.00	3-89	–	–
M. Prabhakar	119.1	20	382	5	76.40	3-123	–	–

Also bowled: W.V. Raman 19-10-23-0; S. Venkatapathy Raju 46-16-113-3.

Statistical Highlights of the Tests

1st Test, Christchurch. Wright scored his 8th Test hundred, his 2nd against India and his highest score in his career. He and Rutherford added 125 for a 4th-wicket record for New Zealand against India. Morrison took 5 wickets for 2nd time, his 1st against India. In the 2nd innings Manjrekar became Hadlee's 400th victim in his 80th Test.

2nd Test, Napier. This was the 2nd scheduled Test for Napier and, like the 1st in February 1979, the match was marred by rain. Morrison took 5 wickets for the 3rd time. Moré, in making his highest Test score, added 128 with Tendulkar for a 7th-wicket record against New Zealand. Wright scored his 9th Test hundred, his 3rd against India. He and Franklin added 149 for a 1st-wicket record against India.

3rd Test, Auckland. Smith scored his 2nd Test hundred, his highest Test score, and added two new record partnerships for New Zealand against India – 103 with Hadlee for 8th wicket and 136 with Snedden for 9th. Azharuddin scored his 8th Test hundred, his 1st against New Zealand. It is the highest score for India against New Zealand in New Zealand. Snedden took his 50th Test wicket. Jones scored his 2nd Test hundred and Crowe his 11th, both for the 1st time against India. Wright at 27* in the 2nd innings became the 1st New Zealand batsman to score 4,000 Test runs. Morrison took 5 wickets for the 4th time and 3rd in successive Tests against India, to finish with a record 16 wickets for a series against India in New Zealand. The match was the highest aggregate (1,505 runs) for a Test between the two countries and India's total was their highest in New Zealand.

India Tour of New Zealand 1989-90

First-Class Matches: Played 6; Won 1, Lost 1, Drawn 4

All Matches: Played: 10; Won 2, Lost 4, Drawn 4

First-Class Averages

Batting and Fielding	M	I	NO	HS	R	Avge	100	50	Ct/St
K.S. Moré	5	8	4	73	301	75.25	–	4	13/1
Gursharan Singh	3	5	1	115	274	68.50	1	2	3
M. Azharuddin	5	8	0	192	505	63.12	2	–	2
W.V. Raman	5	9	1	123	460	57.50	1	4	3
A.K. Sharma	2	4	1	87	160	53.33	–	2	–
M. Prabhakar	4	7	1	95	260	43.33	–	2	3
N.S. Sidhu	2	3	0	51	104	34.66	–	1	–
V.B. Chandrasekhar	3	6	0	92	204	34.00	–	2	6
S.R. Tendulkar	5	8	1	88	211	30.14	–	1	1
S.V. Manjrekar	5	8	0	82	240	30.00	–	2	1
A. Wassan	5	5	2	53	90	30.00	–	1	1
S. Venkatapathy Raju	5	7	2	52*	122	24.40	–	1	2
Kapil Dev	5	7	0	25	101	14.42	–	–	2
D.B. Vengsarkar	3	4	0	47	52	13.00	–	–	–
N.D. Hirwani	5	7	4	11	15	5.00	–	–	1

Also batted: V. Razdan (2 matches) 18, 0; M. Venkataramana (2 matches) 7 (2ct).

Bowling	O	M	R	W	Avge	Best	5wI	10wM
N.D. Hirwani	192	55	480	15	32.00	4-31	–	–
S. Venkatapathy Raju	211	64	496	13	38.15	3-72	–	–
A. Wassan	167.4	25	601	15	40.06	4-108	–	–
M. Prabhakar	154.2	28	493	12	41.08	4-87	–	–
Kapil Dev	148.5	35	398	7	56.85	3-89	–	–

Also bowled: K.S. Moré 1-0-7-0; W.V. Raman 23-10-44-0; V. Razdan 60-10-227-1; A.K. Sharma 24-5-79-1; S.R. Tendulkar 9-2-23-0; M. Venkataramana 74.1-12-289-4.

New Zealand v Australia

The great moment of the Australians' one-Test tour of New Zealand came when they were in the process of beating New Zealand in their opening one-day match at Christchurch. Simon O'Donnell bowled what John Bracewell regarded as a vicious 'beamer' heading straight for his face. Bracewell ducked hastily and did not even see the ball drop sharply, bounce under his bottom, and hit the leg stump. It was the most masterly change-of-pace ball New Zealanders have recently seen, and poor Bracewell went shamefacedly away. It was all a mystery to him.

And the Australians' other one-day expertise was equally a mystery to the New Zealand and Indian sides who played the first tri-series in New Zealand. Dean Jones had scores of 32, 107, 59, and 102 not out in his four one-day matches. O'Donnell, Carl Rackemann, and Terry Alderman bowled expertly, and the fielding was precise as clockwork. The other sides were not in the race. Australia were unbeaten in the preliminary games, and thrashed New Zealand in the final.

In the solitary Test, at the Basin reserve, Allan Border surprised everyone by batting first on a dampish pitch with a slow outfield. Danny Morrison and Richard Hadlee had the first five wickets for 38, and in slightly more than three hours Australia were out for 110.

New Zealand scraped together a first innings lead of 92, only to see Peter Taylor play a nightwatchman innings of 78 in four hours to haul Australia to 269, with Bracewell taking 6 for 85, his last four for only 19 runs. New Zealand needed 178. John Wright started cautiously, but then blazed away to 117 not out, his last 50 from 74 balls. to lead New Zealand to their nine-wicket win.

Statistical Highlights of the Test

Single Test, Wellington. Australia were defeated for the first time in 15 Tests as New Zealand recorded their first win over them at Wellington. Hadlee took 5 wickets for 35th time, his 14th against Australia. It was the 100th time in his first-class career. Then, at 1*, he reached 3,000 Test runs, the 4th player after Botham, Kapil Dev, and Imran Khan to have 3,000 runs and 300 wickets. Alderman became the 11th Australian bowler to take 150 Test wickets. In the 2nd innings Peter Taylor reached his highest Test score. Bracewell took 5 wickets for 4th time, his 2nd against Australia. Wright scored his 10th Test hundred, his 2nd against Australia. Jones, at 4*, reached 1,000 Test runs in his 24th innings. He and Wright added 128* for a record 2nd-wicket partnership for New Zealand against Australia.

New Zealand v Australia 1989-90

New Zealand won by 9 wickets
Played at Basin Reserve, Wellington, 15, 16, 17, 18, 19 March
Toss: Australia. Umpires: R.S. Dunne and S.J. Woodward
Debuts: nil

Australia

M. A. Taylor	lbw b Morrison	4	(2) lbw b Hadlee		5
G.R. Marsh	b Morrison	4	(1) c Rutherford b Bracewell		41
D.C. Boon	lbw b Hadlee	0	c Smith b Bracewell		12
A.R. Border*	lbw b Morrison	1	(5) not out		78
D.M. Jones	c Wright b Snedden	20	(6) lbw b Morrison		0
S.R. Waugh	b Hadlee	25	(7) c Greatbatch b Hadlee		25
I.A. Healy†	b Snedden	0	(8) c Rutherford b Bracewell		10
P.L. Taylor	c Wright b Hadlee	29	(4) c Smith b Morrison		87
G.D. Campbell	lbw b Hadlee	4	b Bracewell		0
C.G. Rackemann	not out	6	b Bracewell		1
T.M. Alderman	b Hadlee	4	st Smith b Bracewell		1
Extras	(LB6, NB7)	13	(LB6, NB3)		9
		110			**269**

New Zealand

T.J. Franklin	c Marsh b P.L. Taylor	28	c Healy b Campbell	18
J.G. Wright*	c Healy b Alderman	36	not out	117
A.H. Jones	c & b Border	18	not out	33
M.C. Snedden	b Alderman	23		
M.J. Greatbatch	c Healy b P.L. Taylor	16		
K.R. Rutherford	c Healy b P.L. Taylor	12		
J.J. Crowe	lbw b Alderman	9		
R.J. Hadlee	lbw b Campbell	18		
I.D.S. Smith†	c M.A. Taylor b Campbell	1		
J.G. Bracewell	not out	19		
D.K. Morrison	c M.A. Taylor b Alderman	12		
Extras	(B2, LB5, NB3)	10	(B2, LB10, NB1)	13
		202	(1 wkt)	**181**

New Zealand	O	M	R	W	O	M	R	W
Hadlee	16.2	5	39	5	25	3	70	2
Morrison	10	4	22	3	24	8	58	2
Snedden	15	3	33	2	25	5	46	0
Rutherford	2	0	8	0				
Bracewell	2	1	2	0	34.2	11	85	6
Jones					1	0	4	0

Australia	O	M	R	W	O	M	R	W
Alderman	29	9	46	4	14	8	27	0
Rackemann	32	17	42	0	15	4	39	0
P.L. Taylor	33	19	44	3	11	3	39	0
Campbell	21	3	51	2	7	2	23	1
Border	6	3	12	1	10.4	5	27	0
Jones					6	3	14	0

Fall of Wickets

Wkt	A 1st	NZ 1st	A 2nd	NZ 2nd
1st	4	48	27	53
2nd	9	89	54	–
3rd	9	89	91	–
4th	12	111	194	–
5th	38	123	194	–
6th	44	150	232	–
7th	70	151	261	–
8th	87	152	261	–
9th	103	171	267	–
10th	110	202	269	–

Nehru Cup

Wasim Akram struck Viv Richards over wide long-on for the memorable six that provided a thrilling climax to the crazy extravaganza that was billed as the 'World Series'. The adage that the finish is everything in the limited-overs game was proved, as much of the rest of the tournament was quite forgettable.

Six of seven Test nations scrambled from centre to centre for an elaborate 15-match preliminary league, which was more a test of nerves than cricket skills. Australia, the World Cup champions in much the same conditions just two seasons previously, were eliminated. But after a long and successful tour of England, their hearts were not in it. Sri Lanka, who shocked the West Indies in their first game, faded after losing close games to India and Pakistan.

The West Indies beat India in a bloodless semi-final, while Pakistan just managed to pass England in a high-scoring, rain-affected game at Nagpur. There was much good cricket in the final, a free-flowing contest that was swung Pakistan's way by the nerveless presence of Imran Khan at the finish after the hectic run chase had earlier been managed so well by Salim Malik's obvious brilliance.

Qualifying Rounds

15 October at Feroz Shah Kotla, Delhi. ENGLAND beat SRI LANKA by 5 wickets. Toss: England. Sri Lanka 193 (48.3 overs) (P.A. De Silva 80). England 196-5 (48.4 overs) (R.A. Smith 81*, A.J. Lamb 52). Award: R.A. Smith (81*).

19 October at Lal Bahadur Shastri Stadium, Hyderabad. ENGLAND beat AUSTRALIA by 7 wickets. Toss: Australia. Australia 242-3 (50 overs) (G.R. Marsh 54, D.M. Jones 50, A.R. Border 84*). England 243-3 (47.3 overs) (W. Larkins 124, G.A. Gooch 56). Award: W. Larkins (124).

19 October at Municipal Ground Rajkot. SRI LANKA beat WEST INDIES by 4 wickets. Toss: Sri Lanka. West Indies 176-9 (50 overs) (D.L. Haynes 42, A.L. Logie 54*). Sri Lanka 180-6 (47.1 overs) (A.P. Gurusinha 66). Award: A.P. Gurusinha (66 & 1ct).

21 October at Chidambaram Stadium, Chepauk, Madras. AUSTRALIA beat WEST INDIES by 99 runs. Toss: Australia. Australia 241-6 (50 overs) (G.R. Marsh 74, A.R. Border 46, S.R. Waugh 53*). West Indies 142 (40.3 overs) (R.B. Richardson 61). Award: A.R. Border (46 & 10-2-20-3).

22 October at Baribati Stadium, Cuttack. ENGLAND beat PAKISTAN by 4 wickets. Toss: Pakistan. Pakistan 148-9 (50 overs) (Salim Malik 42). England 149-6 (43.2 overs) (A.J. Lamb 42). Award: G.A. Gooch (10-4-19-3).

22 October at Gujarat Stadium, Ahmedabad. INDIA beat SRI LANKA by 6 runs. Toss: India. India 227-8 (50 overs) (N.S. Sidhu 80). Sri Lanka 221 (49.4 overs) (A.P. Gurusinha 83). Award: N.S. Sidhu (80 & 1ct).

23 October at Wankhede Stadium, Bombay. PAKISTAN beat AUSTRALIA by 66 runs. Toss: Australia. Pakistan 205-8 (50 overs) (Shoaib Mohammad 73; T.M. Alderman 10-3-22-4). Australia 139 (43.2 overs) (D.M. Jones 58). Award: Imran Khan (8-2-13-3).

23 October at Feroz Shah Kotla, Delhi. WEST INDIES beat INDIA by 20 runs. Toss: India. West Indies 196-9 (45 overs) (R.B. Richardson 57, I.V.A. Richards 44). India 176 (41.4 overs) (R. Lamba 61; I.V.A. Richards 9.4-0-41-6).
Award: I.V.A. Richards (44, 9.4-0-41-6 & 1ct).

25 October at Fatorda Stadium, Margoa. AUSTRALIA beat SRI LANKA by 28 runs. Toss: Australia 222-7 (50 overs) (D.M. Jones 85). Sri Lanka 194 (47.1 overs) (P.A. De Silva 96).
Award: P.A. De Silva (9-0-36-0 & 96).

25 October at Green Park, Kanpur. INDIA beat ENGLAND by 6 wickets. Toss: India. England 255-7 (50 overs) (W. Larkins 42, A.J. Lamb 91, A.J. Stewart 61). India 259-4 (48.1 overs) (N.S. Sidhu 61, C. Sharma 101*). Award: C. Sharma (101*).

25 October at Burlton Park, Jullundur. WEST INDIES beat PAKISTAN by 6 wickets. Toss: Pakistan. Pakistan 223-5 (50 overs) (Aamer Malik 77, Salim Malik 44*). West Indies 226-4 (48.3 overs) (R.B. Richardson 80, P.J.L. Dujon 46, I.V.A. Richards 47*). Award: R.B. Richardson (80).

27 October at Chinnaswamy Stadium, Bangalore. INDIA beat AUSTRALIA by 3 wickets. Toss: Australia. Australia 247-8 (50 overs) (D.C. Boon 49, D.M. Jones 53, A.R. Border 41). India 249-7 (47.1 overs) (K. Srikkanth 58, R. Lamba 57). Award: A.K. Sharma (10-0-41-3 & 32).

27 October at Roop Singh Stadium, Gwalior. WEST INDIES beat ENGLAND by 26 runs. Toss: West Indies. West Indies 265-5 (50 overs) (D.L. Haynes 138*, R.B. Richardson 44). England 239-8 (50 overs) (G.A. Gooch 59, R.A. Smith 65; M.D. Marshall 10-0-33-4). Award: D.L. Haynes (138*).

27 October at K.D. Singh Bahu Stadium, Lucknow. PAKISTAN beat SRI LANKA by 6 runs. Toss: Pakistan. Pakistan 219-6 (50 overs) (Imran Khan 84*). Sri Lanka 213 (49.2 overs) (H.P. Tillekeratne 71, P.A. De Silva 83). Award: Imran Khan (84* & 7-0-29-0).

28 October at Eden Gardens, Calcutta. PAKISTAN beat INDIA by 77 runs. Toss: India. Pakistan 279-7 (50 overs) (Aamer Malik 51, Ramiz Raja 77, Imran Khan 47*). India 202 (42.3 overs) (K. Srikkanth 65, R. Lamba 57). Award: Imran Khan (47*).

Qualifying Table	P	W	L	Run Rate	Points
INDIA	5	3	2	4.63	12
ENGLAND	5	3	2	4.51	12
PAKISTAN	5	3	2	4.30	12
WEST INDIES	5	3	2	4.11	12
Australia	5	2	3	4.36	8
Sri Lanka	5	1	4	4.05	4

Semi-Finals

30 October at Wankhede Stadium, Bombay. WEST INDIES beat INDIA by 8 wickets. Toss: India 165 (48.5 overs). West Indies 166-2 (42.1 overs) (D.L. Haynes 64, R.B. Richardson 58*). Award: I.V.A. Richards (4-0-21-0 & 3ct).

30 October at Vidharba C.A. Stadium, Nagpur. PAKISTAN beat ENGLAND by 6 wickets. Toss: Pakistan. England 194-7 (30 overs) (R.A. Smith 55). Pakistan 195-4 (28.3 overs) (Ramiz Raja 85*, Salim Malik 66). Award: Ramiz Raja (85*).

Final

1 November at Eden Gardens, Calcutta. PAKISTAN beat WEST INDIES by 4 wickets. Toss: West Indies. West Indies 273-5 (50 overs) (D.L. Haynes 107*, P.V. Simmons 40). Pakistan 277-6 (49.5 overs) (Ijaz Ahmed 56, Salim Malik 71, Imran Khan 55*). Award: Imran Khan (9-0-47-3 & 55*).

Player of the Series: Imran Khan (Pakistan).
Pakistan won the Nehru Cup and US$40,000.

Benson & Hedges World Series Cup

Australia won the Benson & Hedges World Series Cup for the fifth time in the triangular competition's 11 seasons by beating Pakistan 2-0 in the best-of-three final. Australia had beaten New Zealand in 1980-81, 1982-83, and 1987-88 and India in 1985-86. This time, Australia defeated Pakistan by seven wickets with 4.1 overs to spare in the first final, under lights in Melbourne (before a crowd of 55,205) and by 69 runs with five overs to spare in the sceond final two days later, in Sydney (34,443).

Prize money and bonuses boosted the Australian's haul from the lucrative limited-overs competition to a massive $A82,500 in their season's total collect of $A155,500. The Pakistanis shared $A48,500, including $A37,500 from the cup. The Sri Lankans earned $A22,000, including $A14,000 from the cup.

Australian batsman Dean Jones won the Player of the Series and Player of the Finals awards, but Pakistan captain Imran Khan was adjudged the International Cricketer of the Year – fractionally ahead of Jones after Imran's votes were weighted slightly (multiplied by 1.182) because Jones had the opportunity to play in more Tests during the Australian season. Imran donated his prize – a $A72,000 Rover motor-car – to a cancer hospital in Pakistan.

The cup competition was again split into two sections, with the first five matches played in late December/early January – just before Australia's three Tests against Pakistan. The other nine, including the two finals, took place from February 10 to 25 – immediately after the third Test. Australia won six of their eight qualifying matches, losing both of their last two against Pakistan, who also beat Sri Lanka three times in four meetings. Sri Lanka's only cup victory was against Pakistan in their first clash – by three wickets with 3.1 overs to spare, under lights in Perth on New Year's Eve.

Jones was easily the outstanding batsman of the competition, with 461 runs (avge. 76.83). The Australians believe he is the best one-day batsman in the world. No other batsman in the three teams reached 300, nor did any others have an average of 50. Jones' scores were: 85 not out, 2, 69 (run out), 32 (run out), 54 (run out), 80 not out, 10, 83 not out, and 46 (run out). Pakistan's teenage quickie Aaqib Javed was the only bowler to dismiss him – bowled in Melbourne and caught in Sydney.

Five Australian batsmen – Jones, David Boon, Allan Border, Geoff Marsh, and Simon O'Donnell – averaged more than 40, although injuries restricted Boon and Marsh to three and four games, respectively. Australia also boasted the five most successful bowlers – O'Donnell (20), Terry Alderman (16), Carl Rackemann (13), Peter Taylor (12), and Greg Campbell (10) – who shared 71 wickets.

Qualifying Rounds

26 December at Melbourne Cricket Ground. AUSTRALIA beat SRI LANKA by 30 runs. Toss: Sri Lanka. Australia 228-5 (48.5 overs) (D.M. Jones 85*, S.P. O'Donnell 57*). Sri Lanka 198 (47.2 overs) (A. Ranatunga 55; S.P. O'Donnell 9-1-36-4). Award: S.P. O'Donnell (57*, 9-1-36-4 & 1ct).

30 December at WACA Ground, Perth (floodlit). AUSTRALIA beat SRI LANKA by 9 wickets. Toss: Sri Lanka. Sri Lanka 203-9 (48 overs) (A. Ranatunga 71*). Australia 204-1 (38.5 overs) (G.R. Marsh 80*, D.C. Boon 49*). Award: G.R. Marsh (80*).

31 December at WACA Ground, Perth (floodlit). SRI LANKA beat PAKISTAN by 3 wickets. Toss: Pakistan. Pakistan 222-7 (47 overs) (Aamer Malik 69, Javed Miandad 43). Sri Lanka 223-7 (45.3 overs) (M.A.R. Samarasekera 60, P.A. De Silva 40). Award: M.A.R. Samarasekera (60).

3 January at Melbourne Cricket Ground (floodlit). AUSTRALIA beat PAKISTAN by 7 wickets. Toss: Pakistan. Pakistan 161 (50 overs). Australia 162-3 (41 overs) (A.R. Border 69*). Award: A.R. Border (69*).

4 January at Melbourne Cricket Ground (floodlit). AUSTRALIA beat SRI LANKA by 73 runs. Toss: Australia. Australia 202-7 (50 overs) (D.M. Jones 69). Sri Lanka 129 (41 overs). Award: D.M. Jones (69).

10 February at Woolloongabba, Brisbane. PAKISTAN beat SRI LANKA by 5 wickets. Toss: Pakistan. Sri Lanka 253-5 (50 overs) (H.P. Tillekeratne 61, A.P. Gurusinha 88). Pakistan 254-5 (47 overs) (Salim Yousuf 52, Ijaz Ahmed 102*). Award: Ijaz Ahmed (102).

11 February at Woolloongabba, Brisbane. AUSTRALIA beat PAKISTAN by 67 runs. Toss: Pakistan. Australia 300-5 (50 overs) (M.A. Taylor 66, T.M. Moody 89). Pakistan 233 (39.1 overs) (Imran Khan 82; C.G. Rackemann 8.1-0-44-4). Award: T.M. Moody (89).

13 February at Sydney Cricket Ground (floodlit). PAKISTAN beat AUSTRALIA by 5 wickets. Toss: Pakistan. Australia 165-8 (50 overs) (D.M. Jones 54). Pakistan 167-5 (48.3 overs) (Imran Khan 56*). Award: Imran Khan (10-1-30-2 & 56*).

15 February at Bellerive Oval, Hobart. PAKISTAN beat SRI LANKA by 6 wickets. Toss: Pakistan. Sri Lanka 195 (47.5 overs) (A.P. Gurusinha 59, A. Ranatunga 42; Waqar Younis 10-2-39-4). Pakistan 198-4 (48.3 overs) (Ramiz Raja 116*, Javed Miandad 42. Award: Ramiz Raja (116*).

17 February at Adelaide Oval. PAKISTAN beat SRI LANKA by 27 runs. Toss: Sri Lanka. Pakistan 315-3 (50 overs) (Ramiz Raja 107*, Saeed Anwar 126). Sri Lanka 288-8 (50 overs) (A. Ranatunga 64, R.S. Mahanama 72). Award: Saeed Anwar (126).

18 February at Adelaide Oval. AUSTRALIA beat SRI LANKA by 7 wickets. Toss: Sri Lanka. Sri Lanka 158 (40.4 overs). Australia 159-3 (40 overs) (D.M. Jones 80*). Award: D.M. Jones (80*).

20 February at Sydney Cricket Ground (floodlit). PAKISTAN beat AUSTRALIA by 2 runs. Toss: Pakistan. Pakistan 220-8 (49 overs) (Saeed Anwar 43, Salim Malik 67, Imran Khan 56). Australia 218-9 (49 overs) (T.M. Moody 74). Award: S.P. O'Donnell (10-0-32-3 & 39.

Qualifying Table	P	W	L	Points
AUSTRALIA	8	6	2	12
PAKISTAN	8	5	3	10
Sri Lanka	8	1	7	2

Final Round Results

23 February at Melbourne Cricket Ground (floodlit). AUSTRALIA beat PAKISTAN by 7 wickets. Toss: Australia. Pakistan 162 (47.5 overs) (Wasim Akram 86). Australia 163-3 (45.5 overs) (D.M. Jones 83*, A.R. Border 44*).

25 February at Sydney Cricket Ground. AUSTRALIA beat PAKISTAN by 69 runs. Toss: Australia. Australia 255-6 (50 overs) (M.A. Taylor 76, T.M. Moody 44, D.M. Jones 46). Pakistan 186 (45 overs) (Salim Yousuf 59).

Player of the Finals Award: D.M. Jones (Australia).

Leading Averages (Qual: 8 innings or 10 wkts)

Batting/Fielding	M	I	NO	HS	R	Avge	100	50	Ct/St
D.M. Jones (Aus)	10	9	3	85*	461	76.83	–	5	2
A. Ranatunga (SL)	8	8	2	71*	273	45.50	–	3	1
A.R. Border (Aus)	10	9	3	69*	271	45.16	–	1	6
Imran Khan (Pak)	10	9	2	82	283	40.42	–	3	2
Wasim Akram (Pak)	9	8	2	86	209	34.83	–	1	2
M.A. Taylor (Aus)	9	9	0	76	294	32.66	–	2	5
Saeed Anwar (Pak)	9	9	0	126	293	32.55	1	–	2
A.P. Gurusinha (SL)	8	8	0	88	250	31.25	–	2	1
Ijaz Ahmed (Pak)	10	9	2	102*	184	26.28	1	–	3
Salim Malik (Pak)	8	8	0	67	190	23.75	–	1	2
H.P. Tillekeratne (SL)	8	8	1	61	151	21.57	–	1	5/1
P.A. De Silva (SL)	8	8	0	40	155	19.37	–	–	1
M.A.R. Samarasekera (SL)	8	8	0	60	143	17.87	–	1	2
S.R. Waugh (Aus)	9	8	2	31*	104	17.33	–	–	4
R.J. Ratnayake (SL)	8	8	1	31	100	14.28	–	–	1

Bowling	O	M	R	W	Avge	Best	5wI
S.P. O'Donnell (Aus)	84.3	7	332	20	16.60	4-36	–
T.M. Alderman (Aus)	75.5	12	283	16	17.68	3-25	–
C.G. Rackemann (Aus)	71.1	9	253	13	19.46	4-44	–
G.D. Campbell (Aus)	52	6	227	10	22.70	3-31	–
P.L. Taylor (Aus)	80	4	301	12	25.08	3-36	–

Other International Competitions

Champions' Trophy

13 October at Sharjah. WEST INDIES beat INDIA by 5 wickets. Toss: India. India 169 (48.1 overs) (C.A. Walsh 10-1-25-4). West Indies 173-5 (47.5 overs) (K.L.T. Arthurton 48, A.L. Logie 59*). Award: I.V.A. Richards (10-0-44-2 & 34).

14 October at Sharjah. PAKISTAN beat WEST INDIES by 11 runs. Toss: West Indies. Pakistan 250-8 (50 overs) (Shoaib Mohammad 45, Salim Malik 74, Imran Khan 45). West Indies 239 (48.4 overs) (D.L. Haynes 59, I.V.A. Richards 46, C.A. Best 53*; Wasim Akram 9.4-1-38-5 including hat-trick). Award: Wasim Akram (9.4-1-38-5).

15 October at Sharjah. PAKISTAN beat INDIA by 6 wickets. Toss: India. India 273-4 (46 overs) (K. Srikkanth 51, N.S. Sidhu 108, M. Amarnath 88). Pakistan 274-4 (44.4 overs) (Shahid Saeed 50, Shoaib Mohammad 65, Salim Malik 68*). Award: N.S. Sidhu (108).

16 October at Sharjah. INDIA beat WEST INDIES by 37 runs. Toss: West Indies. India 211-9 (50 overs) (K. Srikkanth 40, Kapil Dev 41). West Indies 174 (46.4 overs) (M.D. Marshall 40). Award: Kapil Dev (41 & 7.4-1-19-2).

17 October at Sharjah. PAKISTAN beat WEST INDIES by 57 runs. Toss: Pakistan. Pakistan 237-7 (50 overs) (Ijaz Ahmed 50, Imran Khan 60*). West Indies 180 (44.4 overs) (C.A. Best 44). Award: Imran Kahn (60* & 5.4-0-21-1).

20 October at Sharjah. PAKISTAN beat INDIA by 38 runs. Toss: India. Pakistan 252-4 (47 overs) (Shoaib Mohammad 51, Salim Malik 102). India 214-9 (47 overs). Award: Salim Malik (102).

Pakistan won the Champions' Trophy.
Player of the Series Award: Salim Malik

Rothmans Cup

1 March at Carisbrook, Dunedin. NEW ZEALAND beat INDIA by 108 runs. Toss: India. New Zealand 246-6 (47 overs) (M.D. Crowe 104, K.R. Rutherford 78*). India 138 (32.1 overs). Award: M.D. Crowe (104).

3 March at Lancaster Park, Christchurch. AUSTRALIA beat INDIA by 18 runs. Toss: Australia. Australia 187-9 (50 overs). India 169 (45 overs) (T.M. Alderman 10-2-32-5). Award: T.M. Alderman (10-2-32-5).

4 March at Lancaster Park, Christchurch. AUSTRALIA beat NEW ZEALAND by 150 runs. Toss: Australia. Australia 244-8 (50 overs) (D.C. Boon 67, D.M. Jones 107). New Zealand 94 (25.2 overs) (A.H. Jones 43; S.P. O'Donnell 6-0-13-5). Award: D.M. Jones (107).

6 March at Basin Reserve, Wellington. INDIA beat NEW ZEALAND by 1 run. Toss: India. India 221 (48.2 overs) (Kapil Dev 46). New Zealand 220 (48.5 overs) (M.J. Greatbatch 53, K.R. Rutherford 44, R.J. Hadlee 46). Award: Kapil Dev (46 & 9.5-1-45-2).

8 March at Seddon Park, Hamilton. AUSTRALIA beat INDIA by 7 wickets. Toss: India. India 211-8 (50 overs) (W.V. Raman 58, Kapil Dev 48*). Australia 212-3 (48 overs) (G.R. Marsh 86, M.A. Taylor 56). Award: M.A. Taylor (56).

10 March at Eden Park, Auckland. AUSTRALIA beat NEW ZEALAND on faster run-rate. Toss: New Zealand. Australia 239-6 (47 overs) (D.M. Jones 59, S.P.O'Donnell 52). New Zealand 167-2 (34.5 overs) (J.G. Wright 48, M.D. Crowe 51 retired hurt). (New Zealand target 204 from 40 overs but rain stopped play.)

Final 11 March at Eden Park, Auckland. AUSTRALIA beat NEW ZEALAND by 8 wickets. Toss: New Zealand. New Zealand 162 (49.2 overs) (R.J. Hadlee 79). Australia 164-2 (39.1 overs) (D.M. Jones 102*). Award: D.M. Jones (102*).

Austral-Asia Cup

25 April at Sharjah. SRI LANKA beat INDIA by 3 wickets. Toss: Sri Lanka. India 241-8 (50 overs) (N.S. Sidhu 64, M. Azharuddin 108). Sri Lanka 242-7 (49.2 overs) (A. Ranatunga 85*). Award: A. Ranatunga (8-0-40-0 & 85*).

26 April at Sharjah. AUSTRALIA beat NEW ZEALAND by 63 runs. Toss: New Zealand. Australia 258-5 (50 overs) (M.A. Taylor 60, D.C. Boon 92*). New Zealand 195-7 (50 overs) (M.D. Crowe 41). Award: D.C. Boon (92*).

27 April at Sharjah. PAKISTAN beat INDIA by 26 runs. Toss: India. Pakistan 235-9 (50 overs) (Salim Yousuf 62). India 209 (46.3 overs) (M. Azharuddin 78*; Waqar Younis (4-24). Award: Waqar Younis (10-0-42-4).

28 April at Sharjah. NEW ZEALAND beat BANGLADESH by 161 runs. Toss: Bangladesh. New Zealand 338-4 (50 overs) (M.D. Crowe 69, J.G. Wright 93, A.H. Jones 93). Bangladesh 177-5 (50 overs) (Azhar Shantu 54). Award: A.H. Jones (90).

29 April at Sharjah. PAKISTAN beat SRI LANKA by 90 runs. Toss: Sri Lanka. Pakistan 311-8 (50 overs) (Saeed Anwar 40, Salim Yousuf 46, Javed Miandad 75, Ijaz Ahmed 89). Sri Lanka 221 (47.4 overs) (D.S.B.P. Kuruppu 41; Waqar Younis 10-1-26-6). Award: Waqar Younis (10-1-26-6).

30 April at Sharjah. AUSTRALIA beat BANGLADESH by 7 wickets. Toss: Australia. Bangladesh 134-8 (50 overs) (Aminul Islam 41*). Australia 140-3 (25.4 overs) (P.L. Taylor 54*). Award: P.L. Taylor (10-2-22-2 & 54*).

Qualifying Table	P	W	L	Points
PAKISTAN	2	2	0	8
AUSTRALIA	2	2	0	8
NEW ZEALAND	2	1	1	4
SRI LANKA	2	1	1	4
India	2	0	2	0
Bangladesh	2	0	2	0

Semi-Finals

1 May at Sharjah. PAKISTAN beat NEW ZEALAND by 8 wickets. Toss: New Zealand. New Zealand 74 (31.1 overs) (A.H. Jones 47; Waqar Younis 9-2-20-5). Pakistan 77-2 (15.4 overs). Award: Waqar Younis (9-2-20-5).

2 May at Sharjah. AUSTRALIA beat SRI LANKA by 114 runs. Toss: Australia. Australia 332-3 (50 overs) (G.R. Marsh 68, D.M. Jones 117*, S.P. O'Donnell 74). Sri Lanka 218 (45.4 overs) (H.P. Tillekeratne 76). Award: S.P. O'Donnell (74* & 5.4-0-19-1).

Final

4 May at Sharjah. PAKISTAN beat AUSTRALIA by 36 runs. Toss: Pakistan. Pakistan 266-7 (50 overs) (Saeed Anwar 40, Salim Malik 87, Wasim Akram 49*). Australia 230 (46.5 overs) (M.A. Taylor 52, S.R. Waugh 64; Wasim Akram hat-trick). Award: Wasim Akram (49* & 8.5-0-45-3).

Pakistan won the Austral-Asia Cup and £18,500.

AUSTRALIA 197

Cricket in Australia

New South Wales turned Queensland's Sheffield Shield-winning dream into yet another nightmare when they won the final by a whopping 345 runs at the Sydney Cricket Ground. It was the 40th time New South Wales had taken the champion-State title in the 88 seasons (and 98 years) of Lord Sheffield's trophy. And it was the 12th time Queensland – poor old Queensland – had been the bridesmaid. The northernmost State still has not won the Shield since it entered the competition in 1926-27.

Queensland's agony was compounded this time by their leading the Shield table until the last round of qualifying matches, only to lose top spot to New South Wales, who were then afforded the luxury of hosting the final and having only to draw it to win the Shield. New South Wales and Queensland finished level on 26 points, but New South Wales had won three of their 10 matches outright, while Queensland had won only two.

The five-day final could hardly have been more lopsided. Sent in, New South Wales scored 360 and demolished Queensland's first innings for 103. Closing their second innings at 396 for 9, New South Wales left Queensland the impossible target of 654. In the event 308 rated as a respectable fourth-innings tally on Sydney's turner.

In the absence of Geoff Lawson (shoulder injury), New South Wales were led by prolific-scoring Test left-hand opening batsman Mark Taylor, who duly peeled off a century in each innings against a Queensland attack that boasted three front-line fast bowlers – Craig McDermott, Carl Rackemann, and left-armer Dirk Tazelaar – but lacked a quality spinner. New South Wales made off-spinner Peter Taylor 12th man, just a week after he had represented Australia against New Zealand in the Wellington Test. Former Test off-spinning all-rounder Greg Matthews and Taylor's replacement, rookie leg-spinner Adrian Tucker, 20, shared 12 of the 20 Queensland wickets, with Tucker, crucially, dismissing Allan Border in both innings.

Having appointed Mark Taylor, 25, captain for the final – and there are many who now see him as the eventual successor to Border as Australian captain – New South Wales allowed regular skipper Lawson to field late in the match, and to speak on behalf of the team at the presentation ceremony – at which Queensland captain Greg Ritchie (Border had relinquished the job before the start of the season) rightly was miffed at not being asked to respond. Regrettably, Ritchie and other Queenslanders had suffered much abuse from some corporate box spectators throughout the match.

In getting so near, yet so far again, Queensland could reflect ruefully on an early-season match against New South Wales in Newcastle, where their second innings folded for 131 after they had needed only 164 to win outright. The Queenslanders later complained bitterly about the New South Wales umpires in that match, in which they reckoned they had six 'bad' decisions go against them.

Former Test batsman Ritchie, 30, enjoyed a successful personal season, with 928 runs (avge 54.58) in 13 first-class matches. He made three centuries, including 167 not out against Victoria in Melbourne and a career-high 213 not out against South Australia in Adelaide in Queensland's last two matches before the final. But four months later, in July, he stunned Australian cricket by announcing his retirement, stating 'business and personal reasons', while expressing dissatisfaction with some Queensland administrators and disillusionment with a disloyal faction within the team.

Queenslanders aside, few doubted New South Wales's right to the Shield as they had appealed as the most powerful and complete outfit in the competition, especially at the SCG. Even when without Test batsmen Mark Taylor and Steve Waugh, New South Wales could rely on Mark Waugh, Trevor Bayliss, Steve Small, Mark O'Neill, and Matthews for plenty of runs, and Lawson and Matthews were consistently productive spearheads of a versatile bowling squad.

Mark Waugh's 1,009 (avge 77.61), with five centuries, in 12 first-class matches was further proof of the exceptional ability that will force him into Australia's Test team sooner rather than later. It was a measure of Australia's new-found batting riches that Mark Waugh, 25, West Australian Tom Moody, 24, and South Australian Darren Lehmann, 20 – three of the world's finest young batsmen – could not be squeezed into Australia's 13-man team for New Zealand. Left-hander Lehmann, a rare, exciting talent, finished second to Mark Taylor on the national first-class aggregate, with 1,142 (avge 57.10), with five centuries, in 12 first-class matches. Along the way, he became, at 20 years, 32 days, the youngest Australian to score 1,000 runs in an Australian first-class season, eclipsing Doug Walters, who was 20 years, 57 days when he completed 1,000 for New South Wales and Australia in 1965-66.

Mark Waugh won the Shield Player of the Year award, with 21 votes – one more than Lehmann and four more than Tasmanian opening bowler Dave Gilbert.

Under David Hookes, South Australia were an honourable third on the Shield ladder, and Dirk Wellham's Tasmania finished a creditable fourth. Western Australia, winner of the previous three titles, dropped Graeme Wood from the captaincy and the team on a vote of players, after 6 of their 10 Shield matches, and subsequently moved from bottom to fifth position – ahead of Victoria only because of one more outright victory. Western Australia gained end-of-season consolation in their seven-wicket thrashing of South Australia in the FAI Insurance Cup limited-overs final in Perth.

New South Wales v Queensland
1989-90 Sheffield Shield Final

New South Wales won by 345 runs
Toss: Queensland. Umpires: A.R. Crafter and P.J. McConnell

New South Wales

S.M. Small	c Law b Rackemann	75	b Law		58
M.A. Taylor*	c Healy b Tazelaar	127	st Healy b Border		100
T.H. Bayliss	lbw b Border	25	c & b Rackemann		58
S.R. Waugh	c Healy b McDermott	6	c Healy b Rackemann		10
M.E. Waugh	c Healy b Border	3	not out		78
P.E. Emery†	b McDermott	13	(8) c Tazelaar b Rackemann		11
M.D. O'Neill	c Healy b Rackemann	50	(6) b Cantrell		0
G.R.J. Matthews	lbw b Tazelaar	8	(7) b Cantrell		19
A.E. Tucker	b Border	4	run out (McDermott)		16
M.R. Whitney	not out	15	c Border b Cantrell		8
W.J. Holdsworth	b Kasprowicz	7			
Extras	(B2, LB7, NB9)	27	(B13, LB13, W2, NB5)		38
		360	(9 wkts dec)		**396**

Queensland

P.E. Cantrell	b Whitney	0	(2) st Emery b Matthews		60
G.I. Foley	c & b Matthews	0	(1) c Emery b M.E. Waugh		10
G.M. Ritchie*	c Emery b Matthews	16	(5) b Matthews		69
A.R. Border	b Tucker	36	c Emery b Tucker		34
P.S. Clifford	c Emery b M.E. Waugh	0	(6) run out (O'Neill/Matthews)		28
S.G. Law	b Matthews	8	(3) c Small b Whitney		6
I.A. Healy†	not out	21	not out		40
C.J. McDermott	c & b Tucker	2	lbw b M.E. Waugh		16
M.S. Kasprowicz	c Small b Tucker	0	b Whitney		1
D. Tazelaar	lbw b Matthews	0	c Emery b Whitney		10
C.G. Rackemann	b Matthews	9	c & b Matthews		17
Extras	(B2, LB5, NB2)	11	(B2, LB5, NB5)		17
		103			**308**

Note: NB count 2 runs each.
G.I. Foley retired hurt (0*) at 0-0 and resumed at 95-9 (1st innings)

Queensland	O	M	R	W	O	M	R	W
McDermott	38	8	102	2	18	1	81	0
Rackemann	28	6	72	2	22	7	36	3
Tazelaar	18	4	46	2	12	0	53	0
Kasprowicz	12.3	2	40	1	12	2	41	0
Cantrell	15	4	39	0	20.5	5	71	3
Border	24	5	44	3	16	1	58	1
Foley	3	1	8	0				
Clifford					4	1	14	0
Law					3	1	16	1

New Sth Wales	O	M	R	W	O	M	R	W
Whitney	8	2	24	1	28	9	66	3
Holdsworth	5	3	16	0	3	0	17	0
Matthews	16.3	5	31	5	37.3	15	96	3
M.E. Waugh	3	0	8	1	6	0	22	2
Tucker	11	4	17	3	27	3	92	1
O'Neill					2	0	8	0

Fall of Wickets

Wkt	NSW 1st	Q 1st	NSW 2nd	Q 2nd
1st	160	0	133	33
2nd	194	44	205	42
3rd	205	49	242	114
4th	220	64	249	122
5th	261	72	254	216
6th	272	76	282	234
7th	286	76	311	256
8th	309	77	372	257
9th	347	95	396	279
10th	360	103	–	308

Sheffield Shield 1989-90

Final Table	P	W	D	L	1st inngs Pts	Total Pts
NEW SOUTH WALES	10	3	4	3	8	26†
QUEENSLAND	10	2	6	2	14	26
South Australia	10	3	4	3	2	20
Tasmania	10	2	5	3	4	16
Western Australia	10	2	6	2	2	14
Victoria	10	1	9	0	8	14

Outright win 6 pts; 1st innings lead in match drawn or lost 2 pts. † NSW placed first on games won, giving them home advantage over Queensland in final.

Leading First-Class Averages (Top 15)
(Note: including Test played in Wellington, but excluding touring teams)

Batting (Qual: 8 innings)	State	M	I	NO	HS	R	Avge	100	50	Ct/St
M.E. Waugh	NSW	12	17	4	198*	1009	77.61	5	2	18
M.A. Taylor	NSW	13	23	1	199	1412	64.18	7	5	17
D.M. Jones	Vic	11	18	4	149	888	63.42	4	2	4
A.R. Border	Q	10	17	5	144*	700	58.33	1	5	14
D.S. Lehmann	SA	12	20	0	228	1142	57.10	5	3	3
G.J. Shipperd	Tas	11	18	3	200*	845	56.33	3	3	7
T.H. Bayliss	NSW	12	20	2	115	992	55.11	2	6	5
G.M. Ritchie	Q	12	19	2	213*	928	54.58	3	4	17
J.D. Siddons	Vic	10	17	2	159	793	52.86	3	2	15
G.A. Bishop	SA	7	12	1	173	561	51.00	2	1	5
G.R. Marsh	WA	8	13	2	355*	546	49.63	1	–	5
S.P. O'Donnell	Vic	8	13	2	121	544	49.45	2	3	8
G.M. Wood	WA	9	13	4	125*	440	48.88	1	1	3
D.W. Hookes	SA	11	18	1	159	823	48.41	3	3	4
D.C. Boon	Tas	9	16	2	200	669	47.78	3	1	6

Bowling (Qual: 10 wkts)	State	O	M	R	W	Avge	Best	5wI	10wM
C.D. Matthews	WA	304.3	77	806	42	19.19	7-22	3	–
S.P. O'Donnell	Vic	179.3	54	410	20	20.50	4-38	–	–
T.M. Alderman	WA	379.4	119	857	38	22.55	5-62	3	–
C.G. Rackemann	Q	555.2	165	1155	50	23.10	4-39	–	–
G.F. Lawson	NSW	464.2	142	1018	44	23.13	4-26	–	–
G.R.J. Matthews	NSW	470.3	165	1040	44	23.63	7-50	3	1
D.R. Gilbert	Tas	350.1	70	999	42	23.78	7-127	2	–
M.A. Polzin	Q	260.2	65	682	28	24.35	8-51	2	–
C. Owen	SA	100	25	296	12	24.66	3-80	–	–
G.D. Campbell	Tas	382.2	96	939	38	24.71	6-80	1	–
D. Fleming	Vic	234.3	59	693	28	24.75	6-37	1	–
C.R. Miller	SA	402.1	107	1117	44	25.43	6-85	1	–
C.J. McDermott	Q	432	100	1375	54	25.46	8-44	4	–
P. McPhee	Tas	175	54	413	16	25.81	5-73	1	–
A.E. Tucker	NSW	92.5	23	260	10	26.00	4-25	–	–

FAI Insurance Cup Final
31 March at WACA Ground, Perth. WESTERN AUSTRALIA beat SOUTH AUSTRALIA by 7 wickets. Toss: Western Australia. South Australia 87 (34.5 overs) (T.M. Alderman 8-3-14-4). Western Australia 88-3 (19.1 overs). Award: T.M. Alderman (8-3-14-4).

Cricket in South Africa

Kepler Wessels has surplanted Clive Rice as the most successful captain on the South African domestic cricket scene. The former Australian Test player made a clean sweep as captain of Eastern Province last season, when he led his team to victory in all three domestic competitions – the first-class Castle Currie Cup, the Nissan Shield (55 overs), and the Benson & Hedges night series (45 overs). Admittedly, they had to share the Currie Cup with Western Province after a highly forgettable five-day final that ended in an all too predictable draw. But there was little doubt that Eastern Province were the team of the season for their consistency over the six-months period, while Wessels had a strong claim on the player of the season. In the last three seasons he has won the Currie Cup and Nissan Shield (both twice) as well as the night series.

Western Province were the front runners throughout the Currie Cup season and they managed to beat Eastern Province in impressive style by 201 runs in their league match in Port Elizabeth immediately before the Currie Cup final at the same venue. But their form dropped alarmingly in both limited-overs competitions. Eastern Province beat them by an embarrassing 10 wickets in the Nissan Shield match at Newlands, and, for the first time in five seasons, Western Province failed to reach the final of the night series.

The less said about the Currie Cup final the better. Western Province batted for the first two-and-a-half days, making only just over 200 runs on each of the first two days. Once Ken McEwan made a century in reply for the home side, there was little prospect of a result and the Cup was shared. The one highlight was that the young opening batsman from Western Province, Gary Kirsten, made a career-best 175.

But it was obvious that the players were protesting against the system, and were determined not to throw away at least a half-share of the trophy, having been the dominant forces in their respective sections of the league competition. Western province finished a whopping 38 points ahead of Transvaal in Section One, while Eastern Province were somewhat hard pressed, finishing only 3 points ahead of Northern Transvaal in Lee Barnard's final season as captain.

If Wessels was the outstanding captain, then the outstanding player was undoubtedly Western Province's all-rounder Adrian Kuiper. A succession of injuries prevented him from giving of his best in the bowling department, but there was nobody who could match him in the batting stakes. Kuiper has always been renowned for his ability as a big-hitter and a devastating match-winner in limited-overs cricket, but his record in the first-class game has lagged way behind. Up to the start of last season he had only two first-class centuries to his credit. But the burly apple farmer has put all that behind him. Whether his axing as Western Province captain in favour of Lawrence Seeff during the off-season acted as a spur, it is difficult to say. But, whatever the reason, Kuiper was able to boast a Currie Cup average of 95.42 by season's end from an aggregate of 668 runs. Admittedly he was helped by being not out on five occasions, but only Roy Pienaar was able to better his aggregate, and then by only 10 runs. More important, there were three centuries to his credit, including a personal best Currie Cup innings of 161 not out, which showed that he had at last found the ability to make substantial totals in the first-class game.

Pienaar, Gary Kirsten, Clive Rice, England professional Jon Hardy, and Vernon du Preez were others to average more than 50, while established stars, such as Wessels, McEwan, and Peter Kirsten, all had disappointing figures by their standards in the middle to upper 30s.

Another disappointing aspect was the lack of young batsmen making the grade. Gary Kirsten, despite being played out of position as a specialist opener, was a notable exception. But Mark Rushmere and Daryll Cullinan, who earned Springbok colours against Mike Gatting's English side, battled to make the top 25.

There was a similar worry in the fast-bowling department. Australian John Maguire, leading the Eastern Province attack, was way out in front both in terms of wickets taken and average, with 45 victims at a cost of 16.91. And there were two other foreigners in fellow Australian Rod McCurdy, also playing in the colours of Eastern Province, and Barbadian Sylvester Clarke of Northern Transvaal among the top six fast bowlers.

Western Province produced the top three local fast bowlers in Meyrick Pringle, Craig Matthews, and Brian McMillan, as well as the top spinner in David Rundle.

It was not surprising that, at the end of the season, the SACU decided to revert to the old system that the players wanted. This amounts to doing away with the final as well as the controversial two-section league format. The competition will now be played over a double-round between the six competing provinces – Eastern Province, Western Province, Northern Transvaal, Transvaal, Free State, and Natal – with the winner of the league competition taking the championship. The season will be split into three sections, with two rounds being played in October, five rounds in the holiday period from Christmas to mid-January, and the final three rounds from late February to early March.

Border, who shared the B section honours with Western Province B, had their application for promotion turned down, although they will continue to play in the night series against the 'big boys'.

Western Province v Eastern Province, 1989-90
Castle Currie Cup Final

Match Drawn. Trophy shared
Played at St George's Park, Port Elizabeth, on 26, 27, 28, 30, 31 January
Toss: Western Province. Umpires: S.B. Lambson and C.J. Mitchley

Western Province

L. Seeff*	c Richardson b Maguire	65	lbw b Maguire	6
G. Kirsten	b Maguire	175	b Shaw	26
P. Kirsten	c & b Maguire	128	lbw b Hobson	42
D. Cullinan	c Rushmere b McCurdy	41	lbw b Hobson	6
A. Kuiper	c Maguire b McCurdy	28	b Shaw	31
J. Hardy	not out	20	lbw b Shaw	36
B. McMillan	lbw b McCurdy	0	not out	12
M. Pringle	b Maguire	9		
D. Rundle	b McCurdy	4		
R. Ryall†	b Maguire	4		
A. McClement	did not bat			
Extras	(B2, LB16, NB15)	33	(LB4, NB3)	7
	(9 wkts dec)	**507**	(6 wkts dec)	**166**

Eastern Province

M. Rushmere	lbw b Kuiper	81	(2) c Ryall b McClement	4
P. Amm	b McMillan	24	(1) not out	8
K. Wessels*	c McMillan b Rundle	33	b McClement	2
K. McEwan	c Ryall b Pringle	101	not out	4
L. Hobson	c McMillan b Rundle	1		
V. Michau	c Hardy b Pringle	16		
D. Callaghan	c McMillan b Rundle	25		
D. Richardson†	c Seeff b McClement	20		
T. Shaw	run out	36		
J. Maguire	c Cullinan b Kuiper	4		
R. McCurdy	not out	24		
Extras	(B11, LB16, W3, NB9)	39		
		404	(2 wkts)	**18**

Eastern Province	O	M	R	W	O	M	R	W
McCurdy	43	6	129	4	4	0	10	0
Maguire	63.4	16	137	5	11	0	52	1
Shaw	58	14	116	0	16.4	5	35	3
Callaghan	13	1	46	0	2	0	22	0
Hobson	18	3	52	0	9	1	43	2
Michau	3	0	9	0				

Western Province	O	M	R	W	O	M	R	W
Pringle	32	6	79	2				
McMillan	31	6	82	1				
Rundle	51	19	96	3	6.2	4	7	0
McClement	40	11	78	1	6	2	11	2
Kuiper	18	6	32	2				
Seeff	1	0	4	0				

Fall of Wickets

Wkt	WP 1st	EP 1st	WP 2nd	EP 2nd
1st	133	74	16	4
2nd	385	145	77	6
3rd	392	149	85	—
4th	450	160	93	—
5th	461	196	135	—
6th	461	247	166	—
7th	491	313	—	—
8th	502	348	—	—
9th	507	360	—	—
10th	—	404	—	—

Castle Currie Cup Final Tables

Section One	P	W	D	L	Bonus points Batting	Bonus points Bowling	Total points
WESTERN PROVINCE	7	3	4	0	22	32	99
Transvaal	7	1	6	0	21	25	61
Natal	7	0	4	3	23	27	50

Section Two	P	W	D	L	Bonus points Batting	Bonus points Bowling	Total points
EASTERN PROVINCE	7	2	3	2	23	33	86
Northern Transvaal	7	2	3	2	23	30	83
Orange Free State	7	1	4	2	20	26	61

Leading First-Class Averages 1989-90

Batting (Top 10. Qual: 300 runs)

	M	I	NO	HS	R	Avge	100	50
A. Kuiper (WP)	6	12	5	161*	668	95.42	3	1
R. Pienaar (T)	7	13	2	150*	678	61.63	2	4
G. Kirsten (WP)	3	6	0	175	352	58.66	1	1
C. Rice (T)	6	10	1	129*	504	56.00	1	3
J. Hardy (WP)	6	10	3	119	363	51.85	1	1
V. du Preez (NT)	7	13	2	82*	561	51.00	0	6
R. Jennings (T)	7	11	4	66*	326	46.57	0	2
H. Fotheringham (N)	6	11	1	143*	464	46.40	1	3
J. Cook (T)	7	13	1	112*	504	42.00	1	2
J. Strydom (OFS)	7	14	1	104	513	39.46	1	4

Bowling (Top 10. Qual: 15 wkts)

	O	M	R	W	Avge	Best	5wI	10wM
J. Maguire (EP)	359	103	761	45	16.91	6-48	4	1
M. Pringle (WP)	191.1	32	527	25	21.08	7-60	1	1
D. Rundle (WP)	311.3	89	576	26	22.15	5-32	1	–
C. Matthews (WP)	152.3	46	377	17	22.17	4-52	–	–
S. Clarke (NT)	200	49	468	21	22.28	5-46	1	–
B. McMillan (WP)	156.4	34	424	18	23.55	4-28	–	–
R. McCurdy (EP)	293	53	899	38	23.65	5-92	1	–
L. Hobson (EP)	119	17	391	16	24.43	6-62	2	1
R. Snell (T)	210.1	51	626	25	25.04	5-71	2	–
T. Packer (N)	159.5	28	455	18	25.27	4-40	–	–

Wicket-keeping (Qual: 20 dismissals)

27 N. Day (NT, incl. 5 st)
24 R. Brown (OFS)
20 R. Jennings (T)

Fielding (Qual: 10 catches)

16 M. Haysman (NT)
11 K. Wessels (EP)
10 D. Cullinan (WP), A. Hudson (N)

Nissan Shield Final

1st Leg EASTERN PROVINCE beat NORTHERN TRANSVAAL by 2 runs. E. Province 196-6 (M.W. Rushmere 96). N. Transvaal 194-9 (M.D. Haysman 54, A.M. Ferreira 41*).

2nd leg EASTERN PROVINCE beat NORTHERN TRANSVAAL by 7 wickets. N. Transvaal 130 (D.J. Callaghan 4-38). E. Province 131-3.

Cricket in West Indies

As if to make up fully for a long and inexplicable wait, the Leeward Islands not only won the regional first-class tournament for the Red Stripe Cup for the first time in 1990, but created a record in the process by winning all five matches outright. It was a perfect sequence achieved only once previously, by Barbados in the 1980 Shell Shield, when the Leewards played as a combined team with the Windward Islands and each team had only four matches.

With Vivian Richards as captain and including five other Test players, the Leewards were considered strong favourites prior to the season, as they had been more than once before without realizing their potential. This time, they most certainly did. They conceded only one total in ten of over 300, six of them under 200, and themselves recorded the only total in excess of 500 for the tournament, 526 for 8 declared against the Windwards.

The performance was all the more meritorious since Richards fractured his left index finger while fielding on the first day of the season and only returned for the final match when the Cup was already settled. In addition, Winston Benjamin, the Test fast bowler, was eliminated after the opening match by knee and ankle injuries.

In Richards's absence, Richie Richardson took over the captaincy and handled it with the assurance of a veteran. He seemed to thrive on the additional responsibility, his 421 runs, at an average of 70.16 with two centuries, making him the leading batsman of the season. The aggregate was 65 more than Gordon Greenidge, who cut short a club contract in Australia to play for Barbados and abide by the West Indies Board's stipulation that full participation in the Cup was mandatory for Test selection.

Jamaica, champions of the two previous seasons, had cause to feel hard done by as rain prevented any play in their two away matches against the Windward Islands and Guyana. Although the issue was already decided by then, their final match against the Leewards carried considerable significance to both teams, the Leewards proving their point, and their resilience, by recovering from a difficult first innings position to win by three wickets.

Barbados, under Desmond Haynes, their fifth captain in seven seasons, finished second after winning their last three matches. Their defeat at home by the Leewards in the opening match, when they were 15 for 5 inside an hour, was the most decisive result of the season. Guyana suffered through the complete washout of their two matches at home and the Windwards won their first match in four years by defeating Trinidad & Tobago, who, under the youngest captain in tournament history, 20-year-old Brian Lara, lost all four of their played matches outright.

The leading players were mostly those with familiar names and established reputations. Richardson and Greenidge were the top batsmen while other century-makers were Carlisle Best, Haynes and Thelston Payne of Barbados, Keith Arthurton of the Leewards, and Carl Hooper of Guyana, all with Test experience, James Adams of Jamaica, Andy Jackman of Guyana, and Dawnley Joseph of the Windwards, all with 'B' team qualifications, and Roland Holder of Barbados, from the 1988 youth team. The one and only new century maker was Stuart Williams, 20, an opener from the Leewards.

Unsatisfactory pitches, the bane of regional cricket for some time, placed a high premium on batting technique, courage, and luck at several grounds and often flattered the bowlers. As with the leading batsmen, the main wicket-takers were all well known, all medium-pace and above.

Eldine Baptiste of the Leewards took 26 at 17.50 each, Ian Bishop of Trinidad & Tobago 23 at 14.4 each, and Curtly Ambrose of the Leewards 22 at 17.04. Ezra Moseley, reinstated along with fellow Barbadian Franklyn Stephenson following the International Cricket Council (ICC) ruling on players with South African contacts, took 22 at 24.63 and, at 32, earned his first call to West Indies colours.

A transformed Patrick Patterson reclaimed his Test place, if only briefly, on the evidence of 17 wickets in Jamaica's three matches on his home pitch at Sabina Park, cutting his run and bowling straight so that 13 of his victims were either bowled or lbw.

The Leewards not only possessed the strongest, best led, and best balanced team. They also produced the most exciting new player in Hamesh Anthony, a strongly-built 19-year-old who had 17 wickets in four matches with stiff, fast-medium bowling that had played a big part in the Leewards triumph in the junior West Indies tournament the previous August.

Trinidad & Tobago's disappointment in the Red Stripe Cup was assuaged to some extent when they won the one-day tournament for the Geddes Grant Shield, comfortably beating in the final a Barbados team strong on paper but weak in commitment.

With no simultaneous overseas tour, the Board's insistence on involvement by the Test players prevented what might have been an exodus to Australia on enticing contracts to the detriment of the paying public, the sponsors, and the development of West Indies cricket. But injuries that limited the appearances of several, the complete loss of 3 of the 15 matches through rain, the Leewards' early ascendancy, and the arrival of the England team towards the end of the tournament combined to diminish domestic interest.

Red Stripe Cup 1990

Final Table	P	W	D	L	ND	Points
Leeward Islands	5	5	–	–	–	80
Barbados	5	3	1	1	–	52
Jamaica	5	1	1	1	2	37
Windward Islands	5	1	1	2	1	20
Guyana	5	–	1	2	2	16
Trinidad & Tobago	5	–	–	4	1	9

Leading Red-Stripe Averages

Batting (Qual: 200 runs)	M	I	NO	HS	R	Avge	100s
C.G. Greenidge (B)	4	6	1	128	356	71.20	2
R.B. Richardson (LI)	5	9	3	125	421	70.16	2
P.J.L. Dujon (J)	3	5	1	92	252	63.00	–
L.L. Harris (LI)	5	8	3	81	250	50.00	–
D.S. Morgan (J)	3	5	0	94	226	45.20	–
C.B. Lambert (G)	3	6	1	63	212	42.40	–
C.L. Hooper (G)	3	5	0	102	201	40.20	1
C.A. Best (B)	5	8	0	175	310	38.75	1
T.R.O. Payne (B)	5	8	1	101	270	38.57	1
D.L. Haynes (B)	5	9	1	108	285	35.62	1
K.L.T. Arthurton (LI)	5	9	2	101*	230	32.85	1
A.L. Kelly (LI)	5	9	0	46	241	26.77	–

Bowling (Qual: 12 wkts)	O	M	R	W	Avge	Best
I.R. Bishop (T&T)	130.0	23	330	23	14.34	6-81
B.P. Patterson (J)	88.3	13	277	17	16.29	7-53
H.A. Anthony (LI)	105.5	18	285	17	16.76	5-40
C.E.L. Ambrose (LI)	174.2	61	375	22	17.04	6-29
E.A.E. Baptiste (LI)	191.1	60	455	26	17.50	5-99
H.W.D. Springer (B)	136.0	36	290	12	24.16	4-40
E.A. Moseley (B)	175.1	28	542	22	24.63	5-89
K.C.G. Benjamin (LI)	141.4	35	346	14	24.71	3-22
R.C. Haynes (J)	117.0	20	356	14	25.42	5-28
C.G. Butts (G)	131.0	34	307	12	25.58	5-73
F.D. Stephenson (B)	124.4	25	336	12	28.00	3-63

Geddes Grant Shield Final
10 Feb, at Queen's Park Oval, Port-of-Spain. TRINIDAD & TOBAGO beat BARBADOS by five wickets. Barbados 178-9 (47.0 overs) (A.H. Gray 3-22, R. Sieuchan 3-34). Trinidad & Tobago 180-5 (44.2 overs) (D.I. Mohammed 57, B.C. Lara 41). Player of the Match: D.I. Mohammed.

Cricket in New Zealand

The varied components that made up the New Zealand cricket season of 1989-90 offered a marvellous mixture of colour and drama and occasional brilliance – and each element produced a remarkable ending, ranging from the extraordinary to the bizarre.

The three-day Shell Trophy series, extended for the first time to home-and-away matches for the six major associations, produced some sparkling cricket, but an unsavoury end. In their last match, Wellington captain Ervin McSweeney, needing a win to make sure of the title, tried to entice Canterbury's obdurate ninth-wicket pair, Lee Germon and Roger Ford, to pursue an outright result in the last two overs. He had Robert Vance bowl numerous inviting no-balls in a 21-ball over that produced 77 runs, with another five no-balls in the last over from slow left-armer Gray, who conceded 17 runs.

Neither the scorers nor the scoreboard could keep pace with the flood of no-balls and six-hits; otherwise the ruse might well have rebounded on Wellington, as a recount showed that Ford had padded away the last ball not knowing one run was needed for a victory that would also have given Canterbury the Shell Trophy. As it transpired, Wellington won the Trophy – but few friends – by six points from Canterbury, as fourth-placed Central Districts lost their last game to Northern Districts. Ten points covered the first four in the table. A rider to Wellington's tasteless antics saw the authorities rule Vance's over illegal and therefore not the most expensive over in first-class cricket.

The one-day series for the Shell Cup had an equally extraordinary finish. Auckland just qualified for the semi-finals, and when their semi-final against Northern Districts was washed out, the rules had Northern Districts going through to the final. But Auckland managed to have the rules changed on the spot, beat Northern Districts, and then Central Districts in the final.

The tour by India produced Richard Hadlee's 400th Test wicket in the first Test, in which New Zealand's win was the only result in a series that produced some quite astonishing batting.

The Australians started the three-sided one-day series with India and New Zealand all purposeful efficiency, and they soon turned it into a one-sided affair, beating New Zealand in the final with eight wickets and close to ten overs to spare. New Zealand saved the best until the end, with a dominating display over Australia in the solitary Test, at the Basin Reserve.

The final curiosity of such a varied season was that New Zealand Cricket (Inc) should finish with a loss of $116,000. But even that provoked a rather wan smile, for the national administration had lost $480,000 in the previous season.

Shell Trophy 1989-90

Final Table	P	W	NR	1st innings Points	Points
WELLINGTON	10	4	2	12	58*
Canterbury	10	3	–	16	52
Auckland	10	2	–	28	50†
Central Districts	10	2	–	24	48
Otago	10	2	2	20	42*
Northern Districts	10	2	–	16	40

12 pts for win; 4pts for 1st innings lead; NR = no result (2pts).
Bowling penalties: *4pts, † 2pts.

Leading First-Class Averages 1989-90

Batting (Top 20. Qual: 300 runs)	M	I	NO	HS	R	Avge	100	50
J.G. Wright (A, NZ)	9	12	2	185	818	81.80	3	4
M.D. Crowe (CD, NZ)	9	13	2	242	720	65.45	3	1
A.H. Jones (W, NZ)	10	16	4	170*	697	58.08	1	5
K.R. Rutherford (O, NZ)	13	19	2	226*	940	55.29	3	3
B.A. Young (ND)	11	7	6	100*	586	53.27	1	4
B.R. Blair (O)	11	16	0	131	759	47.43	1	5
C.Z. Harris (C)	10	17	6	86	468	42.54	–	3
S.A. Thomson (ND)	9	18	5	74	532	40.92	–	4
J.J. Crowe (A)	11	16	1	110	609	40.60	1	4
D.N. Patel (A)	10	15	1	125*	567	40.50	2	3
B.A. Edgar (W)	10	18	0	167	720	40.00	2	3
G.E. Bradburn (ND)	12	23	1	96	842	38.27	–	6
C.J. Smith (CD)	10	19	3	160*	610	38.12	2	2
R.T. Latham (C)	10	18	2	79	593	37.06	–	4
C.M. Kuggeleijn (ND)	11	19	3	102*	588	36.75	1	3
G.R. Larsen (W)	10	16	4	69	440	36.66	–	3
T.J. Franklin (A)	11	17	1	110	569	35.56	1	2
R.H. Vance (W)	10	17	1	123	545	34.06	1	3
K.A. Wealleans (ND)	12	23	1	112*	730	33.18	2	3
M.W. Priest (C)	9	15	2	68	429	33.00	–	5

Bowling (Top 20. Qual: 15 wkts)	O	M	R	W	Avge	Best	5wI	10wM
J.P. Millmow (W)	249.5	67	699	33	21.18	6-13	3	1
D.J. Leonard (CD)	221.4	51	641	29	22.10	5-52	2	1
M.C. Snedden (A, NZ)	392.3	106	877	39	22.48	6-20	2	1
R.J. Hadlee (C, NZ)	147.1	32	428	19	22.52	5-39	1	–
P.W. O'Rourke (W)	257.4	61	690	29	23.79	5-71	1	–
D.A. Beard (ND)	126	38	357	15	23.80	6-18	1	–
N.A. Mallender (O)	280.2	74	706	29	24.34	4-20	–	–
D.K. Morrison (A, NZ)	310.4	68	999	41	24.36	5-75	3	–
S.J. Roberts (C)	322.4	61	951	39	24.38	4-61	–	–
C. Pringle (A)	180.5	33	565	23	24.56	4-56	–	–
D.N. Patel (A)	225.4	55	568	23	24.69	5-54	1	–
I.D. Fisher (CD)	290.2	95	652	26	25.07	5-43	2	–
S.L. Boock (O)	414.5	153	865	34	25.44	8-57	3	1
S.W. Duff (CD)	305.2	73	810	29	27.93	6-46	2	1
M.W. Priest (C)	393.4	134	882	31	28.45	9-95	1	1
S.B. Doull (ND)	168	41	431	15	28.73	3-17	–	–
C.Z. Harris (C)	225	87	492	17	28.94	3-42	–	–
E.J. Gray (W)	335.4	132	696	24	29.00	8-78	1	1
S.A. Thomson (ND)	227.4	40	736	24	30.66	4-108	–	–
G.E. Bradburn (ND)	334.1	77	928	30	30.93	6-56	1	–

Cricket in India

The season was one of the busiest in recent years for India, though far from being satisfying in terms of results. The national team was away on two major tours, of Pakistan and New Zealand, besides paying two visits to Sharjah and hosting the high-profile Nehru Cup. By inserting domestic first-class tournaments in strategic gaps between international engagements, it became possible to give exposure to all the talent available in the country. Bengal had particular cause to celebrate, winning the Ranji Trophy after 51 years.

The quotient rule (runs scored divided by wickets lost) used to separate teams locked in inconclusive matches (without both first innings completed) came under fire after Bengal beat the defending champions Delhi on home turf at the Eden Gardens. The employment of this curious 'tiebreaker' is indicative of the larger evil of lifeless wickets on which bowlers have been waging unfruitful battles throughout their careers. Coming as it did, though, from a team that benefited in the season under review, the call for reform was genuine. Bengal, who just managed to stay ahead of Delhi's quotient in a rain-affected final, were a vocal critic of a system that seems not to care a fig for the bowler.

Arun Lal, Bengal's leading batsman, topped the averages for the crowded season, while Rakesh Parikh of Baroda was not far behind and made most runs. Atul Wassan, a rarity in that he was a bowler who emerged during the season, was top wicket-taker with 47. He was to be picked for the tour of New Zealand on which his performances as third seamer were rich in promise.

The Duleep Trophy inter-zonal championship, won by South Zone, was staged between the Pakistan and New Zealand series. Apart from providing a new national captain, Azharuddin, in very contentious circumstances, it held little, though there were runs galore. Youngster Praveen Amre of Railways distinguished himself with three hundreds (one of them a double) on the trot, but was not even remotely in contention for a place in the national squad.

Last season's Ranji Trophy champions, Delhi, beat the Rest of India to win the Irani Cup. North Zone won the Deodhar Trophy inter-zonal limited-overs tournament. For the first time, all domestic cricket was sponsored under an umbrella agreement between the board and a tobacco company. Yet it was not as if the players benefited, except, of course, those who were picked to represent their country.

Delhi v Bengal
Ranji Trophy Final, 1989-90

Bengal won on quotient rule
Played at Eden Gardens, Calcutta, on 23, 24, 25, 27, 28 March

Delhi

Manu Nayyar	b Dattatreya Mukherjee	4
Raman Lamba	run out	7
Manoj Prabhakar	c Raja Venkat b Rajeev Seth	11
Ajay Sharma	c Pranob Roy b D. Mukherjee	28
K.P. Bhaskar	c Rajeev Seth b D. Mukherjee	21
Kirti Azad	c Raja Venkat b Rajeev Seth	93
Bantoo Singh	c Arun Lal b Saradindu Mukherjee	36
Sanjeev Sharma	c Arun Lal b Rajeev Seth	17
Maninder Singh	b Utpal Chatterjee	9
Atul Wassan	st Sambaran Banerjee b S. Mukherjee	11
Mohan Chaturvedi	not out	0
Extras	(B10, W1, NB10)	21
		278†

Bengal

Pranob Roy	b Wassan	11
Indu Bhushan Roy	lbw b Prabhakar	7
Arun Lal	not out	52
Saurav Ganguly	c Chaturvedi b Prabhakar	22
Ashok Malhotra	b Maninder	19
Raja Venkat	not out	39
Extras	(B5, LB6, W6, NB9)	26
	(4 wkts)	**216‡**

Bengal	O	M	R	W
Dattatreya Mukherjee	26	6	74	3
Rajeev Seth	25	5	73	3
Saurav Ganguly	6	1	19	0
Utpal Chatterjee	25.3	1	48	1
Saradindu Mukherjee	17	5	34	2
Arun Lal	1	1	0	0

Delhi	O	M	R	W
Prabhakar	19	6	42	2
Wassan	7	0	30	1
Sanjeev Sharma	11	2	33	0
Maninder Singh	21	8	38	1
Kirti Azad	2	0	14	0
Ajay Sharma	3.4	2	8	0

Fall of Wickets

	D	B
Wkt	1st	1st
1st	4	20
2nd	18	20
3rd	47	57
4th	52	97
5th	90	–
6th	184	–
7th	235	–
8th	237	–
9th	258	–
10th	278	–

† Including 20 penalty runs for slow over rate.
‡ Including 40 penalty runs for slow over rate.

Leading First-Class Averages 1989-90

Batting (Qualification: 500 runs)	M	I	NO	R	HS	Avge	100
J. Arun Lal (Bengal)	8	9	2	828	189*	118.28	3
R.B. Parikh (Baroda)	7	11	2	995	218	110.55	4
P.K. Amre (Railways)	7	8	1	667	240*	95.28	3
V.B. Chandrasekar (Tamil Nadu)	6	6	–	516	146	86.00	3
Raja Venkat (Bengal)	7	7	1	500	170	83.33	2
Robin Singh (Tamil Nadu)	7	9	2	563	141	80.42	2
U.R. Radha Krishnan (Railways)	7	11	2	723	214	80.33	3
S.S. Karim (Bihar)	8	10	2	631	148	78.87	3
Kirti Azad (Delhi)	7	9	1	580	120	72.50	3
Yusuf Ali Khan (Railways)	7	8	–	553	233	69.12	2
M.V. Sridhar (Hyderabad)	9	13	–	885	169	68.07	3
V. Vats (U.P.)	8	11	2	569	130*	63.22	1
S.S. Khandkar (U.P.)	8	14	2	740	102*	61.66	1
L.S. Rajput (Bombay)	8	11	2	506	168	56.22	2
V. Jaisimha (Hyderabad)	9	13	1	662	138*	55.16	2
I.B. Roy (Bengal)	8	10	–	537	152	53.70	2
Bantoo Singh (Delhi)	10	12	1	547	136	49.72	2
R. Sapru (U.P.)	8	13	2	528	184	48.00	1

Bowling (Qualification: 20 wickets)	O	M	R	W	Avge
Sunil Subramaniam (Tamil Nadu)	151	40	410	24	17.08
D. Sharma (Haryana)	167.2	49	377	22	17.13
Bharat Vij (Punjab)	228.2	73	455	26	17.50
S. Banerjee (Bihar)	191.2	41	565	30	18.83
A. Wassan (Delhi)	259.3	39	903	47	19.21
A. Kumble (Karnataka)	196.4	52	471	24	19.62
D. Vasu (Tamil Nadu)	152.3	29	462	23	20.08
Abdul Qayyum (J & K)	170.5	18	608	29	20.96
S.L. Venkatapaty Raju (Hyderabad)	337.4	117	683	32	21.34
Sanjeev Sharma (Delhi)	263	55	711	31	22.93
M.V. Rao (Services)	150.3	13	593	25	23.72
R. Bhat (Karnataka)	248.5	65	600	25	24.00
Gopal Sharma (U.P.)	366.5	70	953	37	25.75
T. Chakradhar Rao (Andhra)	156.1	9	572	22	26.00
S. Mohapatra (Orissa)	214.2	36	719	27	26.62
R.R. Kulkarni (Bombay)	236	29	858	32	26.81
J. Srinath (Karnataka)	193.5	28	747	27	27.66
N.D. Hirwani (M.P.)	335.1	46	1081	37	29.21
S.N. Yadav (Hyderabad)	270	56	699	23	30.39
P.S. Vaidya (Vidarbha)	187	23	765	25	30.60
M. Venkataramana (Tamil Nadu)	207.4	29	735	23	31.95
R. Seth (Bengal)	224	37	724	21	34.47
A. Ayub (Hyderabad)	291.2	55	824	21	39.23

Cricket in Pakistan

It was a satisfying season for Pakistan despite the usual hectic international and domestic commitments. They lifted three one-day trophies, the Champions Trophy, the Austral-Asia Cup at Sharjah, and the MRF Nehru Cup in India, besides winning a truncated limited-overs series at home against India. They were unlucky, however, in the Benson & Hedges World Series in Australia, succumbing to the hosts in the final. The four-match Test series against India at home was drawn, and a hard-fought series in Australia lost 1-0.

On the domestic scene, there were the usual disputes and controversies regarding the registration of players, the state of the wickets, and of course umpiring. Protests were lodged and PIA, the airline team, were also heavily fined by the BCCP for flouting the regulations regarding the registration of players.

PIA, however, won Pakistan's premier first-class tournament, the Quaid-e-Azam Trophy, by virtue of their first innings lead against United Bank. In reply to PIA's 287, United Bank had scored 236. The first three days of the final were washed out and play began on the rest day. After a long absence from the domestic scene, the Combined Varsities team also participated in the grade two of the championship, which they deservedly won, defeating the Customs.

In the Patron's Trophy, two teams from Karachi met in the final of the grade-one competition. Karachi Whites were the winners, defeating the Blues. Grade two winners remained undecided, as a disputed game between Hyderabad and Quetta was not replayed. The Wills Cup one-day tournament was regained by Habib Bank who beat PIA by 8 wickets in a one-sided final. Habib Bank required 178 to win, and reached the target with 7.5 overs to spare. Habib Bank, however, lost the Wills Gold Flake League one-day competition, a newly introduced tournament, to ADBP (Agriculture Development Bank) by 7 wickets. A Super Wills Cup was also played, between the Pakistan one-day winners of 1989, United Bank, and the winners of the tournament in India, Delhi. It was won by Delhi, who defeated the Bank at Lahore by 5 wickets.

In the Under-19 matches, Karachi regained the grade-one title by beating Lahore City, the holders. In grade two, Gujranwala beat Sukkur to be elevated to the higher grade. Pakistan Under-19 toured India and lost the four-match Test series 1-0.

No less than 11 batsmen passed 1,000 runs during the season. United Bank and Multan's Inzamam-ul-Haq scored 1,645 runs, making six centuries and six fifties. Although Test opener Shoaib Mohammad averaged 83.20 he played only five matches and it was Mansoor Rana (79.69) who topped the batting averages.

Leading First-Class Averages

Batting (Top 20, qual: 10 innings)

	M	I	NO	R	HS	Avge	100
Mansoor Rana (B/ADBP)	13	18	5	1036	207*	79.69	2
Saeed Anwar (KW/UB)	11	17	1	1082	221	67.62	5
Inzamam-ul-Haq (M/UB)	21	36	9	1645	139*	60.92	6
Asif Mujtaba (KB/PIA)	22	35	5	1587	170	52.90	6
Nasir Khan (PIA)	6	11	2	451	112*	50.11	1
Shahid Saeed (Pak/HBFC)	12	17	2	730	111*	48.66	3
Tariq Mahboob (M)	7	14	2	579	120	48.25	2
Shafiq Ahmed (UB)	15	21	4	813	130*	47.82	3
Basit Ali (KB/PACO)	19	34	3	1479	157	47.70	4
Zahid Ahmed (PIA)	16	23	2	984	128	46.85	4
Rizwan-uz-Zaman (KW/PIA)	18	29	3	1197	217*	46.03	5
Raees Ahmed (UB)	13	20	1	868	138*	45.68	3
Tariq Ismail (B)	7	14	1	593	149*	45.61	1
Perves Shah (LC/UB)	18	29	7	1001	116*	45.50	2
Mohammad Hasnain (S)	5	10	0	446	130	44.60	2
Sajid Ali (KW/NB)	17	27	0	1200	108	44.44	3
Shahid Anwar (B/PACO)	17	30	2	1239	165	44.25	3
Atif Rauf (ADBP)	10	13	1	517	113*	43.08	1
Manzoor Elahi (M/ADBP)	16	25	2	964	119	41.91	3
Rameez Raja (Pak/PNSC)	7	11	0	459	64	41.72	–

Bowling (Top 20, qual: 15 wkts)

	O	R	W	Avge	Best	5wI
Aziz-ur-Rehman (S)	270.5	746	42	17.76	7-47	4
Fakhruddin Baloch (KW)	119.5	405	22	18.40	5-54	2
Mohammad Zahid (B)	263.5	711	37	19.21	6-68	3
Iqbal Qasim (KW/NB)	517.2	1116	58	19.24	8-34	4
Mohammad Riaz (R)	349.4	881	44	20.02	7-90	4
Tausif Ahmed (KW/UB)	263.4	705	35	20.14	6-79	3
Naved Anjum (Pak/HB)	160.2	465	23	20.21	8-87	2
Shakeel Khan (HB)	294	920	45	20.44	7-46	5
Asif Mujtaba (KB/PIA)	517.1	1191	57	20.89	6-19	4
Zahid Ahmed (PIA)	197.4	546	26	21.00	7-14	2
Naved Nazir (F)	191.5	544	25	21.76	9-50	2
Haaris Khan (KB)	376.1	1003	45	22.28	7-90	4
Sajjad Akbar (S/PNSC)	913.1	2328	104	22.38	8-47	10
Zakir Khan (Pak/ADBP)	291.5	910	40	22.75	7-73	2
Iqbal Sikander (KB/PIA)	510.4	1349	58	23.25	6-52	3
Masood Anwar (UB)	441.4	1159	48	24.14	6-52	2
Shakeel Ahmed (R)	199.4	560	23	24.34	6-35	2
Imran Adil (B/UB)	149.3	558	22	25.36	10-92	2
Sajid Bashir (UB)	112	402	15	26.80	3-48	–
Waqar Younis (Pak/UB)	169	656	24	27.33	6-86	2

Wicket-keeping	M	Ct	St	Total
Bilal Ahmed (F/ADBP)	18	39	11	50
Anil Dalpat (K/PIA)	14	25	13	38
Wasim Arif (NB)	12	29	7	36
Sanaullah (PACO)	13	24	11	35
Tahir Rasheed (HB)	12	33	1	34
Ashraf Ali (UB)	12	22	7	29
Nadeem Abbasi (R/Pak)	8	22	4	26

Qual: 25 dismissals. NB Wasim's total
includes 1ct while not keeping wicket.

Fielding (Qual: 15 catches)	M	Ct
Asif Mujtaba (KB/PIA)	22	21
Amin Lakhani (PNSC)	15	20
Sajjad Akbar (S/PNSC)	19	20
Asif Mohammad (PIA)	16	18
Manzoor Elahi (M/ADBP)	16	17
Arshad Pervez (S/HB)	20	17
Shaukat Mirza (KB/HB)	19	16
Sajid Ali (KW/NB)	17	15
Basit Ali (KB/PACO)	19	15

Cricket in Sri Lanka

With conditions returning to normal, the 1989-90 Lakspray Trophy was completed without any hitch, so that all the matches involving 23 clubs were completed on schedule. Singhalese SC emerged as champions for the second time. In the absence of several key players, SSC won with a comparatively inexperienced side, but led by a gutsy captain in Mahinda Halangoda.

The Sri Lanka Cricket Board gave due recognition to the final-round matches, which were of three days' duration, and ranked them as first class. Nine clubs qualified for the final round of which five were from the South – Panadura, Moratuwa, Galle, Sinha, and Old Cambrians, who made a good impression to qualify for the final round in their debut year in the competition. The other debutant club, Navy, were knocked out in the preliminary round along with 13 other clubs, which included such renowned names as NCC, Tamil Union, and Colombo CC.

The tournament format underwent a further change, with the title being decided on the league standings, similar to the English county system, with no final.

Ajith Wasantha, an attractive right-hander from Moratuwa, was the most prolific of all batsmen in the final round, totalling 519 runs for an average of 57.67, including two centuries and three fifties. None of the others topped the 500-run mark.

Also in the top six was former Sri Lanka cricketer Anura Rana-singhe, who was banned from playing cricket for 25 years for going to South Africa. The ban was lifted last year. Nishan Danasinghe of Sinha made the season's only double-century, with 215 in the final weekend of the tournament against Galle. Rupenath Wickremaratne, the Colts captain and all-rounder, smashed the fastest century of the season off 69 balls against Sinha.

The bowling honours once again went to Galle's right-arm medium-pacer Jayananda Warnaweera. The added responsibilities as captain did not deter Warnaweera, who set up a new record for the final round by capturing 71 wickets (avge. 13.48), which included nine hauls of five wickets in an innings. Considering the 53 wickets he took in the preliminary-round matches, Warnaweera's tally of 124 wickets is another record for one season, beating his own mark of 121 set in 1985-86. He also performed the hat-trick against Air Force.

Halangoda had the best innings (8-64) and match (15-91) figures, against Sinha in the final round.

The 1988-89 Lakspray Trophy final eventually took place at the start of the new season, between SSC and NCC, but rain on all three days forced the game to end in a no-result, and the trophy was shared.

Lakspray Trophy 1989-90

Final Table	P	W	W1	L	L1	NR	Pts
SSC	8	6	1	0	0	1	88.615
Panadura SC	8	5	2	1	0	0	87.480
Moratuwa SC	8	3	3	1	0	1	85.485
Galle CC	8	3	0	3	1	1	60.545
Air Force	8	1	1	5	0	1	40.110
Colts	8	1	1	1	4	1	39.390
Sinha SC	8	0	2	4	1	1	36.690
BRC	8	1	0	3	3	1	31.590
Old Cambrians	8	0	1	2	4	1	28.295

W1 = Won 1st innings; L1 = lost 1st innings.

Leading Lakspray Trophy Averages 1989-90

Batting (Min. qual. 300 runs)	M	I	NO	HS	R	Avge	100	50
A. Wasantha (Moratuwa SC)	8	10	1	134	519	57.67	2	3
A. Gunawardena (SSC)	7	11	1	96	469	46.90	0	3
R. Ranjith (Sinha SC)	8	13	1	124	462	38.50	1	3
D. Bulankulame (Colts)	7	12	1	103	420	38.18	1	2
E.R.N.S. Fernando (Air Force)	6	9	0	110	335	37.22	1	2
A.N. Ranasinghe (BRC)	7	9	0	65	329	36.56	0	3

Bowling (Min. qual: 20 wickets)	O	M	R	W	Best	Avge.	5wI	10wM
S.D. Anurasiri (Panadura SC)	235.3	89	380	40	5-50	9.50	1	0
M.B. Halangoda (SSC)	152	35	424	43	8-64	9.86	5	2
K.P.J. Warnaweera (Galle CC)	338.5	72	957	71	7-16	13.48	9	4
F.S. Ahangama (SSC)	192	48	480	33	7-30	14.55	1	1
S. Jayawardena (Panadura SC)	203	23	525	36	6-30	14.58	2	1
C. Mahesh (Moratuwa SC)	184	38	399	24	4-34	16.63	0	0

Lakspray Trophy Final 1988-89

22, 23, 24 September 1989 at Singhalese SC ground, Colombo. MATCH DRAWN. Toss SSC. Nondescripts CC 222 (Karnain 54, E.A.R. de Silva 45; N. Ranatunga 3-42, S. Ranatunga 3-13). SSC 44-4.

EXTRAS

A Record Season – England 1990

Individual Scores of 200 or more (32)

(chronological order)

206*	A. Fordham	Northants v Yorks (Headingley)
235	A.J. Lamb	Northants v Yorks (Headingley)
313*	S.J. Cook	Somerset v Glamorgan (Cardiff)
215	G.A. Gooch	Essex v Leics (Chelmsford)
245	P.J. Prichard	Essex v Leics (Chelmsford)
291*	I.A. Greig	Surrey v Lancs (Foster's Oval)
366	N.H. Fairbrother	Lancs v Surrey (Foster's Oval)
202*	D.A. Reeve	Warwicks v Northants (Northampton)
220*	D.L. Haynes	Middlesex v Essex (Ilford)
227*	B.C. Broad	Notts v Kent (Tunbridge Wells)
204	M.E.Waugh	Essex v Glos (Ilford)
202*	J.P. Stephenson	Essex v Somerset (Bath)
203*	N.H. Fairbrother	Lancs v Warwicks (Coventry)
201*	P.M. Roebuck	Somerset v Worcs (Worcester)
252*	G.A. Hick	Worcs v Glamorgan (Abergavenny)
204*†	R.J. Bailey	Northants v Sussex (Northampton)
224*	A.J. Moles	Warwicks v Glamorgan (Swansea)
234	S.G. Hinks	Kent v Middlesex (Canterbury)
333	G.A. Gooch	ENGLAND v INDIA (Lord's)
210	P.D. Bowler	Derbys v Kent (Chesterfield)
218*	M.D. Moxon	Yorks v Sussex (Eastbourne)
255*	D.L. Haynes	Middlesex v Sussex (Lord's)
207*	M.E. Waugh	Essex v Yorks (Middlesbrough)
256	M.W.Alleyne	Glos v Northants (Northampton)
219	C.J. Tavaré	Somerset v Sussex (Hove)
207	W. Larkins	Northants v Essex (Northampton)
204	N.R. Taylor	Kent v Surrey (Canterbury)
263	D.M. Ward	Surrey v Kent (Canterbury)
200*	K.R. Brown	Middlesex v Notts (Lord's)
221*	P.A. De Silva	Sri Lankans v Hants (Southampton)
220*	R.T. Robinson	Notts v Yorks (Trent Bridge)
208†	D.M. Ward	Surrey v Essex (Foster's Oval)

Highest Totals

863	Lancs v Surrey (Foster's Oval)
761-6 dec	Essex v Leics (Chelmsford)
707-9 dec	Surrey v Lancs (Foster's Oval)
653-4 dec	ENGLAND v INDIA, First Test (Lord's)
648	Surrey v Kent (Canterbury)
636-6†	Northants v Essex (Chelmsford)
613-6 dec†	Surrey v Essex (Foster's Oval)
606-9 dec	INDIA v ENGLAND, Third Test (Foster's Oval)
600-8 dec	Hants v Sussex (Southampton)

Individual Achievements

428 first-class hundreds were scored in 1990. G.A. Gooch scored 12, H. Morris 10. The first batsman to reach 1,000 first-class runs was S.J. Cook (Somerset), who achieved the feat on 4 August, the earliest instance since 1965. Ten batsmen reached 2,000 first-class runs.

*not out; †second innings

Test Career Records

The individual career averages in this section include all official Test matches to the end of the 1990 English season.

England

Batting / Fielding	M	I	NO	HS	R	Avge	100	50	Ct/St
M.A. Atherton	8	15	0	151	808	53.86	2	6	7
R.J. Bailey	4	8	0	43	119	14.87	–	–	–
D.J. Capel	15	25	1	98	374	15.58	–	2	6
P.A.J. DeFreitas	17	25	1	40	301	12.54	–	–	5
N.H. Fairbrother	7	9	1	33*	64	8.00	–	–	4
A.R.C. Fraser	8	9	1	29	61	7.62	–	–	–
G.A. Gooch	81	147	5	333	5910	41.61	12	33	82
D.I. Gower	109	189	15	215	7674	44.10	16	37	72
E.E. Hemmings	15	20	4	95	383	23.93	–	2	4
N. Hussain	3	5	0	35	100	20.00	–	–	1
A.J. Lamb	67	118	10	139	3981	36.86	13	14	64
W. Larkins	10	19	1	54	352	19.55	–	1	7
C.C. Lewis	3	3	0	32	36	12.00	–	–	4
D.E. Malcolm	11	14	6	15*	63	7.87	–	–	1
J.E. Morris	3	5	2	32	71	23.66	–	–	3
R.C. Russell	17	26	5	128*	690	32.85	1	3	49/5
G.C. Small	13	18	6	59	221	18.41	–	1	5
R.A. Smith	18	34	8	143	1397	53.73	4	10	8
A.J. Stewart	7	13	1	54	317	26.41	–	1	7
N.F. Williams	1	1	0	38	38	38.00	–	–	–

Bowling	Balls	R	W	Avge	Best	5wI	10wM
G.A. Gooch	1803	717	15	47.80	2-12	–	–
M.A. Atherton	276	212	1	212.00	1-60	–	–
D.J. Capel	2000	1064	21	50.66	3-88	–	–
P.A.J. DeFreitas	3550	1713	38	45.07	5-53	2	–
N.H. Fairbrother	12	9	9	–	–	–	–
A.R.C. Fraser	2248	944	36	26.22	5-28	3	–
D.I. Gower	36	20	1	20.00	1-1	–	–
E.E. Hemmings	3999	1626	37	43.94	6-58	1	–
A.J. Lamb	30	23	1	23.00	1-6	–	–
C.C. Lewis	636	408	9	45.33	3-76	–	–
D.E. Malcolm	2606	1448	42	34.47	6-77	3	1
G.C. Small	3033	1447	46	31.45	5-48	2	–
N.F. Williams	246	148	2	74.00	2-148	–	–

Australia

Batting/Fielding	M	I	NO	HS	R	Avge	100	50	Ct/St
T.M. Alderman	36	46	19	23	169	6.25	–	–	22
D.C. Boon	48	88	7	200	3186	39.33	8	14	49
A.R. Border	115	199	36	205	8701	53.38	23	48	125
G.D. Campbell	4	4	0	6	10	2.50	–	–	1
I.A. Healy	21	29	2	52	529	19.59	–	1	55/2
M.G. Hughes	23	28	5	72*	449	19.52	–	2	8
D.M. Jones	34	59	8	216	2637	51.70	9	9	19
G.F. Lawson	46	68	12	74	894	15.96	–	4	10
G.R. Marsh	36	66	3	138	2174	34.50	4	9	27
T.M. Moody	4	6	0	106	234	39.00	1	1	3
C.G. Rackemann	11	12	4	15*	43	5.37	–	–	2
P.R. Sleep	14	21	1	90	483	24.15	–	3	4
M.A. Taylor	15	27	2	219	1618	64.72	6	8	20
P.L. Taylor	10	15	3	87	383	31.91	–	2	10
M.R.J. Veletta	8	11	0	39	207	18.81	–	–	12/-
S.R. Waugh	39	60	10	177*	1983	39.66	3	13	30

Bowling	Balls	R	W	Avge	Best	5wI	10wM
T.M. Alderman	9152	4083	153	26.68	6-128	13	1
D.C. Boon	12	5	0	–	–	–	–
A.R. Border	2719	1022	29	35.24	7-46	1	1
G.D. Campbell	951	503	13	38.69	3-79	–	–
M.G. Hughes	5336	2689	88	30.55	8-87	5	1
D.M. Jones	174	55	1	55.00	1-5	–	–
G.F. Lawson	11118	5501	180	30.56	8-112	11	2
T.M. Moody	234	53	1	53.00	1-23	–	–
C.G. Rackemann	2546	1028	39	26.35	6-86	3	1
P.R. Sleep	2982	1397	31	45.06	5-72	1	–
P.L. Taylor	1891	873	24	36.37	6-78	1	–
S.R. Waugh	3638	1800	43	41.86	5-69	2	–

West Indies

Batting / Fielding	M	I	NO	HS	R	Avge	100	50	Ct/St
C.E.L. Ambrose	20	30	7	44	333	14.47	–	–	5
E.A.E. Baptiste	10	11	1	87*	233	23.30	–	1	2
C.A. Best	6	9	1	164	320	40.00	1	1	7
I.R. Bishop	8	12	6	30*	124	20.66	–	–	1
P.J.L. Dujon	68	96	11	139	2994	35.22	5	14	218/5
C.G. Greenidge	100	170	15	223	7134	46.02	18	34	93
D.L. Haynes	89	153	17	184	5711	41.99	14	31	56
C.L. Hooper	19	31	1	100*	710	23.66	1	3	13
A.L. Logie	40	61	6	130	1919	34.89	2	10	42
M.D. Marshall	68	88	9	92	1457	18.44	–	8	25
E.A. Moseley	2	4	0	26	35	8.75	–	–	1
B.P. Patterson	18	23	11	21*	90	7.50	–	–	3
I.V.A. Richards	111	166	10	291	7990	51.21	24	38	116
R.B. Richardson	49	83	7	194	3515	46.25	10	13	60
C.A. Walsh	37	48	17	30*	302	9.74	–	–	4

Bowling	Balls	R	W	Avge	Best	5wI	10wM
C.E.L. Ambrose	4494	1948	80	24.35	8-45	2	1
E.A.E. Baptiste	1362	563	16	35.18	3-31	–	–
C.A. Best	24	19	0	–	–	–	–
I.R. Bishop	1795	790	37	21.35	6-87	2	–
C.G. Greenidge	26	4	0	–	–	–	–
D.L. Haynes	18	8	1	8.00	1-2	–	–
C.L. Hooper	1276	575	7	82.14	2-42	–	–
A.L. Logie	7	4	0	–	–	–	–
M.D. Marshall	15221	6831	329	20.76	7-22	22	4
E.A. Moseley	522	261	6	43.50	2-70	–	–
B.P. Patterson	2972	1844	60	30.73	5-24	3	–
I.V.A. Richards	5002	1857	32	58.03	2-17	–	–
R.B. Richardson	54	12	0	–	–	–	–
C.A. Walsh	7117	3201	134	23.88	6.62	5	1

New Zealand

Batting / Fielding	M	I	NO	HS	R	Avge	100	50	Ct/St
J.G. Bracewell	41	60	11	110	1001	20.42	1	4	31
C.L. Cairns	1	2	0	28	19	14.50	–	–	–
J.J. Crowe	39	65	4	128	1601	26.24	3	6	41
M.D. Crowe	51	83	7	188	3384	44.52	11	12	48
T.J. Franklin	15	25	1	101	569	23.70	1	3	8
M.J. Greatbatch	14	21	4	146*	917	53.94	2	4	5
Sir Richard Hadlee	86	134	19	151*	3124	27.16	2	15	39
A.H. Jones	17	30	4	170*	1190	45.76	2	5	13
D.K. Morrison	16	20	8	27*	70	5.83	–	–	4
A.C. Parore	1	2	1	20	32	32.00	–	–	4/1
D.N. Patel	8	16	0	62	274	17.12	–	1	2
M.W. Priest	1	1	0	26	26	26.00	–	–	–
K.R. Rutherford	22	34	3	107*	524	16.90	1	3	14
I.D.S. Smith	55	75	16	173	1588	26.91	2	5	143/8
M.C. Snedden	25	30	8	33*	327	14.86	–	–	7
S.A. Thomson	1	2	1	43*	65	65.00	–	–	1
R.H. Vance	4	7	0	68	207	29.57	–	1	–
W. Watson	3	3	1	8*	13	6.50	–	–	2
J.G. Wright	71	126	6	185	4377	36.47	10	18	34

Bowling	Balls	R	W	Avge	Best	5wI	10wM
J.G. Bracewell	8403	3653	102	35.81	6-32	4	1
C.L. Cairns	72	60	0	–	–	–	–
J.J. Crowe	18	9	0	–	–	–	–
M.D. Crowe	1239	607	13	46.69	2-25	–	–
M.J. Greatbatch	6	0	0	–	–	–	–
Sir Richard Hadlee	21918	9611	431	22.29	9-52	36	9
A.H. Jones	156	90	1	90.00	1-40	–	–
D.K. Morrison	3053	1826	49	37.26	5-69	4	–
D.N. Patel	427	210	1	210.00	1-80	–	–
M.W. Priest	72	26	1	26.00	1-26	–	–
K.R. Rutherford	244	150	1	150.00	1-38	–	–
M.C. Snedden	4775	2199	58	37.91	5-68	1	–
S.A. Thomson	165	122	2	61.00	2-92	–	–
W. Watson	659	314	4	78.50	2-51	–	–
J.G. Wright	30	5	0	–	–	–	–

India

Batting/Fielding	M	I	NO	HS	R	Avge	100	50	Ct/St
M. Azharuddin	40	60	3	199	2953	51.80	10	10	31
S.A. Ankola	1	1	0	6	6	6.00	–	–	–
A. Ayub	13	19	4	57	257	17.13	–	1	2
Gursharan Singh	1	1	0	18	18	18.00	–	–	2
N.D. Hirwani	13	17	10	17	45	6.42	–	–	5
Kapil Dev	109	158	13	163	4521	31.17	7	23	54
A. Kumble	1	1	0	2	2	2.00	–	–	–
Maninder Singh	34	38	12	15	99	3.80	–	–	9
S.V. Manjrekar	15	24	2	218	1067	48.50	3	5	11
K.S. Moré	34	46	10	73	924	25.66	–	5	68/15
M. Prabhakar	12	20	6	95	621	44.35	–	4	3
S.L.V. Raju	2	3	1	31	55	27.50	–	–	1
W.V. Raman	6	10	1	96	303	33.66	–	3	3
V. Razdan	2	2	1	6*	6	6.00	–	–	–
S.K. Sharma	2	3	1	38	56	28.00	–	–	1
R.J. Shastri	72	109	14	187	3372	35.49	10	11	35
N.S. Sidhu	17	28	2	116	792	30.46	2	4	2
K. Srikkanth	39	64	3	123	1927	31.59	2	12	33
S.R. Tendulkar	10	15	1	119*	577	41.21	1	4	5
D.B. Vengsarkar	110	175	22	166	6703	43.81	17	33	74
A.S. Wassan	4	5	1	53	94	23.50	–	1	1

Bowling	Balls	R	W	Avge	Best	5wI	10wM
M. Azharuddin	6	8	0	–	–	–	–
S.A. Ankola	180	128	2	64.00	1-35	–	–
A. Ayub	3662	1438	41	35.07	5-50	3	–
N.D. Hirwani	3752	1765	57	30.96	8-61	3	1
Kapil Dev	23037	11199	371	30.18	9-83	21	2
A. Kumble	360	170	3	56.66	3-105	–	–
Maninder Singh	7816	3143	81	38.80	7-27	3	2
S.V. Manjrekar	6	7	0	–	–	–	–
K.S. Moré	12	12	0	–	–	–	–
M. Prabhakar	2907	1580	30	52.66	6-132	2	–
S.L.V. Raju	276	113	3	37.66	3-86	–	–
W.V. Raman	258	66	2	33.00	1-7	–	–
V. Razdan	240	141	5	28.20	5-79	1	–
S.K. Sharma	414	247	6	41.16	3-37	–	–
R.J. Shastri	15103	5914	143	41.35	5-75	2	–
N.S. Sidhu	6	9	0	–	–	–	–
K. Srikkanth	210	108	0	–	–	–	–
S.R. Tendulkar	30	25	0	–	–	–	–
D.B. Vengsarkar	47	36	0	–	–	–	–
A.S. Wassan	712	504	10	50.40	4-108	–	–

Pakistan

Batting / Fielding	M	I	NO	HS	R	Avge	100	50	Ct/St
Aamer Malik	12	15	3	117	486	40.50	2	2	13/1
Aaqib Javed	2	2	0	0	0	00.00	–	–	1
Abdul Qadir	63	74	10	61	1022	15.96	–	3	15
Akram Raza	1	–	–	–	–	–	–	–	–
Imran Khan	82	118	22	136	3541	36.88	6	15	28
Ijaz Ahmed	16	21	0	122	637	30.33	2	2	14
Javed Miandad	104	158	18	280*	7891	56.36	22	38	86/1
Mansoor Akhtar	19	29	3	111	655	25.19	1	3	9
Mushtaq Ahmed	1	2	0	4	4	2.00	–	–	–
Nadeem Abbasi	3	2	0	36	46	23.00	–	–	6/-
Nadeem Ghauri	1	1	0	0	0	0.00	–	–	–
Naved Anjum	1	1	0	12	12	12.00	–	–	–
Ramiz Raja	31	49	3	122	1390	30.21	2	9	21
Salim Jaffer	10	10	4	9	22	3.66	–	–	1
Salim Malik	57	79	14	119*	2718	41.81	7	15	43
Salim Yousuf	28	39	5	91*	977	28.73	–	5	73/11
Shahid Mahboob	1	–	–	–	–	–	–	–	–
Shahid Saeed	1	1	0	12	12	12.00	–	–	–
Shoaib Mohammad	29	42	3	203*	1611	41.30	4	8	16
Tausif Ahmed	31	35	18	35*	284	16.70	–	–	8
Waqar Younis	5	6	1	18	43	8.60	–	–	–
Wasim Akram	32	39	6	123	665	20.15	1	3	11
Zakir Khan	2	2	2	9*	9	–	–	–	1

Bowling	Balls	R	W	Avge	Best	5wI	10wM
Aamer Malik	126	73	1	73.00	1-0	–	–
Aaqib Javed	541	262	3	87.33	2-47	–	–
Abdul Qadir	16591	7458	230	32.42	9-56	15	5
Akram Raza	108	58	0	–	–	–	–
Ijaz Ahmed	12	3	0	–	–	–	–
Imran Khan	19290	8188	358	22.87	8-58	23	6
Javed Miandad	1470	682	17	40.11	3-74	–	–
Mushtaq Ahmed	288	141	1	141.00	1-72	–	–
Nadeem Ghauri	48	20	0	–	–	–	–
Naved Anjum	306	149	4	37.25	2-57	–	–
Salim Jaffer	1931	887	25	35.48	5-40	1	–
Salim Malik	254	101	5	20.20	1-3	–	–
Shahid Mahboob	294	131	2	65.50	2-131	–	–
Shahid Saeed	90	43	0	–	–	–	–
Shoaib Mohammad	198	89	4	22.25	2-8	–	–
Tausif Ahmed	7508	2831	92	30.77	6-45	3	–
Waqar Younis	846	461	10	46.10	4-80	–	–
Wasim Akram	7017	2967	111	26.72	6-62	8	2
Zakir Khan	444	259	5	51.80	3-80	–	–

Sri Lanka

Batting/Fielding	M	I	NO	HS	R	Avge	100	50	Ct/St
E.A.R. De Silva	7	11	3	50	146	18.25	–	1	4
P.A. De Silva	17	31	2	167	974	33.58	3	3	9
A.P. Gurusinha	9	15	2	116*	414	31.84	1	–	6
G.F. Labrooy	5	8	2	42	81	13.50	–	–	1
R.S. Mahanama	6	10	0	85	243	24.30	–	1	3
C.P. Ramanayake	4	7	3	10*	27	6.75	–	–	2
A. Ranatunga	26	46	2	135*	1621	36.84	2	12	14
D. Ranatunga	2	3	0	45	87	29.00	–	–	–
R.J. Ratnayake	15	25	4	56	277	13.19	–	1	6
J.R. Ratnayeke	22	38	6	93	807	25.21	–	5	1
M.A.R. Samarasekera	2	3	0	57	75	25.00	–	1	3
H.P. Tillekeratne	1	2	0	6	6	3.00	–	–	5/-
A.G.D. Wickremasinghe	1	1	0	2	2	2.00	–	–	3/-

Bowling	Balls	R	W	Avge	Best	5wI	10wM
E.A.R. De Silva	1440	639	4	159.75	1-10	–	–
P.A. De Silva	234	134	3	44.66	2-65	–	–
A.P. Gurusinha	254	172	7	24.57	2-25	–	–
G.F. Labrooy	1297	778	14	55.57	5-133	1	–
R.S. Mahanama	6	3	0	–	–	–	–
C.P. Ramanayake	674	396	6	66.00	2-81	–	–
A. Ranatunga	1555	688	11	62.54	2-17	–	–
R.J. Ratnayake	3153	1701	49	34.71	6-66	3	–
J.R. Ratnayeke	3833	1972	56	35.21	8-83	4	–
M.A.R. Samarasekera	192	104	3	34.66	2-38	–	–

Newcomers to County Cricket in 1990

Batting/Fielding		M	I	NO	HS	R	Avge	100	50	Ct/St
Derbyshire	D.G. Cork	2	2	1	7	9	9.00	–	–	–
Essex	J.J.B. Lewis	1	1	1	116*	116	–	1	–	1
	K.O. Thomas	1	1	0	2	2	2.00	–	–	–
Glamorgan	H.A.G. Anthony	6	8	0	39	127	15.87	–	–	–
	M. Davies	1	1	1	5*	5	–	–	–	1
Gloucestershire	S.N. Barnes	10	9	3	12*	23	3.83	–	–	3
	R.M. Bell	2	2	0	0	0	–	–	–	–
	E.T. Milburn	2	4	2	35	49	24.50	–	–	–
	P.A. Owen	3	2	0	1	2	1.00	–	–	–
	R.C.J. Williams	8	8	4	50*	132	33.00	–	1	27/4
Hampshire	R.M.F. Cox	4	7	2	104*	220	44.00	1	–	3
	L.A. Joseph	6	5	4	69*	152	152.00	–	1	1
Kent	P.S. De Villiers	12	15	3	37	264	22.00	–	–	6
	N.J. Llong	1	–	–	–	–	–	–	–	1
	T.N. Wren	5	5	2	16	23	7.66	–	–	2
Lancashire	S. Bramhall	2	3	2	1*	1	1.00	–	–	2/-
	J.P. Crawley	3	3	1	76*	103	51.50	–	1	1
	J. Gallian	1	1	1	17*	17	–	–	–	–
	R. Irani	1	–	–	–	–	–	–	–	–
	S.P. Titchard	3	5	0	80	129	25.80	–	1	–
	G. Yates	5	4	2	106	165	82.50	1	–	1
Leicestershire	C. Hawkes	1	2	1	3	5	5.00	–	–	1
	A.D. Mullally	19	18	6	29	113	9.41	–	–	4
	B.F. Smith	2	2	1	15*	19	19.00	–	–	1
Middlesex	C.W. Taylor	2	2	1	13	13	13.00	–	–	–
	N.R. Taylor	1	1	0	0	0	0.00	–	–	1
	M.J. Thursfield	2	–	–	–	–	–	–	–	–
	P.N. Weekes	3	3	0	51	75	25.00	–	1	3
Northamptonshire	J.G. Hughes	4	7	0	2	4	0.57	–	–	–
Nottinghamshire	D.R. Laing	1	1	0	2	2	2.00	–	–	–
Somerset	J.C. Hallett	3	1	0	0	0	0.00	–	–	–
	R.P. Lefebvre	17	16	3	53	214	16.46	–	1	8
	G.T.J. Townsend	2	4	1	15	21	7.00	–	–	3
Surrey	Waqar Younis	14	9	7	14	56	28.00	–	–	4
Sussex	J.W. Hall	20	37	2	125	1140	32.57	2	5	6
	R. Hanley	2	4	0	28	32	8.00	–	–	–
	J.A. North	4	5	1	19*	41	10.25	–	–	1
Warwickshire	T.M. Moody	9	15	2	168	1163	89.46	7	1	4
	D.P. Ostler	11	19	2	71	510	30.00	–	5	9
Worcestershire	R.D. Stemp	2	2	2	3*	3	–	–	–	1

Batting/Fielding		M	I	NO	HS	R	Avge	100	50	Ct/St
Yorkshire	C. Chapman	2	4	0	20	47	11.75	–	–	2
	M.J. Doidge	1	–	–	–	–	–	–	–	–
	P.A. Grayson	5	8	4	44*	145	36.25	–	–	2
	C. White	10	11	2	38	127	14.11	–	–	4

Bowling		O	M	R	W	Avge	Best	5wI	10wM
Derbyshire	D.G. Cork	39	8	123	2	61.50	1-4	–	–
Essex	K.O. Thomas	18.2	3	81	0	–	–	–	–
Glamorgan	H.A.G. Anthony	132.4	32	466	12	38.83	3-95	–	–
	M. Davies	8	1	16	0	–	–	–	–
Gloucestershire	S.N. Barnes	207	45	602	16	37.62	4-51	–	–
	R.M. Bell	44	7	114	3	38.00	2-38	–	–
	E.T. Milburn	32.3	4	150	3	50.00	3-43	–	–
	P.A. Owen	57	7	239	4	59.75	2-37	–	–
Hampshire	R.M.F. Cox	1	0	1	0	–	–	–	–
	L.A. Joseph	102	16	462	7	66.00	2-28	–	–
Kent	P.S. De Villiers	304.5	58	992	25	39.68	6-70	1	–
	N.J. Llong	7	1	24	0	–	–	–	–
	T.N. Wren	122	14	489	6	81.50	2-78	–	–
Lancashire	J. Gallian	21	8	65	1	65.00	1-50	–	–
	R. Irani	22	7	73	2	36.50	1-12	–	–
	G. Yates	167	38	420	8	52.50	4-94	–	–
Leicestershire	C. Hawkes	14	3	40	0	–	–	–	–
	A.D. Mullally	487.2	117	1446	38	38.05	4-59	–	–
Middlesex	C.W. Taylor	47.5	7	139	6	23.16	5-33	1	–
	N.R. Taylor	14	5	44	3	14.66	3-44	–	–
	M.J. Thursfield	42	11	130	2	65.00	1-24	–	–
	P.N. Weekes	80	17	264	4	66.00	2-115	–	–
Northamptonshire	J.G. Hughes	66	12	293	3	97.66	2-57	–	–
Nottinghamshire	D.R. Laing	5	1	21	0	–	–	–	–
Somerset	J.C. Hallett	65.5	9	238	6	39.66	2-40	–	–
	R.P. Lefebvre	506.1	137	1281	31	41.32	5-30	1	–
Surrey	Waqar Younis	423	70	1357	57	23.80	7-73	3	1
Sussex	J.A. North	83.1	17	236	6	39.33	2-43	–	–
Warwickshire	T.M. Moody	59	15	212	3	70.66	1-7	–	–
Worcestershire	R.D. Stemp	45	14	123	1	123.00	1-32	–	–
Yorkshire	M.J. Doidge	24	5	106	0	–	–	–	–
	P.A. Grayson	80	19	270	1	270.00	1-55	–	–
	C. White	159	23	608	13	46.76	5-74	1	–

County caps awarded in 1990

Derbyshire: S.J. Base, I.R. Bishop
Essex: M.A. Garnham
Glamorgan: I.V.A. Richards
Gloucestershire: M.W. Alleyne
Hampshire: D.I. Gower, T.C. Middleton
Kent: R.P. Davis, M.V. Fleming
Lancashire: I.D. Austin
Leicestershire: C.C. Lewis
Middlesex: K.R. Brown, M.R. Ramprakash, M.A. Roseberry,
P.C.R. Tufnell
Northamptonshire: C.E.L. Ambrose, N.A. Felton, A. Fordham
Nottinghamshire: J.A. Afford, K.P. Evans
Somerset: A.N. Hayhurst
Surrey: D.J. Bicknell, C.K. Bullen, M.A. Feltham, Waqar Younis,
D.M. Ward
Sussex: N.J. Lenham
Warwickshire: T.M. Moody
Worcestershire: G.J. Lord
Yorkshire: none

Lawrence Challenge Trophy

Australian all-rounder Tom Moody won the 1990 Lawrence Challenge Trophy for the fastest hundred of the season. Indeed, he made the fastest first-class century of all time – in 26 minutes off 36 balls. On 27 July, playing for Warwickshire against Glamorgan at Swansea – the ground where Sir Garfield Sobers struck 6 sixes in one over for Notts against Glamorgan in 1968 – Moody took advantage of some friendly 'declaration' bowling by Matthew Maynard and Tony Cottey to hit 11 fours and 7 sixes on the way to the new record. This surpassed the previous record of 35 minutes shared by Percy Fender (Surrey v Northants, 1920) and Steve O'Shaughnessy (Lancs v Leics, 1983). But Warwicks didn't win. Set a target of 283 in 55 overs, Glamorgan reached it with five wickets and just two balls to spare.

This kind of 'run-feeding', however, which O'Shaughnessy also benefited from when he won the Trophy, makes a mockery of the national averages, the feats of great players of the past, and of the game of cricket, and, as E.W. Swanton said in 1983, it frustrates the traditional intentions of the donors to reward attacking batting with a prize that dates back to 1934.

The bowling award, for the first to 100 wickets (or, if no one reaches the target, the most wickets), was revived this year, and Neil Foster (Essex) wins the Walter Lawrence Swanton Plate. He took 94 first-class wickets, which, in a batsman's season, put him streets ahead of the next man.

Coopers Deloitte Ratings
by Rob Eastaway

In October 1989, the Deloitte Ratings became the Coopers Deloitte Ratings. This change of name seemed to herald a change in England's fortunes, too. Wins against West Indies, New Zealand, and India have returned England to being a force to be reckoned with in Test cricket. What a pleasant change to see some old *and* new England names featuring prominently in the Ratings table at the end of the 1990 season!

Most prominent of all is Graham Gooch, whose appointment to the captaincy coincided with the best Test match form of his whole career. He became the highest-rated England batsman for five years, climbing 25 places over the year, and he so nearly went top of the batting. Only the relative weakness of India's bowling attack and the easy pitches (both taken into account by the Ratings) prevented him from doing so.

Robin Smith, now in 5th place, has firmly established himself as a world-class batsman in the last two seasons, and in just over a year Mike Atherton has forced himself into the Ratings top ten.

Meanwhile, England have found a new fast-bowling attack in Fraser and Malcolm to replace the injury (and South Africa) prone Dilley and Foster. Fraser is England's highest rated bowler since Richard Ellison's brief rise to 7th in 1985.

The loss of Foster, Dilley, and many other bowlers – dropped or injured – from the Ratings has made it easier to get into the top 25 (421 points as opposed to 506). And whereas last year no players with fewer than 405 points made the top 35, nine do at the end of this season.

England's opponents in 1990 had mixed fortunes in the Ratings. For India, Azharuddin, Shastri, and Tendulkar all enhanced their reputations, climbing impressively in the batting table. But Vengsarkar fell to 19th, his lowest position for five years, and Sidhu dropped out of the top 40. New Zealand, too, fell from their high of last winter: of their batsmen, only John Wright and Trevor Franklin (up 18 places to 53rd) improved over the year.

Of the other Test-playing countries, the West Indies remain the most stable and highest rated of all, with Ian Bishop their most promising young bowler. Their batting is still intimidating although not as all-powerful or as young as it was. Haynes has leap-frogged over Richards and Richardson, who both lost several places.

Australia's batting still has the potential to be the best in the world. Mark Taylor went top of the Ratings in March, while Waugh and Boon will be looking to return to their superb form of 1989. Merv Hughes, meanwhile, is a much improved bowler.

The highest-rated player of them all, however, is Sir Richard Hadlee, who retired from Test cricket as number one bowler in the ratings – a position he has shared with Malcolm Marshall for nearly six years. At the time of writing, Hadlee is the only player with over 850 points, the mark of supreme form.

Top 40 Coopers Deloitte Ratings

	Batting				Bowling	
Rank (†)	**Player**	**‡Rating**		**Rank (†)**	**Player**	**‡Rating**
1 (+6)	Taylor M. (A)	813		1 (–)	Hadlee (NZ)	868
2 (−1)	Miandad (P)	807		2 (–)	Marshall (WI)	836
3 (+25)	Gooch (E)	793		3 (+9)	Bishop (WI)	766
4 (+5)	Haynes (WI)	781		4 (+41)	Fraser (E)	755
5 (+3)	Smith R. (E)	778		5 (−2)	Imran Khan (P)	753
6 (−4)	Richardson (WI)	774		6 (−2)	Alderman (A)	712
7 (−1)	Border (A)	758		7 (+3)	Ambrose (WI)	688
8 (+10)	Azharuddin (I)	721		8 (–)	Akram (P)	688
9 (+86)	Atherton (E)	711		9 (+16)	Hughes M. (A)	680
10 (+9)	Imran Khan (P)	703		10 (−3)	Walsh (WI)	644
11 (+13)	Wright (NZ)	699		11 (−6)	Kapil Dev (I)	625
12 (−1)	Jones (A)	678		12 (+61)	Malcolm (E)	578
13 (−9)	Richards (WI)	678		13 (−7)	Lawson (A)	575
14 (+1)	Greenidge (WI)	657		14 (+42)	Morrison (NZ)	538
15 (−10)	Crowe M. (NZ)	649		15 (−1)	Ratnayeke (SL)	532
16 (−3)	Greatbatch (NZ)	631		16 (+4)	Qadir (P)	506
17 (−5)	Ranatunga (SL)	627		17 (+5)	Tausif (P)	473
18 (+3)	Salim (P)	621		18 (+21)	Small (E)	472
19 (−16)	Vengsarkar (I)	621		19 (–)	Hirwani (I)	462
20 (−4)	Logie (WI)	615		20 (+11)	Bracewell (NZ)	447
21 (+10)	Lamb (E)	614		21 (+5)	Jaffer (P)	445
22 (−12)	Waugh (A)	605		22 (new)	Rackemann (A)	431
23 (–)	Jones (NZ)	597		23 (−14)	Ayub (I)	425
24 (−7)	Shoaib (P)	579		24 (+12)	Waugh (A)	423
25 (+20)	Manjrekar (I)	574		25 (−1)	Shastri (I)	421
26 (new)	Best (WI)	548		26 (+4)	Border (A)	415
27 (−2)	Gower (E)	539		27 (new)	Ratnayake (SL)	401
28 (new)	Tendulkar (I)	516		28 (+5)	Patterson (WI)	379
29 (+21)	De Silva P. (SL)	516		29 (−1)	Maninder (I)	375
30 (+7)	Shastri (I)	492		30 (+34)	Hemmings (E)	373
31 (+13)	Taylor P. (A)	478		31 (+7)	Snedden (NZ)	356
32 (−18)	Boon (A)	474		32 (+6)	Botham (E)	354
33 (−3)	Smith (NZ)	471		33 (+17)	DeFreitas (E)	342
34 (+5)	Ratnayeke (SL)	468		34 (new)	Prabhakar (I)	341
35 (−13)	Russell (E)	463		35 (+5)	Cook N. (E)	336
36 (new)	Prabhakar (I)	462		36 (+6)	Hohns (A)	318
37 (+3)	Ijaz Ahmed (P)	452		37 (new)	Wasson (I)	289
38 (−9)	Dujon (WI)	448		38 (+9)	Sleep (A)	273
39 (−5)	Kapil Dev (I)	444		39 (–)	Pringle (E)	272
40 (−20)	Srikkanth (I)	439		40 (new)	Gurusinha (SL)	264

† Changes in rank over the year 31.8.89 to 31.8.90.
‡ Ratings after England v India 3rd Test, at The Oval (28.8.90).
NB Several bowlers marked 'new' have returned after long absences.

Unibind ICC Trophy 1990

Zimbabwe beat the Netherlands by six wickets in the final of the 1990 Unibind ICC Trophy to earn themselves a place in the 1992 World Cup. They retained their title by going through the 17-nation tournament unbeaten – winning all eight of their matches.

The preliminary round saw the teams divided into four groups, with the top two in each qualifying for the second phase. Another round robin produced the four semi-finalists. Zimbabwe reached this stage without being extended, but against a useful Bangladesh side they had a scare when reduced to 37 for 4 before the inevitable David Houghton came to the rescue.

The Netherlands not only produced a fine cricketing side, but also ran the tournament with splendid efficiency. Thanks to the bowling of Hampshire's Paul-Jan Bakker (6-41) and Somerset's Roland Lefebvre (3-39), they beat Kenya by five wickets in their semi-final. But they found Zimbabwe too strong for them in the final, despite another sterling bowling effort from Lefebvre (11-3-12-2).

Preliminary Group Tables

Group A	P	W	L	Pts	Sc/R	Group C	P	W	L	Pts	Sc/R
ZIMBABWE	3	3	0	12	3.79	USA	3	3	0	12	4.08
CANADA	3	2	1	8	3.18	DENMARK	3	2	1	8	3.45
Singapore	3	1	2	4	2.06	Gibraltar	3	1	2	4	2.52
Malaysia	3	0	3	0	2.08	East & Central Africa	3	0	3	0	2.23

Group B	P	W	L	Pts	Sc/R	Group D	P	W	L	Pts	Sc/R
BANGLADESH	3	3	0	12	3.17	THE NETHERLANDS	4	4	0	16	5.49
KENYA	3	1	2	4	3.45	PAPUA-NEW GUINEA	4	3	1	12	3.27
Fiji	3	1	2	4	3.31	Hong Kong	4	2	2	8	3.81
Bermuda	3	1	2	4	3.15	Israel	4	1	3	4	2.28
						Argentina	4	0	4	0	1.96

The top two teams in Groups A-D went through to the semi-final qualification phase, Groups E and F.

Group E	P	W	L	Pts	Sc/R	Group F	P	W	L	Pts	Sc/R
ZIMBABWE	3	3	0	12	3.72	THE NETHERLANDS	3	2	1	8	3.68
KENYA	3	1	2	4	2.98	BANGLADESH	3	2	1	8	3.62
Papua-New Guinea	3	1	2	4	2.70	Denmark	3	1	2	4	2.93
USA	3	1	2	4	2.68	Canada	3	1	2	4	2.72

1st Semi-Final
20 June at The Hague. THE NETHERLANDS beat KENYA by 5 wickets. Kenya 202 (59.4 overs) (Karim 53, Kanji 52; Bakker 6-41). The Netherlands 205-5 (56.2 overs) (De Leede 56 not out).

2nd Semi-Final
21, 22 June at The Hague. ZIMBABWE beat BANGLADESH by 84 runs. Zimbabwe 231-7 (60 overs). (Houghton 91, Brandes 66). Bangladesh 147 (53.1 overs) (Nannu 57; Duers 4-25).

Man of the Tournament: Roland Lefebvre (Netherlands).

1990 Unibind ICC Trophy Final
The Netherlands v Zimbabwe

Zimbabwe won by 6 wickets
Played at The Hague CC, 23 June
Toss: Holland. Umpires: J.W. Holder (England) and Rodan Singh (Canada)

The Netherlands

G.J.A.F. Aponso	c A.J. Flower b Shah	36
C. Ruskamp†	c A.J. Flower b Brandes	21
R. Gomes	c Jarvis b Traicos	16
N.E. Clarke	c Paterson b Shah	14
R.P. Lefebvre	c Houghton b Shah	8
T. de Leede	c Jarvis b Duers	9
S.W. Lubbers*	run out	47
R. van Oosterom	c Arnott b Shah	2
P-J. Bakker	c A.J. Flower b Brandes	7
A. van Troost	not out	9
E. Dulfer	not out	0
Extras	(B2, LB4, W19, NB3)	28
	(60 overs)	**197-9**

Zimbabwe

G.A. Paterson	c Aponso b Lefebvre	20
G.W. Flower	b Lefebvre	10
A.J. Flower†	not out	69
A.J. Pycroft	c Ruskamp b van Troost	45
D.L. Houghton	c Lefebvre b van Troost	28
A.H. Shah	not out	11
K.J. Arnott	did not bat	
E.A. Brandes	,,	
M.P. Jarvis	,,	
K.G. Duers	,,	
A.J. Traicos	,,	
Extras	(LB8, W7)	15
	(54.2 overs)	**198-4**

Zimbabwe	O	M	R	W
Jarvis	12	2	32	0
Duers	12	1	39	1
Traicos	12	2	19	1
Shah	12	2	56	4
Brandes	12	1	45	2

Netherlands	O	M	R	W
van Troost	12	1	43	2
Bakker	10.2	2	35	0
Lefebvre	11	3	12	2
Dulfer	12	1	52	0
Aponso	5	0	23	0
Lubbers	2	0	10	0
de Leede	2	0	15	0

Fall of Wickets

Wkt	N	Z
1st	49	25
2nd	77	41
3rd	100	134
4th	100	180
5th	117	–
6th	125	–
7th	139	–
8th	166	–
9th	195	–
10th	–	–

Obituary 1989-90

Len Hutton – prince of batsmen

Sir Leonard Hutton died yesterday at Kingston Hospital, Surrey, following an operation for a ruptured aorta, the main artery of the heart. He was 74. Though the end came suddenly, he had been in frail health for some years. At the Oval Test a fortnight ago his appearance saddened his friends.

The quizzical smile peculiarly his own, as though he were enjoying some private joke – the expression by which many will remember him – emerged now and then, but keeping cheerful was plainly an effort.

He was an essentially quiet, reticent man, though capable of sudden shafts of humour. From his earliest days with Yorkshire there was a natural dignity about him which remained through life. Through the most stressful moments he appeared outwardly unruffled. The good name of cricket meant much to him, and he was only caustic about those who sullied it.

Sir Leonard Hutton holds a secure place among the household names of cricket. He will be remembered as in lineal descent from the great players who, before him, wore the white rose of Yorkshire, as the holder of the record score of 364 in Tests between England and Australia, and as the captain who recovered the Ashes in 1953 and retained them 'down under' 18 months later.

The strain of leadership on a sensitive introverted personality, coupled with the responsibility of continuing to open the England innings, led shortly after these successes to what was then considered a premature retirement six months short of his 40th birthday. The award of a knighthood closely followed, the second, and to date the last, bestowed upon an English professional cricketer.

His predecessor was Sir Jack Hobbs, still remembered as 'The Master', whose last days with Surrey in the early summer of 1934 coincided exactly with Hutton's first with Yorkshire. Hutton, like his great forerunner, was far from robust in physique. Each had reached the peak of his skill when war interrupted his cricket, in Hobbs's case for four years, in Hutton's for six.

The course that their careers subsequently took reflects the respective demands made upon them. After the First War Hobbs made only three tours, all to Australia, before his retirement 15 years later at the age of 51. In the decade after the Second War Hutton's shoulders were burdened with 16 series at home and abroad. He toured Australia three times, the West Indies twice, and South Africa for a second time during this period. In all but his last tour he was the mainstay of England's batting. In the Australian series of 1950/51 and 1953 his average was virtually double that of anyone else on either side.

If Hobbs be acknowledged as the greatest of all English professional batsmen, Len Hutton by common consent must rate pre-eminently with two others of equal pedigree, Denis Compton and Walter Hammond. These two were more flamboyant in style than he, as befitted their place at number four in the order.

There was more self-denial about Hutton's opening role, a characteristic inherited in full from his mentor and partner Herbert Sutcliffe. But he too could dazzle when he deemed the time was right.

Leonard Hutton was born a mile from the celebrated cricket nursery of Pudsey, in the adjacent village of Fulneck. Several generations of Huttons had belonged to the self-sufficient community which the mid-European Moravian sect had established there in the 19th century. His father and grandfather were builders. Naturally the village had its cricket ground, where the minister bowled to him as well as his father, uncles, and brothers. All were dedicated cricketers.

Moving on to Pudsey St Lawrence, Len was only 13 when he was bidden to the Yorkshire nets at Headingley. Len never forgot what George Hirst said after he had first seen him bat. 'Well played. Try and improve on that.'

Another great Yorkshire cricketer, Sutcliffe, was much more effusive in his comment, so much so that the question was whether Len had been burdened with prophecies too extravagant for a youngster's good. However, this one always kept a clear head on his shoulders.

He recovered from a duck in his first innings for Yorkshire shortly before his 18th birthday, and from another (his scores 0 and 1) on his debut for England a few days after his 21st. There had never been doubt about his method, while as his career unfolded, his temperament proved equally reliable.

He made the first of his 19 Test hundreds in his second match, against New Zealand, while both he and Compton scored hundreds in their first Tests against Australia at Trent Bridge the following summer.

In the fifth test, in August 1938, the first and the last 'timeless' Test to be played in England, he produced the ultimate marathon of endurance, an innings of 364, which was both the highest Test score and at 13 hours 20 minutes the longest ever played.

As a boy young Len had seen the making of the score he had now surpassed, the 334 at Headingley by Don Bradman, who was thereupon installed as his hero.

The first of his seven MCC tours followed, to South Africa. In 1939 he made 12 hundreds, two for England v West Indies, 10 for Yorkshire.

When war came, Hutton was at the top of the tree, a well-nigh ideal model for imitation. Perfect positioning of the feet and faultless balance at the moment of impact gave him the timing that a modest physique demanded. These attributes became the more important when in 1941 he suffered a serious gymnasium accident, falling on his left arm during Commando training.

This resulted in several operations, the arm in question emerging from 14 months in plaster emaciated and three inches shorter than the right. The lengthy recuperation period naturally involved also an adjustment of his batting technique.

Hutton was at the centre of the pictures in all England's post-war Test series along with Compton, and notably in the duels against the Australian fast-bowling pair of Lindwall and Miller. In 1952, as the most seasoned and level-headed among the leading professionals, he was promoted to the captaincy of England, the first of his kind since the early missionary tours to Australia in the 1870s.

He wore the mantle of leadership with unruffled dignity if little indication of comfort. India were disposed of easily in England in 1952 in preparation for the Australian visit following. After four fluctuating draws, Hutton, himself playing the highest innings of the match, brought the Ashes back home at the Oval after a record absence of 19 years.

So far so very good. In that 1953/4 winter was due another visit to the West Indies, against whom England had already lost two post-war rubbers. Dubious though many were at the prospect of his handling all the problems of a tour to fervent and politically emerging countries, MCC made the cardinal error of departing from established custom, appointing not an experienced tour manager but a player-manager in C.H. Palmer, a younger member of the team who had not hitherto played for England. Wholesale defeats in the first two Tests saw English prestige at its lowest, both on the playing field and off it.

The subsequent recovery, to the point of halving the series, owed most to the captain, who, draining himself to the furthest point of nervous and physical exhaustion, played successive innings of 169, 44, 30 not out, and 205. If it was not a happy tour, much was redeemed by its ending.

In the following English summer, when Pakistan were the visitors prior to the forthcoming MCC tour of Australia and New Zealand, Hutton's hold on the captaincy did not go unquestioned.

In his absence because of 'acute neuritis due to overstrain', the selectors, despite the fact that he was at a theological college, turned to D.S. Sheppard (now Bishop of Liverpool), a batsman of clear leadership credentials although soon to be lost to the game. The implications of this move caused a rare clamour and a Press outcry lasting until Hutton's appointment late in July.

Up to a point, England's fortunes in Australia followed the West Indies course in that the first Test ended in wholesale defeat. Now, however, two young amateur batsmen, Peter May and Colin Cowdrey, saved their side in successive Tests, while Frank Tyson emerged as a match-winning fast bowler. A narrow victory in the second Test was followed by two by wider margins, the second of which secured the retention of the Ashes. Hutton had handled his side with quiet, shrewd assurance, though it has to be said that the tactic of slowing down the over-rate dates from this tour.

The captain returned home to a hero's welcome. He was appointed captain for all five Tests against South Africa, an unprecedented mark of confidence, and by passing a new rule MCC were able to make him an Honorary Cricket Member while still a player.

But in personal terms the cost of Len's three-year span had now to be accepted. His batting in the Australian Tests had been an unaccustomed struggle, and in the MCC-South Africa match in May he was stricken with lumbago and forced to withdraw as he did soon afterwards from the England captaincy.

He managed 10 matches for Yorkshire, in between aches and pains, and in the penultimate one came his 129th and last hundred, against Notts at Trent Bridge.

After reaching a characteristically flawless unhurried hundred in about 3½ hours, he suddenly blossomed into a stream of the most brilliant strokes, so that his last 94 runs actually came in 65 minutes. As at Sydney and Brisbane, for instance, in Test matches, the Roundhead had revealed a Cavalier struggling to burst forth.

Hutton needs no figures to illustrate his mastery as a batsman. Confined to 16 home seasons and seven in the sun and heat of tours, his tally of 40,140 tells its own story. In Tests his 6,971 runs were made at an average of 56. Given a full career without intermission or accident, who can tell what his record might have been?

After retirement he covered Test matches for the *Observer* newspaper and served as a Test selector in 1975-77. A former president of the Forty Club, earlier this year he accepted the presidency of Yorkshire.

E.W. SWANTON
The Daily Telegraph
7 September 1990

Les Ames – wicket-keeper batsman supreme

Leslie Ames, the Kent and England cricketer who has died at Canterbury aged 84, epitomized all that is most admirable in the world of games.

After a distinguished playing career, during which he kept wicket in 47 Tests, 'Les' Ames became the first professional to be appointed a selector, a role he filled to general approval for eight years.

It was one of a number of firsts for a 'pro'. In the 1960s he managed three MCC sides abroad, including the 1967-68 tour to the West Indies, the only series from which England returned victorious. When he relinquished the secretary-managership of Kent in 1975 after 18 years, he was nominated as president. He was also the first professional to be elected to the MCC Committee.

Leslie Ethelbert George Ames was born in 1905, into a cricketing family in the village of Elham, a few miles south of Canterbury. Blessed with a strong physique, young Les speedily rewarded the interest of two men who in his youth offered him particularly warm encouragement.

One was F.A. Mackinnon, later Chief of his Clan, who had played for Kent in the dark ages, and in 1878 had accompanied Lord Harris's team to Australia. The Mackinnon, who lived close by, gave Ames his first bat at the age of four and followed his career closely thereafter.

G.J.V. Weigall was county coach when he spotted Ames shortly after he left Harvey Grammar School, Folkestone. Telling the promising young batsman that he must become 'double-barrelled' (an all-rounder) if he wanted to make cricket his career, Weigall ordered him to keep wicket.

After a due apprenticeship on the Kent staff, Ames became the regular county wicket-keeper in 1927. His first hundred for the county earned him a silver claymore from the Mackinnon.

Two years later he won the first of his England caps. The Second World War brought an end to his Test career, and his double activity as wicket-keeper and batsman. He joined the RAF in 1940, and rose to the rank of squadron leader.

In 1946 a youngster called Godfrey Evans succeeded him behind the stumps. But Ames was batting as well as ever when in 1950, aged 44, he scored his 100th first-class hundred, aptly enough to win a match against the clock in Canterbury Week. Then, in the first match of 1951, he 'went' so severely in the back that he was obliged to give up playing.

Ames's unexpected retirement frustrated the intention of the Kent committee to make him their first professional captain. He was appointed CBE in 1973. He is survived by his wife, Bunty.

The Daily Telegraph
28 February 1990

Gubby Allen – end of an era

Sir George Allen, universally known as 'Gubby', died peacefully at his home overlooking Lord's. He was 87. Although he endured six hip operations spread over a long period, he was in good health and regularly playing golf until taken ill in June. Allen played the first of his 25 Tests in 1930. He captained England both at home and abroad; was elected to the committee of MCC in his early thirties; and served the club as both treasurer and president, as well as on successive committees, for more than 50 years.

Allen, an Australian by birth who came to England at the age of six, had as close a connection with cricket in many capacities as anyone, and over a longer period.

His playing career lasted from his days as an Eton boy, a Cambridge Blue, and Middlesex all-rounder to the England team, whom he captained in 11 Test matches between 1936 and 1948. He took MCC sides to Australia in 1936-37 and to the West Indies in 1947-48.

He was a model touring captain in that he took infinite trouble over every member of his side. At his best Allen was a valuable Test all-rounder, a fast bowler whose speed stemmed from a perfect action, a sound bat, and excellent close fielder.

He gave up playing in 1954 when appointed chairman of the Test selectors. He remained chairman for seven years, after which he became successively president, treasurer, and life vice-president of MCC. He was more or less continuously on the MCC committee for 50 years. There was scarcely a cricket matter of importance in which he was not involved.

His career was singular in that he never had time for more than a few first-class games a year. Thus he never made 1,000 runs or took 100 wickets in a season, though in his prime he was probably the best fast bowler in England.

Allen's most notable feat was in 1929 at Lord's when he took all 10 Lancashire wickets for 40 runs, this after arriving late on the field (by arrangement, naturally) and so missing the new ball. In county cricket at Lord's it was a unique feat, and so it remains.

The Lord's Committee Room was the scene of his work for cricket from 1932 to 1985 – an unprecedented span interrupted only by the Second World War. In 1963-64 he was president, and from 1964 to 1976 held the club's key post of treasurer.

He was awarded the Territorial Decoration in 1945, following outstanding service during the war, appointed CBE in 1962, and knighted in 1986. He never married. His family said he was always wedded to cricket.

Gubby Allen was a friend to all cricketers and took a special interest in the young – he seldom missed a Middlesex second team home match. An era at Lord's ends with his passing.

E.W. SWANTON
The Daily Telegraph
1 December 1989

Colin Milburn – an unfulfilled talent

Colin Milburn, the former England and Northamptonshire batsman, collapsed and died at the age of 48, 20 years after his Test career was cut short by a car accident.

Milburn, the greatest cricketer produced in County Durham, was visiting Alan Edgar, the former Bishop Auckland wicket-keeper, at his pub in Newton Aycliffe when he collapsed in the car park. It is understood that paramedics were able to revive Milburn in the ambulance, but he later died in Darlington Memorial Hospital.

A cheerful, 18-stone Geordie, universally known as 'Ollie', Milburn will always be remembered for his robust hitting, particularly his fearless hooking and savage square cuts. But, sadly for a man who played in nine Test matches for England, his career was cut short when, in 1969 at the age of 28, he was involved in a car accident. He crashed his head against the windscreen and lost his left eye.

Reacting with typical courage to such a shattering blow, he fought back and reappeared for Northamptonshire in 1973. But his batting was severely handicapped and his lack of mobility in the field caused him to retire a year later.

At his peak, his hurricane hitting made him one of the greatest draws of post-war cricket. Only a few days before his accident he hit a brilliant 158 for Northamptonshire against Leicestershire – the last of his 23 first-class centuries.

He made 13,262 runs between 1960 and 1974 at an average of 33.07, but showed he was a man for the big occasion by averaging 46.71, including two centuries, in his nine Tests. He was also a very useful medium-pace bowler who took 99 wickets in his first-class career and also snapped up 224 catches, mainly at forward short-leg, where his massive frame was not a liability.

The Daily Telegraph
1 March 1990

Joe Hardstaff – a chip off the old block

Joe Hardstaff, the Nottinghamshire batsman who played 23 Tests for England before and after the Second World War, died in hospital in Worksop yesterday. He was 78.

E.W. Swanton writes: When war came in 1939, 'Young Joe Hardstaff' was at the top of the tree, an automatic England choice along with Hammond, Hutton, and Compton. Though his batting afterwards scarcely regained its earlier bloom, he remained a heavy scorer until his retirement in 1955.

Hardstaff was born into the game, the son of 'Old Joe', also of Notts and England, a highly respected cricketer and, later, one of the best of Test umpires. A third generation, Air Vice Marshal Joseph Hardstaff, son of Young Joe, a noted figure in Service cricket, is secretary of Middlesex.

Young Joe, in contrast to his stocky father, was tall and willowy, elegant alike in style and turn-out. With an easy, upright stance, he held his bat high on the handle and swung it with an ease and grace that engendered great power.

In 1937, he won the match in Canterbury Week by reaching 100 in 51 minutes, so taking the Lawrence Trophy.

His early Test performances, with MCC in Australia in 1936-37, were not exceptional. However, he followed with two Test 100s the next summer against New Zealand and, in the record innings of 903 for seven against Australia at the Oval in 1938, he made 169 not out, partnering Len Hutton in a stand of 215.

After the war, he marked the resumption of Test cricket with an innings of 205 not out against India at Lord's.

Thereafter, though only in his middle 30s, his play was something of a disappointment on two MCC tours – to Australia and the West Indies – but he remained a formidable county batsman.

His aggregate of 31,847 runs, including 83 hundreds, was made at an average of 44. He reached 1,000 runs 13 times, four times going on to 2,000. In Tests he scored 1,636 runs, averaging 46.

The Daily Telegraph
2 January 1990

Hilton – conqueror of Bradman

As a 19-year-old, Malcolm Jameson Hilton, who has died aged 61, made his mark at Old Trafford by taking Don Bradman's wicket in both innings for Lancashire against Australia – only his third appearance for the county and his first of the season.

Hilton was a left-arm spinner who really gave the ball a tweak. However, he was the third of his kind on the Lancashire staff, and first Bill Roberts and later Bob Berry were often preferred.

Hilton was consistently successful for Lancashire. In 1950 the Old Trafford wickets, following the club's stated policy of watering and rolling less than normal, were often deplorable, and spinners Roy Tattersall (165) and Hilton (125) got most wickets.

Hilton had one MCC tour, in 1951-52 to India, where, at Kanpur, Tattersall's off-breaks and Hilton's orthodox left-arm spin brought England to an easy victory.

In 1956 he took 158 wickets at 13.96 apiece, and in a career that ended in 1961 his bag was 1,006 at 19 runs each. A free and chancy bat, he once hit 100 not out at Northampton.

E.W. SWANTON
The Daily Telegraph
11 July 1990

Career Details

(b – born; d – died; F-c – first-class career)

ALLEN, Sir George Oswald Browning 'Gubby'; b Bellevue Hill, Sydney, Australia, 31.7.02; d 29.11.89, St John's Wood, London. Cambridge Univ., Middlesex, and England. F-c (1921-54): 9,232 runs (28.67); 788 wkts (22.23); 131 ct. (See also full obituary.)

AMES, Leslie Ethelbert George; b Elham, Kent, 3.12.05; d Canterbury 26.2.90. Kent and England. F-c (1926-51): 37,248 runs (43.51); 24 wkts (33.37); 703 ct 418 st. (See also full obituary.)

DYER, Dennis Victor; b Durban, 2.5.14; d Durban, 18.6.90. Natal and South Africa. F-c (1939/40/1948/9): 1,725 runs (37.50); 0 wkts (27 r); 20 ct. His 3 Test appearances came on 1947 tour of England.

HARDSTAFF, Joseph Jr; b Nuncargate, Notts, 3.7.11; d Worksop, 1.1.90. Notts, Auckland, and England. F-c (1930-55): 31,847 runs (44.35) 36 wkts (59.47); 123 ct. (See also full obituary.)

HILTON, Malcolm Jameson; b Chadderton, Lancs, 2.8.28; d Oldham, 8.7.90. Lancashire and England. F-c (1946-61): 3,416 runs (12.11); 1,006 (19.42); 202 ct. (See also full obituary.)

HOLE, Graeme Blake; b Concord West, NSW, 6.1.31; d Adelaide 14.2.90. NSW, South Australia, and Australia. F-c (1949/50-1957/8): 5,647 runs (36.66); 61 wkts (44.03); 82 ct. Right-hand bat and leg-spinner and a brilliant slip fielder; career cut short at 27 after a freak fielding accident in which he ruptured his spleen making a catch; died after a long fight with cancer.

HUTTON, Sir Leonard; b Pudsey, 23.6.16; d Kingston-upon-Thames 6.9.90. Yorkshire and England. F-c (1934-55): 40,140 runs (55.51); 173 wkts (29.51); 400 ct. (See also full obituary.)

McLEOD, Edwin George; b 1900, d 14.9.89. Auckland, Wellington, and New Zealand. F-c (1920-41): 1,407 runs (32.72); 20 wkts (33.20). Left-hand bat and occasional leg-spinner, made only Test appearance against England at Wellington, New Zealand's second official Test. Oldest Test player (88) at time of death; captained New Zealand hockey team.

MILBURN, Colin; b Burnopfield, Co. Durham, 23.10.41; d Darlington, 28.2.90. Northants, Western Australia, and England. F-c (1960-74): 13,262 (33.07); 99 wkts (32.03); 224 ct. (See also full obituary.)

OWEN-SMITH, Harold Geoffrey 'Tuppy'; b Rondebosch, Cape Town, 18.2.09; d 28.2.90. Western Province, Oxford Univ., Middlesex, and South Africa. F-c (1927/8-1949/50): 4,059 runs (26.88); 319 wkts (23.22); 93 ct. A natural all-rounder who won cricket, rugby, and boxing Blues at Oxford, Owen-Smith captained England at rugby. Remembered for his 129 (the first South African to score 100 before lunch in a Test) against England at Headingley in 1929, when he and Sandy Bell put on 103 in 63 minutes for a last-wicket South African Test record that still stands, and above all for his carefree attitude and as a cricketer for the great occasion.

RAJINDERNATH, V.; b 7.1.28; d Madras, 22.11.89. Northern India, United Provinces, Southern Punjab, Bihar, East Punjab, and India. F-c: 844 runs (22.21); 34 ct, 23 st. Kept wicket in his only Test, in Bombay against Pakistan, in which he made 4 stumpings but did not bat.

ROBERTS, Andrew Duncan Glenn; b 6.5.47; d Wellington 26.10.89. Northern Districts and New Zealand. F-c (1967/8-1983/4): 5,865 runs (34.70); 84 wkts (29.88). Right-hand bat and useful change bowler; hit 7 hundreds for ND.

Their Record in Tests

Batting/Fielding	Career	M	I	NO	HS	R	Avge	100	Ct/St
G.O.B. Allen (E)	1930-1947/8	25	33	2	122	750	24.19	1	20
L.E.G. Ames (E)	1929-1938/9	47	72	12	149	2434	40.56	8	74/23
D.V. Dyer (SA)	1947	3	6	0	62	96	16.00	–	–
J. Hardstaff (E)	1935-48	23	38	3	205★	1636	46.74	4	9
M.J. Hilton (E)	1950-51/2	4	6	1	15	37	7.40	–	1
G.B. Hole (A)	1950/1-1954/5	18	33	2	66	789	25.45	–	21
L. Hutton (E)	19371954/5	79	138	15	364	6971	56.67	19	57
E.G. McLeod (NZ)	1929/30	1	2	1	16	18	18.00	–	–
C. Milburn (E)	1966-1968/9	9	16	2	139	654	46.71	2	7
H.G. Owen-Smith (SA)	1929	5	8	2	129	252	42.00	1	4
V. Rajindernath (I)	1952/3	1	0	–	–	–	–	–	-/4
A.D.G. Roberts (NZ)	1976-1976/7	7			84★	254	23.09	–	3

Bowling	R	W	Avge	Best	5wI	10wM
G.O.B. Allen (E)	2379	81	29.37	7-80	5	1
M.J. Hilton (E)	477	14	34.07	5-61	1	–
G.B. Hole (A)	126	3	42.00	1-9	–	–
L. Hutton (E)	232	3	77.33	1-2	–	–
E.G. McLeod (NZ)	5	0	–	–	–	–
H.G. Owen-Smith (SA)	113	0	–	–	–	–
A.D.G. Roberts (NZ)	182	4	45.50	1-12	–	–

1990-91

LOOKING FORWARD

England play safe for Ashes campaign
by Peter Deeley

Continuity and caution are the twin lodestars which guided the England selectors in their choice of the 16 players they hope will wrest back the Ashes in Australia this winter. There are few surprises and only two uncapped players, the Surrey fast bowler Martin Bicknell and the Middlesex left-arm spinner Philip Tufnell.

Bicknell, at 21 the youngest player in the group, is preferred to Philip DeFreitas, despite his five wickets and man-of-the-match award in the NatWest Trophy final.

Micky Stewart, the England team manager, admitted: "DeFreitas will be very disappointed but we felt we needed a swing bowler in that area. Bicknell, who is developing towards a high-class bowler, can swing the ball away from the bat." On the successful 1986-87 Ashes tour, DeFreitas, then 20 and the "baby" of that side, was a surprise success under Mike Gatting.

Wayne Larkins, the Northants batsman, gets the nomination as principally a third opener, a decision which will lead to some criticism despite its predictability. Alec Stewart's selection as the reserve wicket-keeper to Jack Russell was also expected but will not meet universal approval. Some will also consider John Morris rather fortunate to hold his place against strong opposition after his moderate performances against India this summer.

Both Larkins and Stewart were members of the team in the Caribbean last winter and that party has been taken as the basis from which the selectors have built the present formation – in the process giving themselves something of a vote of confidence.

They have, however, in effect conceded that there is no replacement in sight for Ian Botham and have decided not to go to Australia with an all-rounder. David Capel might have been considered, but will be out of action for some time with a broken finger, along with the back trouble that has bothered him this season.

Instead, the selectors have gone for eight batsmen, including Stewart, and seven bowlers. Ted Dexter, chairman of the England committee, conceded that "the all-rounder position was perceived as a major problem. Sadly we didn't feel there was such a player available to us."

The party contains 11 of the players who went to the West Indies plus two who played for England 'A' in Zimbabwe last winter. Mr Dexter said: "The players performed above expectations in the West Indies. It may be thought that to beat New Zealand and India is good but not that significant.

"But I believe that to win any home series these days is a considerable achievement, particularly because of the difficulties our bowlers have encountered. From Test cricket's point of view, all our bowlers suffer considerably from the domestic season. In those circumstances they did remarkably well to win two Tests and draw four this summer. We expect that when they have time for some proper rest, helped by renewed training – technical and physical – to get back to where we were in the West Indies, then we'll have a formidable unit."

Stewart goes as the second wicket-keeper, a choice which will cause some debate. He has been carrying a damaged finger for a full season now and has only recently taken over the gloves again at Surrey. Some will argue that a specialist wicket-keeper should have gone and there will also inevitably be some shouts of nepotism. Mr Stewart Sr said yesterday that he had not – as on previous occasions – stepped out during the selector's discussions about his son.

Larkins, 37 this November, gets the vote ahead of men such as Glamorgan's Hugh Morris, who has had an outstanding county season. In the field he will give a rather venerable tinge to the team. Mr Stewart cited Larkins's century in Hyderabad last autumn against Australia in the Nehru trophy as an example of his quality as an opening bat. But in this case one cannot help feeling that loyalty has won the day over wisdom.

Mr Dexter's view of the Australian party was "a nice blend of experience and youthful enthusiasm. There are plans afoot to winkle out the Australian batsmen after our failure here last summer. We'll be attempting to discover their Achilles' heel – but we aren't saying how."

In all, about 25 players were considered for Australia.

Alan Shiell writes: Allan Border, Australia's captain, said his players must respect the England party, because of the hard work they had put in over the past 12 months.

"Gooch has got them firing pretty well, and he's a stickler for hard work in the nets. They'll be very well prepared for the tour and we have to make sure we are too. The biggest mistake we can make is to think about what happened in '89, and take it easy just because we can see all these familiar names. I can guarantee you there's no way we'll be doing that," the Australian captain said.

"It's a good, all-round, solid side, to be respected on what it has done over the past 12 months," Border said. A squad of Australian players will attend a pre-season training camp in Brisbane from 30 September to 3 October.

Border added: "There are really only two players not many people here have heard much about – Martin Bicknell, the young quickie from Surrey, and Philip Tufnell, the left-arm spinner from Middlesex. I don't know a lot about Bicknell, but he's had some good performances. Tufnell was on the Lord's staff. Most of our guys have faced him in the practice nets, so he's had a brief look at us, too. We certainly know he's a handy young spinner.

The Daily Telegraph, 7 September

Morris gets England 'A' job

by Peter Deeley

Some of the fire and fury steaming out of the Welsh valleys at the omission of Glamorgan's Hugh Morris from the Ashes tour party will have been dampened by his appointment yesterday as captain of the England 'A' side to visit Pakistan early next year.

Morris, 26, has had an outstanding summer with 10 centuries, and surprisingly has been given the job ahead of Essex's John Stephenson, captain of the Under-25 side against India a month ago, who does not even make the party.

Sixteen players have been named for a six or seven weeks' tour, with the possibility of a short visit to Sri Lanka afterwards. The full itinerary has still to be finalized.

Eight of the party were on duty last winter, either in Zimbabwe with the 'A' team or in West Indies with the senior side. Morris has captained the England Under-19 team and led Glamorgan for three seasons before giving up the post last year, saying that the burdens of captaincy were affecting his form.

Micky Stewart, the England team manager, said of Morris's appointment: "He was obviously delighted to accept and is confident that he can cope with the extra responsibility." He added that Morris would benefit particularly from the appointment of Lancashire's Neil Fairbrother as vice-captain and Keith Fletcher as team coach – both of whom have previous experience of Pakistan.

The party has been increased by one to 16 to accommodate a second wicket-keeper – Lancashire's Warren Hegg and Worcestershire's Steve Rhodes are both chosen – "in order to extend their experience," Mr Stewart said. There is a third 'keeper in the group, Richard Blakey of Yorkshire, but Mr Stewart said he would be used as a batsman and fielder.

Neil Williams, who played in the final India Test, becomes the only current England player not to get recognition in any touring side this winter. Mr Stewart said Williams and Stephenson could "consider themselves unlucky but will remain under close observation". Michael Watkinson, who has played an important part in Lancashire's success this season, can also feel unfortunate at being overlooked. Selections that will cause some surprise include Graham Thorpe, the left-hander who went to Zimbabwe but who is currently dropped from the Surrey side for lack of form, and Andy Pick, the Notts quick bowler who has taken 51 wickets this season.

The Daily Telegraph, 13 September

England on Tour 1990-91

Tour Party to Australia and New Zealand

	Age†	Caps		Age†	Caps
G.A. Gooch, captain (Essex)	37	81	C.C. Lewis (Leics)	22	3
A.J. Lamb, vice-capt (Nthants)	36	67	D.E. Malcolm (Derbyshire)	27	11
M.A. Atherton (Lancs)	22	8	J.E. Morris (Derbyshire)	26	3
M.P. Bicknell (Surrey)	21	0	R.C. Russell (Glos)	27	17
A.R.C.Fraser (Middx)	25	8	G.C. Small (Warwicks)	28	13
D.I. Gower (Hants)	33	109	R.A. Smith (Hants)	27	18
E.E. Hemmings (Notts)	41	15	A.J. Stewart (Surrey)	27	7
W. Larkins (Northants)	36	10	P.C.R. Tufnell (Middx)	24	0

† At 1.10.90

Tour Itinerary

October	19	Arrive Perth
	25	Western Australia President's XI (Perth)
	27, 28	Western Australia Country XI (Geraldton)
	30	Western Australia Invitation XI (Perth, d/n)
November	2,3, 4, 5	Western Australia (Perth)
	7	S. Australian Country XI (Port Pirie)
	9, 10, 11, 12	South Australia (Adelaide)
	14	Tasmania (Hobart)
	16, 17, 18, 19	Australian XI (Hobart)
	23, 24, 25, 26, 27	AUSTRALIA (Brisbane) First Test
	29	Australian Cricket Academy (Adelaide)
December	1	New Zealand (Adelaide) B & H
	4	Prime Minister's XI (Canberra)
	7	New Zealand (Perth, d/n)
	9	Australia (Perth) B & H
	11	Bradman XI (Bowral)
	13	New Zealand (Sydney, d/n) B & H
	15	New Zealand (Brisbane) B & H
	16	Australia (Brisbane) B & H
	20, 21, 22, 23	Victoria (Ballarat)
	26, 27, 28, 29,30	AUSTRALIA (Melbourne) Second Test
January 91	1	Australia (Sydney, d/n) B & H
	4, 5, 6, 7, 8	AUSTRALIA (Sydney) Third Test
	10	Australia (Melbourne, d/n) B & H
	13‡	B & H 1st Final (Sydney, d/n)
	15‡	B & H 2nd Final (Melbourne, d/n)
	17‡†	B & H 3rd Final (Melbourne, d/n)
	19, 20, 21, 22	Queensland (Carrara)
	25, 26, 27, 28, 29	AUSTRALIA (Adelaide) Fourth Test
February	1, 2, 3, 5, 6	AUSTRALIA (Perth) Fifth Test
	9	New Zealand (Christchurch) 1st 1-day International
	13	New Zealand (Wellington) 2nd 1-day International
	16	New Zealand (Auckland) 3rd 1-day International

‡If qualifying. †If needed. d/n = day/night game.

England 'A' Tour Party to Pakistan

	Age†	Caps‡
H.A. Morris (Glamorgan, capt)	26	–
N.H. Fairbrother (Lancs, vice-capt)	27	7
D.J. Bicknell (Surrey)	23	–
R.J. Blakey (Yorkshire)	23	–
P.A.J. DeFreitas (Lancashire)	24	17
W.K. Hegg (Lancashire)	22	–
N. Hussain (Essex)	22	3
R.K. Illingworth (Worcestershire)	27	–
K.T. Medlycott (Surrey)	25	–
T.A. Munton (Warwickshire)	25	–
P.J. Newport (Worcestershire)	27	2
R.A. Pick (Nottinghamshire)	26	–
M.R. Ramprakash (Middlesex)	21	–
S.J. Rhodes (Worcestershire)	26	–
I.D.K. Salisbury (Sussex)	20	–
G.P. Thorpe (Surrey)	21	–

Manager: R. Bennett (Lancashire). Team Manager: K.W.R. Fletcher (Essex). Physiotherapist: D. Roberts (Worcestershire).

† At 1.10.90   ‡Full caps for England

Fixtures 1991

Duration of Matches (*including play on Sunday)

Cornhill Insurance Tests	5 days	Texaco Trophy	1 day
Britannic Assurance		Benson & Hedges Cup	1 day
County Championship	3 days or as stated	NatWest Bank Trophy	1 day
Tourist matches	3 days or as stated	Refuge Assurance League/Cup	1 day
Universities v Counties	3 days	Other matches	as stated

APRIL 13, SATURDAY

Fenners	*Cambridge U v Lancs
The Parks	Oxford U v Hampshire

APRIL 16, TUESDAY

Lord's	MCC v Middlesex (4 days)
Fenners	Cambridge U v Northants

APRIL 17, WEDNESDAY

The Parks	Oxford U v Glamorgan

APRIL 19, FRIDAY

Fenners	Cambridge U v Essex

APRIL 21, SUNDAY

Refuge Assurance League

Cardiff	Glamorgan v Northants
Bristol	Glos v Middlesex
Southampton	Hampshire v Yorkshire
Old Trafford	Lancashire v Notts
Leicester	Leics v Derbyshire
The Foster's Oval	Surrey v Somerset
Edgbaston	Warwicks v Sussex
Worcester	Worcs v Kent

APRIL 23, TUESDAY

Benson & Hedges Cup

Derby	Derbyshire v Northants
Bristol	Glos v Combined U
Southampton	Hampshire v Notts
Canterbury	Kent v Leics
Taunton	Somerset v Middlesex
The Foster's Oval	Surrey v Essex
Trowbridge	Minor Counties v Glam
Forfar	Scotland v Lancashire

APRIL 25, THURSDAY

Benson & Hedges Cup

Old Trafford	Lancashire v Kent
Lord's	Middlesex v Surrey
Trent Bridge	Notts v Yorkshire
Hove	Sussex v Leics
Edgbaston	Warwicks v Essex
Worcester	Worcs v Glos
Oxford	Combined U v Derbys
Trowbridge	Minor Counties v Hants

† Rapid Cricketline Champions
‡ Reserve day Sunday

APRIL 27, SATURDAY

Britannic Assurance Championship (4 days)

Derby	Derbys v Northants
Chelmsford	Essex v Surrey
Southampton	*Hants v Kent
Leicester	Leics v Glamorgan
Lord's	Middlesex v Yorkshire
Taunton	Somerset v Sussex
Edgbaston	Warwicks v Lancs
Worcester	Worcs v Glos

Other Matches

The Parks	Oxford U v Notts
Hove	†Sussex 2nd XI v Eng Under-19s (4 days)

APRIL 28, SUNDAY

Refuge Assurance League

Chelmsford	Essex v Yorkshire
Old Trafford	Lancs v Northants
Leicester	Leics v Glamorgan
Lord's	Middlesex v Surrey
Trent Bridge	Notts v Warwicks
Taunton	Somerset v Sussex

MAY 2, THURSDAY

Benson & Hedges Cup

Chelmsford	Essex v Middlesex
Bristol	Glos v Northants
Southampton	Hants v Glamorgan
Canterbury	Kent v Sussex
Leicester	Leics v Scotland
Edgbaston	Warwicks v Somerset
Headingley	Yorks v Minor Counties
Fenners	Combined U v Worcs

MAY 4, SATURDAY

Benson & Hedges Cup

Cardiff	Glamorgan v Notts
Leicester	Leics v Lancs
Lord's	Middlesex v Warwicks
Northampton	Northants v Combined U
Taunton	‡Somerset v Surrey
Hove	‡Sussex v Scotland
Worcester	Worcs v Derbyshire
Headingley	Yorks v Hants

MAY 5, SUNDAY

Refuge Assurance League

Derby	Derbys v Hants
Chelmsford	Essex v Leics
Cardiff	Glamorgan v Notts
Bristol	Glos v Worcs
Canterbury	Kent v Warwicks
Lord's	Middlesex v Northants

MAY 7, TUESDAY

Benson & Hedges Cup

Derby	Derbys v Glos
Chelmsford	Essex v Somerset
Cardiff	Glamorgan v Yorks
Old Trafford	Lancs v Sussex
Northampton	Northants v Worcs
Trent Bridge	Notts v Minor Counties
The Foster's Oval	Surrey v Warwicks
Glasgow (Hamilton Crescent)	Scotland v Kent

MAY 9, THURSDAY

Britannic Assurance Championship (4 days)

Bristol	Glos v Hants
Lord's	Middlesex v Sussex
Northampton	Northants v Essex
Trent Bridge	Notts v Leics
Taunton	Somerset v Glamorgan
The Foster's Oval	Surrey v Kent
Worcester	Worcs v Lancs
Headingley	Yorks v Warwicks

Other Match

Fenners	Cambridge U v Derbys

MAY 12, SUNDAY

Refuge Assurance League

Southampton	Hampshire v Kent
Northampton	Northants v Leics
Trent Bridge	Notts v Essex
Taunton	Somerset v Glamorgan
The Foster's Oval	Surrey v Glos
Hove	Sussex v Middlesex
Worcester	Worcs v Lancs
Headingley	Yorkshire v Warwicks

Tourist Match

Arundel	Lavinia, Duchess of Norfolk's XI v West Indies (1 day)

MAY 14, TUESDAY

Tourist Match

Bristol	Glos v W. Indies (1 day)

MAY 15, WEDNESDAY

Tourist Match

Worcester	Worcs v W. Indies

Other Matches

Fenners	Cambridge U v Middx
The Parks	Oxford U v Glos

MAY 16, THURSDAY

Britannic Assurance Championship (4 days)

Swansea	Glamorgan v Warwicks
Folkestone	Kent v Essex
Old Trafford	Lancs v Derbys
Northampton	Northants v Leics
Hove	Sussex v Hants
Headingley	Yorks v Notts

MAY 18, SATURDAY

Tourist Match

Lord's	*Middlesex v W. Indies

Other Match

Fenners	Cambridge U v Surrey

MAY 19, SUNDAY

Refuge Assurance League

Derby	Derbys v Lancs
Swansea	Glamorgan v Warwicks
Bournemouth	Hampshire v Somerset
Folkestone	Kent v Essex
Leicester	Leics v Yorkshire
Northampton	Northants v Worcs
Hove	Sussex v Glos

MAY 22, WEDNESDAY

Britannic Assurance Championship

Derby	Derbyshire v Somerset
Chelmsford	Essex v Warwickshire
Cardiff	Glamorgan v Northants
Trent Bridge	Notts v Kent
The Foster's Oval	Surrey v Lancs
Hove	Sussex v Middlesex
Sheffield	Yorks v Glos

Other Match

Fenners	Cambridge U v Leics

MAY 23, THURSDAY

Texaco Trophy (1st 1-day international)

Edgbaston	England v West Indies

MAY 25, SATURDAY

Texaco Trophy (2nd 1-day international)

Old Trafford	England v West Indies

MAY 25, SATURDAY (contd)

Britannic Assurance Championship
Cardiff	Glamorgan v Sussex
Bournemouth	Hants v Surrey
Canterbury	Kent v Derbyshire
Leicester	Leics v Notts
Taunton	Somerset v Middx
Edgbaston	Warwicks v Glos
Headingley	Yorks v Northants

Other Match
The Parks	Oxford U v Worcs

MAY 26, SUNDAY

Refuge Assurance League
Swansea	Glamorgan v Sussex
Swindon	Glos v Hants
Canterbury	Kent v Derbys
Leicester	Leics v Notts
Taunton	Somerset v Middlesex
The Foster's Oval	Surrey v Essex
Edgbaston	Warwicks v Worcs
Headingley	Yorks v Northants

MAY 27, MONDAY

Texaco Trophy (3rd 1-day international)
Lord's	England v West Indies

MAY 29, WEDNESDAY

Benson & Hedges Cup
Quarter-Finals

Tourist Match
Taunton or Oval	Somerset or Surrey v West Indies

MAY 31, FRIDAY

Britannic Assurance Championship
Bristol	Glos v Essex
Old Trafford	Lancs v Sussex
Lord's	Middlesex v Kent
Northampton	Northants v Derbys
Trent Bridge	Notts v Hants
Edgbaston	Warwicks v Yorks
Worcester	Worcs v Glamorgan

JUNE 1, SATURDAY

Tourist Match
Leicester	*Leics v West Indies

JUNE 2, SUNDAY

Refuge Assurance League
Chesterfield	Derbyshire v Yorks
Pontypridd	Glamorgan v Essex
Old Trafford	Lancs v Sussex
Southgate	Middlesex v Kent
Northampton	Northants v Hants
Edgbaston	Warwicks v Somerset
Worcester	Worcs v Surrey

JUNE 4, TUESDAY

Britannic Assurance Championship
Ilford	Essex v Leics
Swansea	Glamorgan v Somerset
Bristol	Glos v Middlesex
Basingstoke	Hants v Lancs
Tunbridge Wells	Kent v Warwicks
Northampton	Northants v Worcs
The Foster's Oval	Surrey v Notts

Other Match
The Parks	Oxford U v Yorks

JUNE 6, THURSDAY

First Cornhill Insurance Test
Headingley	*ENGLAND v WEST INDIES

JUNE 7, FRIDAY

Britannic Assurance Championship
Chesterfield	Derbys v Glamorgan
Ilford	Essex v Worcs
Southampton	Hampshire v Glos
Tunbridge Wells	Kent v Sussex
Uxbridge	Middx v Leics
Edgbaston	Warwicks v Somerset

Other Match
The Parks	Oxford U v Lancs

JUNE 9, SUNDAY

Refuge Assurance League
Chesterfield	Derbys v Surrey
Ilford	Essex v Worcs
Moreton-in-Marsh	Glos v Northants
Basingstoke	Hants v Sussex
Old Trafford	Lancs v Glamorgan
Uxbridge	Middx v Leics
Trent Bridge	Notts v Somerset

JUNE 11, TUESDAY

Other Match
Harrogate	Tilcon Trophy (3 days)

JUNE 12, WEDNESDAY

Benson & Hedges Cup
Semi-Finals

Tourist Match
Derby or Old Trafford	Derbys or Lancs v West Indies

JUNE 14, FRIDAY

Britannic Assurance Championship
Cardiff	Glamorgan v Middx
Gloucester	Glos v Notts
Leicester	Leics v Surrey
Hove	Sussex v Worcs
Harrogate	Yorks v Kent

JUNE 15, SATURDAY

Tourist Match
Northampton   *Northants v W. Indies

JUNE 16, SUNDAY

Refuge Assurance League
Checkley	Derbyshire v Somerset
Chelmsford	Essex v Hants
Cardiff	Glamorgan v Middlesex
Gloucester	Glos v Notts
Leicester	Leics v Surrey
Hove	Sussex v Worcs
Edgbaston	Warwicks v Lancs
Scarborough	Yorkshire v Kent

JUNE 18, TUESDAY

Britannic Assurance Championship
Gloucester	Glos v Derbys
Leicester	Leics v Lancs
Bath	Somerset v Hampshire
Coventry	Warwicks v Sussex
Worcester	Worcs v Notts

Other Matches
Fenners	Cambridge U v Glam
The Parks	Oxford U v Kent

JUNE 20, THURSDAY

Second Cornhill Insurance Test
Lord's   *ENGLAND v WEST INDIES

JUNE 21, FRIDAY

Britannic Assurance Championship
Derby	Derbys v Surrey
†	*Glamorgan v Leics
Old Trafford	Lancs v Kent
Northampton	*Northants v Hants
Trent Bridge	Notts v Warwicks
Bath	Somerset v Glos
Horsham	Sussex v Essex
Sheffield	Yorks v Middx

JUNE 22, SATURDAY

Other Match
†   *Ireland v Scotland (3 days)

JUNE 23, SUNDAY

Refuge Assurance League
Old Trafford	Lancs v Kent
Trent Bridge	Notts v Middlesex
Bath	Somerset v Glos
Horsham	Sussex v Essex
Edgbaston	Warwickshire v Surrey
Sheffield	Yorks v Worcs

JUNE 26, WEDNESDAY

NatWest Bank Trophy (1st Round)
Bedford	Beds v Worcs
Reading	Berkshire v Hants
Exmouth	Devon v Essex
Dean Park, Bournemouth	Dorset v Lancs
Darlington	Durham v Glamorgan
Bristol	Glos v Norfolk
Bishops Stortford	Herts v Derbys
†	Ireland v Middx
Canterbury	Kent v Cambridgeshire
Leicester	Leics v Shropshire
Trent Bridge	Notts v Lincs
Edinburgh (Myreside)	Scotland v Sussex
Taunton	Somerset v Bucks
Stone	Staffs v Northants
The Foster's Oval	Surrey v Oxfordshire
Edgbaston	Warwicks v Yorks

Tourist Match
The Parks   Oxbridge v West Indies
                 (2 days)

JUNE 28, FRIDAY

Britannic Assurance Championship
Liverpool	Lancashire v Glamorgan
Lord's	Middlesex v Essex
Luton	Northants v Glos
The Foster's Oval	Surrey v Somerset
Edgbaston	Warwicks v Derbys
Worcester	Worcs v Leics

Tourist Match
Trowbridge   League Cricket Conference
                  v West Indies (1 day)

JUNE 29, SATURDAY

Tourist Match
Southampton   Hants v West Indies

Other Match
Hove   Sussex v Cambridge U

JUNE 30, SUNDAY

Refuge Assurance League
Chelmsford	Essex v Derbys
Canterbury	Kent v Glos
Luton	Northants v Somerset
The Foster's Oval	Surrey v Notts
Worcester	Worcs v Leics
Headingley	Yorks v Glamorgan

† Venue to be decided

JULY 2, TUESDAY

Britannic Assurance Championship

Chelmsford	Essex v Hants
Cardiff	Glamorgan v Notts
Maidstone	Kent v Northants
Hinckley	Leics v Glos
Taunton	Somerset v Lancs
Arundel	Sussex v Surrey
Edgbaston	Warwickshire v Middx
Headingley	Yorks v Worcs

Varsity Match

Lord's   Oxford U v Cambridge U

JULY 4, THURSDAY

Third Cornhill Insurance Test

Trent Bridge   ENGLAND v WEST INDIES

JULY 5, FRIDAY

Britannic Assurance Championship

Derby	Derbys v Sussex
Southampton	Hants v Yorks
Maidstone	Kent v Glamorgan
Leicester	Leics v Northants
The Foster's Oval	Surrey v Essex

JULY 7, SUNDAY

Refuge Assurance League

Derby	Derbyshire v Sussex
Chelmsford	Essex v Warwicks
Southampton	Hants v Worcs
Maidstone	Kent v Glamorgan
Leicester	Leics v Lancs
Lord's	Middlesex v Yorks
Tring	Northants v Surrey

JULY 10, WEDNESDAY

Tourist Match

Darlington	Minor Counties v
	West Indies (2 days)

JULY 11, THURSDAY

NatWest Bank Trophy (2nd Round)

Beds or Worcs v Durham or Glamorgan
Berks or Hants v Dorset or Lancs
Glos or Norfolk v Notts or Lincs
Scotland or Sussex v Devon or Essex
Somerset or Bucks v Ireland or Middx
Staffs or Northants v Leics or Shropshire
Surrey or Oxon v Kent or Cambs
Warwicks or Yorks v Herts or Derbys

JULY 13, SATURDAY

Benson & Hedges Cup

Lord's   Final

Tourist Match

†	Ireland v West Indies
	(1 day)

JULY 14, SUNDAY

‡Refuge Assurance League

Canterbury	Kent v Leics
Trent Bridge	Notts v Hants
Taunton	Somerset v Lancs
The Foster's Oval	Surrey v Sussex
Edgbaston	Warwicks v Middx
Worcester	Worcs v Derbys
Scarborough	Yorks v Glos

JULY 15, MONDAY

Tourist Match

Brecon   Wales v W. Indies (1 day)

JULY 16, TUESDAY

Britannic Assurance Championship

Southend	Essex v Kent
Portsmouth	Hants v Worcs
Uxbridge	Middx v Northants
Trent Bridge	Notts v Lancs
Guildford	Surrey v Glos
Hove	Sussex v Somerset
Scarborough	Yorks v Derbys

Tourist Match

Swansea   Glamorgan v W. Indies

JULY 19, FRIDAY

Britannic Assurance Championship

Southend	Essex v Somerset
Cheltenham	Glos v Glamorgan
Portsmouth	Hants v Warwicks
Uxbridge	Middx v Lancs
Wellingborough	Northants v Notts
Guildford	Surrey v Yorks
Hove	Sussex v Leics
Kidderminster	Worcs v Derbys

JULY 20, SATURDAY

Tourist Match

Canterbury   *Kent v W. Indies

JULY 21, SUNDAY

Refuge Assurance League

Southend	Essex v Somerset
Cheltenham	Glos v Derbys
Portsmouth	Hants v Warwicks
Lord's	Middlesex v Lancashire
Wellingborough	Northants v Notts
The Foster's Oval	Surrey v Yorks
Hove	Sussex v Leics
Worcester	Worcs v Glamorgan

†Venue to be decided
‡ Matches for B & H Cup finalists to be rearranged

JULY 23, TUESDAY

Britannic Assurance Championship
Chesterfield   Derbys v Hants
Cardiff   Glamorgan v Essex
Cheltenham   Glos v Sussex
Old Trafford   Lancs v Warwicks
Northampton   Northants v Somerset
Worksop   Notts v Yorks
Worcester   Worcs v Kent

JULY 24, WEDNESDAY

Tourist Match
†   England Amateur XI v
                    Sri Lanka (1 day)

JULY 25, THURSDAY

Fourth Cornhill Insurance Test
Edgbaston *ENGLAND v WEST INDIES

JULY 26, FRIDAY

Britannic Assurance Championship
Cheltenham   Glos v Worcs
Leicester   *Leics v Warwicks
Lord's   Middx v Notts
Taunton   Somerset v Kent
The Foster's Oval   Surrey v Glamorgan

Tourist Match
Durham   Durham v Sri Lanka
                    (1 day)

JULY 27, SATURDAY

Tourist Match
Headingley   *Yorkshire v Sri Lanka

JULY 28, SUNDAY

Refuge Assurance League
Derby   Derbys v Northants
Cheltenham   Glos v Essex
Southampton   Hants v Lancs
Taunton   Somerset v Kent
The Foster's Oval   Surrey v Glamorgan
Hove   Sussex v Notts

JULY 30, TUESDAY

Tourist Match
Swansea or
  Worcester   Glam or Worcs v Sri Lanka

JULY 31, WEDNESDAY

NatWest Bank Trophy
Quarter-Finals

Tourist Match
Trent Bridge or   Notts or Glos v W. Indies
  Bristol

Other Match
Jesmond   England XI v Rest of
                    World XI (1 day)

AUGUST 1, THURSDAY

Jesmond   England XI v
                    Rest of World XI (1 day)

AUGUST 2, FRIDAY

Britannic Assurance Championship
Canterbury   Kent v Surrey
Old Trafford   Lancs v Yorks
Lord's   Middx v Hants
Weston-super-Mare Somerset v Leics
Eastbourne   Sussex v Northants
Worcester   Worcs v Warwicks

Tourist Match
Derby   Derbys v Sri Lanka

AUGUST 3, SATURDAY

Tourist Match
Chelmsford   *Essex v W. Indies

AUGUST 4, SUNDAY

Refuge Assurance League
Swansea   Glamorgan v Glos
Canterbury   Kent v Surrey
Old Trafford   Lancs v Yorks
Lord's   Middx v Hants
Trent Bridge   Notts v Worcs
Weston-super-Mare Somerset v Leics
Eastbourne   Sussex v Northants
Edgbaston   Warwicks v Derbys

AUGUST 6, TUESDAY

Britannic Assurance Championship
Derby   Derbys v Essex
Canterbury   Kent v Hants
Lytham   Lancs v Northants
Leicester   Leics v Yorks
Weston-super-Mare Somerset v Worcs
Eastbourne   Sussex v Notts
Edgbaston   Warwicks v Surrey

Tourist Match
Bristol   Glos v Sri Lanka

Bull Under-19 International Series
Lord's   England U-19 v
                    Australia U-19 (1st 1-day)

†Venue to be decided

AUGUST 8, THURSDAY

Fifth Cornhill Insurance Test
The Foster's Oval *ENGLAND V WEST INDIES

Bull Under-19 International Series
Trent Bridge   England U-19 v
                      Australia U-19 (2nd 1-day)

AUGUST 9, FRIDAY

Britannic Assurance Championship
Swansea   Glamorgan v Hants
Bristol   Glos v Lancs
Leicester   Leics v Kent
Lord's   Middx v Derbys
Northampton   Northants v Warwicks
Trent Bridge   Notts v Essex
Middlesbrough   Yorks v Sussex

AUGUST 10, SATURDAY

Tourist Match
Taunton   *Somerset v Sri Lanka

AUGUST 11, SUNDAY

Refuge Assurance League
Ebbw Vale   Glamorgan v Hants
Bristol   Glos v Lancs
Leicester   Leics v Warwicks
Lord's   Middlesex v Derbys
Peterborough   Northants v Essex
Trent Bridge   Notts v Kent
Middlesbrough   Yorks v Sussex

AUGUST 12 OR 13, MONDAY OR TUESDAY

Bain Clarkson Trophy
Semi-Finals (1 day)

AUGUST 14, WEDNESDAY

NatWest Bank Trophy
Semi-Finals

Tourist Match
†Old Trafford   England 'A' v Sri Lanka
                   (1 day)

AUGUST 15, THURSDAY

Tourist Match
†Old Trafford   England 'A' v Sri Lanka
                   (1 day)

AUGUST 16, FRIDAY

Britannic Assurance Championship
Derby   Derbys v Lancs
Colchester   Essex v Northants
Bournemouth   Hants v Leics
Trent Bridge   Notts v Somerset
Worcester   Worcs v Surrey
Headingley   Yorks v Glamorgan

Bell Under-19 International Series
Leicester   England U-19 v
                   Australia U-19 (1st
                   Youth Test, 4 days)

AUGUST 17, SATURDAY

Tourist Match
Hove   *Sussex v Sri Lanka

AUGUST 18, SUNDAY

Refuge Assurance League
Derby   Derbys v Glamorgan
Colchester   Essex v Middx
Bournemouth   Hants v Leics
Canterbury   Kent v Northants
Old Trafford   Lancs v Surrey
Edgbaston   Warwicks v Glos
Worcester   Worcs v Somerset
Scarborough   Yorks v Notts

AUGUST 20, TUESDAY

Britannic Assurance Championship
Derby   Derbys v Leics
Colchester   Essex v Yorks
Bournemouth   Hants v Sussex
Canterbury   Kent v Glos
Blackpool   Lancs v Worcs
The Foster's Oval Surrey v Middx
Edgbaston   Warwicks v Glamorgan

AUGUST 22, THURSDAY

Cornhill Insurance Test
Lord's   ENGLAND v SRI LANKA

AUGUST 23, FRIDAY

Britannic Assurance Championship
Old Trafford   Lancashire v Essex
Northampton   Northants v Surrey
Trent Bridge   Notts v Derbys
Taunton   Somerset v Yorks
Worcester   Worcs v Middlesex

AUGUST 25, SUNDAY

Refuge Assurance League
Old Trafford   Lancs v Essex
Leicester   Leics v Glos
Northampton   Northants v Warwicks
Trent Bridge   Notts v Derbys
Taunton   Somerset v Yorkshire
The Foster's Oval Surrey v Hants
Hove   Sussex v Kent
Worcester   Worcs v Middx

AUGUST 27, TUESDAY

Bull Under-19 International Series
Chelmsford   England U-19 v
                   Australia U-19 (2nd
                   Youth Test, 4 days)

†Or at another venue if Lancashire in NWT semi-finals

AUGUST 28, WEDNESDAY

Britannic Assurance Championship (4 days)

Abergavenny	Glamorgan v Glos
Southampton	Hants v Somerset
Canterbury	Kent v Middlesex
Old Trafford	Lancs v Notts
Leicester	Leics v Derbys
Northampton	Northants v Yorks
The Foster's Oval	Surrey v Sussex
Edgbaston	Warwicks v Worcs

Other Match

Scarborough	Michael Parkinson's International (3 days)

SEPTEMBER 1, SUNDAY

Refuge Assurance Cup (1 day)
Semi-Finals

SEPTEMBER 3, TUESDAY

Britannic Assurance Championship (4 days)

Chelmsford	Essex v Derbys
Bristol	Glos v Northants
Trent Bridge	Notts v Middlesex
The Foster's Oval	Surrey v Hants
Hove	Sussex v Kent
Worcester	Worcs v Somerset
Scarborough	Yorks v Lancs

SEPTEMBER 7, SATURDAY

†NatWest Bank Trophy Final (1 day)
Lord's

Other Matches

Hove	Seeboard Trophy (3 days)
Scarborough	Yorkshire v The Yorkshiremen (1 day)

SEPTEMBER 8, SUNDAY

Other Match

Scarborough	Michael Parkinson's XI v Yorkshire (1 day)

SEPTEMBER 9, MONDAY

Bain Clarkson Trophy
Final (1 day)

Bull Under-19 International Series

Foster's Oval	England U-19 v Australia U-19 (3rd Youth Test, 4 days)

SEPTEMBER 10, TUESDAY

Britannic Assurance Championship (4 days)

Derby	Derbys v Notts
Cardiff	Glamorgan v Worcs
Bristol	Glos v Somerset
Leicester	Leics v Essex
Lord's	Middlesex v Surrey
Edgbaston	Warwicks v Northants

†Reserve days Sunday and Monday

SEPTEMBER 15, SUNDAY

Refuge Assurance Cup Final (1 day)
Old Trafford

SEPTEMBER 17, TUESDAY

Britannic Assurance Championship (4 days)

Chesterfield	Derbys v Yorks
Chelmsford	Essex v Middlesex
Southampton	Hants v Glamorgan
Canterbury	Kent v Leics
Old Trafford	Lancs v Surrey
Trent Bridge	Notts v Worcs
Taunton	Somerset v Warwicks
Hove	Sussex v Glos

SEPTEMBER 22, SUNDAY

Britannic Assurance Challenge (1 day)

Champions' ground	Champions v Sheffield Shield Champions 1990-91

SEPTEMBER 23, MONDAY

Britannic Assurance Challenge (4 days)

Champions' ground	Champions v Sheffield Shield Champions 1990-91